D1563463

# THE SONS OF MAXWELL PERKINS

Maxwell E. Perkins

# THE SONS OF
# MAXWELL PERKINS

## Letters of F. Scott Fitzgerald, Ernest Hemingway, Thomas Wolfe, and Their Editor

What a time you've had with your sons, Max—
Ernest gone to Spain, me gone to Hollywood,
Tom Wolfe reverting to an artistic hill-billy.
*Fitzgerald to Perkins, April 23, 1938*

Edited by Matthew J. Bruccoli
with Judith S. Baughman

UNIVERSITY OF SOUTH CAROLINA PRESS

© 2004 University of South Carolina

Published in Columbia, South Carolina, by the
University of South Carolina Press

Manufactured in the United States of America

08  07  06  05  04    5  4  3  2  1

Library of Congress Cataloging-in-Publication Data

The sons of Maxwell Perkins : letters of F. Scott Fitzgerald, Ernest Hemingway, Thomas
Wolfe, and their editor / edited by Matthew J. Bruccoli, with Judith S. Baughman.
   p. cm.
  Includes bibliographical references and index.
  ISBN 1-57003-548-2 (cloth : alk. paper)
  1. Authors, American—20th century—Correspondence. 2. Authors and publishers—
United States—History—20th century. 3. Literature publishing—United States—
History—20th century. 4. Perkins, Maxwell E. (Maxwell Evarts), 1884–1947—
Correspondence. 5. Fitzgerald, F. Scott (Francis Scott), 1896–1940—Correspondence.
6. Hemingway, Ernest, 1899–1961—Correspondence. 7. Wolfe, Thomas, 1900–1938
—Correspondence. 8. Editors—United States—Correspondence. 9. Charles Scribner's
Sons. I. Perkins, Maxwell E. (Maxwell Evarts), 1884–1947. II. Bruccoli, Matthew
Joseph, 1931– III. Baughman, Judith.
  PS129.S63 2004
  813'.5209—dc22                                     2004000829

FRONTISPIECE: Courtesy of Charles Scribner's Sons

The editors gratefully acknowledge permission from Simon and Schuster to use Maxwell
Perkins's correspondence with Thomas Wolfe. Thomas Wolfe's correspondence with Maxwell
Perkins is reprinted by permission of Eugene Winick, Administrator C.T.A. of the Estate of
Thomas Wolfe. One complete letter and excerpts from seventeen letters and telegrams from
Hemingway were reprinted with permission of Scribner, an imprint of Simon & Schuster
Adult Publishing Group, from Ernest Hemingway, *Selected Letters, 1917–1961,* edited by
Carlos Baker. Copyright © 1981, The Ernest Hemingway Foundation. Excerpts from fifteen
letters and telegrams from *The Only Thing That Counts: The Ernest Hemingway / Maxwell
Perkins Correspondence, 1925–1947,* edited by Matthew J. Bruccoli, copyright © 1996, were
reprinted with permission of The Ernest Hemingway Foundation and reprinted with permission of Scribner, an imprint of Simon & Schuster Adult Publishing Group. Copyright
outside the United States: © Hemingway Foreign Rights Trust. Excerpts from fifty-two Fitzgerald letters and telegrams were reprinted with permission of Scribner, an imprint of Simon
& Schuster Adult Publishing Group, from F. Scott Fitzgerald, *A Life in Letters,* edited by
Matthew J. Bruccoli, copyright © 1984 by The Trustees under Agreement Dated July 3,
1975. Created by Frances Scott Fitzgerald Smith. Excerpts from four Fitzgerald letters to
Maxwell Perkins were reprinted with permission of Scribner, an imprint of Simon & Schuster Adult Publishing Group, from *Dear Scott / Dear Max: The Fitzgerald-Perkins Correspondence,* edited by John Kuehl and Jackson Bryer. Copyright © 1971 Charles Scribner's Sons.

For Vern Sternberg: The Best

Max Perkins didn't want to leave himself lying around.

The Notebooks of F. Scott Fitzgerald

▲ ▼ ▲

He is a great editor and in a quiet, devious and unobtrusive fashion, most completely his own man, I think the most extraordinary individual I have ever known.

Thomas Wolfe to Percy MacKaye (July 19, 1933)

▲ ▼ ▲

I loved Max very much too and knew him pretty well and he always trusted me even when I was unjust and mean. . . . Please bury Max's ghost for keeps and cut out this about he, Tom Wolfe and Scott being gods and you etc. It makes me ashamed. Max was Max with five daughters and an idiot wife. Tom Wolfe was a one book boy and a glandular giant with the brains and the guts of three mice. Scott was a rummy and a liar and dishonest about money with the in-bred talent of a dishonest and easily frightened angel.

Hemingway to Charles Scribner III (May 18–19, 1951)

# CONTENTS

# ILLUSTRATIONS

# PREFACE

When I began serious reading in the late Forties, the novels that most excited me were published by Charles Scribner's Sons. I suspected that there was something wrong with writers published elsewhere. By the time I became a Scribners author in the Seventies, the glory years—the Maxwell Perkins years—were over. Charles Scribner, Jr. (i.e., Charles IV), who was head of the firm, insisted that Perkins's commitment to discovering and encouraging novelists had damaged Charles Scribner's Sons by deflecting attention from building a balanced list.* *Scribner* is now a Simon & Schuster imprint. The Scribner Building at 597 Fifth Avenue became a dress shop.

Publication is the mandatory act of authorship: A book is not a book until it is published. The teaching and study of modern literature are flawed because the circumstances of publication for the books are ignored; therefore, the profession of authorship is ignored. Critics and teachers to the contrary notwithstanding, somebody wrote the book, and somebody else published it. Writers' work, writers' careers, and writers' reputations are influenced by how they are published. A grasp of author-editor-publisher relationships augments serious readers' and competent teachers' understanding of the authorial intention for certain works—including *The Great Gatsby* and *Tender Is the Night; The Sun Also Rises* and *A Farewell to Arms; Look Homeward, Angel* and *Of Time and the River.*

I have done most of my research on Scribners authors F. Scott Fitzgerald, Ernest Hemingway, Ring Lardner, and Thomas Wolfe. Concomitantly I have learned about Maxwell Perkins. The more I learn about him, the more I believe that his achievements have been misunderstood and that his character has been legendized. Perkins was not solely responsible for the stature of the House of Scribner during the Twenties, Thirties, and Forties; but the miracle could not have transpired without him. Under his editorial leadership books mattered more than anything else. He understood that there are no great books without great writers. It was a time when authors were still identified with their publishers. There are no brand-names in publishing; but a Scribners writer was something special in American literature during the Perkins decades.

---

*Charles Scribner, Jr., *In the Company of Writers: A Life in Publishing* (New York: Scribners, 1991); Scribner, *In the Web of Ideas: The Education of a Publisher* (New York: Scribners, 1993).

As I brooded about the fall of the House of Scribner and the decline of publishing values, I concluded that a useful way to assess Perkins was by conflating the epistolary evidence of his endeavors to juggle the needs of three of the greatest American writers. Thus, five letters written during December 1929 provide a sense of the calls on Perkins's attention and forbearance. On December 7–10, Hemingway sent him a two-part letter about Robert McAlmon's allegations that Fitzgerald and Hemingway were homosexuals. Perkins wrote to Fitzgerald on the seventeenth about the false reports of Morley Callaghan's boxing match with Hemingway, in which Fitzgerald was the timekeeper. Wolfe wrote to Perkins on the twenty-fourth expressing mixed feelings about the reception of *Look Homeward, Angel.* Perkins replied to Wolfe on the twenty-seventh assuring him of the success of the novel and asking to see some of his work in progress. On the same day Perkins wrote to Hemingway about the Callaghan flap. These letters are included here; at least nine letters were exchanged by Perkins and the three writers that month. There are separate volumes for Perkins's correspondence with Fitzgerald, Hemingway, and Wolfe; but this collection helps readers to make the connections.

## Editorial Note

This volume assembles 206 letters between Perkins and his Big Three, of which 95 were written by him. There are 57 letters from Fitzgerald to Perkins, 32 from Hemingway to Perkins, and 22 from Wolfe to Perkins; Wolfe's letters have the most wordage because that is the way he wrote. The collection also includes 3 letters between Fitzgerald and Hemingway, 2 letters between Fitzgerald and Wolfe, 2 letters from Perkins to Zelda Fitzgerald, 2 letters between Perkins and Fred Wolfe, 1 letter from Perkins to John Biggs about Fitzgerald, 2 letters from Perkins to Charles Scribner II, a letter from Perkins to Charles Scribner III, and 2 letters from Hemingway to Charles Scribner III.

It has been necessary to cut unessential material from the letters—business matters and comments on nonliterary topics—in order to have space for letters about writing, publishing, and the writers' relationships with Scribners and with one another. All cuts are identified. Nothing has been deleted for reasons of decency or decorum.

Except for a few letters that survive only in printed texts, these letters have been transcribed and printed as written or typed. There are no corrections of spelling or punctuation, but spacing has been regularized. Words in brackets are editorial guesses; empty brackets indicate indecipherable words.

## Acknowledgments

These are some of the people and institutions I am obligated to for assistance with this book: Bertha Perkins Frothingham; J. Gerald Kennedy, the Ernest

Hemingway Foundation; Danielle Lake; Steven Lynn, chairman, Department of English, University of South Carolina; Aldo Magi; AnnaLee Pauls, Princeton University Library; Charles Scribner III (actually Charles V); Phyllis Westberg, Estate of F. Scott Fitzgerald, Harold Ober Associates; Eugene Winick, Estate of Thomas Wolfe, McIntosh & Otis; and Lydia Zelaya, Simon & Schuster. The following archives provided primary material: Thomas Wolfe Collection of William B. Wisdom, Houghton Library, Harvard University; Ernest Hemingway Collection, John F. Kennedy Library; F. Scott Fitzgerald Collection and Charles Scribner's Sons Archives, Princeton University Library; and the Matthew J. and Arlyn Bruccoli Collection of F. Scott Fitzgerald, Thomas Cooper Library, the University of South Carolina.

My ideas about the publishing process were shaped by my work with Vernon Sternberg, Albert Erskine, William Jovanovich, Julian Muller, and Patrick O'Connor. My thinking about the profession of authorship in America was influenced by William Charvat.

# Introduction

Maxwell Perkins (1884–1947) is the only literary editor of whom students of American literature and most of their teachers have heard. He is permanently linked with F. Scott Fitzgerald, Ernest Hemingway, and Thomas Wolfe in literary history and literary myth—which are much the same thing. More than fifty years after his death, job applicants present themselves at publishing firms and announce, "I want to do what Maxwell Perkins did." If asked what he did, the aspirants talk about discovering unpublished geniuses and advising them how to write masterpieces. Sounds like a great job.

The ready explanation that Perkins, who had five daughters, made surrogate sons of his three geniuses is probably accurate. It is also incomplete and simplified. A mild misogynist—he felt uneasy in the company of women, despite his effective work with women writers—Perkins enjoyed the companionship of his male authors. Fitzgerald, Hemingway, and Wolfe were alcoholics, and Perkins drank with them: he was a martini man. Alcohol fueled the glory years at the House of Scribner.

Perkins was twelve years older than Fitzgerald, fifteen years older than Hemingway, and sixteen years older than Wolfe. All three had complex feelings about their fathers. Fitzgerald was ashamed of his father's failure. Hemingway was ashamed of his suicide father's cowardice. Wolfe made his father the richest comic figure in American fiction, W. O. Gant.

Literature courses are taught by people without publishing experience who do not know what editors did for authors and how manuscripts became books. Those pedagogues who mention Perkins in connection with a book or author on the syllabus talk about his success in telling authors what to write and how to write—alleging on no evidence that he revised Fitzgerald, Hemingway, and Wolfe. His editorial role was adivsory—especially in matters of structure. Fitzgerald acknowledged that Perkins's response to the typescript of *The Great Gatsby* helped him to "fix" the novel: ". . . in giving deliberately Gatsby's biography when he gives it to the narrator you do depart from the method of the narrative in some degree, for otherwise almost everything is told, and beautifully told, in the regular flow of it;— in the succession of events or in accompaniment with them" (November 20, 1924).

Perkins's close relationships with Fitzgerald and Hemingway were mainly epistolary. He saw Fitzgerald regularly only during parts of 1920 to 1924 when

Fitzgerald was living in Manhattan and the suburbs. Perkins went fishing with Hemingway in Key West four times and hunting in Arkansas once; otherwise they met when Hemingway was embarking or disembarking in New York. Perkins spent more working hours with Wolfe than with the other two combined.

The most distorted aspect of the Perkins legend is his relationship with Thomas Wolfe, which has contaminated the record of the editor's work with the other writers in his stable. Wolfe required and expected extraordinary editorial help; but even in this case Perkins did not function as a collaborator. He worked with Wolfe night after night, suggesting cuts and advising him about form. He did not rewrite Wolfe; but Perkins finally felt compelled to take *Of Time and the River* away from Wolfe and put it into production. Perkins reported to Marjorie Kinnan Rawlings:

> I am engaged in a kind of life and death struggle with Mr. Thomas Wolfe still, and it is likely to last through the summer. I cannot stop while he will go on, and if he will go on for six weeks more at the present rate, the book will be virtually done. I could even now, if I dared, send a third of it to the printer. But Tom is always threatening to go back to the early part, and if he does that, I do not know what the result will be. We might have to go through the whole struggle over again. It has become an obsession with me now,-one of those things that you get to feel you have got to do even if it costs your life.*

Perkins's friends believed that his struggles to persuade Wolfe to shape and cut his work and Wolfe's defection from Scribner broke Perkins's heart and hastened his death. There are no revisions or insertions in Perkins's hand on any of the tens of thousands of pages of Wolfe's manuscripts and typescripts. Perkins reiterated that "The book belongs to the author."†

Perkins did not discover *Look Homeward, Angel* among the unsolicited manuscripts—Scribners first reader Charles Dunn deserves the credit—but it was Perkins's responsibility to take on the long novel that other publishers had rejected; and he worked hard with Wolfe to make it publishable. The decision to cut sixty-six thousand words from "O Lost" and to publish it as *Look Homeward, Angel* was made for literary and business reasons.‡ Fitzgerald would have been published without Perkins's backing; Hemingway had been published by Boni & Liveright before he came to Scribners; but no Perkins, no Wolfe.

Wolfe's account of his first meeting with Perkins about *O Lost* reveals the editor's response to a masterpiece and his treatment of its obscure author:

---

* June 14, 1934; *Max + Marjorie: The Correspondence between Maxwell E. Perkins and Marjorie Kinnan Rawlings,* ed. Rodger L. Tarr (Gainesville: University Press of Florida, 1999), p. 150.

† To Wolfe, January 16, 1937.

‡ See "Introduction," *O Lost: A Story of the Buried Life,* text established by Arlyn and Matthew J. Bruccoli (Columbia: University of South Carolina Press, 2000), pp. xi–xvi.

Then he began cautiously on the book. Of course, he said, he didn't know about its present form—somewhat incoherent and very long. When I saw now that he was really interested, I burst out wildly saying that I would throw out this, that, and the other—at every point he stopped me quickly saying, "No, no—you must let that stay word for word—that scene's simply magnificent." It became apparent at once that these people were willing to go far farther than I had dared hope—that, in fact, they were afraid I would injure the book by doing too much to it. I saw now that Perkins had a great batch of notes in his hand and that on the desk was a great stack of handwritten paper—a complete summary of my whole enormous book. I was so moved and touched to think that someone at length had thought enough of my work to sweat over it in this way that I almost wept. When I spoke to him of this, he smiled and said everyone in the place had read it. Then he went over the book scene by scene—I found he was more familiar with the scenes and the names of characters than I was—I had not looked at the thing in over six months. For the first time in my life I was getting criticism I could really use. The scenes he wanted cut or changed were invariably the least essential and the least interesting: all the scenes that I had thought too coarse, vulgar, profane, or obscene for publication he forbade me to touch save for a word or two. There was one as rough as anything in Elizabethan drama—when I spoke of this he said it was a masterpiece, and that he had been reading it to Hemingway. He told me I must change a few words. He said the book was new and original, and because of its form could have no formal and orthodox unity, but that what unity it did have came from the strange wild people—the family—it wrote about, as seen through the eyes of a strange wild boy. These people, with relatives, friends, townspeople, he said were "magnificent"—as real as any people he had ever read of. He wanted me to keep these people and the boy at all times foremost—other business, such as courses at state university, etc., to be shortened and subordinated. Said finally if I was hard up he thought Scribners would advance money.*

This volume is restricted to Perkins's work with Fitzgerald, Hemingway, and Wolfe; but he was running the trade department of a major publishing house. His list included Ring Lardner, Marjorie Kinnan Rawlings, Willard Huntington Wright (S. S. Van Dine), Arthur Train, Douglas Southall Freeman, Marcia Davenport, Nancy Hale, Taylor Caldwell, Edmund Wilson, Dawn Powell, Caroline Gordon, Hamilton Basso, Will James, and James Boyd. At the time of his death he was encouraging James Jones to write *From Here to Eternity.*

*To Margaret Roberts, January 12, 1929; *The Letters of Thomas Wolfe,* ed. Elizabeth Nowell (New York: Scribners, 1956), p. 169.

THE ADVOCATE

W. FLETCHER   W. GOODWIN   D. W. STREETER   S. C. WHIPPLE   W. L. STODDARD   S. ERVIN   M. DES. VERDI
C. F. STEVENS   F. E. GREENE
E. C. OBERHOLTZER   VAN W. BROOKS   E. B. SHELDON   R. H. WISWALL   J. H. BRECK
K. B. TOWNSEND   G. A. RIVINIUS
E. D. BIGGERS   R. J. WALSH   H. HAGEDORN   J. L. PRICE   J. WEARE   W. M. E. PERKINS   H. W. BELL
S. P. HENSHAW   A. R. MCINTYRE

The *Harvard Advocate* staff included Perkins and three other students who achieved literary distinction: Van Wyck Brooks as a literary historian, Edward Sheldon as a dramatist, and Earl Derr Biggers as a novelist *(1907 Harvard Class Album).*

▲▼▲

The Twenties was a time of hero worship, and literary figures ranked high among gods of that era. Yet Perkins was an unlikely hero of the Jazz Age. William Maxwell Evarts Perkins was born in New York and raised in Plainfield, New Jersey, but he was a Vermonter with a New England conscience. He was named for his grandfather, William Maxwell Evarts, a United States senator who had been attorney general under Andrew Johnson and secretary of state under Rutherford B. Hayes. Perkins's father, a lawyer, died in 1902. There was not much money; Perkins had to leave St. Paul's Academy after one year, but he was able to attend Harvard. As a member of the Class of 1907 he majored in economics, for which he had little aptitude—rather than English, which he enjoyed—because he believed that it was good discipline to do the things he didn't want to do. Nonetheless, in his freshman year the young Puritan was jailed after the Yale game for being with a drunk classmate, and he took a certain pride in being the first member of his class placed on academic probation. Perkins roomed with Van Wyck Brooks, '08. Charles Townsend Copeland, who taught celebrated Harvard courses in English literature and expository writing, became Perkins's friend and mentor. Perkins wrote for the *Harvard Advocate* and formed friendships with literary undergraduates in the Stylus club but expressed no ambition to be a professional author. John Hall Wheelock, '08—who became his colleague at Scribners—stated that in college Perkins's ambition was to become president of the United States.* The generalization that great editors are frustrated writers who create vicariously does not seem to apply to Perkins. He abandoned whatever literary hopes he may have had at Harvard without discernible pain. As an editor he took satisfaction and pride in the work of his authors, but he declined to claim or accept credit for their successes.

After graduation, Perkins secured a job as a *New York Times* reporter—which he enjoyed. But in 1910 he had fallen in love with Louise Saunders, a Plainfield girl from a well-off family, and required a job suitable for a married man. He applied for the position of advertising manager at Charles Scribner's Sons, armed with a letter to Charles Scribner II from Harvard professor Barrett Wendell: "He is really the sort one can depend on." In 1914 Perkins moved from the Scribners advertising department to the editorial staff. He had demonstrated his literary judgment, and the editorial end of publishing interested him more than the sales end. The joke went around the firm that Mr. Scribner had reassigned Perkins to prevent him from ruining the company by overspending on advertising his favorite books. Charles Scribner's Sons was at that time the most respected imprint in America: a profitable and conservative house with a list that included Henry James, Edith Wharton, John Fox Jr., Thomas Nelson Page, Theodore Roosevelt, Richard Harding Davis, and George Washington Cable. The house published *Scribner's Magazine* and had strength in children's books and religion. William Crary Brownell, "the dean of American critics," was the senior editor, and then literary advisor, from 1888 until his death in 1928. The firm owned its building at 597 Fifth Avenue, near the corner of Forty-eighth Street, with an impressive bookstore on the ground floor.

When Perkins entered publishing it was an occupation for gentlemen. Gentlemen did not raid other gentlemen's authors or try to corrupt them with money. Author-to-publisher loyalty was expected: it was unusual for an important author to change publishers. This state of affairs was better for the publishers

*John Hall Wheelock, *The Last Romantic: A Poet Among Publishers,* ed. Matthew J. Bruccoli with Judith S. Baughman (Columbia: University of South Carolina Press, 2003), p. 51.

than for their authors. Writers—even the very successful ones—earned much less, even in the Twenties boom, than now. The great change in authorial finances resulted from the expansion of subsidiary rights: paperbacks, book clubs, movies, television. American mass-market paperbacks commenced in 1939 and sold for twenty-five cents; they did not become a jackpot until the Sixties. Perkins never had to negotiate a "hard-soft" deal. The Book-of-the-Month Club was launched in 1927 but did not reach a great membership until the Forties and Fifties. Serializations might bring high fees—depending on the circulation of the magazine. Radio rights were not lucrative. Movie rights brought comparatively little (one hundred thousand dollars for *For Whom the Bell Tolls* was regarded as a bonanza in 1941), and there was no television. Agents were not powerful. The boiler-plate Scribners contract had two pages. Sub-rights were covered in one sentence: "It is further agreed that the profits arising from any publication of said work, during the period covered by this agreement, in other than book form shall be divided equally between said PUBLISHERS and said AUTHOR."

Unlike current "acquisitions editors" who deal with agents and do not edit, Perkins recruited authors, advised them on work-in-progress, and read their manuscripts. He prepared extensive memos dealing with plot, character, and structure. His letters of rejection were not form letters; he wrote customized letters offering praise and encouragement while regretfully providing reasons for declining the manuscript. His letters of advice were expressed diffidently: "I guess"; "I think"; "or so it seems to me."

Dr. Johnson hyperbolically declared that "No man but a blockhead ever wrote except for money." They write because they have to, but they need money to do it. In an era of stingy advances, Scribners was careful about corrupting authors. However, early payment of accrued royalties was possible. Perkins was a Yankee, a breed not celebrated for lavish spending. Nonetheless he made personal loans to writers—not always expecting to be repaid—although he did not have independent means. The rules of sound business were suspended for Fitzgerald. In addition to advances against anticipated earnings and interest-free loans from Scribners, he borrowed from Perkins. Fitzgerald died in 1940 owing $5,456.92 to Scribners and at least $1,500 to Perkins. Moreover, Perkins contributed to a fund to let Scottie Fitzgerald finish Vassar. He was no doubt surprised when she paid off what she regarded as a debt.

During his early years at Scribners, Perkins's recommendations involved risk to his job. He was always an employee—not a partner. The house was family-owned; Charles Scribner II (1854–1930) had strong literary tastes and guarded the respectable reputation of his imprint. When *This Side of Paradise*—Perkins's first major discovery—was under consideration in 1919, the junior editor obtained grudging permission to publish it despite Mr. Scribner's opposition. This is John Hall Wheelock's eyewitness report:

. . . I've been in on historic occasions when Max showed himself completely in control of the situation. There was, for instance, the day when Scott Fitzgerald's *This Side of Paradise* came up for discussion. This was before I had become an editor, but the occasion is an historic one. What happened on that occasion followed the usual routine: the editors would find something they thought ought to be published; then they would all go—it would be arranged ahead—into Mr. Charles Scribner's office, and the various arguments, the pros and cons, would be heard, and the decision would be made finally by Mr. Scribner himself.

I understand several had read *This Side of Paradise.* I had read it, and Max had read it. It had very serious flaws in it, but it was quite obviously an outstanding work, something belonging to a new order. Mr. Scribner had read it—and he was very much against it. He said, "It's frivolous. I will not have a frivolous book like that on my list." You must remember that the books that Scribners were then publishing were books by such writers as Henry Van Dyke, Richard Harding Davis, George Washington Cable, Frank R. Stockton, John Galsworthy—all pretty much belonging to the past.

Well, then they got through with their discussion, Mr. Scribner looked up at Max, who was standing behind him, and said, "You haven't said anything, Max. How do you feel about it?" Max, who was a very silent New England type, didn't say anything for a while. Then finally he said very quietly: "My feeling, Mr. Scribner, is that if we let a book like this go, we ought to close up and go out of the publishing business." Mr. Scribner was very much upset: "What do you mean by that?"

"Well," Max said, "we can't go on publishing Theodore Roosevelt and Richard Harding Davis and Henry Van Dyke and Thomas Nelson Page forever, you know. We're got to move on with the times."

Mr. Scribner was impressed by this, and he said, "I'd like to think it over." So he did, and, at a later editorial conference, he said, "Have you any recommendations to make, Max, about changes in the Scott Fitzgerald book?" Max said, "Yes, I have. I've made———, and he had a list of the things that ought to be done. Mr. Scribner said, "All right. If you make those changes to your satisfaction, I'll publish the book." Scott was delirious with joy, and he got to work on it and made most of the changes, though he didn't make all of them. And the book was published.*

Hemingway came to Perkins through Fitzgerald's pressure on both of them. Perkins agreed to publish *The Torrents of Spring* in order to get *The Sun Also Rises* as part of a two-book deal—apparently without reading either one. When *The*

*\* The Last Romantic, pp. 58–59.*

*Sun Also Rises* came up at the editorial meeting in 1925, Perkins was able to persuade Mr. Scribner to put his imprint on a book peppered with promiscuity and alcoholism and that included the word *bitch*.* Ring Lardner also came to Scribners through Fitzgerald; Perkins had trouble getting approval to publish *How to Write Short Stories* (1924), which some of his associates regarded as subliterary.

The publication of *A Farewell to Arms* in 1929 occasioned a widely repeated anecdote about Perkins that exists in several versions. The best-known account is that while discussing the novel with Hemingway, Perkins told him that there was a word that could not be printed; but he could not bring himself to say it and instead wrote *fuck* on his desk calendar. When editor and author went out for drinks, Mr. Scribner came to Perkins's office and saw the calendar notations. The punch line is that when Perkins returned to his office Mr. Scribner solicitously said, "Don't you want to take the rest of the day off, Max? You must be exhausted."†

Perkins placed the highest value on "the real thing in fiction."‡ He regarded *War and Peace* as the greatest novel and gave his authors copies to inspire them. Since Perkins did not read Russian, his admiration for Tolstoy's writing had nothing to do with style or expression. He did not care about political or social messages. Perkins responded to Tolstoy's place descriptions, the characters—perhaps the most important element for him—and the depiction of action in *War and Peace*. These are the qualities Perkins looked for in the writers he published.

Perkins was a hunch player who gambled on writers. He believed that he could recognize promise from talking with a writer or from reading his letters. He risked five hundred dollars on an unwritten novel by the unpublished James Jones in 1946 because he detected that Jones had the essential writer's equipment that could not be taught:

> I was greatly pleased by the last sentence in your letter telling of how "a host of hazy memories come back clear and sharp" from looking at your manuscripts. I remember reading somewhere what I thought was a very true statement to the effect that anybody could find out if he was a writer. If he were a writer, when he tried to write out of some particular day, he found that he could recall exactly how the light fell and how the temperature felt, and all the quality of it. Most people cannot do it. If they can do it, they may never be successful in a pecuniary sense, but that ability is at the bottom of

---

* Its earlier appearance in *The Great Gatsby* was applied to a canine.
† Hemingway was not able to print *fucking* in a Scribners volume until *To Have and Have Not* (1937).
‡ To Hemingway, August 30, 1935; *The Only Thing That Counts: The Ernest Hemingway –Maxwell Perkins Correspondence*, ed. Matthew J. Bruccoli with the assistance of Robert W. Trogdon (New York: Scribner, 1996), p. 224.

writing, I am sure. Not that they would use that day exactly, but that it would be part of the frame of reference, for instance, if they were writing fiction. They would use that day in the fiction, and they could get the exact feel of the day.*

This ability identifies the defining quality of Perkins's greatest writers: the *how-it-was* of their fiction. Fitzgerald recognized a "family resemblance between we three" and their attempts "to recapture the exact feel of a moment in time and space, exemplified by people rather than by things . . . an attempt at a mature memory of a deep experience."†

The great literary editor was a notoriously poor copy editor and proofreader. The books by Perkins's favorites that he personally saw through the press are riddled with factual problems and errors of detail—as in *Gatsby, Tender Is the Night,* and *Look Homeward, Angel.* These textual flaws did not result from Perkins's carelessness or ignorance—although his spelling was shaky. They were the product of his concern with the effectiveness of the work as a whole. The impossible retinas on Dr. T. J. Eckleburg's billboard or the wrong location of Astoria in *Gatsby* or the chronological contradictions in *Tender Is the Night* or the inconsistencies in *Look Homeward, Angel* did not really matter to Perkins.

If Perkins expected his three authorial sons to develop brotherly feelings, he was disappointed. Writers are not automatically happy about the success of other writers; moreover, both Hemingway and Wolfe expected Perkins's total loyalty. Hemingway was compulsively competitive and resented Perkins's commitment to other writers—especially to Wolfe, whom he referred to as "L'il Abner" and described as "a pituitary case." Wolfe was suspicious of everyone. The only meeting between Hemingway and Wolfe, arranged by Perkins in 1933, was a cordial failure: "I hoped Hem would be able to influence Tom to overcome his faults in writing, even though they were the defects of his qualities, such as his tendency to repetitions and excessive expression. . . . He wanted to help Tom, and everything went well, except I think Tom was not in the least affected."‡

Fitzgerald regarded 597 Fifth Avenue as the Mermaid Tavern revidivus and appointed himself acquisitions editor for Scribners; he brought Hemingway and Ring Lardner to the house and recommended Thomas Boyd, John Biggs, Erskine

---

* March 27, 1946; *The House of Scribner, 1931–1984,* Dictionary of Literary Biography Documentary Series, vol. 17, ed. John Delaney (Detroit et al: Bruccoli Clark Layman / Gale Research, 1998), p. 326.

† To Perkins, July 30, 1934; *Dear Scott / Dear Max: The Fitzgerald-Perkins Correspondence,* ed. John Kuehl and Jackson R. Bryer (New York: Scribners, 1971), pp. 203–4.

‡ To John Terry, November 21, 1945; *"Always yours, Max": Maxwell Perkins Responds to Questions about Thomas Wolfe . . . ,* ed. Alice R. Cotten (n.p.: The Thomas Wolfe Society, 1997), p. 57.

Caldwell, Morley Callaghan, and André Chamson to Perkins—who published all of them. Caldwell, an unlikely figure for the Scribners list, left after *Tobacco Road* (1932). Fitzgerald hailed Wolfe's genius and was pleased by his success. After reading *Look Homeward, Angel*, Fitzgerald wired Wolfe: "–have spent twenty consecutive lours weth your fifst book an enmousty moved and grate-fil."* Fitzgerald's report to Perkins was sound: "He strikes me as a man who should be let alone as to length, if he has to be published in five volumes."†

At Perkins's urging, Fitzgerald and Wolfe met in Paris in 1930 and subsequently spent an evening together in Montreux. Wolfe distrusted Perkins's motives in arranging the meeting and was put off by Fitzgerald—as documented by his notebook entry:

> There was once a young man who came to have a feeling of great trust and devotion for an older man. He thought that this older man had created liberty and hope for him. He thought that this older man was brave and loyal. Then he found that this older man had sent him to a drunken and malicious fellow, who tried to injure and hurt his work in every way possible. He found moreover that this older man had sent him to this drunk in order to get the drunk's 'opinion' of him. That is the real end of this story.‡

In 1937 Fitzgerald and Wolfe conducted an epistolary debate about the claims of the novel of selected incident and the novel of inclusion.

The Fitzgerald/Hemingway connection is the most celebrated and distorted authorial relationship in American literary history: the subject of books (fiction and nonfiction) and plays, as well as Hemingway's attacks on Fitzgerald in "The Snows of Kilimanjaro" and in *A Moveable Feast.* It was dangerous to help Hemingway; he never forgave assistance from another writer—except for Ezra Pound. Fitzgerald regarded Hemingway as the greatest living American writer. He vetted *The Sun Also Rises* and *A Farewell to Arms,* incurring Hemingway's enmity by providing advice that he acted on. After Fitzgerald's death, Hemingway belittled him for twenty years, attacking *The Last Tycoon* and accusing Fitzgerald of dishonesty. An undated Fitzgerald notebook entry reads: "I talk with the authority of failure–Ernest with the authority of success. We could never sit across the table again."§ After 1929 Fitzgerald and Hemingway mainly sent

---

*August 2, 1930; *Dictionary of Literary Biography 229: Thomas Wolfe: A Documentary Volume,* ed. Ted Mitchell (Detroit: Bruccoli Clark Layman / Gale, 2001), p. 148.
† Ca. September 1, 1930.
‡ *The Notebooks of Thomas Wolfe,* ed. Richard S. Kennedy and Paschal Reeves (Chapel Hill: University of North Carolina Press, 1970), vol. 2, p. 511.
§ *The Notebooks of F. Scott Fitzgerald,* ed. Matthew J. Bruccoli (New York and London: Harcourt Brace Jovanovich / Bruccoli Clark, 1978), #1915. See Bruccoli, *Fitzgerald and Hemingway: A Dangerous Friendship* (New York: Carroll & Graf, 1994).

messages and commented on each other through letters to Perkins. Hemingway adopted the stance of an older brother or uncle expressing dismay about an irresponsible but gifted youth. Perkins maintained the trust of both.

Perkins is supposed to have had more books dedicated to him than any other editor: the accepted count is sixty-eight. Each of the three sons dedicated books to him. Fitzgerald gave *The Beautiful and Damned* a triple dedication to Perkins, Shane Leslie, and George Jean Nathan. After Perkins's death Hemingway way dedicated *The Old Man and the Sea* to Perkins and Charles Scribner III. The dedication that attracted the most attention and caused great trouble was Wolfe's lavish tribute in *Of Time and the River,* which reinforced the charge that Wolfe couldn't write without Perkins. Wheelock became convinced that this dedication was the key ingredient in Wolfe's defection:

> Tom wrote this absurd dedication. I said to Tom, "No, look–you can't. You'll make yourself ridiculous. Don't do this, Tom. Think it over. Cut it down. You've got four pages here; cut it down to four lines, if you can." Oh, he was furious with me. He had this overwhelming emotion, and he wanted to articulate it. I did get it down, I think, to about eighteen lines; but even, so, I knew it was fatal. Max knew it would be, too. Or, at least, I suggested to him: "Why can't you tell Tom that you won't accept anything in the dedication except just 'To my friend Maxwell Perkins'?" But Max was a little bit hipped on Tom. He had no son of his own. He had five daughters. He had a great contempt for women, you know. He sat down to breakfast every morning with six of them. And he made Tom into his son.*

Wolfe did not complete a novel after he left Perkins. *The Web and the Rock* (1939) and *You Can't Go Home Again* (1940) were assembled from work in progress after Wolfe's death by Harper editor Edward Aswell.

Literary editing is a test of character. Perkins's loyalty to his authors and to their work is famous. He believed in the supreme worth of great literature. When Wolfe was forcing a break with Perkins in 1937 and claiming that Perkins had prevented him from publishing what he wanted to write, Perkins responded: "If it were not true that you, for instance, should write as you see, feel, and think, then a writer would be of no importance, and books merely things for amusement. And since I have always thought that there can be nothing so important as a book can be, and some are, I could not help but think as you do."†

There is a publishing wisecrack applied to promising young authors: "What a nice person. Too bad." Great writers have something wrong with them; the greatest ones are deeply flawed. Perkins accepted this condition. He formed close

* *The Last Romantic,* pp. 63–64.
† 16 January 1937.

friendships with his writers, but the books mattered more. Editors protect themselves from their authors beyond a certain point. Maxwell Perkins did not. Perkins worried about Fitzgerald and found money to keep him going. *Tender Is the Night* probably would not have been published without Perkins's support, and Fitzgerald would not have written as much of *The Love of the Last Tycoon* as he did without Perkins's letters of encouragement and personal loans. Although a mean and suspicious man, Hemingway was the least worrisome of Perkins's geniuses—apart from his angry complaints about the division of subsidiary rights income. Perkins kept his geniuses. Fitzgerald never thought of leaving Perkins. Hemingway occasionally threatened to defect, but he was bluffing. No editor or publishing house could have kept Wolfe; only Perkins could have held him for four books.

Perkins's daughter, Bertha Frothingham, has observed that "I think his real genius lay in his ability to understand each individual talent so that he encouraged and stretched their minds to the utmost but never asked more than a writer was capable of delivering."* Perkins was not the eccentric, naive figure that some versions of his legend portray. He knew that great writers are born troublemakers and took the responsibility of making it possible for them to do what only they could do. The tough-minded Yankee Perkins is more convincing than the saintly character. Thus his statement on writers to Van Wyck Brooks: "They are all sons of bitches."† Perkins knew that without the sons of bitches, there are no masterpieces. If Perkins does qualify for editorial sainthood, it is for his commitment to Wolfe's work and his forbearance with this volatile genius. Before Wolfe broke with him, Perkins did not think it could happen. He should have expected it.

Wheelock has testified to Perkins's recognition that Hemingway's claims about progress on major novels after *For Whom the Bell Tolls* were untrue: "Max knew what Hemingway, fortunately, did not know. Max had this extraordinary intuitive, uncanny thing that made him such a great editor. We always kept hearing about the books that Hemingway was working on; always next year there was to be a big one, a new big one ready. I asked Max about it. He said, 'Ernest will never do anything again. He's done for.' I said, 'How do you know that?' Max said, 'I just know. He's absolutely done for.' And he was. That's why he killed himself, in the end."‡

Perkins believed that the ideal of an editor should be to publish great novels—and to encourage novelists to write them. But he was a good businessman and was responsible for publishing profitable lists at Charles Scribner's

---

* To Bruccoli, March 24, 2003.
† *Van Wyck Brooks: An Autobiography* (New York: Dutton, 1965), p. 631.
‡ *The Last Romantic,* p. 61.

Sons.* The spring 1929 Scribners catalogue announced ninety-six forthcoming titles, including lists for Art and Architecture (18), Books for Younger Readers (4), Religion (14), The Scribner Athletic Library (6), and Educational Books (13). Some of these were bumped to the fall catalogue, which listed ninety-one new books. The 1929 list featured S. S. Van Dine's *The Bishop Murder Case*, Winston Churchill's *Aftermath*, Will James's *Sand*, Arthur Train's *Illusion*, Ring Lardner's *Round Up*, André Chamson's *The Road* and *Roux the Bandit*, Thomas Boyd's *Mad Anthony Wayne*, Benito Mussolini's *My Autobiography*, Leon Trotsky's *My Life*, Edmund Wilson's *I Thought of Daisy*, and Morley Callaghan's *A Native Argosy*. Five of the books were by authors Fitzgerald had scouted for Scribners. Although executive responsibilities probably prevented Perkins from personally editing more than a dozen books in a year, he took responsibility for what were known in the house as "Max's books." The 1929 trade line-up included *A Farewell to Arms* (seven printings: about seventy-five thousand copies) and *Look Homeward, Angel* (three printings: about eleven thousand copies).

Great careers require good timing. Maxwell Perkins could not be Maxwell Perkins now in the era of conglomerate publishing controlled by accountants. He would not be able to get his books through the acquisitions committees. Acquisitions editors were not paid to acquire masterpieces. He would not be able to carry Fitzgerald; he would not be able to nurture Wolfe. Perkins worked for a family-owned house. There were editorial meetings, but the only person he really had to convince was named Scribner. From 1932 to 1947 Perkins—whose title was editor-in-chief and vice president—was able to exercise his judgment and act on his hunches with the backing of Charles III, "Young Charlie," a horsey drinker who "adored" him, according to Charles IV, who did not.

When Maxwell Perkins died of pneumonia in 1947, he had been at Charles Scribner's Sons for thirty-seven years, during which time the canon of American fiction was reconstituted by what critics have since imprecisely categorized as "modernism." If that term is usable for American fiction, it works for novels written by William Faulkner and John Dos Passos—who were not Scribners authors—which developed innovative techniques for treating point of view, mental states and time. Perkins's classic novelists were not experimental writers. The editor was committed to fiction rooted in "the real thing": how it was; what the people were like; how they behaved—without fancy tricks or typographical games. During the Twenties and Thirties the American novel became the most effective literary means for recording social history and portraying character since the Victorian novel. The major novelists associated with Perkins wrote

---

*Perkins's publication of Zelda Fitzgerald's novel, *Save Me the Waltz*, in 1932 was an unbusinesslike act of kindness. The three Scribners novels by Martha Gellhorn, Hemingway's third wife, had commercial value, if not literary value.

historical fiction about the present. Wolfe was a traditional nineteenth-century novelist with an infusion of stream-of-consciousness—or stream-of-speech. Hemingway qualifies for membership in the "modern movement" on the basis of his "unliterary" material and stylized dialogue more than for technical innovation. Fitzgerald developed new methods for structure and point-of-view in *The Great Gatsby* and *Tender Is the Night.*

Maxwell Perkins is permanently connected with the three geniuses he served; but his influence extended beyond the books and authors published by Charles Scribner's Sons. Publisher-editor Patrick O'Connor has assessed the scope of Perkins's achievement: "He shaped American literature more than any other editor. He was responsible for the literary popular novel. He found major authors, and he found the readership for their books."*

*To Bruccoli, May 1, 2003.

# CHRONOLOGY

| June 21, 1929 | *Scribner's Magazine* is banned in Boston because of *A Farewell to Arms* segment. |
| September 27, 1929 | Publication of *A Farewell to Arms* |
| October 18, 1929 | Publication of Wolfe's *Look Homeward, Angel* |
| March 15–16, 1930 | Perkins visits Hemingway in Key West. |
| March 1–13, 1931 | Perkins visits Hemingway in Key West. |
| September 23, 1932 | Publication of Hemingway's *Death in the Afternoon* |
| October 7, 1932 | Publication of Zelda Fitzgerald's *Save Me the Waltz* |
| December 16–21, 1932 | Perkins goes duck hunting with Hemingway in Arkansas. |
| October 27, 1933 | Publication of Hemingway's *Winner Take Nothing* |
| January 1934 | Wolfe and Perkins begin work on *Of Time and the River.* |
| January–April 1934 | Serialization of Fitzgerald's *Tender Is the Night* in *Scribner's Magazine* |
| April 12, 1934 | Publication of *Tender Is the Night* |
| Late January 1935 | Perkins visits Hemingway in Key West to discuss terms for *Green Hills of Africa.* |
| March 8, 1935 | Publication of *Of Time and the River*—dedicated to Perkins |
| March 20, 1935 | Publication of Fitzgerald's *Taps at Reveille* |
| May–November 1935 | Serialization of Hemingway's *Green Hills of Africa* in *Scribner's Magazine* |
| October 25, 1935 | Publication of *Green Hills of Africa* |
| November 14, 1935 | Publication of Wolfe's *From Death to Morning* |
| August 21, 1936 | Publication of Wolfe's *The Story of a Novel* |
| November 1936– January 1937 | Wolfe and Perkins exchange letters that result in the termination of Wolfe's relationship with Scribners. |
| August 11, 1937 | Hemingway and Max Eastman brawl in Perkins's office. |
| October 15, 1937 | Publication of Hemingway's *To Have and Have Not* |
| September 15, 1938 | Death of Thomas Wolfe from tuberculosis of the brain |
| October 14, 1938 | Publication of Hemingway's *The Fifth Column and The First Forty-nine Stories* |
| June 22, 1939 | Publication by Harper of Wolfe's *The Web and the Rock* (edited by Edward C. Aswell), in which Perkins is portrayed as Foxhall Edwards |
| November 18, 1940 | Publication by Harper of Wolfe's *You Can't Go Home Again* (edited by Aswell), in which Perkins is again portrayed as Foxhall Edwards |

| | |
|---|---|
| October 21, 1940 | Publication of Hemingway's *For Whom the Bell Tolls* |
| December 21, 1940 | Death of F. Scott Fitzgerald from a heart attack |
| October 27, 1941 | Publication of Fitzgerald's *The Last Tycoon* [*The Love of the Last Tycoon*], edited by Edmund Wilson |
| August 12, 1945 | Publication by New Directions of Fitzgerald's *The Crack-Up,* edited by Wilson |
| June 17, 1947 | Death of Maxwell Perkins from pneumonia |
| September 7, 1950 | Publication of Hemingway's *Across the River and into the Trees* |
| September 8, 1952 | Publication of Hemingway's *The Old Man and the Sea*—dedicated to Perkins and Charles Scribner III |
| October 28, 1954 | Hemingway learns that he has won the Nobel Prize for Literature. |
| July 2, 1961 | Hemingway commits suicide. |

### *Charles Scribner's Sons*

*The Proprietors*

Charles Scribner (1821–1871)
founder of firm in 1846;
it became Charles Scribner's Sons in 1878

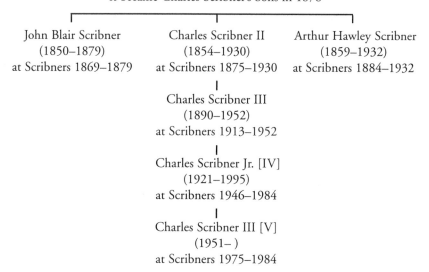

| John Blair Scribner | Charles Scribner II | Arthur Hawley Scribner |
|---|---|---|
| (1850–1879) | (1854–1930) | (1859–1932) |
| at Scribners 1869–1879 | at Scribners 1875–1930 | at Scribners 1884–1932 |

Charles Scribner III
(1890–1952)
at Scribners 1913–1952

Charles Scribner Jr. [IV]
(1921–1995)
at Scribners 1946–1984

Charles Scribner III [V]
(1951– )
at Scribners 1975–1984

In 1979 the company merged with Atheneum; in 1984 it became a subsidiary of Macmillan. Since 1984 the Charles Scribner's Sons imprint has been subsumed successively by Macmillan, Maxwell Communications, and Simon & Schuster.

# LETTERS

Perkins in mid-career (Princeton University Library).

*To: Fitzgerald*
*From: Perkins*                    *TLS, 1 p. Princeton*

Aug. 19, 1918.

Lieutenant F. Scott Fitzgerald,
     Hq. Co. 67th Infantry,
          Camp Sheridan, Ala.
Dear Sir:

    We have been reading "The Romantic Egoist"[1] with a very unusual degree of interest;- in fact no ms. novel has come to us for a long time that seemed to display so much originality, and it is therefore hard for us to conclude that we cannot offer to publish it as it stands at present. Of course, in this we are considerably influenced by the prevailing conditions, including a governmental limitation on the number of publications and very severe manufacturing costs which make profitable publication far more difficult than ordinarily: but we are also influenced by certain characteristics of the novel itself. We generally avoid criticism as beyond our function and as likely to be for that reason not unjustly resented by an author but we should like to risk some very general comments this time because, if they seemed to you so far in point that you applied them to a revision of the ms., we should welcome a chance to reconsider its publication.

    The chief of these is that the story does not seem to us to work up to a conclusion;- neither the hero's career nor his character are shown to be brought to any stage which justifies an ending. This may be intentional on your part for it is certainly not untrue to life; but it leaves the reader distinctly disappointed and dissatisfied since he has expected him to arrive somewhere either in an actual sense by his response to the war perhaps, or in a psychological one by "finding himself" as for instance Pendennis[2] is brought to do. He does go to the war, but in almost the same spirit that he went to college and school,- because it is simply the thing to do. It seems to us in short that the story does not culminate in anything as it must to justify the reader's interest as he follows it; and that it might be made to do so quite consistently with the characters and with its earlier stages.

    It seems to us too that not enough significance is given to some of those salient incidents and scenes, such as the affairs with girls. We do not suggest that you should resort to artificiality by giving a significance inconsistent with that of the life of boys of the age of the hero, but that it would be well if the high points were heightened so far as justifiable; and perhaps this effect could partly be gained by pruning away detail you might find could be spared elsewhere. Quite possibly all that we have said is covered by your own criticism of the ms, as at present a little "crude" and that the revision you contemplate will itself remove the basis of our criticism, and if when you make this you allow us a second reading we shall gladly give it. We do not want anything we have said to make you think we failed to get your idea in the book,- we certainly do not wish you to "conventionalize" it by any means in either form or manner, but only to do those things which it seems to us important to intensify its effect and so satisfy a reader that he will recommend it,- which is the great thing to accomplish toward a success.

We know how busy you are and how absorbed you must be in your present work, and it is rather difficult to think of you as being able to do this revising too; but as you have yourself spoken of it we have less hesitation in making suggestions toward it and in sending back the ms;- we hope we shall see it again and we shall then reread it immediately,- in fact our present delay was due to a misapprehension which led us to think you did not care about an early decision.

Very truly yours,<br>Charles Scribner's Sons[3]

### Notes

1. Fitzgerald's original title for the novel that became *This Side of Paradise*. He performed a fast revision and resubmitted the novel, but it was again rejected.
2. The title hero of William Makepeace Thackeray's 1848–50 novel.
3. This signature is in Perkins's hand.

▲ ▼ ▲

*To: Perkins*
*From: Fitzgerald*                    *ALS, 2 pp. Princeton*

599 Summit Ave<br>St. Paul, Minnesota<br>July 26th, 1919

Dear Mr. Perkins:

After four months attempt to write commercial copy by day and painful half-hearted imitations of popular literature by night I decided that it was one thing or another. So I gave up getting married and went home.

Yesterday I finished the first draft of a novel called

THE EDUCATION OF A PERSONAGE

It is in no sense a revision of the ill-fated Romantic Egotist[1] but it contains some of the former material improved and worked over and bears a strong family resemblance besides.

But while the other was a tedius, disconnected casserole this is definate attempt at a big novel and I really believe I have hit it, as immediatly I stopped disciplining the muse she trotted obediently around and became an erratic mistress if not a steady wife.

Now what I want to ask you is this—if I send you the book by August 20th and you decide you could risk its publication (I am blatantly confident that you will) would it be brought out in October, say, or just what would decide its date of publication?

This is an odd question I realize especially since you havn't even seen the book but you have been so kind in the past about my stuff that I venture to intrude once more apon your patience.

Sincerely<br>F Scott Fitzgerald

*Note*

1. Fitzgerald apparently used "Egoist" and "Egotist" interchangeably.

▲ ▼ ▲

*To: Fitzgerald*
*From: Perkins*                     *CC, 2 pp. Princeton*

Sept. 16, 1919

Dear Mr. Fitzgerald:

I am very glad, personally, to be able to write to you that we are all for publishing your book, "This Side of Paradise". Viewing it as the same book that was here before, which in a sense it is, though translated into somewhat different terms and extended further, I think that you have improved it enormously. As the first manuscript did, it abounds in energy and life and it seems to me to be in much better proportion. I was afraid that, when we declined the first manuscript, you might be done with us conservatives. I am glad you are not. The book is so different that it is hard to prophesy how it will sell but we are all for taking a chance and supporting it with vigor. As for terms, we shall be glad to pay a royalty of 10% on the first five thousand copies and of 15% thereafter,– which by the way, means more than it use to now that retail prices upon which the percentage is calculated, have so much advanced.

Hoping to hear from you, we are,

Sincerely yours,

P.S. Our expectation would be to publish your book in the early Spring. Now, if you are ready to have us do this, and have the time, we should be glad to have you get together any publicity matter you could for us, including a photograph. You have been in the advertising game long enough to know the sort of thing.

▲ ▼ ▲

To: Perkins
From: Fitzgerald                              *ALS, 5 pp. Princeton*

599 Summit Ave.
St. Paul, Minn
Sept 18th, 1919

Dear Mr Perkins:

Of course I was delighted to get your letter and I've been in a sort of trance all day; not that I doubted you'd take it but at last I have something to show people. It has enough advertisement in St. Paul already to sell several thousand copies + I think Princeton will buy it (I've been a periodical, local Great-Expectations for some time in both places)

Terms ect I leave to you but one thing I can't relinquish without at least a slight struggle. Would it be utterly impossible for you to publish the book Xmas—or say by February? I have so many things dependent on its success—including of course a girl—not that I expect it to make me a fortune but it will have a psychological effect on me and all my surroundings and besides open up new fields. I'm in that stage where every month counts frantically and seems a cudgel in a fight for happiness against time. Will you let me know more exactly how that difference in time of publication influences the sale + what you mean by "early Spring"?

Excuse this ghastly hand writing but I'm a bit nervous today. I'm beginning (last month) a very ambitious novel called "The Demon Lover"[1] which will probably take a year also I'm writing short stories. I find that what I enjoy writing is always my best— Every young author ought to read Samuel Butler's Note Books.[2]

I'm writing quite a marvelous after-the-war story.[3] Does Mr Bridges[4] think that they're a little passé or do you think he'd like to see it?

I'll fix up data for advertising + have a photo taken next week with the most gigantic enjoyment. (I'm trying H.G. Well's use of vast garagantuan [sp.] words)

Well thank you for a very happy day and numerous other favors and let me know if I've any possible chance for earlier publication and give my thanks or whatever is in order to Mr. Scribner or whoever else was on the deciding committee.

Probably be East next month or Nov.

                                                    Sincerely
(over for P.S.)                                     F Scott Fitzgerald

P.S. Who picks out the cover? I'd like something that could be a set—look cheerful + important like a Shaw Book. I notice Shaw, Galesworthy + Barrie do that. But Wells doesn't— I wonder why. No need of illustrations is there? I knew a fellow at College who'd have been a wonder for books like mine—a mixture

**Memorandum of Agreement,** *made this* twenty-third *Day of* September *19* 19

*between* **F. SCOTT FITZGERALD**

*of* St. Louis, Missouri, Paul Minn - - - - *hereinafter called "the* AUTHOR,"

*and* CHARLES SCRIBNER'S SONS, *of New York City, N. Y., hereinafter called "the*

PUBLISHERS." *Said* - - F. Scott Fitzgerald - - - *being the* AUTHOR

*and* PROPRIETOR *of a work entitled:*

THIS SIDE OF PARADISE

*in consideration of the covenants and stipulations hereinafter contained, and agreed to be per-*
*formed by the* PUBLISHERS, *grants and guarantees to said* PUBLISHERS *and their successors the*
*exclusive right to publish the said work in all forms during the terms of copyright and renewals*
*thereof, hereby covenanting with said* PUBLISHERS *that he is the sole* AUTHOR *and*
PROPRIETOR *of said work.*

Said AUTHOR *hereby authorizes said* PUBLISHERS *to take out the copyright on said*
*work, and further guarantees to said* PUBLISHERS *that the said work is in no way whatever a*
*violation of any copyright belonging to any other party, and that it contains nothing of a scandal-*
*ous or libelous character; and that he and* **his** *legal representatives shall and will hold*
*harmless the said* PUBLISHERS *from all suits, and all manner of claims and proceedings which*
*may be taken on the ground that said work is such violation or contains anything scandalous or*
*libelous; and he further hereby authorizes said* PUBLISHERS *to defend at law any and all*
*suits and proceedings which may be taken or had against them for infringement of any other copy-*
*right or for libel, scandal, or any other injurious or hurtful matter or thing contained in or*
*alleged or claimed to be contained in or caused by said work, and pay to said* PUBLISHERS *such*
*reasonable costs, disbursements, expenses, and counsel fees as they may incur in such defense.*

Said PUBLISHERS, *in consideration of the right herein granted and of the guarantees*
*aforesaid, agree to publish said work at their own expense, in such style and manner as they*
*shall deem most expedient, and to pay said* AUTHOR, *or* - **his** - *legal representatives,*
**TEN (10)** —————————— *per cent. on their Trade-List (retail) price, cloth style, for* **the**
**first five thousand (5000) copies of said work sold by them in the United States**
**and FIFTEEN (15) per cent. for all copies sold thereafter in the United States.**
Provided, *nevertheless, that one-half the above named royalty shall be paid on all copies*
*sold outside the United States; and provided that no percentage whatever shall be paid on any*
*copies destroyed by fire or water, or sold at or below cost, or given away for the purpose of aiding*
*the sale of said work.*

It is further agreed that the profits arising from any publication of said work, during
*the period covered by this agreement, in other than book form shall be divided equally between*
*said* PUBLISHERS *and said* AUTHOR.

First page of the contract for Fitzgerald's first novel; he did not receive an advance (Bruccoli Collection, Thomas Cooper Library, University of South Carolina).

of Aubrey Beardsly, Hogarth + James Montgomery Flagg. But he got killed in the war.[5]

Excuse this immoderately long and rambling letter but I think you'll have to allow me several days for recuperation[6]

Yrs.

F.S.F

*Notes*

1. Unpublished and probably never written.
2. *The Note-Books of Samuel Butler,* ed. Henry Festing Jones (1912). Fitzgerald praised it in his copy as "The most interesting human document ever written" (Matthew J. and Arlyn Bruccoli Collection of F. Scott Fitzgerald, Thomas Cooper Library, University of South Carolina).
3. Possibly "May Day," published in the July 1920 *Smart Set.*
4. Robert Bridges, editor of *Scribner's Magazine.*
5. J. V. Newlin, Princeton '19.
6. *This Side of Paradise* was an immediate success when published in March 1920; it was widely reviewed and required nine printings (41,075 copies) in 1920.

▲ ▼ ▲

*To: Perkins*
*From: Fitzgerald*                              *ALS, 1 p. Princeton*

38 W 59th St.
New York City
Dec 31st, 1920

Dear Mr. Perkins:

The bank this afternoon refused to lend me anything on the security of stock I hold—and I have been pacing the floor for an hour trying to decide what to do. Here, with the novel[1] within two weeks of completion, am I with six hundred dollars worth of bills and owing Reynolds[2] $650 for an advance on a story that I'm utterly unable to write. I've made half a dozen starts yesterday and today and I'll go mad if I have to do another debutante which is what they want.

I hoped that at last being square with Scribner's I could remain so. But I'm at my wit's end. Isn't there some way you could regard this as an advance on the new novel rather than on the Xmas sale which won't be due me till July? And at the same interest that it costs Scribner's to borrow? Or could you make it a month's loan from Scribner + Co. with my next ten books as security? I need $1600.00

Anxiously
F. Scott Fitzgerald

*Notes*

1. *The Beautiful and Damned.*
2. Paul Revere Reynolds literary agency, in which Harold Ober, Fitzgerald's long-time agent, was then a partner.

▲ ▼ ▲

*To: Fitzgerald*
*From: Perkins*                                    *CC, 3 pp.*[1] *Princeton*

Dec. 6, 1921

Dear Fitzgerald:

   I think almost every change you have made in "The Beautiful and Damned" has been a good one except that passage about the Bible.[2] I made a comment

Perkins drew this sketch of the Fitzgeralds in his August 31, 1920, letter to his daughter Bertha: "This picture shows me doing what I have been doing for five whole hours —talking. I have been trying to tell a writer and his wife how he should write. Isn't that funny when I don't know how to do it myself. I even told him a story *to* write that I made up;– and he was delighted with it" (From *Father to Daughter*, by permission of Bertha Perkins Frothingham).

on the proof on that point, and I cannot add much to it. I think I know exactly what you mean to express, but I don't think it will go. Even when people are altogether wrong, you cannot but respect those who speak with such passionate sincerity. You may think Carlyle is all rubbish, for instance but you cannot but admire him, or at least feel strong about him. What Maurey says is quite consistent with his character but this will seem to have been your point of view and I don't think it would be that.

. . . . .
. . . . .
. . . . .

Yours as ever,

## Notes

1. 197 words have been omitted from this letter.
2. In the "Symposium" section Maury Noble describes the Bible as a work expressing "profound scepticism" and "universal irony."

▲ ▼ ▲

*To: Perkins*                           *ca. December 10, 1921*
*From: Fitzgerald*                      *ALS, 8 pp. Princeton*

626 Goodrich Ave.
St. Paul, Minn

Dear Mr. Perkins–

Have just recieved your letter in re Bible anecdote in novel and I'm rather upset about it. You say:

"Even when people are wrong you cannot but respect those who speak with such passionate sincerity about it."

Now in that remark lies, I think, the root of your objection—except to substitute "be intimidated by" for "respect." I don't suppose any but the most religious minded people in the world believe that such interludes as The Song of Solomon, the story of Ruth have or ever had even in the minds of the original chroniclers the faintest religious significance. The Roman church insists that in the song of Solomon the bride is the church + the lover is Christ but it is almost universally doubted if any such thing was even faintly intended.

Now I feel sure that most people will know that my sketch refers to the old testament, and to Jehovah, the cruel hebrew God, agint whom such writers as even Mark Twain not to mention Anatole France + a host of others have delivered violent pyrotechnics from time to time.

As to the personal side of it don't you think all changes in the minds of people are brought about by the assertion of a thing–startling perhaps at first but later often becoming, with the changes of the years, bromidic. You have read Shaw's preface to Androcles and the Lion—that made no great stir—in fact to the more sophisticated of the critics it was a bit bromidic. His preface, moreover, is couched with very little reverence even tho it treats of <u>Christ</u> who is much less open to discussion than merely that beautiful epic of the bible. If you object to my phrasing I could substitute "deity" for "godalmighty" + get a better word than bawdy—in fact make it more dignified—but I would hate to cut it out as its very clever in its way + Mencken—who saw it—and Zelda were very enthusiastic about it. It's the sort of thing you find continually in Anatole France's <u>Revolt of the Angels</u>—as well as in <u>Jurgen</u>[1] + in Mark Twain's <u>Mysterious Stranger</u>. The idea, refusing homage to the Bible + it's God, runs thru many of Mark Twain's essays + all through Paine's biography.[2]

In fact Van Wyke Brooks in <u>The Ordeal</u>[3] critisizes Clemens for allowing many of his statements to be toned down at the request of Wm. Dean Howells or Mrs. Clemens. If it was an incident which I felt had no particular literary merit I should defer to your judgement without question but that passage belongs beautifully to that scene and is exactly what was needed to make it more than a beautiful setting for ideas that fail to appear. You say:

"Even when people are altogether wrong, you cannot but respect those who speak with such passionate sincerity."

I can imagine that remark having been made to Gallileo and Mencken, Samuel Butler + Anatole France, Voltaire and Bernard Shaw, George Moore and even, if you will pardon me, in this form once upon a time.

"You don't like these scribes and Pharisees. You call them whitened sepulcheres but even when people are altogether wrong— ect"

I havn't seen the proof with your notation and have only read your letter. But I do feel that my judgement is right in this case. I do not expect in any event that I am to have the same person for person public this time that <u>Paradise</u> had. My one hope is to be endorsed by the intellectually élite + thus be <u>forced</u> on to people as Conrad has. (Of course I'm assuming that my work grows in sincerity and proficiency from year to year as it has so far). If I cut this out it would only because I would be afraid and I havn't done that yet + dread the day when I'll have to.

Please write me frankly as I have you—and tell me if you are speaking for yourself, for the Scribner Co. or for the public. I am rather upset about this whole thing. Will wait until I hear from you

As Ever

<u>See next Page</u>

P.S. Besides, as to the position of the thing in the story. It is nessesary to show the growth of Maury's pessimism and to do this I have invented a fable in which the <u>hoi poloi</u> do more than refuse to believe their wise men—but they twist the very wisdom of the wise into a justification of their own maudlin and self-satisfactory creeds. This would discourage anyone.

F.S.F.

*Notes*

1. James Branch Cabell's 1919 novel, which was regarded as sexually suggestive.
2. *Mark Twain* (1912) by Albert Bigelow Paine.
3. *The Ordeal of Mark Twain* (1920) by Van Wyck Brooks.

▲ ▼ ▲

*To: Fitzgerald*
*From: Perkins*                  *CC, 4 pp. Princeton*

Dec. 12, 1921

Dear Fitzgerald:

Don't ever <u>defer</u> to my judgment. You won't on any vital point, I know, and I should be ashamed, if it were possible to have made you; for a writer of any account must speak solely for himself. I should hate to play (assuming V.W.B.'s position to be sound) the W. D. Howells to your Mark Twain.

It is not to the <u>substance</u> of this passage that I object. Everyone of any account, anyone who could conceivably read this book, under forty, agrees with the substance of it. If they did not there would be less objection to it in one way —it would then startle them as a revelation of a new point of view which, by giving a more solid kind of value, would lessen the objection on account of flippancy (I hate the word. I hate to be put in the position of using such words as "respect" and "flippancy" which have so often enraged me, but there is some meaning in them). The old testament ought not to be treated in a way which suggests a failure to realize its tremendous significance in the recent history of man, as if it could simply be puffed away with a breath of contempt, it is so trivial. That is the effect of the passage at present. It is partly so because Maury is talking and is talking in character;- and that is the way men do talk too, so far as ability enables them, even when they fully appreciate every side of the matter. It is here that the question of the public comes in. They will not make allowance for the fact that a character is talking extemporaneously. They will think F. S. F. is writing deliberately. Tolstoi did that even, and to Shakespeare. Now, you are, through Maury, expressing your views, of course; but you would do so differently if you were deliberately stating them as your views. You speak of Gallileo: he and

Bruno showed themselves to have a genuine sense of the religious significance of the theories they broke down. They were not in a state of mind to treat the erroneous beliefs of men with a light contempt. France does not so treat Christ in that story of Pilate in his old age. And "Whited Sepulchre" is an expression of high contempt, although applied to an object which had no such quality of significance as the Bible.

My point is that you impair the effectiveness of the passage—of the very purpose you use it for—by giving it that quality of contempt and I wish you would try so to revise it as not to antagonize even the very people who agree with the substance of it. You would go a long way toward this if you cut out "God Almighty" and put "Deity". In fact if you will change it on the line indicated by that change you will have excised the element to which I object.

I do agree that it belongs in Maury's speech; that it does bring it to a focus. But you could so revise it that it would do this without at the same time doing the thing to which we object.

I hope this gets over to you. If I saw you for ten minutes I know you would understand and would agree with me.

As ever,

▲▼▲

*To: Perkins*                    *ca. December 16, 1921. St. Paul, Minnesota*
*From: Fitzgerald*                        *ALS, 5 pp.*[1] *Princeton*

626 Goodrich Ave

Dear Mr. Perkins—

Your second letter came and I want to apologize to you for mine. I might have known you did not mean what in haste I imagined you did. The thing <u>was</u> flippant—I mean it was the sort of worst of Geo. Jean Nathan.[2] I have changed it now—changed "godalmighty" to deity, cut out "bawdy" + changed several other words so I think it is all right.[3]

Why, really, my letter was so silly with all those absurd citations of "Twain," Anatole France, Howells ect was because I was in a panic because I was afraid I might have to cut it out and as you say it does round out the scene.

I hope you'll accept my apology.

  . . . . .

I have put a new ending on the book—that is on the last paragraph, instead of the repetition of the Paradise scene of which I was never particularly fond. I think that now the finish will leave the "taste" of the whole book in the reader's mouth as it didn't before—if you know what I mean.[4]

I can't tell you how sorry I am about that silly letter. I took that "Oh Christ" out as you suggested. As you say "Oh, God" won't fill the gap but "oh my God" does it pretty well.

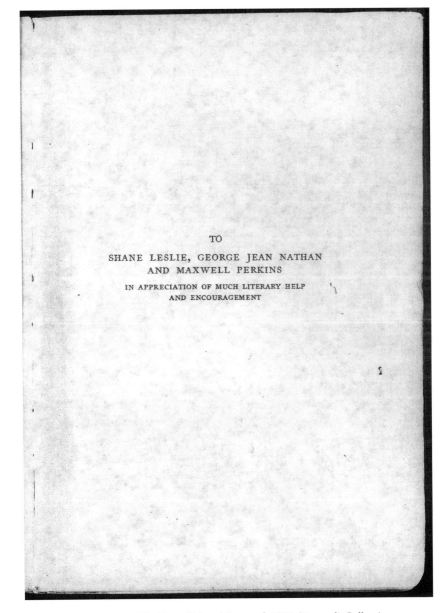

TO

SHANE LESLIE, GEORGE JEAN NATHAN
AND MAXWELL PERKINS

IN APPRECIATION OF MUCH LITERARY HELP
AND ENCOURAGEMENT

The dedication page in *The Beautiful and Damned,* 1922 (Bruccoli Collection,
Thomas Cooper Library, University of South Carolina).

With my changing of the extreme last + fixing up the symposium I am almost, but not quite, satisfied with the book. I prophecy that it will go about 60,000 copies the first year[5]—that is, assuming that Paradise went about 40,000 the first year. Thank God I'm thru with it

As Ever

F Scott Fitzg—

*Notes*

1. 53 words have been omitted from this letter.
2. Co-editor with H. L. Mencken of *The Smart Set,* Nathan was a model for Maury Noble and one of the three dedicatees of *The Beautiful and Damned.*
3. Fitzgerald revised the sentence so that it read, "'We'll choose the keenest satirist alive to compile a deity from all the deities worshipped by mankind, a deity who will be more magnificent than any of them, and yet so weakly human that he'll become a byword for laughter the world over—and we'll ascribe to him all sorts of jokes and vanities and rages, in which he'll be supposed to indulge for his own diversion, so that the people will read our book and ponder it, and there'll be no more nonsense in the world.'"
4. The serial version ended with Gloria's return to heaven; Fitzgerald replaced it with a description of Anthony's broken state.
5. The novel sold about fifty thousand copies in America during 1922.

▲ ▼ ▲

*To: Fitzgerald*
*From: Perkins*                                    *CC, 2 pp. Princeton*

Dec. 31, 1921

Dear Fitzgerald:

The letter from Reynolds which you sent and which I return is rather pathetic,[1] but so far as it concerns your writing, I think it represents a temporary condition. The time ought to come when whatever you write will go through and where its irony and satire will be understood. They will know what you stand for in writing and they do not really know yet. It is in recognition of this that I want very much to have this book so announced in our lists and so on, that it will be regarded as "important" as well as the other things.

There is especially in this country, a rootless class of society into which Gloria and Anthony drifted,– a large class and one which has an important effect on society in general. It is certainly worth presenting in a novel. I know that you did not deliberately undertake to do this but I think "The Beautiful and Damned" has in effect, done this; and that this makes it a valuable as well as brilliant commentary upon American society. Perhaps you have never even formulated the idea that it does do this thing, but don't you think it is true? The book is not written according to the usual conventions of the novel, and its greatest interest is not that of the usual novel. Its satire will not of itself be understood by the great simple minded public without a little help. For instance, in talking to one man about the book, I received the comment that Anthony was unscathed; that he came through with his millions, and thinking well of himself. This man completely missed the extraordinarily effective irony of the last few paragraphs.

As ever,

*Note*

1. Unlocated; possibly about the difficulty in selling "The Diamond as Big as the Ritz."

▲ ▼ ▲

To: Perkins                                    *ca. June 20, 1922*
From: Fitzgerald                               *ALS, 3 pp. Princeton*

The Yatch Club, White Bear Lake, Minn

Dear Mr. Perkins:

The first four stories, those that will comprise the section "My Last Flappers" left here several days ago.[1] The second four, "Fantasies" leave either this afternoon or tomorrow morning. And the last three "And So Forth" will leave here on the 24th (Sat.) + should reach you Tuesday without fail. I'm sorry I've been so slow on this—there's no particular excuse except liquor and of course that isn't any. But I vowed I'd finish a travel article + Thank God its done at last.[2]

Don't forget that I want another proof of the Table of Contents.[3] There's been one addition to the first section and one substitution in the 3d. Its damn good now, far superior to Flappers[4] and the title, jacket + other books ought to sell at least 10,000 copies and I hope 15,000.[5] You can see from the ms. how I've changed the stories. I cut out my last Metropolitan story not because it wasn't technically excellent but simply because it lacked vitality.[6] The only story about which I'm in doubt is The Camel's Back. But I've decided to use it—it has some excellent comedy + was in One O. Henry Collection—though of course that's against it. Here are some suggested blurbs.

1.    Contains the famous "Porcelain and Pink Story"—the bath-tub classic—as well as "The Curious Case of Benjamin Button" and nine other tales. In this book Mr. F. has developed his gifts as a satiric humorist to a point rivalled by few if any living American writers. The lazy meanderings of a brilliant and powerful imagination.

2. TALES OF THE JAZZ AGE

Satyre apon a Saxaphone by the most brilliant of the younger novelists. He sets down "My Last Flappers" and then proceeds in section two to fresher and more fantastic fields. You may like or dislike his work but it will never bore you.

3. TALES OF THE JAZZ AGE

Have you met "Mr. Icky" and followed the ghastly carreer of "Benjamin Button"? A medly of Bath-tubs, diamond mountains, Fitzgerald Flappers and Jellybeans.

Ten acts of lustrous farce—and one other.

That's probably pretty much bunk but I'm all for advertising it as a cheerful book and not as "eleven of Mr. Fitzgerald's best stories by the y.a. of T.S.O.P."

———————

Thank you immensely for the $1000.00. and also for the Phila. Ledger picture. Has the book gone over 40,000 yet? I'm delighted you like Boyd.[7] He hasn't a very original mind—that is: he's too young to be quite his own man intellectually but he's on the right track + if he can read much more of the 18th century—and the middle ages and ease up on the moderns he'll grow at an amazing rate. When I send on this last bunch of stories I may start my novel and I may not. Its locale will be the middle west and New York of 1885 I think. It will concern less superlative beauties that I run to usually + will be centered on a smaller period of time. It will have a catholic element. I'm not quite sure whether I'm ready to start it quite yet or not. I'll write next week + tell you more definate plans.[8]

As Ever

F Scott Fitzgerald

*Notes*

1. For *Tales of the Jazz Age* (1922), Fitzgerald's second collection of short stories.
2. "The Cruise of the Rolling Junk," *Motor* (February–April 1924).
3. Fitzgerald annotated the table of contents of the collection with facetious descriptions of each story.
4. Fitzgerald's first collection of stories, *Flappers and Philosophers,* which was published in 1920.
5. *Tales of the Jazz Age* went through three printings (11,000 copies) and earned Fitzgerald royalties of $3,056 in 1922.
6. "Two for a Cent," *Metropolitan* (April 1922).
7. Thomas Boyd, whose first novel, *Through the Wheat,* was published by Scribners in 1923 at Fitzgerald's recommendation.

8.  *The Great Gatsby* developed from Fitzgerald's projected novel, but no manuscript material from 1922 survives.

▲ ▼ ▲

To: Perkins                                  Mid-July 1922
From: Fitzgerald                             ALS, 1 p. Princeton

> The yatch club,
> White Bear Lake.
>
> Dear Mr. Perkins:
>     Glad you liked the addenda to the Table of Contents.
> I feel quite confident the book will go. How do you think
> The Far Legend will sell? You'll be glad to know that
> nothing has come of the movie idea + I'm rather glad
> myself. At present I'm working on my play —
> the same one. Trying to arrange for an 't
> production in New York. Bunny Wilson
> (Edmund Wilson Jr.) says that it's without
> doubt the best American comedy to date
> (that's just between you and me.)
>     Did you see that in that Literary
> Digest contest I stood 6th among the novelists?
> Not that it matters. I suspect you of
> having been one of the voters.
>     Will you see that the semi-yearly account
> is mailed to me by the 1st of the month — or
> before if it is ready? I want to see where
> I stand. I want to write something new —
> something extraordinary and beautiful and
> simple + intricately patterned.
>                         As Usual
>                             F Scott Fitzgerald

In the final sentence of this letter, Fitzgerald anticipates the structural achievement of the novel that became *The Great Gatsby* (Princeton University Library).

▲ ▼ ▲

*To: Fitzgerald*                    *ca. December 26, 1922*
*From: Perkins*                     *CC, 2 pp. Princeton*

## COMMENT ON "FROST"[1]

(To save space I've omitted most of the "I thinks," "It seems to mes," and "I may be wrong buts": they should, however, be understood)

I've read your play three times and I think more highly of its possibilities on the third reading than ever before;– but I am also more strongly convinced that these possibilities are far from being realized on account of the handling of the story in the second act. The reader feels, at the end, confused and unsatisfied:– the underlying motive of the play has not been sent home. And yet this motive, or idea, has been sufficiently perceived to prevent the play from being a sheer burlesque, like a comic opera. In the second act it seems to me that you yourself have almost thought it <u>was</u> that.

The underlying idea, a mighty good one, is expressed, or should be, in the story of Jerry Frost. ¶God meant Jerry to be a good egg and a postman; but having been created, in a democratic age, Free and Equal, he was persuaded that he ought to want to rise in the world and so had become a railroad clerk against his taste and capacity, and thought he ought to want to become President. He is therefore very unhappy, and so is his wife, who holds the same democratic doctrine.

Your story shows, or should, that this doctrine is sentimental bunk; and to do this is worthwhile because the doctrine is almost universal: Jerry and his wife are products of a theory of democracy which you reduce to the absurd. The idea is so good that if you hold to it and continuously develop it, your play, however successful simply as fun, will be deeply significant as well.

Moreover, the means you have selected to develop the idea are superb – the bootlegger, the super-jag his concoction induces, Jerry thereby becoming President, etc. (and dreams have a real validity nowadays on account of Freud). In fact all your machinery for expressing the idea is exactly in the tune of the time and inherently funny and satirical.

But when you come to the second act, which is the critical point in the play, and so in the expression of your idea, you seem to lose sense of your true motive. Partly, this is because you have three motives here, the main motive of Jerry's story and its meaning, and two subordinate motives – (1) of conveying through the fantastic visions and incidents which are the stuff of a dream caused by a 1923 prohibition brew, <u>the sense of a comic nightmare</u>, and (2) of satirizing the general phenomena of our national scene. You have, I think, simply got more or less lost in the maze of these three motives by a failure to follow the green line of the chief one – Jerry's actual story, or that stage of it which shows him that he <u>doesn't</u> want to be President. Satirize as much as you can, the government, the army, and everything else, and be as fantastic as you please, but keep one eye always on your chief motive. Throughout the entire wild second act there should still be a kind of wild logic.

Aside then from imparting in this act the sense of a dream, you are using the difficult weapon of double edged satire—you are satirizing the conception held by Jerry and his like of the High Offices of President, Secretary of the Treasury, etc., and you are at the same time satirizing those high offices themselves. You begin excellently by making all the appertenances of the Presidency, like the house, white; and the behavior of Jerry's wife and sister-in-law are all within the scope of your purpose. The conduct of Dada as Secretary of the Treasury seems as though it ought to be a fine piece of two edged satire cutting both against the popular idea of the business of that official and against the official himself as he usually is, but the psychology of it is not made quite comprehensible; and the best instance of double satire is seen when General Pushing appears with fifer and drummer and medals—that is just the right note. Why couldn't you do the same for bankers, and senators, etc.?

Maybe I can better express what I mean by examples. The selection of so obscure a man as Jerry for President is itself the stuff of satire in view of present political methods, and much could be made of it. The coffin episode as you use it results as things do in a dream from Jerry's talk with Fish etc. and so it helps to give the sense of a dream, and that is all it does. But suppose coffins were being cornered by "The He-Americans Bloodred Preparedness League" as a preparedness measure, and that this was tied up with General Pushing's feeling that a war was needed:– that would be a hit at extravagant patriotism and militarism as well as having its present value as part of a dream. Suppose the deal over the Buzzard Isles resulted in the Impeachment of Jerry   what a chance that would give to treat the Senate as you have the general and the Army, and also to bring Jerry's affairs to a climax. You could have Jerry <u>convicted</u>, and then (as a hit at a senatorial filibuster) you could have his party place the Stutz-Mozart Ourangatang Band outside the Capitol (it would have appeared for the wedding of Fish), and every time the Justices of the Supreme Court began in chorus to pronounce the sentence, Stutz-Mozart would strike up the National Anthem in syncopated time and everyone would have to stand at attention. At present, the narrative of the second act lacks all logic: the significance of the approaching end of the world eludes me,– except as a dreamer's way of getting release from a desperate situation.

I've now used a great many words to make this single point:– each part of the second act should do three things—add to the quality of a fantastic dream, satirize Jerry and his family as representing a large class of Americans, and satirize the government or army or whatever institution is at the moment in use. And my only excuse for all this verbiage is, that so good in conception is your motive, so true your characters, so splendidly imaginative your invention, and so altogether above the mere literary the whole scheme, that no one could help but greatly desire to see it all equaled in execution. If it were a comparative trifle, like many a short story, it wouldn't much matter.[2]

*Notes*

1. Jerry Frost is the protagonist in Fitzgerald's play that was published as *The Vegetable* in 1923. In 1976 Scribners published the play in "A new edition with unpublished scenes and corrections and an introduction by Charles Scribner III."

2. Fitzgerald had expected that *The Vegetable* would appear on Broadway, but it failed in its out-of-town tryout.

▲ ▼ ▲

*To: Perkins*                    *ca. April 10, 1924. Long Island, New York*
*From: Fitzgerald*                      *ALS, 2 pp. Princeton*

Great Neck.

Dear Max:

A few words more relative to our conversation this afternoon. While I have every hope + plan of finishing my novel in June you know how those things often come out. And even if takes me 10 times that long I cannot let it go out unless it has the very best I'm capable of in it or even as I feel sometimes, something better than I'm capable of. Much of what I wrote last summer was good but it was so interrupted that it was ragged + in approaching it from a new angle I've had to discard a lot of it—in one case 18,000 words (part of which will appear in the Mercury as a short story).[1] It is only in the last four months that I've realized how much I've—well, almost <u>deteriorated</u> in the three years since I finished the Beautiful and Damned. The last four months of course I've worked but in the two years—over two years—before that, I produced exactly <u>one</u> play, <u>half a dozen</u> short stories and three or four articles—an average of about one <u>hundred</u> words a day. If I'd spent this time reading or travelling or doing anything—even staying healthy—it'd be different but I spent it uselessly, niether in study nor in contemplation but only in drinking and raising hell generally. If I'd written the B. + D. at the rate of 100 words a day it would have taken me <u>4 years</u> so you can imagine the moral effect the whole chasm had on me.

What I'm trying to say is just that I'll have to ask you to have patience about the book and trust me that at last, or at least for the 1st time in years, I'm doing the best I can. I've gotten in dozens of bad habits that I'm trying to get rid of

1.  Laziness
2.  Referring everything to Zelda—a terrible habit, nothing ought to be referred to anybody until its finished
3.  Word consciousness + self doubt

ect. ect. ect. etc.

I feel I have an enormous power in me now, more than I've ever had in a way but it works so fitfully and with so many bogeys because I've <u>talked so much</u> and not lived enough within myself to develop the nessessary self reliance. Also I don't know anyone who has used up so [much per]sonel experience as I have at 27. Copperfield + Pendennis were written at past forty while This Side of Paradise was three books + the B. + D. was two. So in my new novel I'm thrown directly on purely creative work—not trashy imaginings as in my stories but the sustained imagination of a sincere and yet radiant world. So I tread slowly and carefully + at times in considerable distress. This book will be a consciously artistic acheivment + must depend on that as the 1st books did not.

If I ever win the right to any liesure again I will assuredly not waste it as I wasted this past time. Please believe me when I say that now I'm doing the best I can.

Yours Ever<br>Scott F——

*Note*

1.  This reference to "Absolution" has generated speculation about the lost early version of *The Great Gatsby.*

▲ ▼ ▲

*To: Fitzgerald*
*From: Perkins*                    *CC, 3 pp. Princeton*

April 16, 1924

Dear Scott:

I delayed answering your letter because I wanted to answer it at length. I was delighted to get it. But I have been so pressed with all sorts of things that I have not had time to write as I meant and I am not doing so now. I do not want to delay sending some word on one or two points.

For instance, I understand exactly what you have to do and I know that all these superficial matters of exploitation and so on are not of the slightest consequence along side of the importance of your doing your very best work the way you want to do it;– that is, according to the demands of the situation. So far as we are concerned, you are to go ahead at just your own pace, and if you should finish the book when you think you will, you will have performed a very considerable feat even in the matter of time, it seems to me.

My view of the future is—particularly in the light of your letter—one of very great optimism and confidence.

The only thing is, that if we had a title which was likely, but by no means sure to be the title, we could prepare a cover and a wrap and hold them in readiness for use.[1] In that way, we would gain several weeks if we should find that we were to have the book this fall. We would be that much to the good. Otherwise we should have done no harm. If we sold the book under a title which was later changed, no harm would have been done either. I always thought that "The Great Gatsby" was a suggestive and effective title,– with only the vaguest knowledge of the book, of course. But anyway, the last thing we want to do is to divert you to any degree, from your actual writing, and if you let matters rest just as they are now, we shall be perfectly satisfied. The book is the thing and all the rest is inconsiderable beside it.

Yours,

### Note

1. There has been considerable speculation about the putative connection between the dust jacket art and the novel's material. See Perkins to Fitzgerald, November 18, 1924.

▲ ▼ ▲

*To: Perkins*                    *ca. October 10, 1924*
*From: Fitzgerald*               *ALS, 2 pp.[1] Princeton*

Villa Marie,<br>Valescure<br>St Raphael, France

Dear Max:

The royalty was better than I'd expected. This is to tell you about a young man named Ernest Hemmingway, who lives in Paris, (an American) writes for the transatlantic Review + has a brilliant future. Ezra Pount published a collection of his short pieces in Paris, at some place like the Egotist Press.[2] I havn't it hear now but its remarkable + I'd look him up right away. He's the real thing.

My novel goes to you with a long letter within five days. Ring arrives in a week.[3] This is just a hurried scrawl as I'm working like a dog. I thought Stalling's book was disappointingly rotten.[4] It takes a genius to whine appealingly. Have tried to see Struthers Burt[5] but he's been on the move. More later.

Scott

. . . . .

*Notes*

1. 61 words have been omitted from this letter.
2. Probably *in our time* (1924), published by the Three Mountains Press in a series edited by Ezra Pound.
3. Humorist Ring Lardner (1885–1933), who became a friend of Fitzgerald in 1922 when they both lived in Great Neck, wrote an account of this visit collected in *What of It?* (Scribners, 1925).
4. *Plumes* (1924), a World War I novel by Laurence Stallings.
5. Maxwell Struthers Burt, Scribners author.

▲ ▼ ▲

*To: Perkins*                            *ca. November 7, 1924*
*From: Fitzgerald*                       *ALS, 1 p. Princeton*

Hotel Continental, St. Raphael, Sun.
(Leaving Tuesday)

Dear Max:

By now you've received the novel. There are things in it I'm not satisfied with in the middle of the book—Chapter 6 + 7. And I may write in a complete new scene in proof.[1] I hope you got my telegram.

<u>Trimalchio[2] in West Egg</u>

The only other titles that seem to fit it are <u>Trimalchio</u> and <u>On the Road to West Egg</u>. I had two others Gold-hatted Gatsby and The High-bouncing Lover but they seemed too light.

We leave for Rome as soon as I finish the short story I'm working on.

As Ever

Scott

I was interested that you've moved to New Canann. It sounds wonderful. Sometimes I'm awfully anxious to be home.

But I am confused at what you say about Gertrude Stien.[3] I thought it was one purpose of critics + publishers to educate the public up to original work. The first people who risked Conrad certainly didn't do it as a commercial venture. Did the evolution of startling work into accepted work cease twenty years ago?

Do send me Boyds (Ernest's) book when it comes out.[4] I think the Lardner ads are wonderful.[5] Did the Dark Cloud flop?[6]

Would you ask the people down stairs to keep sending me my monthly bill for the encyclopedia?[7]

Fitzgerald at the time he was writing *The Great Gatsby* (Bruccoli Collection, Thomas Cooper Library, University of South Carolina)

## Notes

1. In the galley proofs Fitzgerald moved Gatsby's account of falling in love with Daisy from chapter 7 to chapter 6.

| Sequence in MS & TS (unrevised galleys) | Sequence in Book (revised galleys) |
|---|---|
| **MS VI (TS 6)** | **6** |
| | Biography of Gatsby (Cody) |
| Tom & friends visit Gatsby | Tom & friends visit Gatsby |
| Buchanans attend party | Buchanans attend party |
| | Gatsby tells Nick about love for Daisy |
| **MS VI (TS7)** | **7** |
| Gatsby replaces servants | Gatsby replaces servants |
| Gatsby tells Nick about love for Daisy | |
| Lunch at Buchanan home | Lunch at Buchanan home |
| Tom stops for gas | Tom stops for gas |
| [Polo Grounds—Central Park & confrontation] | |
| Plaza & confrontation | Plaza & confrontation |
| Death of Myrtle | Death of Myrtle |
| Nick & Gatsby outside Buchanan home | Nick & Gatsby outside Buchanan home |
| **MS VII (TS 8)** | **8** |
| Biography of Gatsby (Cody) | |
| Gatsby's courtship & Daisy's marriage | Gatsby's courtship & Daisy's marriage |
| Nick & Jordan | Nick & Jordan |
| Flashback to garage | Flashback to garage |
| Murder of Gatsby | Murder of Gatsby |

2. Trimalchio was an ostentatious party giver in Petronius's *Satyricon* written in Latin during the first century A.D.

3. Perkins to Fitzgerald, October 18, 1924: "I am reading the Gertrude Stein [*The Making of Americans*] as it comes out, and it fascinates me. But I doubt if the reader who had no <u>literary</u> interest, or not much, would have patience with her method, effective as it does become. Its peculiarities are much more marked than in 'Three Lives.'"

4. *Portraits: Real and Imaginary* (Scribners, 1924) includes a chapter on Fitzgerald.

5. For *How to Write Short Stories* (Scribners, 1924). See illustration.

6. Thomas Boyd novel published by Scribners in 1924.

7. Fitzgerald purchased a set of the *Encyclopaedia Britannica* from the Scribner bookstore.

▲▼▲

1. My Life and Loves
   High school article        (American)
   How I built my house      Bill takes up the story
   On being Thirty five (American)
   ~~How I got my start in life~~
   My four weeks in France
2. Adventures in Idiocy
3. The Art of The Short Story
4. You know me Al
5. Gullible's Travers
6. The Big Town <

Short Stories:

—— Harmony (McClures)
> The Facts (metropolitan)
—— My Roomy (The Post)
—— Horseshoes (The Post)
~~The young immigrants~~
~~(The Post)~~
? ~~Our story in Cosmopolitan~~
~~files~~

Gooseberry Soul
Jun 26 -1916

The Bib Ballads
Treat 'em Rough

Fitzgerald and Perkins discussed Ring Lardner's first Scribners volume, *How to Write Short Stories* (1924), during luncheon at the Hotel Chatham on December 11, 1923; and Fitzgerald made notes on the menu verso (Princeton University Library).

*To: Fitzgerald*
*From: Perkins*                                    *CC, 2 pp. Princeton*

Nov. 18, 1924

Dear Scott:

I think the novel is a wonder. I'm taking it home to read again and shall then write my impressions in full;– but it has vitality to an extraordinary degree, and glamour, and a great deal of underlying thought of unusual quality. It has a kind of mystic atmosphere at times that you infused into parts of "Paradise" and have not since used. It is a marvelous fusion, into a unity of presentation, of the extraordinary incongruities of life today. As for sheer writing, it's astonishing.

Now deal with this question: various gentlemen here don't like the title,– in fact none like it but me. To me, the strange incongruity of the words in it sound the note of the book. But the objectors are more practical men than I. Consider as quickly as you can the question of a change.

But if you do not change, you will have to leave that note off the wrap.[1] Its presence would injure it too much;– and good as the wrap always seemed, it now seems a masterpiece for this book.[2] So judge of the value of the title when it stands alone and write or cable your decision the instant you can.

With congratulations, I am,

Yours,

### Notes

1. An explanatory note intended for the dust jacket was not used and has not been located. See Fitzgerald to Perkins, ca. December 1, 1924.

2. In a ca. August 27, 1924, letter to Perkins, Fitzgerald had written: "For Christs sake don't give anyone that jacket you're saving for me. I've written it into the book." This remark and Perkins's reply above have generated guesswork. The published jacket art by Francis Cugat depicts a woman's face above an amusement-park night scene. It is not known whether Fitzgerald had seen the final art or an earlier version. See "Appendix 3: Note on the Dust Jacket," *The Great Gatsby*, ed. Bruccoli (Cambridge & New York: Cambridge University Press, 1991), pp. 209–10, and Charles Scribner III, "Celestial Eyes: From Metamorphosis to Masterpiece," *Princeton University Library Chronicle*, 53 (Winter 1992): 140–55.

▲▼▲

*To: Fitzgerald*
*From: Perkins*                                    *CC, 4 pp. Princeton*

November 20, 1924

Dear Scott:

I think you have every kind of right to be proud of this book. It is an extraordinary book, suggestive of all sorts of thoughts and moods. You adopted exactly the right method of telling it, that of employing a narrator who is more of a spectator than an actor: this puts the reader upon a point of observation on a higher level than that on which the characters stand and at a distance that gives perspective. In no other way could your irony have been so immensely effective, nor the reader have been enabled so strongly to feel at times the strangeness of human circumstance in a vast heedless universe. In the eyes of Dr. Eckleberg various readers will see different significances; but their presence gives a superb touch to the whole thing: great unblinking eyes, expressionless, looking down upon the human scene. It's magnificent!

I could go on praising the book and speculating on its various elements, and meanings, but points of criticism are more important now. I think you are right in feeling a certain slight sagging in chapters six and seven, and I don't know how to suggest a remedy. I hardly doubt that you will find one and I am only writing to say that I think it does need something to hold up here to the pace set, and ensuing. I have only two actual criticisms:–

One is that among a set of characters marvelously palpable and vital—I would know Tom Buchanan if I met him on the street and would avoid him— Gatsby is somewhat vague. The reader's eyes can never quite focus upon him, his outlines are dim. Now everything about Gatsby is more or less a mystery i.e. more or less vague, and this may be somewhat of an artistic intention, but I think it is mistaken. Couldn't he be physically described as distinctly as the others, and couldn't you add one or two characteristics like the use of that phrase "old sport",– not verbal, but physical ones, perhaps. I think that for some reason or other a reader—this was true of Mr. Scribner and of Louise[1] —gets an idea that Gatsby is a much older man than he is, although you have the writer say that he is a little older than himself. But this would be avoided if on his first appearance he was seen as vividly as Daisy and Tom are, for instance;– and I do not think your scheme would be impaired if you made him so.

The other point is also about Gatsby: his career must remain mysterious, of course. But in the end you make it pretty clear that his wealth came through his connection with Wolfsheim. You also suggest this much earlier. Now almost all readers numerically are going to be puzzled by his having all this wealth and are going to feel entitled to an explanation. To give a distinct and definite one would be, of course, utterly absurd. It did occur to me though, that you might here and there interpolate some phrases, and possibly incidents, little touches of various kinds, that would suggest that he was in some active way mysteriously engaged. You do have him called on the telephone, but couldn't he be seen once or twice consulting at his parties with people of some sort of mysterious significance, from the political, the gambling, the sporting world, or whatever it may be. I know I am floundering, but that fact may help you to see what I mean. The total lack of an explanation through so large a part of the story does seem to me a defect;– or not of an explanation, but of the suggestion of an explanation. I wish you were here so I could talk about it to you for then I know I could at least make you understand what I mean. What Gatsby did ought never to be definitely imparted, even if it could be. Whether he was an innocent tool in the hands of somebody else, or to what degree he was this, ought not to be explained. But if some sort of business activity of his were simply adumbrated, it would lend further probability to that part of the story.

There is one other point: in giving deliberately Gatsby's biography when he gives it to the narrator you do depart from the method of the narrative in some degree, for otherwise almost everything is told, and beautifully told, in the regular flow of it,– in the succession of events or in accompaniment with them. But you can't avoid the biography altogether. I thought you might find ways to let the truth of some of his claims like "Oxford" and his army career come out bit by bit in the course of actual narrative.[2] I mention the point anyway for consideration in this interval before I send the proofs.

The general brilliant quality of the book makes me ashamed to make even these criticisms. The amount of meaning you get into a sentence, the dimensions and intensity of the impression you make a paragraph carry, are most extraordinary. The manuscript is full of phrases which make a scene blaze with life. If one enjoyed a rapid railroad journey I would compare the number and vividness of pictures your living words suggest, to the living scenes disclosed in that way. It seems in reading a much shorter book than it is, but it carries the mind through a series of experiences that one would think would require a book of three times its length.

The presentation of Tom, his place, Daisy and Jordan, and the unfolding of their characters is unequalled so far as I know. The description of the valley of ashes adjacent to the lovely country, the conversation and the action in Myrtle's apartment, the marvelous catalogue of those who came to Gatsby's house,– these are such things as make a man famous. And all these things, the whole pathetic episode, you have given a place in time and space, for with the help of T.J. Eckleberg and by an occasional glance at the sky, or the sea, or the city, you have imparted a sort of sense of eternity. You once told me you were not a natural writer—my God! You have plainly mastered the craft, of course; but you needed far more than craftsmanship for this.

As ever,

Maxwell E. Perkins

P.S. Why do you ask for a lower royalty on this than you had on the last book where it changed from 15% to 17½% after 20,000 and to 20% after 40,000?[3] Did you do it in order to give us a better margin for advertising? We shall advertise very energetically anyhow and if you stick to the old terms you will sooner overcome the advance. Naturally we should like the ones you suggest better, but there is no reason you should get less on this than you did on the other.

### Notes

1. Perkins's wife.
2. For his restructuring of the novel in galleys to break up Gatsby's autobiography, see Fitzgerald's ca. November 7, 1924, letter, note 1.
3. *The Great Gatsby* was priced at $2.00; the 15 percent royalty amounted to 30 cents per copy. The first printing of 20,870 copies earned Fitzgerald about $6,000. Copies of the first printing in dust jacket now bring up to $150,000 each.

▲ ▼ ▲

*To: Perkins*  
*From: Fitzgerald*

*ca. December 1, 1924*  
*ALS, 3 pp. Princeton*

> Hotel des Princes  
> Piazza di Spagna  
> Rome, Italy

Dear Max:

Your wire + your letters made me feel like a million dollars—I'm sorry I could make no better response than a telegram whining for money. But the long siege of the novel winded me a little + I've been slow on starting the stories on which I must live.

I think all your critisisms are true

(a) About the title. I'll try my best but I don't know what I can do. Maybe simply "Trimalchio" or "Gatsby." In the former case I don't see why the note shouldn't go on the back.

(b) Chapters VI + VII I know how to fix

(c) Gatsby's business affairs I can fix. I get your point about them.

(d) His vagueness I can repair by making more pointed—this doesn't sound good but wait and see. It'll make him clear

(e) But his long narrative in Chap VIII will be difficult to split up. Zelda also thought it was a little out of key but it is good writing and I don't think I could bear to sacrifice any of it.

(f.) I have 1000 minor corrections which I will make on the proof + several more large ones which you didn't mention.

Your critisisms were excellent + most helpful + you picked out all my favorite spots in the book to praise as high spots. Except you didn't mention my favorite of all—the chapter where Gatsby + Daisy meet.

Two more things. Zelda's been reading me the cowboy book[1] aloud to spare my mind + I love it—tho I think he learned the American language from Ring rather than from his own ear.

Another point—in Chap. II of my book when Tom + Mytre go into the bedroom while Carraway reads Simon called Peter[2]—is that raw? Let me know. I think its pretty nessessary.

I made the royalty smaller because I wanted to make up for all the money you've advanced these two years by letting it pay a sort of interest on it. But I see by calculating I made it too small—a difference of 2000 dollars. Let me call it 15% up to 40,000 and 20% after that. That's a good fair contract all around.

By now you have heard from a smart young french woman who wants to translate the book. She's equeal to it intellectually + linguisticly I think—had read all my others—If you'll tell her how to go about it as to royalty demands ect.

Anyhow thanks + thanks + thanks for your letters. I'd rather have you + Bunny[3] like it than anyone I know. And I'd rather have you like it than Bunny. If its as good as you say, when I finish with the proof it'll be perfect.

Remember, by the way, to put by some cloth for the cover uniform with my other books.

As soon as I can think about the title I'll write or wire a decision. Thank Louise for me, for liking it. Best Regards to Mr. Scribner. Tell him Galsworthy[4] is here in Rome. As Ever, Scott

*Notes*

1. Will James, *Cowboys North and South* (Scribners, 1924).
2. Fitzgerald regarded this popular 1921 English novel by Robert Keable as immoral; the protagonist is an army chaplain who becomes involved in passionate episodes.
3. Edmund Wilson (1895–1972); a friend of Fitzgerald's at Princeton, he became an influential literary and social critic.
4. English novelist John Galsworthy, who was published in the United States by Scribners.

▲ ▼ ▲

To: *Perkins*                                 *ca. December 20, 1924*
From: *Fitzgerald*                            *ALS, 5 pp. Princeton*

Hotel des Princes, Piazza de Spagna, Rome.

Dear Max:

I'm a bit (not very—not dangerously) stewed tonight + I'll probably write you a long letter. We're living in a small, unfashionable but most comfortable hotel at $525.00 a month including tips, meals ect. Rome does <u>not</u> particularly interest me but its a big year here, and early in the spring we're going to Paris. There's no use telling you my plans because they're usually just about as unsuccessful as to work as a religious prognosticaters are as to the End of the World. I've got a new novel to write—title and all, that'll take about a year.[1] Meanwhile, I don't want to start it until this is out + meanwhile I'll do short stories for money (I now get $2000.00 a story but I hate worse than hell to do them) and there's the never dying lure of another play.

Now! Thanks enormously for making up the $5000.00. I know I don't technically deserve it considering I've had $3000.00 or $4000.00 for as long as I can remember. But since you force it on me (inexecrable [or is it execrable] joke) I will accept it. I hope to Christ you get 10 times it back on Gatsby——and I think perhaps you will.

For:

I can now make it perfect but the proof (I will soon get the immemorial letter with the statement "We now have the book in hand and will soon begin to send you proof" [what is 'in hand'—I have a vague picture of everyone in the office holding the book in the right and and reading it]) will be one of the most expensive affairs since Madame Bovary. <u>Please</u> charge it to my account. If its possible to send a second proof over here I'd love to have it. Count on 12 days each way—four days here on first proof + two on the second. I hope there are other good books in the spring because I think now the public interest in <u>books</u> per se rises when there seems to be a group of them as in 1920 (spring + fall), 1921 (fall), 1922 (spring). Ring's + Tom's (first) books, Willa Cathers <u>Lost Lady</u> + in an inferior, cheap way Edna Ferber's are the only American fiction in over two years that had a really excellent press (say, since Babbit).[2]

With the aid you've given me I can make "Gatsby" perfect. The chapter VII (the hotel scene) will never quite be up to mark—I've worried about it too long + I can't quite place Daisy's reaction. But I can improve it a lot. It isn't imaginative energy thats lacking—its because I'm automaticly prevented from thinking it out over again <u>because I must get all these characters to New York</u> in order to have the catastrophe on the road going back + I must have it pretty much that way. So there's no chance of bringing the freshness to it that a new free conception sometimes gives.

The rest is easy and I see my way so clear that I even see the mental quirks that queered it before. Strange to say my notion of Gatsby's vagueness was O.K. What you and Louise + Mr Charles Scribner found wanting was that: <u>I myself didn't know what Gatsby looked like or was engaged in</u> + you felt it. If I'd known + kept it from you'd have been <u>too impressed with my knowledge to protest</u>. This is a complicated idea but I'm sure you'll understand. But I know now—and as a penalty for not having known first, in other words to make sure I'm going to tell more.

It seems of almost mystical significance to me that you thot he was older— the man I had in mind, half unconsciously, <u>was</u> older (a specific individual) and evidently, without so much as a definate word, I conveyed the fact. —or rather, I must qualify this Shaw-Desmond[3]–trash by saying, that I conveyed it without a word that I can not present and for the life of me, trace. (I think Shaw Desmond was one of your bad bets—I was the other)

Anyhow after careful searching of the files (of a man's mind here) for the Fuller Magee case[4] + after having had Zelda draw pictures until her fingers ache I know Gatsby better than I know my own child. My first instinct after your letter was to let him go + have Tom Buchanan dominate the book (I suppose he's the best character I've ever done—I think he and the brother in "Salt"[5] + Hurstwood in "Sister Carrie" are the three best characters in American fiction in the last twenty years, perhaps and perhaps not) but Gatsby sticks in my heart. I had him for awhile then lost him + now I know I have him again. I'm sorry Myrtle is better than Daisy. Jordan of course was a great idea (perhaps you know its Edith Cummings)[6] but she fades out. Its Chap VII thats the trouble with Daisy + it may hurt the book's popularity that its a <u>man's book</u>.

Anyhow I think (for the first time since The Vegetable failed) that Im a wonderful writer + its your always wonderful letters that help me to go on believing in myself.

Now some practical, very important questions. Please answer every one.

①  Montenegro has an order called <u>The Order of Danilo</u>. Is there any possible way you could find out for me there what it would look like—whether a courtesy decoration given to an American would bear an English inscription —or anything to give versimilitude to the medal which sounds horribly amateurish.[7]

②  Please have <u>no blurbs of any kind on the jacket</u>!!! No Mencken or Lewis or Sid Howard or any thing. I don't believe in them one bit any more.

③  Don't forget to change name of book in the list of works

④  Please shift exclamation point from end of 3d line to end of 4th line in title page poem.[8] <u>Please</u>! Important!

⑤  I thought that the whole episode (2 paragraphs) about their playing the Jazz History of the world at Gatsby's first party was rotten.[9] Did you? Tell me frank reaction—personal. Don't think! We can all think!

Got a sweet letter from Sid Howard—rather touching. I wrote him first. I thought <u>Transatlantic</u> was great stuff—a really gorgeous surprise. Up to that I never believed in him 'specially + I was sorry because he did in me. Now I'm tickled silly to find he has power, and his own power. It seemed tragic too to see <u>Mrs. Viectch</u> wasted in a novelette when, despite Anderson the short story is at its lowest ebb as an art form. (Despite Ruth Suckow, Gertrude Stien, Ring there is a horrible impermanence on it because the overwhelming number of short stories are impermanent.[10]

Poor Tom Boyd! His cycle sounded so sad to me—perhaps it'll be wonderful but it sounds to me like a ploughing in a field (whose) first freshness has gone.

See that word?[11] The ambition of my life is to make that use of it correct. The temptation to use it as a writer is one of the vile fevers in my still insecure prose.

Tell me about Ring! About Tom—is he poor? He seems to be counting on his short story book, frail cane! About Biggs[12]—did he ever finish the novel? About Peggy Boyd.[13] I think Louise might have sent us her book![14]

I thot the White Monkey was stinko. On second thoughts I didn't like Cowboys, West + South either. What about Bal de Compte Orgel? and Ring's set? and his new book? + Gertrude Stien?[15] and Hemmingway?

I still owe the store almost $700 on my Encyclopedia but I'll pay them on about Jan 10th—all in a lump as I expect my finances will then be on a firm footing. Will you ask them to send me Ernest Boyd's book? Unless it has about my drinking in it that would reach my family. However, I guess it'd worry me more if I hadn't seen it than if I had. If my book is a big success or a great failure (financial—no other sort can be imagined, I hope) I don't want to publish stories in the fall. If it goes between 25,000 and 50,000 I have an excellent collection for you. This is the longest letter I've written in three or four years. Please thank Mr. Scribner for me for his exceeding kindness. Always Yours

Scott Fitz——

*Notes*

1. Fitzgerald apparently abandoned this project.
2. *A Lost Lady* (1923), Ferber's *So Big* (1924), and Sinclair Lewis's *Babbit* (1922).
3. Shaw Desmond, author of *Gods* (Scribners, 1921).
4. Edward M. Fuller and William F. McGee, partners in a stock brokerage firm, were convicted of embezzlement; Arnold Rothstein—the model for Meyer Wolfshiem in *The Great Gatsby*—was allegedly involved in their peculations.
5. 1918 novel by Charles Norris.
6. Golfer, who had been a school friend of Ginevra King, Fitzgerald's first love when he was at Princeton.
7. The Orderi di Danilo is enameled on both sides and could not have been engraved for Gatsby.
8. The epigraph poem was written by Fitzgerald but credited to Thomas Parke D'Invilliers, a character in *This Side of Paradise* who was based on poet John Peale Bishop, a friend of Fitzgerald's at Princeton.
9. The long description was shortened in proof.
10. Howard's stories "Transatlantic" and "Mrs. Vietch" had been collected in his *Three Flights Up* (1924); Ruth Suckow was known for her stories and novels of midwestern life.
11. The word *whose* in the previous paragraph.
12. John Biggs Jr. (1895–1979), Fitzgerald's Princeton friend who became his literary executor. Scribners published Biggs's fiction in 1926 and 1928.

13. The wife of Thomas Boyd, she wrote under the name Woodward Boyd.

14. Mrs. Perkins published *The Knave of Hearts* (Scribners, 1925) under the name Louise Saunders.

15. *The White Monkey* (1924), by John Galsworthy, was published by Scribners, as was Will James's *Cowboys North and South*. Neither Raymond Radiguet nor Gertrude Stein was published by Scribners.

▲ ▼ ▲

*To: Perkins*
*From: Fitzgerald.*                    *TLS, 3 pp., with holograph postscript. Princeton*

Hotel des Princes
Rome, Italy.
January 24th=1925
(But address the American Express
Co. because its damn cold here
and we may leave any day.

Dear Max:

This is a most important letter so I'm having it typed. Guard it as your life. 1) Under a separate cover I'm sending the first part of the proof. While I agreed with the general suggestions in your first letters I differ with you in others. I want Myrtle Wilson's breast ripped off—its exactly the thing, I think, and I don't want to chop up the good scenes by too much tinkering. When Wolfshiem says "sid" for "said", it's deliberate. "Orgastic" is the adjective from "orgasm" and it expresses exactly the intended ecstasy.[1] It's not a bit dirty. I'm much more worried about the disappearance of Tom and Myrtle on Galley 9—I think it's all right but I'm not sure. If it isn't please wire and I'll send correction.

2) Now about the page proof—under certain conditions never mind sending them (unless, of course, there's loads of time, which I don't suppose there isn't. I'm keen for late March or early April publication)

The conditions are two.

a) That someone reads it very carefully twice to see that every one of my inserts are put in correctly. There are so many of them that I'm in terror of a mistake.

b) That no changes whatsoever are made in it except in the case of a misprint so glaring as to be certain, and that only by you.

If there's some time left but not enough for the double mail send them to me and I'll simply wire O.K. which will save two weeks. However don't postpone for that. In any case send me the page proof as usual just to see.

3) Now, many thanks for the deposit. Two days after wiring you I had a cable from Reynolds that he'd sold two stories of mine for a total of $3,750.= but before that I was in debt to him and after turning down the ten thousand dollars from College Humor[2] I was afraid to borrow more from him until he'd

made a sale. I won't ask for any more from you until the book has earned it. My guess is that it will sell about 80,000 copies but I may be wrong. Please thank Mr. Charles Scribner for me. I bet he thinks he's caught another John Fox now for sure.[3] Thank God for John Fox. It would have been awful to have had no predecessor

4) This is very important. Be sure not to give away <u>any</u> of my plot in the blurb. Don't give away that Gatsby <u>dies</u> or is a <u>parvenu</u> or <u>crook</u> or anything. Its a part of the suspense of the book that all these things are in doubt until the end. You'll watch this won't you? And remember about having no quotations from critics on the jacket—<u>not even about my other books!</u>

5) This is just a list of small things.

   a) What's Ring's title for his Spring Book?

   b) Did O'Brien star my story <u>Absolution</u> or any of my others in his trash-album?[4]

   c) I wish your bookkeeping department would send me an account on Feb. 1st. Not that it gives me pleasure to see how much in debt I am but that I like to keep a yearly record of the sales of all my books.

Do answer every question and keep this letter until the proof comes. Let me know how you like the changes. I miss seeing you, Max, more than I can say.

As ever,

Scott

P.S. I'm returning the proof of the title page ect. It's O.K. but my heart tells me I should have named it <u>Trimalchio</u>. However against all the advice I suppose it would have been stupid and stubborn of me. <u>Trimalchio in West Egg</u> was only a compromise. Gatsby is too much like <u>Babbit</u> and <u>The Great Gatsby</u> is weak because there's no emphasis even ironically on his greatness or lack of it. However let it pass.

*Notes*

1. Edmund Wilson incorrectly emended *orgastic* to *orgiastic* in the 1941 edition of *The Great Gatsby;* this blunder was perpetuated in most of the subsequent editions.

2. For a proposed serialization of *Gatsby.*

3. John Fox Jr., author of the popular southern romances *The Little Shepherd of Kingdom Come* (Scribners, 1903) and *The Trail of the Lonesome Pine* (Scribners, 1908), was often in debt to his publisher.

4. Edward J. O'Brien, editor of the annual *Best Short Stories* collections, listed five of Fitzgerald's stories in the 1924 volume. He did not include "Absolution" in his list and gave single stars (three stars marked the best stories) to "John Jackson's Arcady" and to "The Unspeakable Egg."

▲▼▲

BY F. SCOTT FITZGERALD

Author of "This Side of Paradise," etc.                    $2.00

## The Great Gatsby

This novel is about one Gatsby—an attractive, mysterious young man of great wealth who keeps an open house at West Egg and gives the most sumptuous, brilliant entertainments—and his love for Daisy Buchanan. It is a story of infinite pathos about one whose whole life, including his wealth, was an accident—a satirical commentary upon the strange chances of our day, when a man may become a millionaire overnight and without meaning to —a marvellous fusion into unity of the extraordinary incongruities of the life of this time.

It is an account of how Gatsby has taken this house at West Egg in order to watch the green light at the end of Daisy's dock across the bay at fashionable East Egg, of the stark brutality of the scenes in which Daisy's husband, the ex-football-player, figures, of the extraordinary entertainments at the Gatsby house, and the horror of the motor accident, to the touching end, when Gatsby shows himself a true man.

The narrative has an extraordinary vitality and glamour underlaid by shrewd thought of unusual quality. It has also a kind of mystic atmosphere that characterized some parts of "This Side of Paradise," but has not since appeared in Fitzgerald's writings. It is a thrilling and extraordinary novel—all that any one could have asked of the brilliant author.

Catalogue entry for Fitzgerald's third novel; it is not known whether Perkins wrote catalogue copy for any of his authors' books; the final paragraph here echoes his November 18 letter to Fitzgerald (Princeton University Library).

*To: Perkins*                    *ca. February 18, 1925*
*From: Fitzgerald*                    *ALS, 1 p. Princeton*

Hotel Tiberio

New Adress

Capri

Dear Max:

After six weeks of uninterrupted work the proof is finished and the last of it goes to you this afternoon. On the whole its been very successful labor

(1.) I've brought Gatsby to life

(2.) I've accounted for his money

(3.) I've fixed up the two weak chapters (VI and VII)

(4.) I've improved his first party

(5.) I've broken up his long narrative in Chap. VIII

This morning I wired you to hold up the galley of Chap 40. The correction
—and God! its important because in my other revision I made Gatsby look too
mean[1]—is enclosed herewith. Also some corrections for the page proof.

We're moving to Capri. We hate Rome. I'm behind financially and have to
write three short stories. Then I try another play, and by June, I hope, begin my
new novel.

Had long interesting letters from Ring and John Bishop. Do tell me if all
corrections have been received. I'm worried

Scott

[*in left margin*] I hope you're setting publication date at first possible moment.

### Note

1.  In Fitzgerald's holograph insert for galley 40, he has Tom Buchanan say, "'They
[Gatsby and Wolfshiem] had the taxi-starters in front of hotels lined up as bookmakers,
squeezing money out of taxi-drivers and drunks and the poor bums that hang around
the streets. And every night one of Wolfshiem's men collected the money,' He turned to
Gatsby with a sneer, 'Who went to jail for you when the police stopped that game?'"
This passage does not appear in the printed book. See *F. Scott Fitzgerald Manuscripts III:
The Great Gatsby, The Revised and Rewritten Galleys,* ed. Bruccoli (New York & London:
Garland, 1990), pp. 139–40.

▲ ▼ ▲

*To: Hemingway*
*From: Perkins*                    *CC, 2 pp. Princeton*

Feb. 21, 1925

Dear Mr. Hemingway:

I have just read "in our time" published by the Three Mountains Press. I had
heard that you were doing very remarkable writing and was most anxious to see
it and after a great deal of effort and correspondence, I finally did manage to get
this book which seems not to be in circulation in this country. At all events I
could not find it. I was greatly impressed by the power in the scenes and incidents pictured, and by the effectiveness of their relation to each other, and I am
venturing to write to you to ask whether you have anything that you would
allow us to consider as publishers. I am bound to say at the same time that I
doubt if we could have seen a way to the publication of this book itself, on
account of material considerations:– it is so small that it would give the booksellers no opportunity for substantial profit if issued at a price which custom
would dictate. The trade would therefore not be interested in it. This is a pity
because your method is obviously one which enables you to express what you
have to say in very small compass, but a commercial publisher cannot disregard
these factors. It occurred to me, however, that you might very well be writing

something which would not have these practical objections and in any case, whatever you are writing, we should be most interested to consider.

Sincerely yours,

▲ ▼ ▲

*To: Charles Scribner's Son*
*From: Fitzgerald*          *Wire. Princeton*

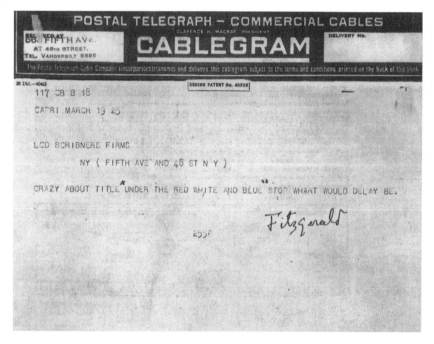

Fitzgerald never felt confident about "The Great Gatsby" as a title and tried to change it shortly before publication. Perkins wired that changing the title would delay publication and that he preferred "The Great Gatsby." On March 22 Fitzgerald wired: YOURE RIGHT (Princeton University Library).

▲ ▼ ▲

*To: Fitzgerald*
*From: Perkins*          *CC, 3 pp. Princeton*

March 19, 1925

Dear Scott:

This is not a letter, but a sort of bulletin. All the corrections came safely, I am sure, and all have been rightly made. I had to make two little changes: there are no tides in Lake Superior, as Rex Lardner told me and I have verified the fact, and this made it necessary to attribute the danger of the yacht to wind.[1]

The other change was where in describing the dead Gatsby in the swimming pool, you speak of the "leg of transept". I ought to have caught this on the galleys. The transept is the cross formation in a church and surely you could not figuratively have referred to this. I think you must have been thinking of a transit, which is an engineer's instrument. It is really not like compasses, for it rests upon a tripod, but I think the use of the word transit would be psychologically correct in giving the impression of the circle being drawn. I think this must be what you meant, but anyway it could not have been transept. You will now have page proofs and you ought to deal with these two points and make them as you want them, and I will have them changed in the next printing. Otherwise we found only typographical errors of a perfectly obvious kind. I think the book is a wonder and Gatsby is now most appealing, effective and real, and yet altogether original. We publish on April 10th.

I am awfully sorry that Zelda has been ill, and painfully. I hope it is all over now. Pain is regarded altogether too likely[2] in this world. It is about the worst thing there is.

I am sending you a wonderful story by Ring Lardner in Liberty.[3] We worked his "Young Immigrunts" and "Symptoms of Being 35" into the set.[4]

As ever,

### Notes

1. Ring Lardner's brother, Rex, was an editor at *Liberty*, which declined to serialize *The Great Gatsby*.
2. Perkins's typist probably misheard the word *lightly*.
3. "Haircut" (March 28, 1925).
4. Scribners had published a uniform edition of Lardner.

▲ ▼ ▲

To: Perkins　　　　　　　　　　　1925. En route to Paris
From: Fitzgerald　　　　　　　　　ALS, 5 pp. Princeton

April 10

Dear Max:

The book comes out today and I am overcome with fears and forebodings. Supposing women didn't like the book because it has no important woman in it, and critics didn't like it because it dealt with the rich and contained no peasants borrowed out of <u>Tess</u>[1] in it and set to work in Idaho? Suppose it didn't even wipe out my debt to you—why it will have to sell 20,000 copies even to do that! In fact all my confidence is gone—I wouldn't tell you this except for the fact that by the this reaches you the worst will be known. I'm sick of the book myself—I wrote it over at least five times and I still feel that what should be the strong scene (in the Hotel) is hurried and ineffective. Also the last chapter, the burial,

Gatsby's father ect is faulty. Its too bad because the first five chapters and parts of the 7th and 8th are the best things I've ever done.

"The best since Paradise". God! If you know how discouraging that was. That was what Ring said in his letter together with some very complementary remarks. In strictest confidence I'll admit that I was disappointed in <u>Haircut</u>— in fact I thought it was pretty lousy stuff—the crazy boy as the instrument of providence is many hundreds of years old. However please don't tell him I didn't like it.

Now as to the changes I don't think I'll make any more for the present. Ring suggested the correction of certain errata—if you can make the changes all right—if not let them go. Except on Page 209 old dim La Salle Street Station should be old dim Union Station and should be changed in the second edition.[2] Transit will do fine though of course I really meant compass. The page proofs arrived and seemed to be O.K. though I don't know how the printer found his way through those 70,000 corrections. The cover (jacket) came too and is a delight. Zelda is mad about it (incidently she is quite well again.

When you get this letter adress me c/o Guaranty Trust Co. 1 Rue Des Italennes, Paris.

Another thing—I'm convinced that Myers[3] is all right but have him be sure and keep all such trite phrases as "Surely the book of the Spring!" out of the advertising. That one is my pet abomination. Also to use no quotations <u>except those of unqualified and exceptionally entheusiastic praise from eminent individuals</u>. Such phrases as

"Should be on everyones summer list"
    Boston Transcript
"Not a dull moment ... a thoroughly sound solid piece of work"
        havn't sold a copy of any book in three years. I thought your advertising for Ring was great.
I'm sorry you didn't get Wescotts new book. Several people have written me that <u>The Apple of the Eye</u> is the best novel of the year.[4]

Life in New Cannan sounds more interesting than life in Plainfield. I'm sure anyhow that at least two critics Benet + Mary Column[5] will have heard about the book. I'd like her to like it—Benets opinion is of no value whatsoever.

And thanks mightily for the $750.00 which swells my debt to over $6000.00

When should my book of short stories be in?
                                                            Scott
P.S.

I had, or rather saw, a letter from my uncle who had seen a preliminary announcement of the book. He said:

"it sounded as if it were very much like his others."

This is only a vague impression, of course, but I wondered if we could think of some way to advertise it so that people who are perhaps weary of assertive jazz and society novels might not dismiss it as "just another book like his others." I confess that today the problem baffles me—all I can think of is to say in general to avoid such phrases as "a picture of New York life" or "modern society"—though as that is exactly what the book is its hard to avoid them. The trouble is so much superficial trash has sailed under those banners. Let me know what you think

Scott

### Notes

1. Thomas Hardy, *Tess of the D'Urbervilles* (1891).
2. Incorrectly changed to "Union Street Station" in the second printing.
3. Wallace Meyer of the Scribners advertising department.
4. Glenway Wescott's *The Apple of the Eye* was published by MacVeagh/Dial in 1924.
5. William Rose Benét favorably reviewed *Gatsby* in the May 9, 1925, *Saturday Review of Literature*; Mary Colum did not review the novel.

▲ ▼ ▲

*To: Perkins*
*From: Hemingway*                    *ALS, 3 pp.[1] Princeton*

113 Rue Notre Dame des Champs,
Paris VI, France
April 15, 1925

Dear Mr. Perkins:

On returning from Austria I received your letter of February 26 inclosing a copy of a previous letter which unfortunately never reached me. About ten days before your letter came I had a cabled offer from Boni and Liveright to bring out a book of my short stories in the fall.[2] They asked me to reply by cable and I accepted.

I was very excited at getting your letter but did not see what I could do until I had seen the contract from Boni and Liveright. According to its terms they are to have an option on my next three books, they agreeing that unless they exercise this option to publish the second book within 60 days of the receipt of the manuscript their option shall lapse, and if they do not publish the second book they relinquish their option on the third book.

So that is how matters stand. I cannot tell you how pleased I was by your letter and you must know how gladly I would have sent Charles Scribner's Sons the manuscript of the book that is to come out this fall. It makes it seem almost worth while to get into Who's Who in order to have a known address.

I do want you to know how much I appreciated your letter and if I am ever in a position to send you anything to consider I shall certainly do so.

I hope some day to have a sort of Daughty's Arabia Deserta of the Bull Ring, a very big book with some wonderful pictures.[3] But one has to save all winter to be able to bum in Spain in the summer and writing classics, I've always heard, takes some time. Somehow I don't care about writing a novel and I like to write short stories and I like to work at the bull fight book so I guess I'm a bad prospect for a publisher anyway. Somehow the novel seems to me to be an awfully artificial and worked out form but as some of the short stories now are stretching out to 8,000 to 12,000 words may be I'll get there yet.

. . . . .

Very Sincerely,
Ernest Hemingway

113 Rue Notre Dame des Champs
is a permanent address

*Notes*

1. 49 words have been omitted from this letter.
2. *In Our Time* (1925), which printed the vignettes of the Paris *in our time* as inter-chapters between longer Hemingway stories.
3. Hemingway refers to Charles Montagu Doughty's *Travels in Arabia Deserta.* Hemingway's book on bullfighting was published by Scribners in 1932 as *Death in the Afternoon.*

▲▼▲

*To: Perkins*        *April 18, 1924*
*From: Fitzgerald*      *Wire. Princeton*

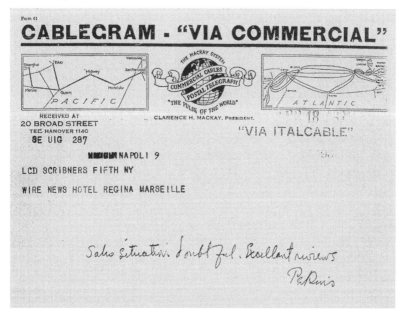

The note in Perkins's hand is his reply.

▲▼▲

*To: Fitzgerald*
*From: Perkins*                                    *CC, 4 pp. Princeton*

April 20, 1925

Dear Scott:

I wired you today rather discouragingly in the matter of the sales and I could send no qualifications in a cable. A great many of the trade have been very skeptical. I cannot make out just why. But one point is the small number of pages in the book,– an old stock objection which I thought we had got beyond. To attempt to explain to them that the way of writing which you have chosen and which is bound to come more and more into practice is one where a vast amount is said by implication, and that therefore the book is as full as it would have been if written to much greater length by another method, is of course utterly futile. The small number of pages, however, did in the end lead a couple of big distributors to reduce their orders immensely at the very last minute. The sale is up to the public and that has not yet had time to reveal itself fully. On the other hand, we have had a very good review, a very conspicuous one, in the Times, and an excellent one also in the Tribune from Isabelle Patterson. William Rose Benet has announced preliminary to a review in the Saturday Review, that this is distinctly your best book. And the individuals whom I encounter like Gilbert Seldes (who will write also), Van Wyck Brooks, John Marquand, John Bishop, think this too. Marquand and Seldes were both quite wild about it. These people understand it fully, which even the Times and Tribune reviewers did not.[1]

I will send you anything that has much significance by cable. I know fully how this period must try you: it must be very hard to endure, because it is hard enough for me to endure. I like the book so much myself and see so much in it that its recognition and success mean more to me than anything else in sight at the present time,– I mean in any department of interest, not only that of literature. But it does seem to me from the comments of many who yet feel its enchantment, that it is over the heads of more people than you would probably suppose.

In the course of this week when they have had time to accumulate, I will get together ads. and reviews and send them on. The situation has really not developed sufficiently yet to say anything decisive, but you can at least have the satisfaction of knowing that I shall watch it with the greatest anxiety imaginable in anyone but the author.

Yours,

*Note*

1. Edwin Clark, "Scott Fitzgerald Looks into Middle Age," *New York Times Book Review* (April 19, 1925), and Isabel Paterson, "Up to the Minute," *New York Herald Tribune Book Review* (April 19, 1925). Gilbert Seldes reviewed the novel twice: in the August 1925 issue of the *Dial*, and in the January 1926 issue of *New Criterion*. In the *Dial* Seldes declared: "Fitzgerald has more than matured; he has mastered his talents and gone soaring in beautiful flight, leaving behind him everything dubious and tricky in his earlier work, and leaving even farther behind all the men of his own generation and most of his elders."

▲▼▲

*To: Perkins*　　　　　　　　　　*ca. April 24, 1925*
*From: Fitzgerald*　　　　　　　 *ALS, 2 pp. Princeton*

Marsielle, en route to Paris

Dear Max:

Your telegram depressed me—I hope I'll find better news in Paris and am wiring you from Lyons. There's nothing to say until I hear more. If the book fails commercially it will be from one of two reasons or both

1st.　The title is only fair, rather bad than good.

2nd.　And most important—the book contains no important woman character, and women controll the fiction market at present. I don't think the unhappy end matters particularly.

It will have to sell 20,000 copies to wipe out my debt to you. I think it will do that all right—but my hope was it would do 75,000. This week will tell.

Zelda is well, or almost but the expense of her illness and of bringing this wretched little car of ours back to France which has to be done, by law, has wiped out what small progress I'd made in getting straight financially.

In all events I have a book of good stories for this fall.[1] Now I shall write some cheap ones until I've accumulated enough for my next novel. When that is finished and published I'll wait and see. If it will support me with no more intervals of trash I'll go on as a novelist. If not I'm going to quit, come home, go to Hollywood and learn the movie business. I can't reduce our scale of living and I can't stand this financial insecurity. Anyhow there's no point in trying to be an artist if you can't do your best. I had my chance back in 1920 to start my life on a sensible scale and I lost it and so I'll have to pay the penalty. Then perhaps at 40 I can start writing again without this constant worry and interruption

Yours in great depression
Scott

P.S. Let me know about Ring's Book. Did I tell you that I thought <u>Haircut</u> was mediochre?

P.S. (2) Please refer any movie offers to Reynolds.

*Note*

1. *All the Sad Young Men,* published in February 1926, included four important stories related to *The Great Gatsby.* "The Rich Boy," "Winter Dreams," "Absolution," and "'The Sensible Thing.'"

▲ ▼ ▲

*To: Perkins*                    *1925*
*From: Fitzgerald*               *ALS, 3 pp. Princeton*

Guaranty Trust Co.
Paris. May 1st

Dear Max:

There's no use for indignation against the long suffering public when even a critic who likes the book fails to be fundamentally held—that is Stallings, who has written the only intelligent review so far[1]—but its been depressing to find how quick one is forgotten, especially unless you repeat yourself ad <u>nauseam</u>. Most of the reviewers floundered around in a piece of work that obviously they completely failed to understand and tried to give it reviews that committed them neither pro or con until some one of culture had spoken. Of course I've only seen the <u>Times</u> and the <u>Tribune</u>—and, thank God, Stallings, for I had begun to believe no one was even glancing at the book.

Now about money. With the $1000. for which I asked yesterday (and thank you for your answer) I owe you about $7200, or if the book sells 12,000 about $4000.00. If there is a movie right I will pay you all I owe—if not, all I can offer for you at present is an excellent collection of stories for the fall entitled "All the Sad Young Men"—none of the stories appeared in the <u>Post</u>—I think <u>Absolution</u> is the only one you've read. Thank you for all your advertising and all the advances and all your good will. When I get ahead again on trash I'll begin the new novel.

I'm glad Ring is getting such a press and hope he's selling. The boob critics have taken him up and always take a poke at the "intelligentia" who patronize him. But the "intelligentsia"—Seldes + Mencken discovered him (after the people) while the boob critics let <u>The Big Town</u> and <u>Gullibles Travels</u> come out in dead silence. Let me know the sale.

A profound bow to my successor Arlen[2]—when I read <u>The London Venture</u> I knew he was a comer and was going to tell you but I saw the next day that Doran had already published <u>Piracy</u>. That was just before I left New York.

Which reminds me—it seems terrible that all the best of the young English-men have been snapped up. I tried to get Louis Golding[3] for you in Capri but he'd signed a rotten cash contract with Knopf a week before. Also they've just signed Brett Young[4] who might have been had any time in the last two years and who'll be a big seller and now I see <u>The Constant Nymph</u>[5] is taken. Wouldn't it pay you to have some live young Londoner watch the new English books. I imagine Kingsley[6] gets his information a month late out of the <u>London Times Supplement</u>. This sounds ill-natured but I am really sorry to see you loose so many new talents when they are appearing as fast now in England as they did here in 1920. Liverite has got Hemminway! How about Radiguet?

We have taken an apartment here from May 12th to Jan 12th, eight months, where I shall do my best. What a six months in Italy! Christ!

I'm hoping that by some miracle the book will go up to 23,000 and wipe off my debt to you. I haven't been out of debt now for three years and with the years it grows heavy on my ageing back. The happiest thought I have is of my new novel—it is something really NEW in form, idea, structure—the model for the age that Joyce and Stien are searching for, that Conrad didn't find.

Write me any news—I havn't had a written line since publication except a pleasant but not thrilling note from the perennial youth, Johnny Weaver.[7] I am bulging with plans for—however that's later. Was Rings skit which was in Mencken's American Language incorporated into What of it? If not it should have been—its one of his best shorter things.[8] And doesn't it contain his famous world's series articles about Ellis Lardners Coat? If not they'd be a nucleous for another book of nonsense. Also his day at home in imitation of F.P.A.'s diary.[9]

My adress after the 12th is 14 Rue de Tilsitt. If you have my Three Lives by Gertrude Stien don't let anybody steal it.

Many Thanks to Mr. Scribner and to all the others and to you for all you've done for me and for the book. The jacket was a hit anyhow

Scott

P.S. And Tom Boyd's Book?[10]

*Notes*

1. Laurence Stallings reviewed *The Great Gatsby* in the *New York World* on April 22.

2. Michael Arlen, author of English society novels; his best-known work was *The Green Hat* (1924).

3. English novelist and critic.

4. Francis Brett Young, English novelist.

5. By English novelist Margaret Kennedy.

6. Charles Kingsley was in charge of the Scribners London office.

7. Poet John V. A. Weaver.

8. "Baseball-American" and "Ham-American," *The American Language,* (1921) were not included in *What of It?* (Scribners, 1925).

9. Franklin Pierce Adams, who signed his work "F.P.A.," wrote newspaper columns titled "The Diary of Our Own Samuel Pepys."

10. Probably *Samuel Drummond* (Scribners, 1925).

▲ ▼ ▲

*To: Perkins*                     *ca. May 22, 1925*
*From: Fitzgerald*                *ALS, 2 p.*[1] *Princeton*

> 14 Rue de Tillsit
> Paris
> (Permanent adress)

Dear Max:

. . . . .

I've had entheusiastic letters from Mencken and Wilson—the latter says he's reviewing it for that Chicago Tribune syndicate he writes for.[2] I think all the reviews I've seen, except two, have been absolutely stupid and lowsy. Some day they'll eat grass, by God! This thing, both the effort and the result have hardened me and I think now that I'm much better than any of the young Americans without exception.

Hemingway is a fine, charming fellow and he appreciated your letter and the tone of it enormously. If Liveright doesn't please him he'll come to you, and he has a future. He's 27.

. . . . .

. . . . .                                                Scott

. . . . .

*Notes*

1. 185 words have been omitted from this letter.

2. Wilson did not review *The Great Gatsby*; Mencken reviewed the novel in the Baltimore *Evening Sun* (May 2, 1925).

▲ ▼ ▲

*To: Perkins*                     *ca. June 1, 1925*
*From: Fitzgerald*                *ALS, 8 pp. Princeton*

> 14 Rue de Tilsitt, Paris, France

Dear Max:

This is the second letter I've written you today—I tore my first up when the letter in longhand from New Cannan telling me about Liveright arrived. I'm wiring you today as to that rumor—but also it makes it nessessary to tell you something I didn't intend to tell you.

Yesterday arrived a letter from T. R. Smith[1] asking for my next book—saying nothing against the Scribners but just asking for it: "if I happened to be dissatisfied they would be delighted" ect. ect. I answered at once saying that you were one of my closest friends and that my relations with Scribners had always been so cordial and pleasant that I wouldn't think of changeing publishers. That letter will reach him at about the time this reaches you. I have never had any other communication <u>of any sort</u> with Liveright or any other publisher except the <u>very definate and explicit letter</u> with which I answered their letter yesterday.

So much for that rumor. I am both angry at Tom who must have been in some way responsible for starting it and depressed at the fact that you could have believed it enough to mention it to me. Rumors start like this.

Smith: (<u>a born gossip</u>) "I hear Fitzgerald's book isn't selling. I think we can get him, as he's probably blaming it on Scribners.

The Next Man: It seems Fitzgerald is disatisfied with Scribners and Liveright is after him.

The Third Man: I hear Fitzgerald has gone over to Liverite

Now, Max, I have told you many times that you are my publisher, and permanently, as far as one can fling about the word in this too mutable world. If you like I will sign a contract with you immediately for my next three books. The idea of leaving you has never for <u>one single moment</u> entered my head.

<u>First</u>. Tho, as a younger man, I have not always been in sympathy with some of your publishing ideas, (which were evolved under the pre-movie, pre-high-literacy-rate conditions of twenty to forty years ago), the personality of you and of Mr. Scribner, the tremendous squareness, courtesy, generosity and open-mindedness I have always met there and, if I may say it, the special consideration you have all had for me and my work, much more than make up the difference.

<u>Second</u>. You know my own idea on the advantages of one publisher who backs you and not your work. And my feeling about uniform books in the matter of house and binding.

<u>Third</u>. The curious advantage to a rather radical writer in being published by what is now an ultra-conservative house

<u>Fourth</u>. (and least need of saying) Do you think I could treat with another publisher while I have a debt, which is both actual and a matter of honor, of over $3000.00?

If Mr. Scribner has heard this rumor please show him this letter. So much for Mr. Liveright + Co.

Your letters are catching up with me. Curtis in <u>Town + Country</u> + Van Vetchten in <u>The Nation</u> pleased me.[2] The personal letters: Cabell, Wilson, Van Wyke Brooks ect. have been the best of all. Among people over here Ernest Hemminway + Gertrude Stien are quite entheusiastic. Except for Rascoe[3] it has been, critically only a clean sweep—and his little tribute is a result of our having snubbed his quite common and cheaply promiscuous wife.

Ring's book has been a terrible disappointment to everyone here.[4] He didn't even bother to cut out the connecting tags at the end of his travel articles and each of the five plays contain the same joke about "his mother—afterwards his wife." I shouldn't press him about his new collection, if I were you, because if you just took the first nine stories he writes, they couldn't be up to the others and <u>you know how reviewers are quick to turn on anyone in whom they have believed and who now disappoints them</u>. Of course I've only read <u>Haircut</u> and I may be wrong. I do want him to believe in his work + not have any blows to take away his confidence. The reviews I have seen of <u>What of It?</u> were sorry imitations of Seldes stuff and all of them went out of their way to stab Seldes in the back. God, cheap reviewers are low swine—but one must live.

As I write word has just come by cable that Brady has made an offer for the dramatic rights of <u>Gatsby</u>, with Owen Davis, king of proffessional play doctors, to do the dramatization.[5] I am, needless to say, accepting, but please keep it confidential until the actual contract is signed.

═══════════

As you know, despite my admiration for <u>Through the Wheat</u>, I haven't an enormous faith in Tom Boyd either as a personality or an artist—as I have, say, in E.E. Cummings and Hemminway. His ignorance, his presumptious intolerance and his careless grossness which he cultivates for vitality as a man might nurse along a dandelion with the hope that it would turn out to be an onion, have always annoyed me. Like Rascoe he has never been known to refuse an invitation from his social superiors—or to fail to pan them with all the venom of a James-Oliver-Curwood[6]–He-Man when no invitations were forthcoming.

All this is preparatory to saying that his new book sounds utterly lowsy—Shiela Kaye-Smith[7] has used the stuff about the farmer having girls instead of boys and being broken up about it. The characters you mention have every one, become stock-props in the last ten years—"Christy, the quaint old hired man" after a season in such stuff as Owen Davis' <u>Ice Bound</u> must be almost ready for the burlesque circuit.

<u>History of the Simple inarticulate Farmer and his Hired Man Christy</u>
(Both guaranteed to be utterly full of the Feel of the Soil)
<u>1st Period</u>
1855—English Peasant discovered by Geo. Elliot in <u>Mill on the Floss</u>, <u>Silas Marner</u> ect.

1888—Given intellectual interpretation by Hardy in <u>Jude</u> and <u>Tess</u>

1890—Found in France by Zola in <u>Germinal</u>

1900—Crowds of Scandanavians, Hamsun, Bojer[8] ect, tear him bodily from the Russian, and after a peep at Hardy, Hamlin Garland[9] finds him in the middle west.

===

Most of that, however, was literature. It was something pulled by the individual out of life and only partly with the aid of models in other literatures.

### 2nd Period

1914—Shiela Kaye-Smith frankly imitates Hardy, produces two good books + then begins to imitate herself.

1915—Brett Young discovers him in the coal country

1916—Robert Frost discovers him in New England

1917—Sherwood Anderson discovers him in Ohio

1918—Willa Cather turns him Swede

1920—Eugene O'Niell puts him on the boards in <u>Different</u> + <u>Beyond Horizon</u>

1922—Ruth Suckow <u>gets</u> in before the door closes

These people were all good second raters (except Anderson) Each of then brought something to the business—but they exhausted the ground, the type was set. All was over.

===

### 3d Period

The Cheap skates discover him—Bad critics and novelists ect.

1923    Homer Croy[10] writes <u>West of the Water Tower</u>

1924    Edna Ferber turns from her flip jewish saleswoman for a strong silent earthy carrot grower and the Great Soul of Charley Towne thrills to her passionately.[11] Real and Earthy struggle

1924    <u>Ice Bound</u>[12]. by the author of <u>Nellie the Beautiful Cloak Model</u> wins Pulitzer Prize

<u>The Able Mcgloughlins</u>[13] wins $10,000 prize + is forgotten the following wk.

1925    <u>The Apple of the Eye</u> pronounced a masterpiece

<u>1926</u>—TOM, BOYD, WRITES, NOVEL, ABOUT, INARTICULATE, FARMER WHO, IS, CLOSE, TO SOIL, AND, HIS, HIRED, MAN CHRISTY!

"STRONG! VITAL! REAL!"

As a matter of fact the American peasant as "real" material scarcely exists. He is scarcely 10% of the population, isn't bound to the soil at all as the English + Russian peasants were—and, if has any sensitivity whatsoever (except a most sentimental conception of himself, which our writers persistently shut their eyes to) he is in the towns before he's twenty. Either Lewis, Lardner and myself have been badly fooled, or else using him as typical American material is simply <u>a stubborn seeking for the static in a world that for almost a hundred years has simply not been static</u>. Isn't it a 4th rate imagination that can find only that old property farmer in all this amazing time and land? And anything that ten people a year can do well enough to pass muster has become so easy that it isn't worth the doing.

I can not disassociate a man from his work.— That this Wescott (who is an effeminate Oxford fairy) and Tom Boyd and Burton Rascoe (whose real ambition is to lock themselves into a stinking little appartment and screw each others' wives) are going to tell us mere superficial "craftsmen" like Hergeshiemer, Wharton, Tarkington and me about the Great Beautiful Appreciation they have of the Great Beautiful life of the Manure Wielder—rather turns my stomach. The real people like Gertrude Stien (with whom I've talked) and Conrad (see his essay on James) have a respect for people whose materials may not touch theirs <u>at a single point</u>. But the fourth rate + highly derivative people like Tom are loud in their outcry against any subject matter that doesn't come out of the old, old bag which their betters have used and thrown away.

For example there is an impression among the thoughtless (including Tom) that Sherwood Anderson is a man of profound ideas who is "handicapped by his inarticulateness". As a matter of fact Anderson is a man of practically no ideas—<u>but he is one of the very best and finest writers in the English language today</u>. God, he can write! Tom could never get such rythms in his life as there are on the pages of <u>Winesburg, Ohio</u>— Simple! The words on the lips of the critics makes me hilarious: Anderson's style is about as simple as an engine room full of dynamos. But Tom flatters himself that he can sit down for five months and by dressing up a few heart throbs in overalls produce literature.

It amazes me, Max, to see you with your discernment and your fine intelligence, fall for that whole complicated fake. Your chief critical flaw is to confuse mere earnestness with artistic sincerity. On two of Ring's jackets have been statements that he never wrote a dishonest word (maybe it's one jacket). But Ring and many of the very greatest artists have written thousands of words in plays, poems and novels which weren't even faintly sincere or ernest and were yet <u>artisticly sincere</u>. The latter term is <u>not</u> a synonym for plodding ernestness. Zola did not say the last word about literature; nor the first.

I append all the data on my fall book, and in closing I apologize for seeming impassioned about Tom and his work when niether the man or what he writes has ever been personally inimical to me. He is simply the scapegoat for the mood Rascoe has put me in and, tho I mean every word of it, I probably wouldn't have wasted all this paper on a book that won't sell + will be dead in a month + an imitative school that will be dead by its own weight in a year or so, if the news about Liveright hadn't come on top of the Rascoe review and ruined my disposition. Good luck to <u>Drummond</u>.[14] I'm sure one or two critics will mistake it for profound stuff—maybe even Mencken who has a weakness in that direction. But I think you should look closer.

With best wishes as always, Max,

Your Friend. Scott

DATA ON NEW FITZGERALD BOOK.

Title

<u>ALL THE SAD YOUNG MEN</u>

(9 short stories)

Print list of previous books as before with addition of this title under "Stories". Binding uniform with others.

Jacket plain, as you suggest, with text instead of picture
Dedication: To Ring and Ellis Lardner
The Stories (now under revision) will reach you by July 15th. No proofs need be sent over here.

It will be fully up to the other collections and will contain only one of those <u>Post</u> stories that people were so snooty about. You have read only one of the stories. ("Absolution")—all the others were so good that I had difficulty in selling them, except two.

They are, in approximately order to be used in book:

1. The Rich Boy (Just finished. Serious story and
   very good)     13,000 wds.
2. Absolution (From <u>Mercury</u>)     6,500 "
3. Winter Dreams (A sort of 1st draft of the Gatsby idea
   from <u>Metropolitan</u> 1923)     9,000 "
4. Rags Martin-Jones and the Pr-nce of Wales (Fantastic Jazz,
   so good that Lorimer + Long[15] refused it. From <u>McCalls</u>)   6,000 "
5. The Baby Party (From <u>Hearsts</u>. A fine story)     5,000 "
6. Dice, Brass knuckles and Guitar (From <u>Hearsts</u>.
   Exuberant Jazz in my early manner)     8,000 "
7. The Sensible Thing (Story about Zelda + me.
   All True. From <u>Liberty</u>)     5,000 "
8. Hot + Cold Blood (Good Story, from <u>Hearsts</u>)     6,000 "
9. Gretchen's Forty Winks (from Post. Farrar, Christian
   Gauss and Jesse Williams thought it my best.[16] It isn't.)   7,000 "
   Total — about— — — — — — — —     64,500
   (And possibly one other short one)

This title is because seven stories deal with young men of my generation in rather unhappy moods. The ones to mention on the outside wrap are the 1st five or the 1st three stories.

———————

Rather not use advertising appropriation in <u>Times</u>—people who read <u>Times Book Review</u> won't be interested in me. Recommend <u>Mercury</u>, the F. P. A. page of the <u>World</u>, <u>Literary Review</u> and Fanny Bucher page of <u>Chicago Tribune</u>.

No blurbs in ad. as I think the blurb doesn't help any more. Suggestion.

Charles Scribners Sons
Announce a new book of short stories
By
F. Scott Fitzgerald

<u>Advertising Notes</u>

Suggested line for jacket:—"Show transition from his early exuberant stories of youth which created a new type of American girl and the later and more serious mood which produced <u>The Great Gatsby</u> and marked him as one of the half dozen masters of English prose now writing in America. . . .[17] What other writer has shown such unexpected developments, such versatility, changes of pace"

ect — ect — ect — I think that, toned down as you see fit, is the general line. Don't say "Fitzgerald has done it!" + then in the next sentence that I am an artist. People who are interested in artists aren't interested in people who have "done it." Both are O.K. but don't belong in the same ad. This is an author's quibble. All authors have one quibble.

However, you have always done well by me (except for Black's memorable execretion in the <u>Allumni Weekly</u>: do you remember "Make it a Fitzgerald Christmas!") and I leave it to you. If 100,000 copies are not sold I shall shift to Mitchell Kennerley.[18]

By the way what has become of Black? I hear he has written a very original and profound novel. It is said to be about an inarticulate farmer and his struggles with the "soil" and his sexual waverings between his inarticulate wife and an inarticulate sheep. He finally chooses his old pioneering grandmother as the most inarticulate of all but finds her in bed with none other than our old friend THE HIRED MAN CHRISTY!

CHRISTY HAD DONE IT!

[*In left margin*] [In 1962 Fitzgerald's famous letter to Perkins was sold at auction at Chrystie's (not old man Christy's) for £7000.][19]

## Notes

1. Thomas R. Smith, editor at Boni & Liveright.

2. Reviews of *The Great Gatsby* by William Curtis (May 15, 1925) and Carl Van Vechten (May 20, 1925).

3. This attack on *The Great Gatsby* by book reviewer Burton Rascoe has not been located.

4. *What of It?*

5. Broadway impresario William A. Brady and playwright Owen Davis; the Davis version of *The Great Gatsby* opened on Broadway on February 2, 1926, and ran for 112 performances.

6. James Oliver Curwood, author of western adventure fiction.

7. English novelist.

8. Knut Hamsun and Johan Bojer, Norwegian novelists.

9. American realist writer.

10. Midwestern novelist and humorist.

11. Ferber's *So Big* won the 1925 Pulitzer Prize for fiction; Charles H. Towne was a journalist and editor.

12. *Icebound,* a play by Owen Davis, won the 1923 Pulitzer Prize for drama.

13. *The Able McLaughlin,* by Margaret Wilson, won the 1924 Pulitzer Prize for fiction.

14. *Samuel Drummond* (1925), novel by Boyd.

15. George Horace Lorimer, editor of the *Saturday Evening Post,* and Ray Long, editor of *Hearst's International.*

16. John Farrar, critic; Jesse Lynch Williams, playwright and short-story writer; Dean Christian Gauss of Princeton, whom Fitzgerald admired.

17. Fitzgerald's ellipsis marks.

18. Publisher known for his parsimonious dealings with authors.

19. Fitzgerald's marginal note. This letter was never sold at auction.

▲ ▼ ▲

To: *Perkins*               ca. *July 10, 1925*
From: *Fitzgerald*          *ALS, 1 p. Princeton*

14 Rue de Tilsitt.
Paris, France

Dear Max:

(1.) I'm afraid in sending the book[1] I forgot the dedication, which should read

### TO RING AND ELLIS LARDNER

will you see to this?

(2.) I've asked <u>The Red Book</u> to let you know the first possible date on "The Rich Boy"[2]

(3.) I'm terribly sorry about the whooping cough but I'll have to admit it did give me a laugh.

(4.) Max, it amuses me when praise comes in on the "structure" of the book[3]—because it was you who fixed up the structure, not me. And don't think I'm not grateful for all that sane and helpful advice about it.

(5)   The novel has begun. I'd rather tell you nothing about it quite yet. No news. We had a great time in Antibes and got very brown + healthy. In case you don't place it its the penninsula between Cannes + Nice on the Rivierra where Napoeleon landed on his return from Elba.

As Ever
Scott.

### Notes

1. *All the Sad Young Men.*
2. "The Rich Boy" was published in the January and February 1926 issues of *Red Book Magazine* and collected in *All the Sad Young Men,* the publication of which was delayed until the novella appeared in the magazine.
3. *The Great Gatsby.*

▲ ▼ ▲

To: Perkins                          *ca. December 30, 1925*
From: Fitzgerald                     *ALS, 3 pp. Princeton*

14 Rue de Tilsitt
[New adress
Guaranty Trust Co.
1 Rue des Italiennes]

Dear Max:

(1.)  To begin with many thanks for all deposits, to you and to the Scribners in general. I have no idea now how I stand with you. To set me straight will you send me my account <u>now</u> instead of waiting till February 1st. It must be huge, and I'm miserable about it. The more I get for my trash the less I can bring myself to write. However this year is going to be different.

(2.)  Hemmingways book (not his novel) is a 28,000 word satire on Sherwood Anderson and his imitators called The <u>Torrents of Spring</u>. I loved it, but believe it wouldn't be popular, + Liveright have refused it—<u>they are backing Anderson</u> and this book is almost a vicious parody on him. You see I agree with Ernest that Anderson's last two books have let everybody down who believed in him—I think they're cheap, faked, obscurantic and awful. Hemmingway thinks, but isn't yet sure to my satisfaction, that their refusal sets him free from his three book (letter) agreement with them. In that case I think he'll give you his novel (on condition you'll publish satire first—probable sale 1000 copies) which he is now revising in Austria. Harcourt has just written Louie Bromfield[1] that to get the novel they'll publish satire, sight unseen (utterly confidential) and Knopf is after him via Aspinwall Bradley.[2]

He and I are very thick + he's marking time until he finds out how much he's bound to Liveright. If he's free I'm almost sure I can get satire to you first + then if you see your way clear you can contract for the novel <u>tout ensemble</u>. He's anxious too to get a foothold in your magazine—one story I've sent you— the other, to my horror he'd given for about $40 to an "arty" publication called <u>This Quarter</u>,[3] over here.

He's <u>dead set</u> on having the satire published first. His idea has always been to come to you + his only hesitation has been that Harcourt might be less conservative in regard to certain somewhat broad scenes. His adress is:

Herr Ernest Hemmingway
Hotel Taube
Vorarlburg
Austria

As soon as he has definate dope I'll pass it on to you I wanted a strong wire to show you were as interested, and more, than Harcourt. Did you know your letter just missed by two weeks getting <u>In Our Time</u>. It had no sale of course but I think the novel may be something extraordinary—Tom Boyd and E. E. Cummings + Biggs combined.

Wasn't Dos Passos' book astonishingly good.[4] I'm very fond of him but I had lost faith in his work.

(3.) Tell me all about my play.
(4.) I can't wait to see the book your sending me. Zelda says it might be <u>Gatsby</u> but I don't think so.
(5 ) Poor Eleanor Wylie! Poor Bill Benet! Poor everybody![5]
(6 ) My novel is wonderful.
(7 ) The translation of Gatsby sounds wonderful.
(8 ) Will you ask the bookstore to send The Beautiful and Damned to <u>M. Victor Llona, 106 Rue de La Tour, Paris</u> Thanks. Charge to my account, of course.
(9 ) I thought Dunns remark about Biggs book[6] was wonderful. Tell me about it. Also about Tom Boyd's work and Ring's. You never do.

As Ever    Scott

[*To the right of Hemingway's Schrunns address*]. Don't even tell him I've discussed his Liveright + Harcourt relations with you.

### Notes

1. Alfred Harcourt, a founder of Harcourt, Brace publishing company; novelist Louis Bromfield, who lived in France.
2. William Aspinwall Bradley, American literary agent in Paris.
3. Probably "Big Two-Hearted River."
4. *Manhattan Transfer* (1925).

5. Poet and novelist Elinor Wylie had separated from her husband, editor William Rose Benét.

6. According to Perkins's December 17, 1925, letter to Fitzgerald, Scribners first reader Charles Dunn said that Biggs's book "had become a classic in this office without ever having been written."

▲ ▼ ▲

*To: Fitzgerald*
*From: Hemingway*                          *ALS, 5 pp.*[1] *Princeton*

December 31, 1925

Dear Scott—

Have just received following cable from Liveright—Rejecting Torrents of Spring Patiently awaiting manuscript Sun Also Rises Writing Fully—

I asked them in the letter I sent with the Ms. to cable me their decision. I have known all along that they could not and would not be able to publish it as it makes a bum out of their present ace and best seller Anderson. Now in 10th printing. I did not, however, have that in mind in any way when I wrote it.

Still I hate to go through the hell of changing publishers etc. Also the book should come out in the late Spring at latest. That would be best. Later would not be bad but Spring would be ideal.

My contract with Liveright—only a letter—reads that in consideration of they're publishing my first book at their own expense etc. they are to have an option on my first three books. If they do not exercise this option to publish within 60 days of receipt of Ms. it lapses and if they do not exercise their option on the 2nd book it lapses for 3rd book. So I'm loose. No matter what Horace may think up in his letter to say.

As you know I promised Maxwell Perkins that I would give him the first chance at anything if by any chance I should be released from Liveright.

. . . . .
. . . . .
. . . . .
. . . . .
. . . . .
. . . . .
. . . . .

In any event I am not going to Double Cross you and Max Perkins to whom I have given a promise.

I will wire Liveright tomorrow a.m to Send Manuscript to Don Stewart[2] care of the Yale Club, New York (only address I can think of tonight) and summarize by cable any propositions he may be making me in his letter.

It's up to you how I proceed next. Don I can wire to send Ms. to Max Perkins. You can write Max telling him how Liveright turned it down and why and your own opinion of it. I am re-writing The Sun Also Rises and it is damned good. It will be ready in 2–3 months for late fall or later if they wish.

As you see I am jeopardizing my chances with Harcourt by first sending the Ms. to Scribner and if Scribner turned it down. It would be very bad as Harcourt have practically offered to take me unsight unseen. Am turning down a sure thing for delay and a chance but feel no regret because of the impression I have formed of Maxwell Perkins through his letters and what you have told me of him. Also confidence in Scribners and would like to be lined up with you.

. . . . .
. . . . .
. . . . .
. . . . .
. . . . .
. . . . .
. . . . .
. . . . .
. . . . .
. . . . .
. . . . .
. . . . .

Best to you always,
Ernest/

*Notes*

1. 759 words have been omitted from this letter.
2. American humorist Donald Ogden Stewart (1894–1980).

▲ ▼ ▲

*To: Perkins*      *January 8, 1926*
*From: Fitzgerald*      *Wire. Princeton*

YOU CAN GET HEMINGWAYS FINISHED NOVEL PROVIDED YOU PUBLISH UNPROMISING SATIRE HARCOURT HAS MADE DEFINITE OFFER WIRE IMMEDIATELY WITHOUT QUALIFICATIONS
FITZGERALD

▲ ▼ ▲

*To: Fitzgerald*                    *January 8, 1926*
*From: Perkins*                       *TS draft for wire with holograph*
                                      *revisions by Perkins. Princeton*

Publish novel at fifteen percent and advance if desired. Also satire unless objectionable other than financially. Hemingways stories splendid. Scribners

▲ ▼ ▲

*To: Fitzgerald*
*From: Perkins*                      *CC, 4 pp. Princeton*

Jan. 13, 1926

Dear Scott:

I enclose three wraps.[1] Don't judge them without putting them around books, because that is the only way in which you can get any idea of how they will look. They are rather shabby specimens but they are all I can get hold of.

I thought Hemingway's stories astonishingly fine and so does everyone who reads them. It seems strange that Liveright has put so little behind them. I speak of this on the assumption that for some reason he is not to publish any more for Hemingway. Otherwise your cable would not have come. I did my best with that cable, but there was a fear that this satire—although in the hands of such a writer it could hardly be rightly so upon any theory—might be suppressible. In fact we could tell nothing about it of course in those respects and it is not the policy obviously of Scribners to publish books of certain types. For instance, if it were even Rabelasian to an extreme degree, it might be objected to. It was only this point that prevented me from wiring you without any qualification because those stories are as invigorating as a cold, fresh wind.

I am afraid though that the qualification was fatal.— But in any case, I think it was bully of you to have acted in our behalf in that way. I was much pleased that you did it. As for Harcourt, I think him an admirable publisher and I haven't any criticism of him. But I believe that as compared with most others, Hemingway would be better off in our hands because we are absolutely true to our authors and support them loyally in the face of losses for a long time, when we believe in their qualities and in them. It is that kind of a publisher that Hemingway probably needs, because I hardly think he could come into a large public immediately. He ought to be published by one who believes in him and is prepared to lose money for a period in enlarging his market.— Although he would certainly, even without much support, get recognition through his own powers.

I have not tried to communicate with him because I did not know how far I ought to go, particularly after getting your second telegram. The fact is that we would publish the satire however certain it might be of financial failure because of our faith in him,— and perhaps also because of the qualities of the work itself, of which I cannot speak.

As ever yours,

*Note*

1. Trial dust jackets for *All the Sad Young Men*.

▲ ▼ ▲

*To: Fitzgerald*                          *January 11, 1926*
*From: Perkins*                          *TS draft for wire. Princeton*

Confidence absolute. Keen to publish him. Cabled you Friday care of Guaranty Trust. Scribners

▲ ▼ ▲

*To : Perkins*                          *ca. January 19, 1926*
*From: Fitzgerald*                          *ALS, 3 pp. Princeton*

c/o Guaranty Trust Co.
Paris, France

Dear Max:

Your thoughtful cablegram came today and I can't imagine how the rumor got started—unless from Zelda using an imaginary illness as a protection against the many transients who demand our time.[1] Somehow if one lives in Paris one is fair game for all the bores one wouldn't look at and who wouldn't look at one in New York. (If there's one thing I hate it's a sentence full of "ones")

We have escaped to a small town in the Pyrenes where Zelda is to take a cure. Our adress for cables is

Fitzgerald, Bellevue, Salies-de-Béarn, France

but for letters the Guaranty, Paris is best. We are living in an absolutely deserted hotel. We move on to Nice the first of March. Here are my usual list of things.

(1) Thanks a million times for the bound copy of my book—it is beautiful and, Max, I'm enormously obliged.[2] I wish you'd written in the front— but that will wait till I get home. Your thought of me touched me more than I can say.

(2.) Now about the many deposits. They are past all reckoning but must total $5000 which is a record advance (?) on a book of short stories. I'm terribly sorry, Max. Could he send me my account this year on the 1st of February really instead of February 15th. We won't be able to tell about The Sad Young anyhow and I'm frantic to know if I'm helplessly in debt.

(3) What is the date of the book? How are advance sales, compared with Gatsby? Did the latter ever reach 25,000?

(4) Now, confidentially, as to Hemminway. He wrote a satire 28,000 words long on Sherwood Anderson, very funny but very cerebral, called <u>The Torrents of Spring</u>. It is <u>biting</u> on Anderson—so Liveright turns it down. Hemminways contract <u>lapses when Liveright turns down a book, so Hemminway says</u>. But I think Horace will claim this isn't a book and fight it like the devil, according to a letter I saw which he wrote Ernest—because he's crazy to get Ernests almost completed novel <u>The Sun Also Rises</u>. It is such a mess that Ernest goes to N.Y next month.

Meanwhile Harcourt + Knopf are after him but he's favorably disposed toward you because of your letters and of the magazine. He's very excitable, though and I can't promise he'll know his own mind next month. I'll tip you off the moment he arrives. Of course if Bridges likes his work + if you'll take Torrents he's yours absolutely—contingent, of course, on the fact that he isn't bitched by some terrible contract with Liveright. To hear him talk you'd think Liveright had broken up his home and robbed him of millions—but thats because he knows nothing of publishing, except in the cucoo magazines, is very young and feels helpless so far away. You won't be able to help liking him—he's one of the nicest fellows I ever knew.

In addition to the critics will you send my new book to the following people[3] and charge my account (except in cases like Hergeshiemer + Van Vetchten,[4] who actually reviewed Gatsby. Send me only 3 copies.

Thanks again for my beautiful copy

As ever     Scott

### Notes

1. Perkins's telegram to Zelda Fitzgerald was prompted by a newspaper report that Fitzgerald was ill.

2. Perkins sent Fitzgerald a leatherbound copy of *The Great Gatsby.*

3. Fitzgerald's list is missing.

4. American novelists Joseph Hergesheimer (1880–1954) and Carl Van Vechten (1880–1964).

▲ ▼ ▲

*To: Hemingway*
*From: Perkins*                                    *CC, 4 pp. Princeton*

Feb. 1, 1926

Dear Mr. Hemingway:

I, and, we, think your "Fifty Grand" is a magnificent story. Scott sent it here,– I suppose with your authorization, and as I had just recently read "In Our Time" I naturally read this without a moment's delay.– And the magazine people read it immediately thereafter, and everyone here was roused up by it. It makes you see how poor most of the material is that is thought pretty good. Naturally we want to have it in the magazine and we would pay two hundred and fifty dollars for it, which is more than we usually do pay for short stories. There is this one great obstacle: it is too long. If we run a story of over eight thousand words, we have to give it too much room; we are not like the large-page magazines, which run the text back into the advertisements. We have to hold the stories down, and we have lost some good ones on that account. But we have lost none as good as this one, I guess, if we must lose it. I had a hope that you might be able and willing to cut it by fifteen hundred words, for then it would fit. Could you do this, and if so have you a copy to do it from? It looks to me as if it would be difficult, but I do hope you can manage it, and will. I might as well say frankly that you would get more money—I suppose you know it—from Liberty, which Scott suggested I send this story to if we could not take it; but I do think that it might well be better to have it in Scribner's. Still, I won't urge this point for you will know the situation well enough. I am awfully sorry to hold up matters until you get this letter, and have written an answer, but we cannot bring ourselves to surrender the story without this attempt to get it. If the delay seems a bad one to you, and you feel that you cannot do as we want, wire me the one word "No" and I shall understand that I must send it on to Liberty. Address it simply Scribners, New York, and the message will come to me. You won't even have to sign it. If you wire "Yes" I shall know that it is all right, but that you must have the copy back, but if you have a carbon copy to cut, don't wire at all, but simply go ahead and send that to us. Certainly nobody else ought to attempt to cut the story by any possibility, even if you were willing to let them.[1]

You would be pleased if you heard what people said of "In Our Time", those people who are quick to catch on to notable publications. It is vastly admired and this admiration is bound to spread. I think stories in Scribner's would help in that respect more than stories in Liberty, or the Post, or any of those more popular magazines, but as I am naturally prejudiced, it will hardly do for me to argue the point too much.

Reading "In Our Time" makes me even more disgusted with having failed to communicate with you more quickly last summer. I did not realize that you had so much material as that, by any means. I judged mainly by the Three Mountain Press book. I saw in one of the papers a note that you were writing a novel. It will certainly be awaited eagerly by a considerable number over here, including myself.

Sincerely yours,

### Note

1. The story was published in the *Atlantic Monthly* (July 1927).

▲▼▲

*To: Perkins*                                        *ca. March 1, 1926*
*From: Fitzgerald*                                   *ALS, 2 pp.[1] Princeton*

Hotel Bellevue
Saliés-de-Béarn

Dear Max:

Ernest will reach N.Y. as soon as this. Apparently he's free so its between you
and Harcourt. He'll get in touch with you.

There are several rather but not very Rabelaisian touches in Torrents of
Spring (the satire) <u>No worse than Don Stuart</u> or Benchley's[2] Anderson parody.
Also Harcourt <u>is said</u> to have offered $500. advance <u>Torrents</u> and $1000. on
almost completed novel. (Strictly confidential.) If Bridges takes <u>50 Grand</u> I
don't think Ernest would ask you to meet those advances but here I'm getting
involved in a diplomacy you can handle better. I don't say hold <u>50 Grand</u> over
him but in a way he's holding it over you—one of the reasons he verges toward
you is the magazine.

In any case he is tempermental in business. Made so by these bogus publishers over here. If you take the other two things <u>get a signed contract</u> for <u>The
Sun Also Rises</u> (novel) Anyhow this is my last word on the subject—confidential
between you + me. Please destroy this letter.

. . . . .
. . . . .
. . . . .
. . . . .
. . . . .

As Ever
Scott Fitz—

. . . . .

*Notes*

1. 105 words have been omitted from this letter.
2. American humorist Robert Benchley (1889–1945) parodied Anderson in "A
Ghost Story (As Sherwood Anderson Would Write It If He Weren't Prevented)," *Life*
(December 3, 1925), 21, 64.

▲▼▲

*To: Fitzgerald*
*From: Perkins*                                      *CC, 3 pp.[1] Princeton*

March 4, 1926

Dear Scott:

. . . . .

. . . . .

. . . . .

As for Hemingway, whom I enjoyed very much, we have contracted to publish "Torrents of Spring" and the novel. He was willing to give us options on other books, but I never thought well of that way of doing:– if a man does not like us after we have published two of his books, he ought not to be compelled to publish through us, and we do not want to publish for anyone who is not square enough to recognize that what we have done is good, if it is, and to give us the advantage over anybody else. If a writer can get better terms from another publisher on his third or fourth book, it is only fair that he can also demand better terms of us. The relations you have with an author cannot be satisfactory if they are absolutely cut and dried business relations, anyhow. I am extremely grateful to you for intervening about Hemingway. He is a most interesting chap about his bull fights and boxing. His admirable story, "Fifty Grand" was too long to be got into the magazine, and it has been declined by Colliers and the Post,– although Lorimer spoke highly of it. Liberty could not use it because of its length. . . .

. . . . .

. . . . .

As ever yours,

. . . . .

*Note*

1. 449 words have been omitted from this letter.

▲ ▼ ▲

*To: Hemingway*
*From: Perkins*                    *CC, 4 pp.[1] Princeton*

May 18, 1926

Dear Mr. Hemingway:

"The Sun Also Rises"[2] seems to me a most extraordinary performance. No one could conceive of a book with more life in it. All the scenes, and particularly those when they cross the Pyrenees and come into Spain, and when they fish in that cold river, and when the bulls are sent in with the steers, and when they are fought in the arena, are of such a quality as to be like actual experience. You have struck our pet phrase, "pity and irony,"[3] to death so I can't use it; but the humor in the book and the satire—especially expressed by Gorton, and by the narrator,—are marvelous; and not in the least of a literary sort. But in connection with this there is one hard point—a hard one to raise too, because the passage in question comes in so aptly and so rightly. I mean the speech about Henry James.[4] I swear I do not see how that can be printed. It could not by any conception be printed while he was alive, if only for the fear of a lawsuit; and in a way it seems almost worse to print it after he is dead. I am not raising this you must believe, because we are his publishers. The matter referred to is peculiarly a personal one. It is not like something that a man could be criticized for,—some part of his conduct in life and which might therefore be considered open for comment. I want to put this before you at the very beginning.

Hemingway received a combined $1,500 advance for his first two Scribners books (Princeton University Library).

There are also one or two other things that I shall bring up in connection. with the proof, but there is no need to speak of them here.

The book as a work of art seems to me astonishing, and the more so because it involves such an extraordinary range of experience and emotion, all brought together in the most skillful manner—the subtle ways of which are beautifully concealed—to form a complete design. I could not express my admiration too strongly.

As ever yours,

. . . . .

Expenses incurred for alterations in type or plates, exceeding twenty per cent. of the cost of composition and electrotyping said work are to be charged to the AUTHOR's account.

The first statement shall not be rendered until six months after date of publication; and thereafter statements shall be rendered semi-annually, on the AUTHOR's application therefor, in the months of February and August; settlements to be made in cash, four months after date of statement.

If, on the expiration of **five** years from date of publication, or at any time thereafter, the demand for said work should not, in the opinion of said PUBLISHERS, be sufficient to render its publication profitable, then, upon written notice by said PUBLISHERS to said AUTHOR, this contract shall cease and determine; and thereupon said AUTHOR shall have the right, at **his** option, to take from said PUBLISHERS, at cost, whatever copies of said work they may then have on hand; or, failing to take said copies at cost, then said PUBLISHERS shall have the right to dispose of the copies on hand as they may see fit, free from any percentage or royalty, and to cancel this contract.

Provided, also, that if, at any time during the continuance of this agreement, said work shall become unsalable in the ordinary channels of trade, said PUBLISHERS shall have the right to dispose of any copies on hand, paying to said AUTHOR – **fifteen (15)** – per cent. of the net amount received therefor, in lieu of the percentage hereinbefore prescribed.

Said Publishers shall pay to said Author the sum of fifteen hundred dollars ($1,500.) as an advance on royalty account, said amount to be reimbursed to said Publishers from the first monies accruing under said royalties.

In consideration of the mutuality of this contract, the aforesaid parties agree to all its provisions, and in testimony thereof affix their signatures and seals.

Witness to signature of
Ernest Hemingway

*Ernest Hemingway.*

Witness to signature of
Charles Scribner's Sons

{ L. S. }

*Notes*

1. 52 words have been omitted from this letter.
2. Fitzgerald vetted both *The Sun Also Rises* and *A Farewell to Arms* in typescript and wrote Hemingway detailed letters of advice; see *Fitzgerald and Hemingway: A Dangerous Friendship*, by Bruccoli (New York: Carroll & Graf, 1994), pp. 64–67 and pp. 111–15.
3. In *The Sun Also Rises*, Bill Gorton uses this phrase in a nonsense song ridiculing literary critics.
4. In chapter 12 of *The Sun Also Rises*, Gorton alludes to the claim that James was rendered impotent by a horseback- or bicycle-riding accident. The passage was revised for the book, and James is referred to as "Henry" without his surname.

▲ ▼ ▲

*To: Charles Scribner III*
*From: Perkins*                                          *ALS, 4 pp.*[1] *Princeton*

May 27th 1926

Dear Charley:–

You wanted to know the decision on Hemingway: We took it,- with misgiving. In the course of the debate I argued that the question was a crucial one in respect to younger writers;- that we suffered by being called "ultra-conservative" (Even if unjustly + with malice) + that this would become our reputation for the present when our declination of this book should, as it would, get about. That view of the matter influenced our decision largely. Wheelock[2] was called in, with a curious result: I thought he had been so much out of the world on that balcony of his, + in his generally hermitlike life, as to be out of touch with modern tendencies in writing + therefore over sensitive; but to my amazement he thought there was no question whatever but that we should publish. There was of course a great one. I simply thought in the end that the balance was slightly in favor of acceptance, for all the worry + general misery involved. -But you wont see Hemingway: he's in Spain, Bull fighting I suspect.

. . . . .
. . . . .
. . . . .

*Notes*

1. 380 words have been omitted from this letter.
2. John Hall Wheelock, poet and associate editor at Scribners. See his account of this meeting in *The Last Romantic: A Poet among Publishers*, p. 59.

▲ ▼ ▲

*To: Fitzgerald*
*From: Perkins*                                    *AL, 3 pp.*[1] *Kennedy*

May 29th 1926

Dear Scott:-

When you think of Hemingways' book you recall Scenes as if they were memories,-glorious ones of Spain, + fishing in a cold river, + bull fights, all full of life + color; + you recall people as hard + actual as real ones. That is the way you remember the book,-not as you do Thackeray where the style + all, the literary quality, is always a part of the recollection. Here the ms. wriggles with vitality. The art is marvelously concealed, + yet the whole is composed to the last word.-Yet the book is not an unmixed pleasure because it is almost unpublishable. It is about such people as I suppose you know in Paris. Hemingway must have known them,-that is, their like. They belong to "a lost generation." Several including the girl are what are now called "disintegrated personalities," I suppose. They are the war generation + have had too long + too fierce a dose of reality. They conceal nothing, + neither does Hemingway. The principle characters are naturally fine people + their situation is tragic. The true principles are a girl + a man who belong together; but they are always + inivitably parted by the fact-+ what an ironic fact-that he (who tells the tale) has been so wounded that he can not sexually play the part of a man!-You may know all this so I wont go into it. You can guess that it presents a problem;-but the book is never erotic, +, in a true sense, it is always clean + healthy. There is one passage-a part of one of the best + most humorous conversations in the book-that simply must come out:-its about Henry James supposed incapacity in the matter of sex. During his life no one could have dreamed of printing it, + to do it now would really be worse. And there are many words seldom if ever used before in print;-possibly some can come out without damage, or with less than their presense will cause. Altogether it is a very strange + remarkable book, with many aspects. The beauty + cruelty of the world are curiously blent in it. One would naturally fall back on "irony + pity" to describe it, but there's a chap in the book, + he's a good one, who laughs that fine old phrase out of usage. What we publishers are to do for blurbs I don't know!

### Note

1. Fitzgerald apparently gave Hemingway the first three pages of this letter; the rest of the letter has not been located.

▲ ▼ ▲

*To: Perkins*
*From: Hemingway*          *TLS with holograph additions, 2 pp.*[1] *Princeton*

Dear Mr. Perkins =

   . . . . .

   . . . . .

   . . . . .

   . . . . .

I believe that, in the proofs, I will start the book at what is now page 16 in the Mss. There is nothing in those first sixteen pages that does not come out, or is explained, or re-stated in the rest of the book—or is unnecessary to state. I think it will move much faster from the start that way. Scott agrees with me. He suggested various things in it to cut out—in those first chapters—which I have never liked—but I think it is better to just lop that off and he agrees. He will probably write you what he thinks about it—the book in general. He said he was very excited by it.

As for the Henry James thing—I haven't the second part of the Ms. here—it is over at Scott's—so I can't recall the wording. But I believe that it is a reference to some accident that is generally known to have happened to Henry James in his youth. To me Henry James is as historical a name as Byron, Keats, or any other great writer about whose life, personal and literary, books have been written. I do not believe that the reference is sneering, or if it is, it is not the writer who is sneering as the writer does not appear in this book. Henry James is dead and left no descendants to be hurt, nor any wife, and therefore I feel that he is as dead as he will ever be. I wish I had the ms. here to see exactly what it said. If Henry James never had an accident of that sort I should think it would be libelous to say he had no matter how long he were dead. But if he did I do not see how it can affect him—now he is dead. As I recall Gorton and Barnes are talking humourously around the subject of Barnes' mutilation and to them Henry James is not a man to be insulted or protected from insult but simply an historical example. I remember there was something about an airplane and a bicycle—but that had nothing to do with James and was simply a non-sequitor. Scott said he saw nothing off-color about it.

   . . . . .

   . . . . .

   . . . . .

   . . . . .

                       Yours very sincerely
                         Ernest Hemingway

Villa Paquita
Juan les Pins
   (A.M)
June 5, 1926

*Note*

1. 334 words have been omitted from this letter.

▲ ▼ ▲

To: *Perkins*     *ca. June 25, 1926*
From: *Fitzgerald*     *ALS, 2 pp.*[1] *Princeton*

> Villa St. Louis
> Juan-les-Pins
> A—M.

Dear Max:

Thanks for both letters. We were in Paris having Zelda's appendix neatly but firmly removed or I would have answered before.

First as to Ernests book. I liked it but with certain qualifications. The fiesta, the fishing trip, the minor characters were fine. The lady I didn't like, perhaps because I don't like the original.[2] In the mutilated man I thought Ernest bit off more than can yet be chewn between the covers of a book, then lost his nerve a little and edited the more vitalizing details out. He has since told me that something like this happened. Do ask him for the absolute minimum of nessessary changes, Max—he's so discouraged about the previous reception of his work by publishers and magazine editors. (Tho he loved your letter) From the latter he has had a lot of words and until Bridges offer for the short story (from which he had even before cut out a thousand words on my recommendation) scarcely a single dollar. From the <u>Torrents</u> I expect you'll have little response. Do you think the Bookman article[3] did him any good?

. . . . .

. . . . .

Will you ask them (your accounting dept.) to send me an account the 1st of August. I'd love to see what a positive statement looks like for the first time in three years.

I am writing Bridges today. I have an offer now for a story at $3,500.00 (rather for six stories). To sell one for $1,000.00 would mean a dead loss of $2,500 and as I average only six stories a year I don't see how I can do it. I hope he'll understand

The novel, in abeyance during Zelda's operation now goes on apace. This is confidential but <u>Liberty</u>, with certain conditions, has offered me $35,000. sight unseen. I hope to have it done in January.

Do send out a picture to everyone that got that terrible one.

> Ever Your Friend
> Scott.

*Notes*

1. 17 words have been omitted from this letter.
2. Duff Twysden, the model for Brett Ashley.
3. Fitzgerald had written "How to Waste Material: A Note on My Generation," an essay-review of *In Our Time,* for the *Bookman* (May 1926).

▲▼▲

To: *Hemingway*
From: *Perkins*                          *CC, 3 pp. Princeton*

July 20, 1926

Dear Hemingway:

The complete galley proof goes out today, C/o The Guaranty Trust Company. I have hardly made a mark on it,- though I can see the point about cutting at the start. What is there said is later said, and in the course of narrative; but it is well said here if not according to the method of the book, and a reader to whom your way of writing will be new, and in many cases strange, would be helped by this beginning. But you write like yourself only, I shall not attempt criticism. I couldn't with confidence. But there are two points to consider that bear on this publication: the danger of trouble from referring to real people in a way to reflect upon them, and the danger of suppression.

As for the first, it is slight, and rest upon passages:

(1.) I know who Roger Prescott is quite well.[1] Would not others recognize him? You might say, so much the better; but you cannot be sure about these birds, and why injure him? You will if certain people who guess point out his identity. Why not call him Prentiss. You don't want to harm him.

(2) An Englishman will actually sue for libel on the slightest provocation. This we know to our cost. The reference to Hillaire Belloc[2] though apparently the most absolutely harmless of the lot, is really the most dangerous, so far as material results are concerned. The English have a reticence and a sense of the right to it, a right to privacy, unknown in the U.S.A. I think we'll have to disguise the name of Belloc in some way.

(3) I don't know what Hergesheimer[3] might do about being announced as a "garter snapper",- probably not much. We can quote what a man has written but not what he has reported to have said, or even is known for sure to have <u>said</u>, without his permission. Besides, he and Mencken are friends. I don't think we have a right to impair their relationship.

(4) As for the Henry James, you know how we feel about it. I know too, how you feel about it,- that he is as much a historic character as Balzac is. But in truth, this town and Boston are full of people who knew him and who cannot regard him as you do. There are four right in this office who were his friends,- two his close friends.

Then, as to the fact, I have inquired into it and it is at most, extremely doubtful. Van Wyck Brooks who questioned everyone who knew James, does not believe it, nor Willard Huntington Wright, nor anyone here. There are a variety of rumors, and many obvious lies, but no certainty.

As for the other aspect I question:-

The book is of course a healthy book with marked satirical implications upon novels which are not.- Sentimentalized, subjective novels, marked by sloppy, hazy thought. That is one of the first things it is. But as I said, people are afraid of words. We don't want to divert attention from its intrinsic qualities to details of purely extrinsic importance. It would be a pretty thing if the very significance of so original a book should be disregarded because of the howls of a lot of cheap, prurient, moronic yappers. You probably don't appreciate this disgusting possibility because you've been too long abroad, and out of that atmosphere. Those who breathe its stagnant vapors now attack a book, not only on grounds of eroticism which could not hold here, but upon that of "decency", which means <u>words</u>.

In view of this, I suggest that a particular adjunct of the Bulls, referred to a number of times by Mike, be not spelled out, but covered by a blank;[4] and I rather inconsistently suggest that in the passage about Irony and Pity, you do not so plainly indicate the second line, but leave it as if Barnes did not hear it well, for Gorton was humming.-[5] By this you would lose little and would tend to avoid the raising of an utterly false issue which might give your book an entirely false reputation and identify it with that very type of book which it should counteract.

But in general I recommend doing nothing that would <u>really</u> <u>harm</u> the text in this matter of words, but large reducing so far as you rightly can the profanity, etc.

I hope Pamplona has been as wonderful this time as in your manuscript. I'm afraid I've misled you about The Younger Son.[6] I see it gets to be theatrical. I was so impressed by the killing of that terrible Raven (like that of Rasputin) and then by the news of Trafalgar, that I thought the book must be a marvel. Maybe it is later. I've been too busy to find out.

Yours as ever,

*Notes*

1. Novelist Glenway Wescott.
2. The anecdote about Braddocks (based on English novelist Ford Madox Ford) mistaking diabolist Aleister Crowley for Belloc was cut from the opening. Hemingway recycled this anecdote in "Ford Madox Ford and the Devil's Disciple" (*A Moveable Feast*).
3. Joseph Hergesheimer's name was changed to *Hoffenheimer* in *The Sun Also Rises*.
4. The word *balls* was emended to *horns*.
5. The implied rhyme word is *shitty*. No revision was made.
6. Edward John Trelawny's *Adventures of a Younger Son* (1831).

▲ ▼ ▲

*To: Perkins*
*From: Hemingway*                          *TLS, 2 pp.*[1] *Princeton*

Hotel Valencia—Valencia—Spain
July 24, 1926.

Dear Mr. Perkins:

. . . . .

    I imagine we are in accord about the use of certain <u>words</u> and I never use a word without first considering if it is replaceable. But in the proof I will go over it all very carefully. I have thought of one place where Mike when drunk and wanting to insult the bull fighter keeps saying—tell him bulls have no balls. That can be changed—and I believe with no appreciable loss to—bulls have no horns. But in the matter of the use of the <u>Bitch</u> by Brett—I have never once used this word ornamentally nor except when it was absolutely necessary and I believe the few places where it is used must stand. The whole problem is, it seems, that one should never use words which shock altogether out of their own value or connotation—such a word as for instance <u>fart</u> would stand out on a page, unless the whole matter were entirely rabelaisian, in such a manner that it would be entirely exaggerated and false and overdone in emphasis. Granted that it is a very old and classic English word for a breaking of wind. But you cannot use it. Altho I can think of a case where it might be used, under sufficiently tragic circumstances, as to be entirely acceptable. In a certain incident in the war of conversation among marching troops under shell fire.

    I think that words—and I will cut anything I can—that are used in conversation in The Sun etc. are justified by the tragedy of the story. But of course I haven't seen it for some time and not at all in type.

. . . . .
. . . . .
. . . . .
. . . . .
. . . . .
. . . . .

Yours always,
Ernest Hemingway.

*Note*

1. 255 words have been omitted from this letter.

▲ ▼ ▲

### BY ERNEST HEMINGWAY
Author of "In Our Times"

**The Sun Also Rises**        $2.00

This, the first novel by Mr. Hemingway, quivers with life. The characters, who belong to that group of English and American expatriates who frequent the Quarter in Paris to-day, are so palpable that one, after reading, would recognize them upon the street. They belong to that war generation too strongly dosed with raw reality of which Gertrude Stein is quoted as saying, "You are all a lost generation." Through the Cafés of Paris, the Fiesta in Pamplona, the bull-fights, one accompanies them with amusement sometimes tinged with horror, and a deep sense of underlying tragedy; for their sense of life—all illusions being shattered, all reticences dissipated—is that of the futile repetitions of the Book of Ecclesiastes from which the title comes.

In the narrative one seems to observe life directly, not through a literary medium—and with a curious consciousness of its beauty and its cruelty. Yet the book is full of humor, sometimes pure fun, but often of a satirical sort. In fact, one can see that it was written in a spirit of literary revolt; in disgust with hazy, subjective, sentimentalized presentations which result in certain popular novels. Life is hard and bright, and in the eyes of persons of vitality, objective. Let us face it at any cost—so Hemingway seems to say.

**THE TORRENTS OF SPRING**     *Second printing*
A ROMANTIC NOVEL IN HONOR OF THE PASSING OF A GREAT RACE    $1.50

"An elaborate and exceedingly witty parody of the Chicago school of literature in general, and of Sherwood Anderson in particular. It is the kind of parody which is real criticism. . . . Mr. Hemingway is a genuine humorist, and a critic so shrewd that I almost hope he may cure the disease he so well diagnoses."
—*The Independent.*

"The delightful entertainment of 'The Torrents of Spring' . . . is full-blooded comedy, with a sting of satire at the expense of certain literary affectations. . . . It is a somewhat specialized satire. . . . He is not parodying merely a manner but a philosophy and an attitude, a fundamental approach, as well . . . 'The Torrents of Spring' reveals Mr. Hemingway's gift for high-spirited nonsense . . . it contributes to that thoughtful gayety which true wit should inspire. . . . The book sets out to amuse. This it does."—*New York Times.*

Catalogue entry for Hemingway's two 1926 books (Princeton University Library)

*To: Hemingway*
*From: Perkins*            *CC, 3 pp. Princeton*

April 13, 1927

Dear Hemingway:

It so often happened that when I wrote you, a letter crossed mine which gave me the information I asked for, that I have lately rather delayed, awaiting news from you. I thought it best now, though, to write to say that although we are making up a dummy on "Men Without Women", using "The Killers" for text material, we could now with great advantage use the manuscript itself. I hope you will therefore send it as soon as you can. It is short according to your figuring, and we do not above all things want to make it look padded. This we shall not do in any case, beyond putting in half titles between stories, which is proper. But Scott thinks that you must have much more material than forty-five or fifty thousand words. He spoke of various things that I had never heard of. If you have other stories that would go into this book without any regret on your part, send them too.- But if you are not satisfied that they are good ones, let the book remain short, and we shall do very well that way. Anyhow I suspect there are many more words according to our figuring than you think.[1]

I am forwarding a letter today to Mr. Scott Fitzgerald, which is evidently one from you. I wish there were one for me. You ought to come over and see Ellersley Mansion,[2] Brandywine Hundred, with the big Delaware River right beyond it. You had better come soon too, because nobody could live in such a house and not be modified. Zelda will soon be a stately lady of the manor, and the drinking will be port by candle light, accompanied with walnuts.

As ever yours,

### Notes

1.  The Scribners edition of *Men Without Women* had fourteen stories, making 232 text pages.
2.  The Fitzgeralds returned to America in December 1926 and rented "Ellerslie," a mansion near Wilmington, Delaware, in March 1927.

▲ ▼ ▲

*To: Hemingway*
*From: Perkins*                              *CC, 4 pp. Princeton*

June 8, 1927

Dear Hemingway:

I thought the two stories that came with your letter of the 27th were most excellent. The book will have a great deal of variety, among its other qualities. It is a notable collection. I still hope for the other bull fight story by July first or thereabouts, and perhaps some others. "Italy"[1] we already had got, and I am trying to find the Little Review story.[2]

Here is an advertisement, the first in a new series. Something different from what we have used before. The book goes on.[3] It has been suppressed in Boston, but not until about a dozen other books had been. Boston suppressions do not even have a publicity value any longer.

The Liveright incident is definitely closed apparently and so I should like to say that the terms they offered you are the terms we will give you any time. And if you want any more money in advance on "Men Without Women" as the summer goes on, you have only to let us know. And do always let us know when you are in the position. I always hesitate to propose advances myself, or to suggest a high figure, because unless it is necessary for some reason, it is better that an author should not be running behind the game. With Scott, for instance —and I am sure you know about it in general from him, so I can speak of it freely—we have never stated an advance. We have simply given him what he required when he wanted it; and this has worked very well excepting that he has sometimes got royalty reports which showed a considerable earning, and yet has received no money with them. The only trouble with Scott has been that being unusually strict about money matters, and accurate, he has often felt as if he were in debt to us, and has apologized for asking for money which he could just as easily have had without any obligation whatever, as an advance. This I have often told him because his conscience seemed to trouble him.– It was only the other day I got an apologetic telegram asking for money which we would have given him long ago without a quiver as an advance on a novel he is now finishing. I say all this so that you will understand that you can call on us, either for large advances, or for money against your work when you require it.

I was very much pleased to get your letter, and appreciated to the full your attitude. I hope you have a wonderful summer.

As ever yours,

### Notes

1. "Italy—1927," *New Republic* (May 18, 1927); reprinted as "Che Ti Dice La Patria?" in *Men Without Women.*

2. "Banal Story," *The Little Review* (Spring–Summer 1926); reprinted in *Men Without Women.*

3. *The Sun Also Rises.*

▲ ▼ ▲

*To: Hemingway*
*From: Perkins*                              *CC, 4 pp.*[1] *Princeton*

Oct. 31, 1927

Dear Hemingway:

I hope you won't mind our sending the enclosed cheque without waiting till the regular royalty time which is far off. "Men Without" has earned $400 odd beyond this $1000, after deducting the $750 advanced. It's a hard feature of book writing that an author has to wait from six months to a year to realize a penny. "Men Without" is being wonderfully received and it ought to sell; and we should like to give you some advantage from this now. We shall gladly send more at any moment.– That's a fact.

Scott (as I implied by cable) is much better. He was here ten days ago and had a bad nervous spell, but the first in some days. He had to walk, he said, and wanted me to go for a drink. I said, "Well, I'll go if it's just one drink." He said,

"You talk to me as if I were a Ring Lardner." So we did go and had a grand talk, and he was most keen about "Men Without",– not only about particular stories, but about the book as a whole, so generally uniform and solid in quality.– He'll have written you though.

He was much improved that day and then I saw John Biggs from Wilmington, who had been worried about him. He said Scott was now quite different, in really good shape. I put him on to a denicotinized cigarette called Sano. They're horrible and did me no good, but Scott has managed to stick to them. I think tobacco was hurting him more than drink,– which he had lately gone easy on anyway.

. . . . .

. . . . .

Ever yours,

*Note*

1. 152 words have been omitted from this letter.

▲ ▼ ▲

*To: Hemingway*
*From: Perkins*                           *CC, 3 pp.*[1] *Princeton*

April 10, 1928

Dear Hemingway:

. . . . .

Scott I believe, is to go abroad with Zelda on the 21st of April. I saw him last Friday. We had lunch at the Plaza with the Seldes, and afterward Scott said we must have a talk, and selected the Plaza roof for it. So we sat in the sunshine and overlooked the Park. He has got entirely over his nervous attacks, but he was very depressed,– perhaps partly because of a party the night before with Ring Lardner. It was evident that he would have to make some kind of change, and although he had not decided when I left him, I thought that it would mean Europe. I had hoped he would stay here now for a long time, but after seeing him the way he was, I am glad that he won't. He seemed to have no resilience at all, which is most unusual in Scott. He has made no progress with his novel for a long time, always having to stop to write stories.

As for when you will have something done, I could not make out definitely at all from your letter. But we will just wait patiently and be mighty quick to jump when anything does come,– both here and in the Magazine.

I shall be sending you a royalty report in a day or two, and money whenever you want it.

Ever yours,

*Note*

1. 135 words have been omitted from this letter.

▲ ▼ ▲

*To: Perkins*
*From: Hemingway*

*TLS with holograph inserts and*
*postscripts, 3 pp.[1] Princeton*

April 21—1928

Key West     Fla.

Dear Mr. Perkins,

I'm terribly sorry to hear about Scott. Could you tell me the name of his ship and I will send him a cable. Perhaps it would be better to wire it the name of hid boat or where he is in a night letter as this place seems to be a long way from New York by mail. I wish he would finish his novel or throw it away and write a new one. I think he has just gotten stuck and does not believe in it any more himself from having foole with it so long and yet dreads giving it up. So he writes stories and uses any excuse to keep from having to bite on the nail and finish it. But I believe that everybody has had to give them up (novels) at some time and start others. I wish I could talk to him. He believes that this novel is so important because people came out and said such fine things about him after the Gatsby and then he had a rotten book of stories[2] (I mean there were cheap stories in it) and he feels that he must have a GREAT novel to live up to the critics. All that is such (     ) because the thing for Scott to do is WRITE novels and the good will come out with the bad and in the end the whole thing will be fine. But critics like Seldes[3] etc. are poison for him. He is scared and builds up all sorts of defences like the need for making money with stories etc. all to avoid facing the thing through. He could have written three novels in this length of time—and what if two of them were bad if one of them was a Gatsby. Let him throw away the bad ones. He is prolific as a Gueinea pig (mis-spelled) and instead he has been bamboozled by the critics (who have ruined every writer that reads them) into thinking he lays eggs like the Ostrich or the elephant.

. . . . .

. . . . .

Have been going very well. Worked every day and have 10,000 to 15,000 words done on the new book.[4] It won't be awfully long and has been going finely. I wish I could have it for Fall because that seems like the only decent time to bring out a book but suppose, with the time necessary to leave it alone before re-writing, that is impossible. I forget when I got the mss. for the Sun to you but think it was sometime pretty early in the Spring. Please tell me if I am wrong. Would like to finish this down here—if possible—put it away for a couple or three months and then re-write it. The re-writing doesn't take more than six weeks or two months once it is done. But it is pretty important for me to let it cool off well before re-writing. I would like to stay right here until it is done as I have been going so very well here and it is such a fine healthy life and the fishing keeps my head from worrying in the afternoons when I don't work. But imagine we will have to go someplace for the baby to be born around the end of June.[5] Ought to leave a month before. Still if I keep on going there will be a lot done by then.

. . . . .

After I get the novel done—if it is too late for this fall—I could do quite a lot of stories and that would keep the stuff going until the next fall and then the novel would come out and we would have stories enough for a book of them to follow it.

. . . . .

. . . . .

Yrs always
Hemingway

. . . . .

*Notes*

1. 355 words have been omitted from this letter.

2. *All the Sad Young Men* (1926) included four major Fitzgerald stories—"Winter Dreams," "The Rich Boy," "'The Sensible Thing,'" and "Absolution."

3. Gilbert Seldes's warmly admiring review of *The Great Gatsby* in the *Dial* annoyed Hemingway because he nurtured a grudge against the *Dial*.

4. *A Farewell to Arms.*

5. Patrick Hemingway was born in Kansas City.

▲ ▼ ▲

*To: Perkins*                                          *ca. July 21, 1928. Paris*
*From: Fitzgerald*                                   *ALS, 2 pp. Princeton*

Dear Max

(1)   The novel goes fine. I think its quite wonderful + I think those who've seen it (for I've read it around a little) have been quite excited. I was encouraged the other day, when James Joyce came to dinner, when he said "Yes, I expect to finish my book in three or four years more at the latest" + he works 11 hrs a day to my intermittent 8. Mine will be done sure in September.

(2)   Did you get my letter about André Chamson?[1] Really Max, you're missing a great opportunity if you don't take that up. Radiguet was perhaps

obscene—Chamson is absolutely <u>not</u>—he's head over heals the best young man here, like Ernest + Thornton Wilder rolled into one. This Hommes de la Route (Road Menders) is his 2nd novel + all but won the Prix Goncourt—the story of men building a road, with all of the force of K. Hamsun's <u>Growth of the Soil</u>—not a bit like Tom Boyds bogus American husbandmen. Moreover, tho I know him only slightly and have no axe to grind, I have every faith in him as an extraordinary personality like France + Proust. Incidently King Vidor (who made <u>The Crowd</u> + <u>The Big Parade</u>) is making a picture of it next summer.[2] If you have any confidence in my judgement do at least get a report on it + let me know what you decide. Ten years from now he'll be beyond price.

(3)   I plan to publish a book of those <u>Basil Lee</u> Stories after the novel. Perhaps one or two more serious ones to be published in the Mercury or with Scribners if you'd want them, combined with the total of about six in the Post Series, would make a nice <u>light</u> novel, almost, to follow my novel in the season <u>immediately</u> after, so as not to seem in the direct line of my so-called "work." It would run perhaps 50 or 60 thousand words.[3]

(4)   Do let me know any plans of ⓐErnest ⓑ Ring ⓒTom (reviews poor, I notice) ⓓ John Biggs

(5)   Did you like Bishops story?[4] I thought it was grand.

(6)   Home Sept 15th I think. Best to Louise

(7)   About Cape—won't you arrange it for me + take the 10% commission? That is if Im not committed <u>morally</u> to Chatto + Windus who did, so to speak, pick me up out of the English gutter. I'd <u>rather</u> be with Cape.[5] Please decide + act according if you will. If you don't I'll just ask Reynolds. As you like. <u>Let me know</u>

[*In left margin*] Ever yr Devoted + Grateful Friend

Scott

### Notes

1. The only French writer with whom Fitzgerald formed a friendship, Chamson became a Scribners author. *Hommes de la Route*, translated by Van Wyck Brooks with a foreword by Ernest Boyd, was published by Scribners as *The Road* in 1929.

2. American movie director. Vidor's *Our Daily Bread* (1934) was partially based on Chamson's novel.

3. Fitzgerald abandoned this project.

4. "The Cellar," collected in John Peale Bishop's *Many Thousands Gone* (Scribners, 1931).

5. Jonathan Cape never published Fitzgerald in England.

▲▼▲

To: Perkins                          *Piggot, Arkansas*
From: Hemingway          *TLS with holograph inserts, 2 pp.*[1] *Princeton*

Oct 11, 1928

Dear Mr. Perkins—

. . . . .

. . . . .

. . . . .

. . . . .

. . . . .

   Instead of thinking Zelda a possible good influence (what a phrase) for
Scott—I think 90% of all the trouble he has comes from her.[2] Almost Every
bloody fool thing I have ever seen or known him to do has been directly or indirectly Zelda inspired. I'm probably wrong in this. But I often wonder if he
would not have been the best writer we've ever had or likely to have if he hadnt
been married to some one that would make him waste Every thing. I know no
one that has ever had more talent or wasted it more. I wish to god he'd write a
good book and finish it and not poop himself away on those lousy Post stories.
I dont blame <u>Lorimer</u> I blame Zelda.
[*In left margin beside last paragraph*] I would not have Scott imagine I believed
<u>this for the world</u>.

Yours always,
Ernest Hemingway

. . . . .

*Notes*

   1. 261 words have been omitted from this letter.
   2. In an October 2, 1928, letter, Perkins had told Hemingway: "Scott sailed on the
29th. Zelda is so able and intelligent, and isn't she also quite a strong person? that I'm
surprised she doesn't face the situation better, and show some sense about spending
money. Most of their trouble, which may kill Scott in the end, comes from extravagance.
All of his friends would have been busted long ago if they'd spent money like Scott and
Zelda. Well, I'll let you know how Scott seems the moment I can. Perhaps the news will
be really good."

▲ ▼ ▲

To: Wolfe
From: Perkins                          *CC, 2 pp. Princeton*

Oct. 22, 1928

Dear Mr. Wolfe:

   Mrs. Ernest Boyd left with us some weeks ago, the manuscript of your
novel, "O Lost".[1] I do not know whether it would be possible to work out a plan

by which it might be worked into a form publishable by us, but I do know that setting the practical aspects of the matter aside, it is a very remarkable thing, and that no editor could read it without being excited by it, and filled with admiration by many passages in it, and sections of it.

Your letter[2] that came with it, shows that you realize what difficulties it presents, so that I need not enlarge upon this side of the question. What we should like to know is whether you will be in New York in a fairly near future, when we can see you and discuss the manuscript. We should certainly look forward to such an interview with very great interest.

Ever truly yours,

*Notes*

1. New York literary agent Madeleine Boyd had delivered the 275,000-word typescript that was published in an edited version as *Look Homeward, Angel;* 66,000 words were cut from "O Lost" and 5,000 words were added by Wolfe.

2. Perkins refers to Wolfe's general statement about the novel—"Notice For The Publisher's Reader"—not to a letter.

▲ ▼ ▲

*To: Perkins*                          *Delaware*
*From: Fitzgerald*                  *ALS, 2 pp. Princeton*

Edgemoor<br>Nov. '28

Dear Max:

It seems fine to be sending you something again, even though its only the first fourth of the book (2 chapters, 18,000 words). Now comes another short story, then I'll patch up Chaps. 3 + 4 the same way, and send them, I hope, about the 1st of December.[1]

Chap I. here is good.

Chap II. has caused me more trouble than anything in the book. You'll realize this when I tell you it was once 27,000 words long! It started its career as Chap I. I am far from satisfied with it even now, but won't go into its obvious faults. I would appreciate it if you jotted down any critisisms—and <u>saved them until</u> I've sent you the whole book, because I want to <u>feel</u> that each part is finished and not worry about it any longer, even though I may change it enormously at the very last minute. All I want to know now is if, in general, you like it + this will have to wait, I suppose, until you've seen the next batch which finishes the first half. (My God its good to see those chapters lying in an envelope!

I think I have found you a new prospect of really extraordinary talent in a Carl Van Vechten way. I have his first novel at hand—unfortunately its about Lesbians. More of this later.

I think Bunny's title is <u>wonderful!</u>[2]

Remember novel is confidential, even to Ernest.

Always Yrs.<br>Scott

### Notes

1. Fitzgerald sent only one installment of the first version of the novel, in which the central figure is Francis Melarky, a young American in France. This material was recycled in *Tender Is the Night.* The working titles were "Our Type" and "The Boy Who Killed His Mother."

2. *I Thought of Daisy* (Scribners, 1929).

▲ ▼ ▲

*To: Fitzgerald*
*From: Perkins*                                   *CC, 1 p. Princeton*

Nov. 13, 1928

Dear Scott:

I have just finished the two chapters. About the first we fully agree. It is excellent. The second I think contains some of the best writing you have ever done—some lovely scenes, and impressions briefly and beautifully conveyed. Besides it is very entertaining, including the duel. There are certain things one could say of it in criticism, but anyhow I will make no criticism until I read the whole book, and so see the relationships of the chapters. I think this is a wonderfully promising start off. Send on others as soon as you can.

I wish it might be possible to get this book out this Spring, if only because it promises so much that it makes me impatient to see it completed.

Ever yours,

▲ ▼ ▲

*To: Perkins*
*From: Wolfe*                                   *ALS, 7 pp. Princeton*

Vienna, Saturday Nov 17, 1928

Dear Mr Perkins: Your letter of October 22 which was addressed to Munich, was sent on to me here. I have been in Budapest for several weeks and came here last night. I got your letter at Cook's[1] this morning.

Mrs Ernest Boyd wrote me a few weeks ago that she was coming abroad, and said that you had my book. I wrote her to Paris but have not heard from her yet.

I can't tell you how good your letter has made me feel. Your words of praise have filled me with hope, and are worth more than their weight in diamonds to me. Sometimes, I suppose, praise does more harm than good, but this time it was badly needed, whether deserved or not.—I came abroad over four months ago determined to put the other book out of my mind, and to get to work on a new one. Instead, I have filled one note book after another, my head is swarming with ideas—but I have written nothing that looks like a book yet. In Munich I did write thirty or forty thousand words; then I got my head and my nose broken, and began to have things happen thick and fast with a great many people, including the police. I have learned to read German fairly well, and have learned something of their multitudinous books. But I had indigestion from seeing and trying to take in too much, and I was depressed at my failure to settle down to work. Now I feel better. I have decided to come back to New York in December, and I shall come to see you very soon after my arrival.

I have not looked at my book since I gave a copy to Mrs. Boyd—at the time I realized the justice of all people said—particularly the impossibility of printing it in its present form and length. But at that time I was "written out" on it—I could not go back and revise. Now I believe I can come back to it with a much fresher and more critical feeling.—I have no right to expect others to do for me what I should do for myself, but, although I am able to criticize wordiness and over-abundance in others, I am not able practically to criticize it in myself. The business of selection, and of revision is simply hell for me—my efforts to cut out 50000 words may sometimes result in my adding 75000.

—As for the obscene passages and the dirty words, I know perfectly well that no publisher could print them. Yet, I swear to you, it all seemed to me very easy and practical when I wrote them.—But already I have begun to write a long letter to you, when all I should do is to thank you for your letter and say when I am coming back Then the other things can come out when I see you.

But your letter has given me a new hope for the book—I have honestly always felt that there are parts of it of which I need not be ashamed, and which might justify some more abiding form. I want you to know that you have no very stiff necked person to deal with as regards the book—I shall probably agree with most of the criticisms, although I hope that my own eagerness and hopefulness will not lead me into a weak acquiescence to everything.

I want the direct criticism and advice of an older and more critical person. I wonder if at Scribners I can find Someone who is interested enough to talk over the whole huge Monster with me—part by part. Most people will say "it's too long," "its got to be cut," "parts have to come out," and so on—but obviously this is no great help to the poor wretch who has done the deed, and who knows all this, without always knowing how he's going to remedy it.

I am sorry that Mrs Boyd sent you the letter that I wrote for the Reader. She said it was a very foolish letter, but added cheerfully that I would learn as I grow older. I wish I had so much faith. I told her to tear the letter out of the binding;[2] but if it indicated to you that I did realize some of the difficulties, perhaps it was of some use. And I realize the difficulties more than ever now.

I am looking forward to meeting you, and I am still youthful enough to hope that something may come of it. It will be a strange thing indeed to me if at last I shall manage to make a connection with such a firm as Scribner's which, in my profound ignorance of all publishing matters, I had always thought vaguely was a solid and somewhat conservative house. But it may be that I am a conservative and at bottom very correct person. If this is true, I assure you I will have no very great heartache over it, although once it might have caused me trouble. At any rate, I believe I am through with firing off pistols just for the fun of seeing people jump—my new book has gone along 40000 words without improprieties of language—and I have not tried for this result.

Please forgive my use of the pencil—in Vienna papers and pen and ink, as well as many other things that abound in our own fortunate country, are doled out bit by bit under guard. I hope you are able to make out my scrawl which is more than many people do—and that you will not forget about me before I come back.

Cordially Yours<br>Thomas Wolfe

My address in New York is The Harvard Club—I get my mail there. Here in Vienna, at Thomas Cook's, but as I'm going to Italy in a week, I shall probably have no more mail before I get home[3]

### Notes

1. Thomas Cook and Sons, travel agency.
2. The ribbon copy for *O Lost* submitted to Scribners does not survive; it was apparently bound.
3. Wolfe ended his first draft of this letter, mistakenly addressed to "Mr. Peters," with "Is there someone on Scribner's staff who might be interested enough in my book to *argue* with me? On many points I am sure he would not have to argue at all. But it would be wrong for me to say 'Yes, sir,' to everything in a spirit of a weak agreement" (*The Notebooks of Thomas Wolfe*, ed. Richard S. Kennedy and Paschal Reeves [Chapel Hill: University of North Carolina Press, 1970], p. 243).

▲▼▲

*To: Wolfe*
*From: Perkins*                     *CC, 2 pp. Princeton*

Jan. 8, 1929

Dear Mr. Wolfe:

This is to tell you that we have formally considered "O Lost" and shall be delighted to publish it on the basis of a 10% royalty on the first 2,000 copies and of 15% thereafter;– and as soon as we hear that the terms suit you, we shall send a cheque for five hundred dollars as an advance. The question of terms would naturally be taken up with Mrs. Boyd who brought us the book and acts as literary agent. I'd be glad to get into touch with her if she's in New York, or you might do it;– or if she's out of reach, we could make the terms dependent on her approval, which I hardly doubt she would give, and send you the advance immediately. You could simply give us a note accepting provisionally.

Ever sincerely yours,

▲▼▲

Memorandum of Agreement, *made this* – **ninth** – *day of* **January** *19* **29**

*between* **THOMAS WOLFE**

*of* **New York City, N.Y.,** – – – *hereinafter called "the* AUTHOR,"

*and* CHARLES SCRIBNER'S SONS, *of New York City, N. Y., hereinafter called "the* PUBLISHERS." *Said* – – **Thomas Wolfe** – – *being the* AUTHOR *and* PROPRIETOR *of a work entitled:* published as

– – **LOST** ——→ LOOK HOMEWARD, ANGEL

*in consideration of the covenants and stipulations hereinafter contained, and agreed to be performed by the* PUBLISHERS, *grants and guarantees to said* PUBLISHERS *and their successors the* in the United States and Canada after first serialization *exclusive right to publish the said work in all forms during the terms of copyright and renewals thereof, hereby covenanting with said* PUBLISHERS *that he is the sole* AUTHOR *and* PROPRIETOR *of said work.*

*Said* AUTHOR *hereby authorizes said* PUBLISHERS *to take out the copyright on said work, and further guarantees to said* PUBLISHERS *that the said work is in no way whatever a violation of any copyright belonging to any other party, and that it contains nothing of a scandalous or libelous character; and that* he *and* **his** *legal representatives shall and will hold harmless the said* PUBLISHERS *from all suits, and all manner of claims and proceedings which may be taken on the ground that said work is such violation or contains anything scandalous or libelous; and* he *further hereby authorizes said* PUBLISHERS *to defend at law any and all suits and proceedings which may be taken or had against them for infringement of any other copyright or for libel, scandal, or any other injurious or hurtful matter or thing contained in or alleged or claimed to be contained in or caused by said work, and pay to said* PUBLISHERS *such reasonable costs, disbursements, expenses, and counsel fees as they may incur in such defense.*

*Said* PUBLISHERS, *in consideration of the right herein granted and of the guarantees aforesaid, agree to publish said work at their own expense, in such style and manner as they shall deem most expedient, and to pay said* AUTHOR, *or* – **his** – *legal representatives,* **TEN (10)** —————— *per cent. on their Trade-List (retail) price, cloth style, for* the **first Two Thousand (2000) copies** of said work sold by them in the United States and **FIFTEEN (15) per cent. for all copies sold thereafter.** *Provided, nevertheless, that one-half the above named royalty shall be paid on all copies sold outside the United States; and provided that no percentage whatever shall be paid on any copies destroyed by fire or water, or sold at or below cost, or given away for the purpose of aiding the sale of said work.*

*It is further agreed that the profits arising from any publication of said work, during the period covered by this agreement, in other than book form shall be divided equally between said* PUBLISHERS *and said* AUTHOR.

Wolfe received a $500 advance for his first novel (Princeton University Library).

*To: Perkins*                          *Harvard Club letterhead*
*From: Wolfe*                          *ALS, 4 pp. Princeton*
                                       Jan 9, 1929

Dear Mr Perkins: I got your letter this morning and I have just come from a talk with Mrs Madeleine Boyd, my literary agent.

I am very happy to accept the terms you offer me for the publication of my book, <u>O Lost</u>. Mrs Boyd is also entirely satisfied.

I am already at work on the changes and revisions proposed in the book, and I shall deliver to you the new beginning some time next week.

Although this should be only a business letter I must tell you that I look forward with joy and hope to my connection with Scribner's. To-day—the day of your letter—is a very grand day in my life. I think of my relation to Scribner's thus far with affection and loyalty, and I hope this marks the beginning of a long association that they will not have cause to regret. I have a tremendous lot to learn, but I believe I shall go ahead with it and I know that there is far better work in me than I have yet done.

If you have any communication for me before I see you next, you can reach me at 27 West 15th Street (2nd Floor Rear).
                     Faithfully Yours,
                     Thomas Wolfe

▲ ▼ ▲

*To: Hemingway*                        *Havana Special letterhead*
*From: Perkins*                        *ALS, 4 pp.[1] Kennedy*

Feb 9, 1929

Dear Ernest:– I've just finished re-reading the book.[2] It's a most beautiful book I think,—perhaps. Especially the last part, after they get into Switzerland. I got a different kind of pleasure out of it this time, knowing the Story, + so not being diverted either by the interest of some of the material, as I was the first time, or by anxiety to see what happened + how things ended. Its full of lovely things. The characters are marvelously + deeply disclosed, all their qualities, not the 'good' or 'bad' only, coming out. The interest of the material is itself immensely strong + many readers may miss the deeper + rare things at first on that account. —As for the proprieties, I'm in complete agreement with You personally, + have argued that way all my life. I guess You understand that. I said all this before + this letter is superfluous as well as really illigible.—But when you put down such a book you've got to say Something. If I Knew anyone on the train I could have taken it out on them.

Now I'm going to take Your absynthe + drink a lonely health to you all in the wash room. It was a grand time for me.

Ever yours
Maxwell Perkins

. . . . .

*Notes*

1. 50 words have been omitted from this letter.
2. Perkins, who had gone to Key West to get the typescript of *A Farewell to Arms*, read it on the train.

▲ ▼ ▲

*To: Charles Scribner II*
*From: Perkins*                     *TLS with holograph postscript, 5 pp.*[1] *Princeton*

New York, February 14, 1929

Dear Mr. Scribner:

I'd meant to write you the moment I got back from Key West—after a splendid, refreshing week of sunshine and outdoors—but found an accumulation of little time-taking troubles.– And I thought it better to wait perhaps till Mr. Bridges and Dashiel[2] had read, "A Farewell to Arms."

This title is a bitter phrase: war taints and damages the beautiful and the gallant, and degrades everyone;– and this book which is a <u>farewell</u> to it, as useless and hateful, would be only grim reading if it were not illuminated with the beauty of the world, and of the characters, even though damaged, of some people, and by love; and if it were not also lively with incident and often, in spots, amusing. Its quality is that of "The Sun", though its range is much larger and its implications consequently more numerous and widely scattered. Its story in outline is not objectionable but many words and some passages in it are: we can blank the words and the worst passages can be revised.– The reading of the book will still be a violent experience because of the force, directness, and poignance of the writing. We wired Hemingway yesterday naming a price of $16,000 and the first instalment is being set.[3]

The story begins after a year or so of war, with some such phrase as, "That summer we were in the mountains." You get the idea of a place of charm and beauty hurt and saddened by war; of troops and guns passing up and down, and of a fatigued, raw-nerved group of men in the officer's mess,– one of whom, the narrator, an American boy, named Henry, is in charge of an ambulance section. A likable, dissolute surgeon named Rinaldi, persuades him to go to a hospital to see a "lady English". She is a tall, 'tawny' beauty. Henry who has frankly been all over the place with all low sorts of girls approaches her like one of them;– but this approach is somewhat resented and he feels the cheapness of it. He goes to the front with a little "St. Anthony" she gives him for luck around his neck.–

There while eating cheese with his men in a dugout, he is wounded in the legs by a shell.– All this is fiercely vivid, sharp, and painful.– It almost happens to the reader.

A couple of days after he arrives at the hospital—certain disagreeable physiological aspects in the care of him having been frankly described—Katharine Barker arrives. The moment they meet Henry discovers that he is in love.– He had not meant to fall in love, his idea had been quite different, but he finds that he has, and it is a wholly new experience in spite of all his amorous adventures. She is a gallant, winning girl, and she also has fallen in love. And though not his nurse, she manages, by taking on more than her share of undesired night work, to stay with him at night. And as he recuperates, they go to hotels once or twice together. He wants her to marry him, but if she does this she will be sent home on account of regulations, and will be separated from him, and she keeps saying that she already is his wife,– that a ceremony is a mere technicality. At the same time he is worried, and before he goes back to the front he knows that he has cause to be. He gets back in time to be a part of the great Caparetto retreat. This is a magnificent episode in the book. It is the account of the experience of several individuals,– Henry, and his companions, ambulance drivers. The episode as described differs from conventional descriptions of a retreat in much the same way as Stendhal's account of Waterloo differs from conventional accounts of battles. Henry gets loose from the great column of retreat which is constantly blocked, loses his cars in mud on a side road, loses one man by desertion, and another by a bullet, an Italian one too, finds himself at one time among detachments of Germans, finally rejoins the column at night as it approaches a river. On the other side of the river is a group of officers with battle police. They are flashing lights into the column and calling out officers from it. Two police come and seize Henry. He finds that all officers separated from their men are instantly shot. This is happening on the spot. He is indignant because he has behaved manfully throughout and has been true in every sense, and yet he knows he will be shot. He will be thought to be a German in Italian uniform. He breaks away, dives into the river, and with the help of a timber escapes. He is through with the Italian army.– He knows that they will finish him off if they get him anyhow. He gets civilian clothes from a friend, makes his way to a lake near the Swiss border where he hears that Katherine is, and is with her in the hotel there when late on a stormy night his friend the bar man tells him a squad has come to arrest him. He and Katherine get into a row boat and row up the lake in the storm with the help of the wind (a fine episode) until in the morning they have crossed the Swiss line. The rest of the book is most beautiful. It records the life of Katherine and Henry in Switzerland throughout the fall and the winter. It has the pathos of a happy time that is tinged with sorrow because those having it feel that it must end soon, and tragically. That sense of the beauty of nature and of its permanence, in contrast to the brevity and fluidity of an individual's affairs, pervades it. It is beautiful and affecting reading.

Henry tries several times to persuade Katherine to marry him, but she will not do it now because she says she looks too "matronly". They will get married later in America, when this is over with.– The reader knows by the tone of the narrative that when it is over with, Henry will have nobody to marry.

The last twenty pages of the book tell of the birth of the child which results in her death,– and rather fully, although not naturalistically. The reason it is recounted is to show what a brave, gallant person Katherine is. It is most painful and moving reading because of her bravery in suffering.

Mr. Bridges thinks the book a very strong one and its motif—a revelation of the tragic degradation of war, of which this love affair is a part—a fine one. Dashiel is very enthusiastic and regrets that even a word must be changed. I do not think that given the theme and the author, the book is any more difficult than was inevitable. It is Hemingway's principle both in life and literature never to flinch from facts, and it is in that sense only, that the book is difficult. It is not at all erotic, although love is represented as having a very large physical element.

I had a splendid eight days in Key West, and formed a very high opinion of Hemingway's character. Nobody could be more altogether healthy and decent in every sense, and no household could be more natural and simple than his, with his wife and sister and two children. We spent almost all of every day on the water fishing. Hemingway was determined I should get a tarpon, although I had considerable doubts of my ability to land one after quite exhausting struggles even with barracudas. At the very last possible moment, on my last day, it was Hemingway, and not I, who hooked a tarpon. He instantly wanted me to take his rod and was so violently insistent that I did it, and after about fifty fine and quite exhausting minutes made more exciting by a sudden storm which kept the spray flying over us all the time, and, added to the strength of the tarpon, kept me staggering all over the boat, we landed him. In view of the rarity of tarpons, and the value set upon them by sportsmen, I think this was a remarkably generous thing of Hemingway to do.

. . . . .

Ever sincerely yours,
Maxwell E. Perkins

P.S. I was somewhat constrained in bringing out the difficult points in "A Farewell" by dictating this to Miss Wyckoff,[4] but I thought your familiarity with Hemingway's way would sufficiently suppliment what I have said

MEP

*Notes*

1. 30 words have been omitted from this letter.
2. Alfred ("Fritz") Dashiell was managing editor of *Scribner's Magazine.*
3. *A Farewell to Arms* was serialized in *Scribner's Magazine* (May–October 1929).
4. Irma Wyckoff, Perkins's secretary.

▲ ▼ ▲

To: Perkins                              *1929. Key West, Florida*
From: Hemingway                      *ALS, 4 pp.*[1] *Princeton*

Feb 16—

. . . . .

Dear Max—

. . . . .

I'm awfully glad they are going to serialize and the Price is fine.

About omissions—They can only be discussed in the concrete examples—
I told you I would not be unreasonable—dont mind the leaving out of a word
if a blank is left if the omission is unavoidable and as for passages—almost every
part of the book depends on almost every other part—You know that—So if a
passage is dropped—there should be something to show it—That will not hurt
the serial and will help the book. People might be curious to see the book and
see what that passage contained. It's not a regular serial anyway.

My point is that the operation of emasculation is a tiny one—It is very simple and easy to perform on men—animals and books—It is not a Major operation but its effects are great—It is <u>never</u> performed <u>intentionally</u> on books—
What we must both watch is that it should not be performed unintentionally—

I know, on the other hand, that you will not want to print in a magazine
certain words and, you say, certain passages. In that event what I ask is that
when omissions are made a blank or some sign of omission be made that isnt
to be confused with the dots that writers employ when they wish to avoid bit-
ing on the nail and writing a hard part of a book to do.

Still the dots may be that sign—I'm not Unreasonable—I know we both
have to be careful because we have the same interest <u>ie</u> (literature or whatever
you call it) and I know that you yourself are shooting for the same thing that I
am. And I tell you that emasculation is a small operation and we dont want to
perform it without realizing it.

Anyway enough of talking—I am not satisfied with the last page and will
change it[2]—but the change will in no way affect the serializability—(what a
word.)

I think you are very fine about the price—If I havent said more about it it
is because while we are friends I am no blanket friend of the entire organization

and have the feeling, from experience, that the bull fighter is worth whatever he gets paid. However I think you are fine about the price. You are generous and I appreciate it. I may want some of the money quite soon Will write. This letter in great haste. Best to you always, Ernest Hemingway.

. . . . .

### Notes

1. 326 words have been omitted from this letter.
2. Hemingway claimed to have rewritten the final paragraph of the novel thirty times.

▲▼▲

*To: Hemingway*
*From: Perkins*                          *CC, 3 pp.*[1] *Princeton.*

February 19, 1929

Dear Ernest:

. . . . .

Bridges is sending you today the proofs of the first installment, and there is one passage where he thinks a cut should be made, where cutting will go hard. I believe he is telling you why he thinks it necessary,– circulation as collateral reading in schools, and consideration of subscribers, etc. You as an ex-newspaperman know about such things, and that there is a practical side to running periodicals.– On the other hand, there is this other side which I cannot wholly overlook:– there was a great deal of hostility. to "The Sun". It was routed and driven off the field by the book's qualities, and the adherence which they won. The hostility was very largely that which any new thing in art must meet, simply because it is disturbing. It shows life in a different aspect, and people are more comfortable when they have got it all conventionalized and smoothed down, and everything unpleasant hidden. Hostility also partly came from those who actually did not understand the book because its method of expression was a new one. Sisley Huddleston expressed their view.[2] It was the same failure to be understood that a wholly new painter meets. People simply do not understand because they can only understand what they are accustomed to.

Now this serialization is not the real thing, as the book <u>is</u>. If we considered "A Farewell to Arms" only in respect to its intrinsic quality, and refused to regard the question from any practical point of view, we would all be dead against serialization. It is an incidental and outside thing, and the best reason for it, to my mind, was on account of the practical aspects of it in widening your public, and in making you understandable to a great many more people, and generally in helping you to gain complete recognition. It is in view of all this that I think— as I judge you do by yo.ur letter of today—that cuts can be philosophically made, for if we can keep people from being diverted from the qualities of the material itself, by words and passages which have on account of <u>conventions</u>, an astonishingly exaggerated importance to them, a great thing will have been done. Your mind is so completely free of these conventions—and it is fortunate it is—that you do not realize the strength with which they are held. If you knew a few of the genteel!

I am afraid this discourse is not very well put, but what I am trying to argue is that if we can bring out this serial without arousing too serious objection, you will have enormously consolidated your position, and will henceforth be further beyond objectionable criticism of a kind which is very bad because it prevents so many people from looking at the thing itself on its merits.

. . . . .

Ever yours,

*Notes*

1. 169 words have been omitted from this letter.
2. Sisley Huddleston, *Paris Salons, Cafés, Studios: Being Social, Artistic and Literary Memories* (Philadelphia: Lippincott, 1928), pp. 121–23.

▲ ▼ ▲

*To: Perkins.*          *ca. March 1, 1929. "Ellerslie," Edgemoor, Delaware.*
*From: Fitzgerald*                    *ALS, 3 pp. Princeton*

Dear Max: I am sneaking away like a thief without leaving the chapters—there is a weeks work to straighten them out + in the confusion of my influenza + leaving, I havn't been able to do it. I'll do it on the boat + send it from Genoa. A thousand thanks for your patience—just trust me a few months longer, Max —it's been a discouraging time for me too but I will never forget your kindness and the fact that you've never reproached me.

I'm delighted about Ernest's book—I bow to your decision on the modern library without agreeing at all.[1] $100 or $50 advance is better than 1/8 of $40 for a years royalty, + the Scribner collection sounds vague + arbitrary to me. But its a trifle + I'll give them a new + much inferior story instead as I want to be represented with those men, i e Forster, Conrad, Mansfield ect.

Herewith an ms. I promised to bring you—I think it needs cutting but it just might sell with a decent title + no forward.[2] I don't feel certain tho at all—

Will you watch for some stories from a young Holger Lundberg[3] who has appeared in the Mercury; he is a man of some promise + I headed him your way.

I hate to leave without seeing you—and I hate to see you without the ability to put the finished ms in your hands. So for a few months good bye + my affection + gratitude always

Scott.

*Notes*

1. Scribners selected "At Your Age" for the Modern Library *Great Modern Short Stories* (1930). Fitzgerald did not want to be represented in this collection by what he considered a weak story. The word *inferior* in this letter is Fitzgerald's blunder for the intended word *superior*.
2. Unidentified.
3. Lundberg was not published by Scribners.

▲ ▼ ▲

*To: Hemingway*
*From: Perkins*                                  *CC, 3 pp. Princeton*

May 24, 1929

Dear Ernest:

I'm about to send you the book proof. Don't delay the reading because of the fact that we have a good margin in time, but still don't feel hurried. The book is so remarkable that if you want to work further on any parts of it, you ought to do it. A book that can touch one more deeply on the third reading than on the first, ought not to be rushed through the final stages.– So take the time you need.

It has been read now here by those who will be most active in "pushing" it: their interest in it is not less than fanatical. I have thought and talked about it for some three months now, and beyond the few slight comments on the margin of the proof I have one or two more serious ideas on it which I dare give you because I know you will know easily whether to reject them, and won't mind doing it;– and if you do it I'll believe you're right: I see plainly that you go down to the very bottom at any cost to test the truth of everything. Only you can do that—not many writers, even, have the strength to—and that brings the right decision.

The first point relates to the combination of the two elements of the book,– Love and War. They combine, to my mind, perfectly up to the point where Catherine and Lieutenant Henry get to Switzerland;– thereafter, the war is almost forgotten by them and by the reader,– though not quite. And psychologically it should be all but forgotten;– it would be by people so profoundly in love, and so I do not think what I at first thought, that you might bring more news of it or remembrances of it into this part. Still, I can't shake off the feeling that War, which has deeply conditioned this love story—and does so still passively—should still do so actively and decisively. It would if Catherine's death might probably not have occurred except for it, and I should think it likely that the life she had led as nurse, and all the exposure, etc., might have been largely responsible. If it were, and if the doctor said so during that awful night, in just a casual sentence, the whole story would turn back upon War in the realization of Henry and the reader.

I say this with the realization that a man in this work may make a principle into an obsession, as professors do. Unity? Nothing is so detestable as the <u>neat</u> ending. But Catherine was in a physical condition which made her unable to come through the Caesarian even if the Caesarian were required only because of her type of physical form. If it is true that the War produced that condition, I don't think it would make the conclusion <u>artificial</u>, or too <u>neat</u> if it were said, or implied. Of course in a deeper sense the reader does feel that War permeated the entire thing.– I can argue either way but even that fact makes the question worth raising.[1]

I know, by the way, that Wister[2] wrote you about these two elements of War and Love, and that he saw the question differently,– as if the story was really only one of Love with War as the impressive and conditioning background; or almost only that. But I could not quite see it that way. The elements are so fully interfused up to the Switzerland section that I hardly think War should be regarded as secondary to that degree.[3]

The other point regards the intense pain of the hospital episode. It's physical painfulness is such as by itself—apart from all the rest of the story—to completely absorb the reader, and this may not be right. You might lessen it by reducing the physical detail, perhaps. Wister felt this strongly I know, and I needn't go further into it.– Wheelock here did not feel this way about it. But the bad thing is that Catherine is made to suffer so, and to die, and if the physical aspects of the affair are too intensely presented, the reader suffers and shudders not because it is Catherine, but merely because of the horror of the thing itself,– while Henry, on the spot, poor devil, would suffer because it was Catherine. This is confused, but will suggest whatever need be thought of, I guess. The pain is after all mainly due simply to Catherine's situation, which perhaps seems to a male especially awful.– Besides, I know that I am super-sensitive to the physical. I only want the matter brought up for your consideration.

Otherwise, there's nothing much to say, except that if you could reduce somewhat the implications of physical aspects in the relationship I doubt that harm would be done. But here I may be influenced by the dangers of censorship. My whole intention is to put these things in mind.– I have most absolute confidence in your judgment and wouldn't want to influence it if I could.

I hope you're all well now. Write if you can.

Ever yours,

*Notes*

1. Hemingway did not act on Perkins's suggestions.
2. Novelist Owen Wister (1860–1938), author of *The Virginian*.

3. Fitzgerald had also argued for this connection of the themes of love and war at the end of the novel; Hemingway ridiculed this idea.

▲ ▼ ▲

To: Perkins                        [*August 1929*]. *Santiago de Compostela, Spain*
From: Hemingway                        ALS [*letter fragment*], *2 pp. Princeton*

Have an idea for the next book. Maybe it is punk—but started to write some things about fishing—hunting—about Bull fights and bull fighters—About eating and drinking—About different places—Mostly things and places. Not so much people—though I know some funny ones about people. Several about fishing—If there were enough of these and they were good enough they might make a book. Started to write because my Goddamned imagination wasn't functioning—still tired may be—and still I know a lot of things—Thought it's better to write than constipate trying to write Masterpieces—When I'm writing then I can write stories too.—But when cant write then cant write anything— Maybe if I got some ahead the Magazine might publish some—They are quiet and not awfully exciting—More like that Big Two Hearted River story—and not so long—Might be good for the magazines—Somewhere between Essays and Remeniscences—The two worst qualifecations I could find—What do you think?—

I dont want to have any correspondence with Dr. Bridges about them yet— Want to write a bunch first—Will divide them into three kinds—Quiet ones— Funny ones—Immoral ones—He can have the quiet ones. Will help the magazine as much as that piece by Doc Phelps[1] about how awful we pornographers are. Who are the other pornographers? What was funniest was where he said what the beastly public interest in murder stories was and stories of Crime. I thought there were 10 commandments and adultry was only the 7th!

But am going to write—I think that's Scott's trouble with his novel. Among other things of course more complicated. But he thought he had to write a masterpiece to follow The Gatsby—as good as Seldes etc. said he was—And to consciously write such a thing that had to be great just constipated him—

Then too you have to use up your material—You never use Anything you save. I thought I'd used up everything in In Our Time—Should always write as though you were going to die at the end of the book—(This doesnt seem to go with what's before but it's a good idea too!) Never for gods sake use or turn over to the advt. dept. anything I say in a letter—

I think I could write some pretty good things—About Key West—Here— Paris—Constantinople—Try to have more than meets the eye and the old ice-berg stuff[2]—but no more stories than that Che Ti Dice La Patria thing. What do you think? You'll say fine whether you think so or not because that is what you have to do with these bloody authors—But I could write some pretty good ones I think—Did you ever read Far Away and Long Ago—by W.H. Hudson— Like that only not so good—That's a swell book—Swell is a dreadful word— When I hear somebody say it that thinks I would like to hear it—Jews usually —my stomach turns over—

There wont be anything like Sherwood Anderson in Vanity Fair[3]—

Yours always

Ernest—

I'll write when I want the advances—

*Notes*

1. William Lyon Phelps's "As I Like It" in the August 1929 *Scribner's Magazine;* it does not mention Hemingway.

2. Hemingway subsequently elaborated on his comparison of good prose and an iceberg: the power of each results from concealed elements.

3. Beginning in 1926, Anderson had been publishing articles in *Vanity Fair* about places where he had lived.

▲ ▼ ▲

*To: Hemingway*
*From: Fitzgerald*                                    *ALS, 2 pp. Princeton.*

Villa Fleur des Bois
Cannes. Sept 9th 1929

Dear Ernest:

I'm glad you decided my letter wasn't snooty—it was merely hurried (incidently I thought you wanted a word said to Ruth G.[1] If it came about naturally —I merely remarked that you'd be disappointed if you lost your apartment— never a word that you'd been exasperated.) But enough of pretty dismal matters —let us proceed to the really dismal ones. First tho let me say that from Perkins last your book like Pickwick has become a classic while still in serial form. Everything looks bright as day for it and I envy you like hell but would rather have it happen to you than to anyone else.

Just taken another chapter to typists + its left me in a terrible mood of depression as to whether its any good or not. In 2 ½ mos. I've been here I've written 20,000 words on it + one short story, which is suberb for me of late years. I've paid for it with the usual nervous depressions and such drinking manners as the lowest bistrop (bistrot?) boy would scorn. My latest tendency is to collapse about 11.00 and with the tears flowing from my eyes or the gin rising to their level and leaking over, + tell interested friends or acquaintances that I havn't a friend in the world and likewise care for nobody, generally including Zelda and often implying current company—after which the current company tend to become less current and I wake up in strange rooms in strange palaces. The rest of the time I stay alone working or trying to work or brooding or reading detective stories—and realizing that anyone in my state of mind who has in addition never been able to hold his tongue is pretty poor company. But when drunk I make them all pay and pay and pay.

Among them has been Dotty Parker.[2] Naturally she having been in an equivalent state lacks patience—(this isn't snooty—no one likes to see people in moods of despair they themselves have survived. Incidently the Murphys[3] have given their whole performance for her this summer and I think, tho she would be the last to admit it, she's had the time of her life.

We are coming to Paris for 2 mos the 1st of October.

Your analysis of my inability to get my serious work done[4] is too kind in that it leaves out dissipation, but among acts of God it is possible that the 5 yrs between my leaving the army + finishing Gatsby 1919–1924 which included 3 novels, about 50 popular stories + a play + numerous articles + movies may have taken all I had to say too early, adding that all the time we were living at top speed in the gayest worlds we could find. This au fond is what really worries me—tho the trouble may be my inability to leave anything once started—I have worked for 2 months over a popular short story that was foredoomed to being torn up when completed. Perhaps the house will burn down with this ms + preferably me in it

Always Your Stinking Old Friend

Scott

I have no possible right to send you this gloomy letter. Really if I didn't feel rather better with one thing or another I couldn't have written it. Here's a last flicker of the old cheap pride:—the Post now pay the old whore $4000. a screw. But now its because she's mastered the 40 positions—in her youth one was enough.

*Notes*

1. The Hemingways were subletting a Paris apartment from Ruth Obre-Goldbeck-de Vallombrosa.

2. Dorothy Parker (1893–1967), writer and celebrated wit.

3. Gerald Murphy (1888–1964) and Sara Murphy (1883–1975) were Riviera hosts who befriended Fitzgerald and Hemingway; *Tender Is the Night* is dedicated to them. See Honoria Murphy Donnelly, *Sara & Gerald: Villa America and After* (New York: Times Books, 1982).

4. In his September 4, 1929, letter to Fitzgerald, Hemingway reiterated his charge that Fitzgerald had been blocked by Gilbert Seldes's glowing review of *Gatsby.*

▲▼▲

*To: Perkins*                          *1929. Paris*
*From: Hemingway*                  *ALS, 3 pp.[1] Princeton*

November 30

Dear Max—

    Have read, heard and received cables about a report that I was going to leave Scribners. You offered to publish what I was writing before any one else did. It was only by luck that I was in Austria and so did not get your letter which was waiting in Paris and accepted the cabled offer of another firm to publish my first book. You published a book which was refused by this first publisher. You published The Sun Also intact with the exception of one word which you have now published in this last book.[2] You have been constantly loyal and you have been wholly admirable. If we have fought over you cutting words out of this last book you at least left blanks wherever you Cut and it has been our own fight and no outsider is going to profit by it. I have absolutely no intention of leaving Scribners and I hope to live long enough so you may publish my Collected Works if my kidneys hold out and I have luck enough to write any works worth Collecting.
. . . . .

Yours always
Ernest Hemingway

*Notes*

    1. 242 words have been omitted from this letter.
    2. The word *balls*. See Hemingway to Perkins, July 24, 1926.

▲ ▼ ▲

*To: Perkins*                          *1929. Paris.*
*From: Hemingway*                  *ALS, 6 pp.[1] Princeton*

Sunday Dec 7

Dear Max—
    . . . . .
    Had a letter from A Knopf asking to see me so went in order to tell him and his wife there was absolutely no truth in report I was leaving you—nor was I dis satisfied in any way. He is returning to N Y in a week and I asked him to deny the report wherever he heard it—which they both promised to do.
    . . . . .
    . . . . .

Dec 10

Started to write you Sunday— Now it's Tuesday— Scott came to dinner last night and while drunk told me he had heard from you that McAlmon[2] had told you various stories about me. He also told me of particularly filthy story Morley Calloghan[3] had told him about me. Morley had gotten it from McAlmon.

So I write to ask if McAlmon has any new stories— His stories that I am familiar with are (1) That Pauline is a lesbian (2) that I am a homosexual (3) that I used to beat Hadley and as a result of one of these beatings Bumby was born prematurely.

Did he tell you these or did he have new ones? I'd appreciate not a general but a particular answer.

Morley, it seems, asked Scott on meeting him if he knew it were true that I was a homo-sexual. He had just gotten the news from McAlmon! He may therefore be counted on to have spread it fairly thoroughly. He seems also to be having a great deal of success with a story about how I sneered at his boxing ability, he challenged me and knocked me cold.

I sent McAlmon with a letter to you because I have tried to help materially everyone I know who is writing whether a friend or an enemy. Have tried especially to help people I did not like since my judgement might be warped in favor of my friends and hate to see people bitter about never having had a chance even though I may feel sure personally there is good and abundant cause for their failure. I do not try to get them published That's your business not mine. but to obtain them an extra-fair presentation to the publisher.

But this has gone a little too far. There should be a limit to what lies people are allowed to tell under jealousies.

I did not know until last night that Calloghan was definitely in that class. It is all pretty disgusting. Pauline says it is my own fault for having had any thing to do with such swine. She is right enough. There will be a certain satisfaction in beating up Calloghan because of his boasting and because he is a good enough boxer. There is none in beating up McAlmon— I would have done it years ago if he wasnt so pitiful. But I will go through with it as I should have long ago because the only thing such people fear is physical correction— They have no moral feelings to hurt.

I have, as far as I know, only one one other—perhaps two other enemies, that is people willfuly seeking to do you harm through malice. One in a very minor way would seem to be Isabel Patterson whom I've never even seen and the other is a Russian Jew with a name like Lipschitzky who calls himself Pierre Loving and lies about every one. He is a disappointed writer.[4]

Scott is the soul of honor when sober and completely irresponsible when drunk. If it's all the same I would rather you wrote me when you hear stories about me—not Scott. Please do not reproach Scott with a breach of confidence as he is absolutely incapable of such a thing sober and drunk he is no more responsible than an insane man. He did not say you had written him any definite stories— but told me stories he had heard from Calloghan as a type of thing McAlmon had probably told you.

I had to sit, drinking Vichey, cold sober, and listen to an hour or more of that sort of thing last night. When McAlmon told one of those stories in the presence of Evan Shipman[5]—Evan called him a liar and hit him. When McAlmon called Scott a homosexual to me (It is one of his manias) I told him he was a liar and a damned fool. It was not until after he had left for N.Y. that I heard the story he was telling about Pauline. Frankly I think he is crazy. Calloghan has no such excuse. He is a cheap, small town gossip anxious to believe and retail any filth no matter how improbable.

This seems to be the end of the letter— Your wires about the sale being 57,000 and 59,000 came yesterday and today. Thanks ever so much for sending them. I am glad it is going so well.

Yours always—

Ernest Hemingway

[*Two lines crossed out by Hemingway*]

This is nothing—I was starting to make a reflection about people waiting 6 ms. to tell you when drunk some filthy story about you which they apparently never challenged physically or in any way but realized that since last night I have reflected entirely too damned much— But Ill be damned glad be in Key West and see people like Charles,[6] Mike Strater[7] and yourself and have no filth and jealousy. What the hell are they jealous of?— I dont want the publicity and I dont get the money. All I want is to work and be let alone and I damned well will be.

### Notes

1. 251 words have been omitted from this letter.
2. Robert McAlmon (1896–1956), American writer, whose Contact Press had published Hemingway's *Three Stories and Ten Poems* (1923) in Paris.
3. Callaghan (1903–90), who had worked with Hemingway on the *Toronto Star,* became a Scribners author in 1928.
4. Paterson wrote the "Turns With a Bookworm" column for the Sunday *New York Herald Tribune Books* section. Loving wrote fiction and criticism.
5. Shipman was a minor poet and horse-racing fancier; he met Hemingway in 1924, and the two remained lifelong friends.
6. Charles Thompson, Hemingway's fishing and hunting companion in Key West and Africa.
7. American artist Henry Strater (1896–1987) was referred to as Mike.

▲▼▲

To: *Fitzgerald*
From: *Perkins* *TLS, 4 pp. University of South Carolina*

Dec. 17, 1929

Dear Scott:

I am enclosing a letter I got from Callaghan, and a note which he sent to the Herald Tribune, and which was printed there. They will show you how things stand.[1] The girl who started this story is one Caroline Bancroft. She wanders around Europe every year and picks up what she can in the way of gossip, and prints it in the Denver paper, and it spreads from there. Callaghan told me the whole story about boxing with Ernest, and the point he put the most emphasis on was your time-keeping. That impressed him a great deal. He did say that he knew he was more adept in boxing than Ernest, and that he had been practising for several years with fighters. He was all right about the whole matter. He is much better than he looks.

As for Tom Boyd, he is in Reno where that Mrs. Bartlett is getting a divorce. This takes until January, and if Peggy goes ahead with her side of the divorce matter and gets Tom free, those two will be married and apparently plan to live in Woodstock, Vermont. All reports indicate that Tom is satisfied, but I think he has got himself badly hooked. He got into some kind of a fight out in Reno during a party, and was arrested and fined, and I guess he feels pretty badly about that. The story that appeared in the News was awful, but I suppose the fact was that he wanted to kill some man,—as it seems he generally does when he gets drunk—once he was for laying out Harrison Smith[2] at a party in New Canaan—and in the resulting struggle other people got more or less hurt too.

Ernest's book should have sold very close to 70,000 by Christmas, and then the question is whether we can carry it actively on into the next season;- and that is chiefly a question because of the fact that we are evidently in for a period of depression. We have come out well here for the year—probably the best year we have had—but it is largely because of four or five very good books.[3] Most books have failed this year, and most publishers have had bad years because of the fall season.

I hope you and Zelda will be coming back sometime early in 1930. Why don't you think of going down to Key West, if I go, in the spring?

Ever your friend,
Maxwell Perkins

### Notes

1. Some of Hemingway's antipathy to Callaghan resulted from an episode that had occurred in Paris in June 1929. Fitzgerald, who was keeping time for a sparring match between Hemingway and Callaghan, inadvertently let a round go long, and Hemingway was knocked down. The story spread that Callaghan—who was smaller than

Hemingway—had knocked him out. The boxing match led to bad feelings among the three men. See Bruccoli, *Fitzgerald and Hemingway: A Dangerous Friendship* (New York: Carroll & Graf, 1994), pp. 120–28.

    2. Book publisher.

    3. The 1929 Scribners list included Wolfe's *Look Homeward, Angel*, Lardner's *Round Up*, and S. S. Van Dine's *The Bishop Murder Case*.

▲ ▼ ▲

| | |
|---|---|
| *To: Perkins* | *Harvard Club letterhead* |
| *From: Wolfe* | *ALS, 5 pp. Princeton* |

New York, Dec 24, 1929

Dear Mr. Perkins: One year ago I had little hope for my work, and I did not know you. What has happened since may seem to be only a modest success to many people; but to me it is touched with strangeness and wonder. It is a miracle.

You are now mixed with my book in such a way that I can never separate the two of you. I can no longer think clearly of the time I wrote it, but rather of the time when you first talked to me about it, and when you worked upon it. My mind has always seen people more clearly than events or things—the name "Scribners" naturally makes a warm glow in my heart, but you are chiefly "Scribners" to me: you have done what I had ceased to believe one person could do for another—you have created liberty and hope for me.

Young men sometimes believe in the existence of heroic figures, and wiser than themselves, to whom they can turn for an answer to all their vexation and grief. Later, they must discover that such answers have to come out of their own hearts; but the powerful desire to believe in such figures persists. You are for me such a figure: you are one of the rocks to which my life is anchored.

I have taken the publication of my first book very hard—all the happy and successful part of it as well as the unhappy part: a great deal of the glory and joy and glamour with which in my fantasy I surrounded such an event has vanished. But, as usual, life and reality supplant the imaginary thing with another glory that is finer and more substantial than the visionary one.

I should have counted this past year a great one, if it had allowed me only to know about you. I am honored to think I may call you my friend, and I wish to send to you on Christmas Day this statement of my loyal affection.

Faithfully Yours,<br>Thomas Wolfe.<br>Dec 24, 1929

▲ ▼ ▲

## CHARLES SCRIBNER'S SONS

### Look Homeward, Angel
BY THOMAS WOLFE $2.50

This novel is a strange and deep picture of American life, the cyclic curve of a large family—genesis, union, disintegration. It touches not only their visible, outer lives, but explores their buried lives as well.

The rich variety of its characters and the freedom of their portrayal give it a vividness seldom matched in fiction. The early pages are dominated by the lusty, Gargantuan figure of Oliver Gant, in whose stone-cutter's shop stood the angel of Carrara marble that was the secret symbol of his buried life. Then there is Eliza, his wife, stubborn with the patience of avarice, and their odd brood of children—Frank, with all the taints of his heredity; Helen, slapping her father out of his drunkenness; Luke, who quivers with wild laughter; Ben, bitter, secretive, attractive, aloof in his brief life, aloof in his death; and the youngest, Eugene, the stranger who never ceases to view life with something of a child's innocency and wonder. It is Eugene's life thread which the author weaves ever more firmly into the fabric of his novel, writing with sweeping intensity and moments of free beauty.

Catalogue entry for Wolfe's first novel (Princeton University Library)

*To: Wolfe*
*From: Perkins*          *CC, 1 p. Princeton*

Dec 27 '29

Dear Wolfe:- I'm mighty glad you feel as you do,- except for a sense of not deserving it. I hope anyway that there could be no serious thought of obligation between us but, as a matter of convenience in speech, I would point out that even if you really 'owed' me a great deal it would be cancelled by what I owe you.- The whole episode, from receipt of Ms. up to now was for me a most happy, interesting, + exciting one.

Come in soon,- + bring the story. What you last told me of the October Fair[1] made me eager to have you get to it,- it gave me a real glimpse into the quality + character of it

Ever yours,
Maxwell Perkins

### Note

1. Wolfe's projected second novel was never published although some of its material was recycled in other volumes.

To: *Hemingway*
From: *Perkins*                              *CC, 5 pp.*[1] *Princeton*

Dec. 27, 1929

Dear Ernest:

. . . . .

The only reason I spoke to Scott at all about McAlmon was that you sent him over here and wrote me a letter all about him,– and all presumably to help him. It was only on that account that his talk as I told it to you in a letter yesterday,[2] impressed me. People like that are always depreciating other people, and it was only because you had played the friend to him that it seemed worth any comment. And I am sorry I said a word about it, for it had no significance of any kind in reality. Of course, he is not what you would want a man to be, by a considerable sight, but everyone who knows him knows that, I suppose.

When Callaghan got back here, I was having lunch with him. Bunny Wilson had told me the story you speak of, and it had seemed very improbable, and I said, "How about this story of you and Hemingway having a boxing bout?" and then he told me in an altogether decent way about how you asked him what he wanted to do, and mentioned boxing among other things, and how he, who had done a lot of it since he knew you, had said he was for that.– Then he gave an account of how you boxed, and the way Scott kept time. There was nothing about anyone getting knocked out or anything of the kind, but he only did so with pride, but not bragging that he had been able to hold you off through this heart-breaking round. He told me how he did not think he could last through the round, and could not imagine why it held out so long until he caught a glimpse of Scott out of the corner of his eye, apparently not taking any interest in his watch at all, or in the bout. This story was disseminated, as she admits, by Caroline Bancroft, of the Denver Post. She has admitted this and has corrected it so far as is possible. Scott wrote Callaghan about it, and so I sent Scott Callaghan's letter about it, and the statement he sent the Tribune which was printed.

. . . . .
. . . . .

Ever yours,

. . . . .

*Notes*

1. 201 words have been omitted from this letter.
2. On December 26, 1929, Perkins had written to Hemingway: "The McAlmon part. If he is talking on the line you tell me about I guess he knew it wouldn't interest me. I haven't hit anybody since I was fourteen so I don't believe I would have done that, but I would somehow have shut off that line of talk."

▲ ▼ ▲

*To: Perkins*
*From: Fitzgerald*                    *AL, 7 pp. Princeton*

10 Rue Pergolèse
Paris, France
Jan 21st 1930

[*In upper left corner of first page*] This has run to seven long close-written pages so you better not read it when you're in a hurry.

Dear Max: There is so much to write you—or rather so many small things that I'll write 1st the personal things and then on another sheet a series of suggestions about books and authors that have accumulated in me in the last six months.

(1.) To begin with, because I don't mention my novel it isn't because it isn't finishing up or that I'm neglecting it—but only that I'm weary of setting dates for it till the moment when it is in the Post Office Box.

(2) I was very grateful for the money—it won't happen again but I'd managed to get horribly into debt + I hated to call on Ober, who's just getting started,[1] for another cent

(3.) Thank you for the documents in the Callaghan case. I'd rather not discuss it except to say that I don't like him and that I wrote him a formal letter of apology. I never thought he started the rumor + never said nor implied such a thing to Ernest.

(4.) Delighted with the success of Ernest's book. I took the responsibility of telling him that McAlmon was at his old dirty work around New York. McAlmon, by the way, didn't have anything to do with founding <u>Transition</u>. He published Ernest's first book over here + some books of his own + did found some little magazine but of no importance.

(5) Thank you for getting Gatsby for me in foreign languages

(6) Sorry about John Biggs but it will probably do him good in the end. <u>The Stranger in Soul Country</u> had something + the <u>Seven Days Whipping</u> was respectable but colorless. <u>Demigods</u> was simply oratorical twirp. How is his play going?

(7.) Tom Boyd seems far away. I'll tell you one awful thing tho. Lawrence Stallings was in the West with King Vidor at a <u>huge</u> salary to write an equivalent of <u>What Price Glory</u>. King Vidor told me that Stallings in despair of showing Vidor what the war was about gave him a copy of <u>Through the Wheat</u>. And that's how Vidor so he told me made the big scenes of the <u>Big Parade</u>. Tom Boyd's profits were a few thousand—Stallings were a few hundred thousands. Please don't connect my name with this story but it is the truth and it seems to me rather horrible.

(8) Lastly + most important. For the English rights of my next book Knopf made me an offer so much better than any in England (advance $500.00; royalies sliding from ten to fifteen + twenty; guaranty to publish next book of short stories at same rate) that I accepted of course.[2] My previous talk with Cape was encouraging on my part but conditional. As to Chatto + Windus—since they made no overtures at my <u>All the Sad Young Men</u> I feel free to take any advantage of a technicality to have my short stories published in England, especially as they answered a letter of mine on the publication of the book with the signature (Chatto + Windus, per Q), undoubtedly an English method of showing real interest in one's work.

I must tell you ( + privately) for your own amusement that the first treaty Knopf sent me contained a clause that would have required me to give him $10,000 on date of publication—that is: 25% of <u>all</u> serial rights (not specifying only <u>English</u> ones,) for which <u>Liberty</u> have contracted, as you know, for $40,000.[3] This was pretty Jewish, or maybe an error in his office, but later I went over the contract with a fine tooth comb + he was very decent. Confidential! Incidently he said to me as Harcourt once did to Ernest that you were the best publishers in America. I told him he was wrong—that you were just a lot of royalty-doctors + short changers.

No more for the moment. I liked Bunny's book[4] + am sorry it didn't go. I thot those Day Edgar stories made a nice book, didn't you?[5]

Ever Your Devoted Friend<br>Scott

I append the sheet of brilliant ideas of which you may find one or two worth considering. Congratulations on the Eddy Book[6]

① (Suggestion list)

(1.) Certainly if the ubiquitous and ruined MacAlmon deserves a hearing then John Bishop, a poet and a man of really great talents and intelligence does. I am sending you under another cover a sister story of the novelette you refused, which together with the first one and, three shorter ones will form his Civil-War-civilian-in-invaded-Virginia-book,[7] a simply grand idea + new, rich field. The enclosed is the best thing he has ever done and the best thing about the <u>non-combatant</u> or rather behind-the-lines war I've ever read. I <u>hope</u> to God you can use this in the magazine—couldn't it be run into small type carried over like Sew Collins did with <u>Boston</u> + you <u>Farewell to Arms</u>? He <u>needs</u> the encouragement + is <u>so</u> worth it.

(2) In the new American Caravan amid much sandwiching of Joyce and Co is the first work of a 21 year old named <u>Robert Cantwell</u>.[8] Mark it well, for my guess is that he's learned a better lesson from Proust than Thornton Wilder did and has a destiny of no mean star.

(3.) Another young man therein named <u>Gerald Sykes</u> has an extraordinary talent in the line of heaven knows what, but very memorable and distinguished.[9] (4) Thirdly (and these three are all in the whole damn book) there is a man named Erskine Caldwell,[10] who interested me less than the others because of the usual derivations from Hemmingway and even Callaghan—still read him. He + Sykes are 26 yrs old. I don't know any of them.

If you decide to act in any of these last three cases I'd do it within a few weeks. I know none of the men but Cantwell will go quick with his next stuff if he hasn't gone already. For some reason young writers come in groups— Cummings, Dos Passos + me in 1920–21; Hemmingway, Callaghan + Wilder in 1926–27 and no one in between and no one since. This looks to me like a really new generation

(5) Now a personal friend (but he knows not that I'm you)—Cary Ross (Yale 1925)[11]—poorly represented in this <u>American Caravan</u>, but rather brilliantly by poems in the <u>Mercury</u> + <u>Transition</u>, studying medicine at Johns Hopkins + one who at the price of publication or at least examination of his poems might prove a valuable man. Distinctly <u>younger</u> that <u>post</u> war, later than my generation, sure to turn to fiction + worth corresponding with. I believe these are the cream of the young people

(6) [general] Dos Passos wrote me about the ms. of some protegée of his but as I didn't see the ms. or know the man the letter seemed meaningless. Did you do anything about Murray Godwin (or Goodwin?). Shortly I'm sending you some memoirs by an ex-marine, doorman at my bank here. They might have some documentary value as true stories of the Nicaruguan expedition ect.

(7.) In the foreign (French) field there is besides Chamson one man, and at the opposite pole, of great great talent. It is not Cocteau nor Arragon but young <u>René Crevel</u>.[12] I am opposed to him for being a fairy but in the last <u>Transition</u> (number 18.) there is a <u>translation</u> of the beginning of his current novel which simply knocked me cold with its beauty. The part in <u>Transition</u> is called <u>Mr. Knife and Miss Fork</u> and I wish to God you'd read it immediately. Incidently the novel is a great current success here. I know its not yet placed in America + if you're interested <u>please</u> communicate with me <u>before</u> you write Bradley.

(8) Now, one last, much more elaborate idea. In France any military book of real tactical or strategical importance, theoretical or fully documented ( + usually the latter) (and I'm not referring to the one-company battles between "<u>Red</u>" + "Blue" taught us in the army under the name of Small Problems for Infantry). They are mostly published by Payots here + include such works as <u>Ludendorf's Memoirs</u>; and the <u>Documentary Preparations for the German break-thru in 1918</u>—how the men were massed, trained, brought up to the line in 12 hours in 150 different technical groups from flame throwers to field kitchens, the whole inside story <u>from captured orders</u> of the greatest <u>tactical</u>

attack in history; a study of <u>Tannenburg</u> (German); several, both French + German of the 1st <u>Marne</u>; a thorough study of gas warfare, another of Tanks, no dogmatic distillations complied by some old dodart, but original documents.

<u>Now</u>—believing that so long as we have service schools and not much preparation ( I am a political cynic and a big-navy-man, like all Europeans) English Translations should be available in all academies, army service schools, staff schools ect (I'll bet there are American army officers with the rank of Captain that don't know what "infiltration in depth" is or what Colonel Bruckmüller's idea of artillery employment was.) It seems to me that it would be a great patriotic service to consult the war-department bookbuyers on some subsidy plan to bring out a tentative dozen of the most important as "an original scource tactical library of the lessons of the great war." It would be a parallel, but <u>more</u> essentially <u>military</u> rather than <u>politics-military</u>, to the enclosed list of Payot's collection. I underline some of my proposed inclusions. This, in view of some millions of amateurs of battle now in America might be an enormous popular success as well as a patriotic service. Let me know about this because if you shouldn't be interested I'd like to for my own satisfaction make the suggestion to someone else. Some that I've underlined may be already published.[13]

My God—this is 7 pages + you're asleep + I want to catch the Olympic with this so I'll close. Please tell me your response to <u>each</u> idea.

Does Chamson sell at all? Oh, for my income tax will you have the usual statement of lack of royalties sent me— + for my curiosity to see if I've sold a book this year except to myself.

*Notes*

1. Ober had left the Reynolds agency and started his own literary agency. Fitzgerald went with him.
2. Knopf did not publish *Tender Is the Night* in England; it was published there by Chatto & Windus.
3. *Liberty* did not serialize *Tender Is the Night.*
4. *I Thought of Daisy.*
5. *In Princeton Town* (Scribners, 1929).
6. Scribners had published Edwin Franden Dakin's *Mrs. Eddy: The Biography of a Virginal Mind* (1929) despite opposition from the Christian Science church. See John Hall Wheelock's account in *The Last Romantic: A Poet among Publishers,* pp. 98–99.
7. Bishop's "The Cellar" had been rejected by *Scribner's Magazine,* which then accepted "Many Thousands Gone" (September 1930). The novelette won the *Scribner's Magazine* prize for 1930 and became the title story for Bishop's first Scribners book in 1931.
8. Cantwell later published a well-regarded proletarian novel, *The Land of Plenty* (New York: Farrar & Rinehart, 1934).
9. Scribners did not publish Sykes.

10. Scribners published Caldwell's *American Earth* (1931) and *Tobacco Road* (1932). See John Hall Wheelock's account of Scribners' postpublication suppression of *Tobacco Road* (*The Last Romantic: A Poet among Publishers,* pp. 90–91).

11. Scribners did not publish a volume by Ross.

12. Scribners did not publish Crevel.

13. Perkins did not act on Fitzgerald's plan for a military series.

▲ ▼ ▲

To: Perkins
From: Fitzgerald

May 1930. Paris
ALS, 1 p. Princeton

Dear Max:

I was delighted about the Bishop story—the acceptance has done wonders for him. The other night I read him a good deal of my novel + I think he liked it. Harold Ober wrote me that if it couldn't be published this fall I should publish the Basil Lee stories, but I know too well by whom reputations are made + broken to ruin myself completely by such a move—I've seen Tom Boyd, Michael Arlen + too many others fall through the eternal trapdoor of trying cheat the public, no matter what their public is, with substitutes—better to let four years go by. I wrote young + I wrote a lot + the pot takes longer to fill up now but the novel, my novel, is a different matter than if I'd hurriedly finished it up a year and a half ago. If you think Callaghan hasn't completely blown himself up with this death house masterpiece[1] just wait and see the pieces fall. I don't know why I'm saying this to you who have never been anything but my most loyal and confident encourager and friend but Ober's letter annoyed me today + put me in a wretched humor. <u>I know what I'm doing</u>—honestly, Max. How much time between <u>The Cabala</u> + <u>The Bridge of St Lois Rey</u>, between <u>The Genius</u> + <u>The American Tragedy</u> between <u>The Wisdom Tooth</u> + <u>Green Pastures</u>.[2] I think time seems to go by quicker there in America but time put in is time eventually taken out—and whatever this thing of mine is its certainly not a mediocrity like <u>The Woman of Andros</u> + <u>The Forty Second Parallel</u>.[3] "He through" is an easy cry to raise but its safer for the critics to raise it at the evidence in print than at a long silence.

Ever yours
Scott

*Notes*

1. *Strange Fugitive* (1928).

2. *The Cabala* (1926) and *The Bridge of San Luis Rey* (1927) by Thornton Wilder; *The "Genius"* (1915) and *An American Tragedy* (1925) by Theodore Dreiser; *The Wisdom Tooth* (1926) and *The Green Pastures* (1929) by Marc Connelly.

3. *The Woman of Andros* (1930) by Wilder; *The 42nd Parallel* (1930) by Dos Passos.

▲ ▼ ▲

*To: Perkins*          *Hotel Lorius letterhead, Montreux, Switzerland*
*From: Wolfe*                    *ALS, 39 pp. Princeton*

July 17,
1930

Dear Mr. Perkins: Your letter was sent on here from Paris, and I got it this morning. I suppose by now you have the letter I sent you from Paris several weeks ago. I have been here five or six days. I came down from Paris and stopped off at Dijon for two days. A few days after I wrote you, I believe, Fritz Dashiell came to Paris and found me one morning in the Guaranty Trust Co—together with Mrs Dashiell we spent two or three days together, visited one or two museums, and did some very fancy eating. Every time we went to a new place we wished you were there. I think I told you I saw Scott Fitzgerald and Jim Boyd.[1] I was with Jim for a day or two—after that I did not see him: before he left Paris he wrote me, he had had another attack of sinus trouble and was off for Mont 'Dore.'[2]

The other night at the Casino here I was sitting on the terrace when I saw Scott Fitzgerald and a friend of his, a young man I met in Paris. I called to them, they came over and sat with me: later we gambled at roulette and I won 15 francs—then Scott took us to a night club here. This sounds much gayer than it is: there is very little to do here, and I think I saw all the night life there is on that occasion. Later Scott and his friend drove back to Vevey, a village a mile or two from here on the lake: they are staying there. They asked me to come over to dine with them, but I am not going: I do not think I am very good company to people at present. It would be very easy for me to start swilling liquor at present but I am <u>not</u> going to do it. I am here to get work done, and in the next three months, I am going to see whether I am a bum or a man. I shall not try to conceal from you the fact that at times now I have hard sledding: my life is divided between just two things;—thought of my book, and thought of an event in my life which is now, <u>objectivally</u>, finished.[3] I do not write any more to anyone concerned in that event—I received several letters, but since none have come for some time I assume no more will come. I have been entirely alone since I left New York, save for these casual meetings I have told you about: Something in me hates being alone like death, and something in me cherishes it: I have always felt that somehow, out of this bitter solitude, some fruit must come. I lose faith in myself with people. When I am with someone like Scott I feel that I am morose and sullen—and violent in my speech and movement part of the time—later I feel that I have repelled them.

Physically my life is very good. My nerves are very steady, I drink beer and wine, mostly beer, I do not think to excess, and I have come to what is, I am sure, one of the most beautiful spots in the world. I am staying at a quiet and excellent hotel here; have a very comfortable room with a writing desk and a stone balcony that looks out on the lake of Geneva, and on a garden below filled with rich trees and grass and brilliant flowers. On all sides of the lake the mountains soar up: everything begins to climb immediately, this little town is built in three or four shelving terraces, and runs along the lake shore. Something in me wants to get up and see places, the country is full of incredibly beautiful places, but also something says 'stay here and work.'

That, in a way, is what my book is about. I hope in these hasty scrawls I have been able to communicate the idea of my book, and that it seems clear and good to you. I told you that the book begins with "of wandering forever, and the earth again," and that these two opposing elements seem to me to be fundamental in people. I have learned this in my own life, and believe I am at last beginning to have a proper use of a writer's material: for it seems to me he ought to see in what has happened to him the elements of the universal experience. In my own life my desire has fought between a hunger for isolation, for getting away, for seeking new lands, and a desire for home, for permanence, for a piece of this earth fenced in and lived on and private to oneself, and for a person or persons to love and possess. This is badly put, but I think it expresses a desire that all people have. I think the desire for wandering is more common to men, and for fixity and a piece of the earth to women, but I know these things are rooted in most people. I think you have sometimes been puzzled when I have talked to you about parts of this book—about the train as it thunders through the dark, and about the love for another person—to see how they could be reconciled or fit into the general scheme of a story, but I think you can get some idea of it now: the great train pounding at the rails is rushing across the everlasting and silent earth—here the two ideas of wandering and eternal repose—and the characters, on the train, and on the land, again illustrate this. Also, the love theme, the male and female love, represent this again: please do not think I am hammering this in in the book. I let it speak for itself—I am giving you a kind of key.

There is no doubt at all what the book is about, what course it will take, and I think the seething process, the final set of combinations, has been reached. I regret to report to you that the book will be very long, probably longer than the first one, but I think that each of its four parts makes a story in itself and, if good enough, might be printed as such. I have been reading your favorite book, War and Peace—it is a magnificent and gigantic work—if we are going to worship anything let it be something like this: I notice in this book that the personal story is interwoven with the universal—you get the stories of private individuals, particularly of members of Tolstoy's own family, and you get the whole tremendous panorama of nations, and of Russia. This is the way a great writer uses his material, this is the way in which every good work is "autobiographical"—and I am not ashamed to follow this in my book. The four parts of the book as they now stand are: (1) <u>Antaeus</u> or <u>Immortal Earth</u> (Title to be chosen from one of these)

(2) Antaeus or <u>The Fast Express</u>

(3) Faust and Helen (?)

(4) The October Fair.

—I do not think <u>Immortal Earth</u> or <u>The Immortal Earth</u> is a bad title; and if you are not keen upon <u>The Fast Express</u>—we might call part I <u>Immortal Earth</u>—and Part II <u>Antaeus</u>—since in part I the idea of eternal movement, of wandering and the earth, of flight and repose is more manifest, and in Part II, even though we have the fast train, the idea of redoubling and renewing our strength by contact with the earth (Antaeus) is more evident.

Now, the general movement of the book is from the universal to the individual: in Part I <u>The Immortal Earth</u> (?), we have a symphony of many voices (I described this briefly in my other letter) through which the thread of the particular story begins to run. I think this can be done with entire clearness and unity: we have a character called David (chapter II is called <u>The Song of David</u>) but this character appears at first only as a window, an eye, a wandering seer: he performs at first exactly the same function as the epic minstrel in some old popular epic like Beowulf—who makes us very briefly conscious of his presence from time to time by saying "I have heard," or "it has been told me." Thus in Part I, in the chapter called <u>The River</u>, the woman telling the story of the river in flood refers to him once by name, in the chapter Pioneers, O Pioneers, we understand that David is a member of an American family, two or three hundred of whose members are buried in different parts of the American earth, and we get the stories and wanderings of some of these people; in the letter of the tourist from Prague he is referred to by name; in the chapter On the Rails we know that he is on the train, although the story is that of the engineer; in the chapter <u>The Bums at Sunset</u>[4] we know he has seen them waiting for the train at the water-tower; in the chapter called The Congo, the wandering negro who goes crazy and kills people and is finally killed by the posse as he crosses a creek is known to David, the boy—etc.[5]

So much for some of the general movement: now among the twenty Chapters of this first part is interspersed the first element of the particular story—the figure of David remains almost entirely a window, but begins to emerge as an individual from what is told about him by other people—and by the way all these episodes, even the general ones—Pioneers, O Pioneers, The Congo, etc—give flashes of his life—but in this first part, not to tell about him, but to tell about his country, the seed that produced him, etc. It will be seen in the particular story that the desire and longing of David is also the desire and longing of the race—"wandering forever and the earth again"—these half dozen chapters, moreover, are concerned with the <u>female</u> thing: the idea of the earth, fructification, and repose—these half dozen chapters interspersed among the twenty are almost entirely about women and told in the language of women: the mother, the mistress, and the child—sometimes all included in one person, some times found separately in different women

Now, if you will follow me a little farther in this, here is another development. I have said that wandering seems to me to be more of a male thing, and the fructification of the earth more a female thing—I don't think there can be much argument about this, as immediately we think of the pioneers, the explorers, the Crusaders, the Elizabethan mariners, etc. I am making an extensive use of old myths in my book, although I never tell the reader this: you know already that I am using the Heracles (in my book the City is Heracles) and Antaeus myth; and you know that the lords of fructification and the earth are almost always women: Maya in the Eastern legends; Demeter in the Greek; Ceres in Latin, etc.

Now I hope you dont get dizzy in all this, or think I am carrying the thing to absurdity: all intense conviction has elements of the fanatic and the absurd in it, but they are saved by our belief and our passion: Contained in the book like a kernel from the beginning, but unrevealed until much later is the idea of a man's quest for his father: the idea becomes very early apparent that when a man returns he returns always to the female principle—he returns, I hope this is not disgusting, to the womb of earthly creation—to the earth itself, to a woman, to fixity. But I dare go so far as to believe that the other pole—the pole of wandering is not only—a masculine thing, but that in some way it represents the quest of a man for his father—I dare mention to you the wandering of Christ upon this earth, the wanderings of Paul, the quests of Crusaders, the wanderings of the Ancient Mariner who makes his confession to the Wedding Guest —please don't laugh:

"The moment that his face I see

I know the man that must hear me,

To him my tale I teach."

I could mention also a dozen myths, legends, or historical examples, but you can supply them quite as well for yourself. Suffice it to say that this last theme— the quest of a man for his father—does not become fully revealed until the very end of the book: under the present plan I have called the final chapter of the fourth and last part (The October Fair), Telemachus.

Now, briefly, in the first part on which I am now at work (to be called Antaeus or The Immortal Earth.) I want to construct my story on the model of the old folk epic: Beowulf, for example. I want the character of David to be the epic minstrel who sings of the experience of his race, and I want to do this with eloquence, with passion and with simplicity. I want my book of poetry—that is I want it to be drenched in a poetic vision of life: I believe at this moment in the truth and the passion of what I have to say, and I hope, in spite of this fast scrawl, I have been able to make parts of it clear to you, and to show you it has a coherent plan and purpose.

In the first chapter of the first part (after the prelude)—the first chapter is called The Ship—I think I have done a good piece of writing: I tell about the sea and the earth—I tell why they are different—of the sea's eternal movement, and the earths eternal repose. I tell why men go to sea, and why they have made harbours at the end; I tell why a ship is always called "she"; I tell of the look in the eyes of men when the last land fades out of sight, and when land comes first in view again; I tell of the earth; I describe the great ship, and the people on it— and, so help me, when I am through, I am proud of that ship and of man, who built her, who is so strong because he is so weak, who is so great because he is so small, who is so brave because he is so full of fear—who can face the horror of the ocean and see there in that unending purposeless waste the answer to his existence—I insist, by the way, in my book that men are wise, and that we all know we are lost, that we are damned together—and that man's greatness comes in knowing this and then making myths; like soldiers going into battle who will whore and carouse to the last minute, nor have any talk of death and slaughter.

Well, I have almost written you a book, and I hope you have stayed awake thus far. I don't know if it makes sense or not, but I think it does: remember, although this letter is very heavy, that my book, as I plan it will be full of rich- ness, talk and humor—please write me and tell me if all this has meant any- thing to you, and what you think of it. Please don't talk about it to other people. Write me as often as you can, if only a note. We like to get letters when we are in a strange land.

Please forgive me for talking so much about myself and my book. I hope I can do a good piece of work, and that any little personal distress does not get the best of me—I do not think it will.

One final thing: please understand—I think you do—that my new book will make use of experience, things I have known and felt, as the first one did— but that now I have created fables and legends and that there will be no ques- tion of identification (certainly not in the first two parts) as there was in the first. The David I have referred to is part of me, as indeed are several other char- acters, but nothing like, in appearance or anything else, what people think me) this is very naive and foolish, and for God's sake keep it to yourself: in mak- ing the character of David, I have made him out of the inside of me, of what I have always believed the inside was like: he is about five feet nine, with the long arms and the prowl of an ape, and a little angel in his face—he is part beast, part spirit—a mixture of the ape and the angel—there is a touch of the monster in him)[6]

But no matter about this—at first he is the bard and, I pray God, that is what I can be. Please write me soon I'll tell you how things come

Yours Faithfully, Tom Wolfe

P.S. My book came out in England last Monday, July 14. I hope it goes well and gets good notices, but I have instructed them not to send any reviews—I can't be bothered by it now. Some <u>kind</u> friend probably will send reviews, but I hope for the best.

My address will continue to be The Guaranty Trust Co, Paris I hope you have a nice vacation and get a good rest.

### Notes

1. James Boyd, historical novelist published by Scribners.
2. Mont-Dore, spa in south-central France.
3. Wolfe is referring to his relationship with his patron and lover Aline Bernstein.
4. Published as a story in *Vanity Fair,* October 1935.
5. The Congo story was published as "The Child by Tiger" in the *Saturday Evening Post,* September 11, 1937. The David character was not retained in *Of Time and the River.*
6. This is descriptive of Wolfe's character Monk Webber.

▲ ▼ ▲

*To: Wolfe*          *Harvard Club letterhead*
*From: Perkins*          *ALS, 8 pp. Harvard*

Tuesday July 30th, 1930

Dear Wolfe:—

I had to go to Baltimore for two weeks for medical purposes—not serious. I was never better except my nose which it was thought an expert could improve—+ I took with me your letter meaning to answer it there at leisure. It was hardly ever less than 100 + for three days 104 in the shade; + never a drop of rain. The ink in the ink wells coagulated + caked on the pens;— + the hotel stenographer was "overcome" + went to the seashore, + so I came back, letter unwritten, today, + found another letter. Don't think I ever worry about the book.—All you say of it interests me deeply, + in fact excites my imagination. It sounds like a very Leviathan of a book as you describe it, now lying in the depths of your consciousness; + I believe you are the man who can draw out such a Leviathan. So far as I can judge—by a sort of instinct—all of your plan + intention is right + true.—But chasten yourself. You know your danger, the rarer sort, comes from lack of restraint. Your talent seems to me a truly great one, + that sort requires to be disciplined + curbed. Length itself is so important as with the first book,— though there is a limit to a volume + I think you'd gain by the compression needed to subscribe to it.—By keeping that always in your mind.

I wish you were here,—that we might now cool ourselves with a long Tom Collins. When will you be here? Baltimore I liked much. I tramped the entire city from waterfront to Druid Hill Park. There seemed to be a sort of kindly preciousness about it,—quite different from the tone of Philadelphia which I hate,— + from that of N.Y. which I like.

I'm glad you saw Scott, but he's in trouble: Zelda is still very seriously ill in a nervous breakdown. I don't know how it will end. Scott is blameable I know for what has come to Zelda, in a sense. But he's a brave man to face trouble as he does, always facing it squarely.—no self-deceptions.

Everything goes on well in the office. Will James "Lone Cowboy"—his autobiography—was taken for August by the Book of the Month Club. It should be a great success, as Van Dine's "Scarab" was this spring,[1]—So in spite of bad business conditions we make out reasonably well.

Ever yours,<br>Maxwell Perkins

*Note*

1. *The Scarab Murder Case.*

▲ ▼ ▲

*To: Hemingway*
*From: Perkins*                    *CC, 4 pp.*[1] *Princeton*

Aug. 1, 1930

Dear Ernest:

. . . . .

. . . . .

"In Our Time" is certainly your book, and not mine, so make it exactly as you please,– I will admit that in most of the arguments between us, you have turned out to be right, but sometime, in some way, the original "In Our Time" pieces ought to be printed consecutively, so that they could be read in that way.[2] I agree that the big thing is that you should go on writing while it goes well, and anyhow that the important book is the one that is not done.– Still we ought to get out "In Our Time" not later than October, so if it comes in right, get it fixed the way you want.

. . . . .

. . . . .

I'll tell you, Ernest, I think Scott is in a bad way, on account of Zelda. She has evidently been desperately sick, and I infer on the edge of insanity,– if not beyond it. In very recent and brief letter, he says, "Zelda is still sick as Hell" and he speaks of himself as "somewhat harassed and anxious about life." I wouldn't quote these phrases to anyone else but you, but you ought to know about it. He does not like to admit—at least to me—that he is worried, and when he does, there is no doubt of it. I sometimes even think of going over there,– but

I never could do anything with him anyhow,– and anyhow, what's to be done? Of course he can't work in these circumstances. I shall certainly give him your messages, anyway.

Remembrances to Pauline.
Always yours

*Notes*

1. 330 words have been omitted from this letter.
2. Perkins refers to the 1924 Paris edition *in our time,* which consisted of vignettes. They were printed as interchapters in the 1925 Boni & Liveright edition *In Our Time* and in the 1930 Scribners edition.

▲ ▼ ▲

To: Perkins                  *Grand Hotel Bellevue letterhead*
From: Wolfe                  *ALS, 2 pp. Princeton*

Geneva Aug 18, 1930

Dear Mr. Perkins: Will you please have Mr Darrow[1] send me, at his convenience, a statement of whatever money is due me? I shall not write any more books and since I must begin to make other plans for the future, I should like to know how much money I will have.[2] I want to thank you and Scribner's very sincerely for your kindness to me, and I shall hope Someday to resume and continue a friendship which has meant a great deal to me.

I hope this finds you well, and entirely recovered from the trouble you had that took you to Baltimore. Please get a good vacation and a rest away from the heat and confusion of New York.

Yours Faithfully,
Tom Wolfe.

I have stopped all mail by telegraph, but my mail will be held for me at the Guaranty Trust Co, Paris, and that will be my address.

*Notes*

1. Whitney Darrow, chief financial officer for Charles Scribner's Sons.
2. This decision resulted from Wolfe's response to the British reviews of *Look Homeward, Angel.*

▲ ▼ ▲

To: Wolfe
From: Perkins                  *CC, 2 pp. Princeton*

Aug. 28, 1930

Dear Tom:

If I really believed you would be able to stand by your decision, your letter would be a great blow to me. I cannot believe it, though. If anyone were ever destined to write, that one is you. As for the English reviews, I saw one from an important source which was adverse,– though it recognized the high talent displayed. It argued that the book was at fault because it was chaotic and that the function of an artist is to impose <u>order</u>. That was the only review that could be called unfavorable, and as I say, it recognized that the book showed great talent. Otherwise the reviews—and I must have seen all the really important ones— were very fine.

For heaven's sake write me again. I am sending you herewith a royalty report showing the money due.

Always and anxiously yours,

▲ ▼ ▲

| | |
|---|---|
| *To: Perkins* | *ca. September 1, 1930* |
| *From: Fitzgerald* | *ALS, 2 pp. Princeton* |

Geneva, Switzerland

Dear Max:

All the world seems to end up in this flat and antiseptic smelling land—with an overlay of flowers. Tom Wolfe is the only man I've met here who isn't sick or hasn't sickness to deal with. You have a great find in him—what he'll do is incalculable. He has a deeper culture than Ernest and more vitality, if he is slightly less of a poet that goes with the immense surface he wants to cover. Also he lacks Ernests quality of a stick hardened in the fire—he is more susceptible to the world. John Bishop told me he needed advice about cutting ect, but after reading his book I thought that was nonsense. He strikes me as a man who should be let alone as to length, if he has to be published in five volumes. I liked him enormously.

I was sorry of course about Zelda's stories[1]—possibly they mean more to me than is implicit to the reader who doesn't know from what depths of misery and effort they sprang. One of them, I think now, would be incomprehensible without a Waste-Land footnote. She has those series of eight portraits that attracted so much attention in <u>College Humor</u>[2] and I think in view of the success of Dotty Parkers <u>Laments</u>[3] (25,000 copies) I think a book might be got together for next Spring if Zelda can add a few more during the winter.

Wasn't that a nice tribute to C.S. from Mencken in the Mercury?[4]

The royalty advance or the national debt as it might be called shocked me. The usual vicious circle is here—I am now exactly $3000. ahead which means 2 months on the Encyclopedia.[5] I'd prefer to have all above the $10,000 paid back to you off my next story (in October). You've been so damn nice to me.

Zelda is almost well. The doctor says she can never drink again (not that drink in any way contributed to her collapse), and that I must not drink anything, not even wine, for a year, because drinking in the past was one of the things that haunted her in her delerium.

Do please send me things like Wolfe's book when they appear. Is Ernest's book a history of bull-fighting? I'm sending you a curious illiterate ms written by a chasseur at my bank here. Will you skim it + see if any parts, like the marines in Central America, are interesting as pure data? And return it, if not, directly to him? You were absolutely right about the dollar books—it's a preposterous idea and I think the author's league went crazy[6]

Always Yours                    Scott

[*In left margin*] This illness has cost me a fortune—hence that telegram in July. The biggest man in Switzerland gave all his time to her— + saved her reason by a split second.

## Notes

1. Fitzgerald had sent Perkins three of Zelda Fitzgerald's short stories, which Perkins rejected on August 5, 1930: ". . . they show an astonishing power of expression, and have and convey a curiously effective and strange quality.– But they are for a selected audience, and not a large one, and the magazine thinks that on that account, they cannot use them." These stories were not published.

2. A series of stories published as by F. Scott and Zelda Fitzgerald.

3. *Laments for the Living* (1930).

4. "An American Publisher," *American Mercury,* 20 (August 1930): 408. Of Charles Scribner II, who had died on April 19, 1930, Mencken wrote: "Just as, in his earlier days, he was quick to combine his fortunes with those of Robert Louis Stevenson, James M. Barrie, Thomas Nelson Page, Henry James and John Galsworthy, and, a bit later on, with those of such a revolutionary as James Huneker, so he was ready, at seventy, to see the virtues of such youngsters as F. Scott Fitzgerald, Thomas Boyd, Ring Lardner and Ernest Hemingway."

5. Fitzgerald ironically referred to his novel in progress as *The Encyclopaedia Britannica.*

6. In spring 1930, four publishers—Doubleday, Doran; Simon & Schuster; Farrar & Rinehart; and Coward-McCann—announced plans to sell popular books for $1.00 a copy rather than for the standard $2.00 or $2.50 per copy. The price reduction was supported by the Authors' League on the grounds that lower prices would increase sales of books and thus improve writers' royalty income. Ten major publishing houses— including Charles Scribner's Sons—refused to cut prices on their books.

▲ ▼ ▲

*To: Wolfe*
*From: Perkins*                    *TLS, 4 pp. Harvard*

Sept. 10, 1930

Dear Tom:

I wrote you very hurriedly at the end of August: I was then on the edge of a ten days' vacation which is now ended. I hoped when I got back there might be another letter telling me you felt differently than in your last, and I have had that letter on my mind ever since you wrote it. I could not clearly make out why you had come to your decision, and surely you will have to change it;– but certainly there never was a man who had made more of an impression on the best judges with a single book, and at so early an age. Certainly you ought not to be affected by a few unfavorable reviews—even apart from the overwhelming number of extremely and excitedly enthusiastic reviews.– By the way, Scott Fitzgerald wrote me how much better things were with him now;– but most of his letter was taken up with you. I daresay it would be a good thing if you could avoid him at present, but he was immensely impressed with you, and with the book,– and however you may regard him as a writer, he is certainly a very sensitive and sure judge of writers.– Not that there is any further need of confirmation with respect to you. There is no doubt of your very great possibilities,– nor for that matter of the great accomplishment of the "Angel."

Somewhere, perhaps to Jack, you referred to a young man of our friend Madeleine's having run you down and taken observations.[1] I daresay this was not pleasant, but I have seen the letter he wrote her—she came in with it—and it was extremely interesting. He also has great admiration for you, and he quoted some of your sayings which I could recognize as authentic, and which were extremely discerning. There was one about Scott.

It seems rather futile to write this letter in view of your having stopped all communications. I hope somehow it will break through to you. If you do not write me some good news pretty soon, I shall have to start out on a spying expedition myself. You know it has been said before that one has to pay somehow for everything one has or gets, and I can see that among your penalties are attacks of despair,– as they have been among the penalties great writers have generally had to pay for their talent.

Please do write me.

Always your friend,
Maxwell Perkins

*Note*

1. In a August 18, 1930, letter to John Hall Wheelock, Wolfe mentioned that his privacy in Montreux, Switzerland, had been violated by several people, including a young man employed by Wolfe's literary agent, Madeleine Boyd.

▲▼▲

*To: Perkins*                    *September 13, 1930. Freiburg, Germany*
*From: Wolfe*                          *Wire. Princeton*

WORKING AGAIN EXCUSE LETTER WRITING YOU
TOM ROLFE

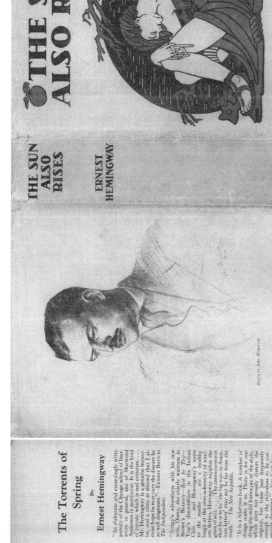

Dust jacket for Hemingway's first Scribners novel, published in 1926 (Speiser and Easterling-Hallman Foundation Collection of Ernest Hemingway, Thomas Cooper Library, University of South Carolina)

Dust jacket for the book-length parody Perkins published in 1926 to acquire *The Sun Also Rises* (Speiser and Easterling-Hallman Foundation Collection of Ernest Hemingway, Thomas Cooper Library, University of South Carolina)

Dust jacket for Hemingway's 1932 "Baedeker of the bullfight" (Speiser and Easterling-Hallman Foundation Collection of Ernest Hemingway, Thomas Cooper Library, University of South Carolina)

Dust jacket for Hemingway's second novel, published in 1929 (Speiser and Easterling-Hallman Foundation Collection of Ernest Hemingway, Thomas Cooper Library, University of South Carolina)

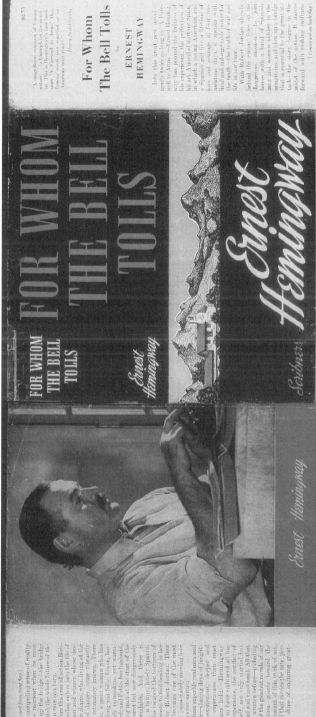

Dust jacket for Hemingway's 1940 novel of the Spanish Civil War, the copy inscribed to Fitzgerald (Matthew J. and Arlyn Bruccoli Collection of F. Scott Fitzgerald, Thomas Cooper Library, University of South Carolina)

Dust jacket for Fitzgerald's first novel, published in 1920 (Matthew J. and Arlyn Bruccoli Collection of F. Scott Fitzgerald, Thomas Cooper Library, University of South Carolina)

Dust jacket for Fitzgerald's third novel, published in 1925. It is the most valuable dust jacket in American literature. Dust jacket art by Francis Cugat (Matthew J. and Arlyn Bruccoli Collection of F. Scott Fitzgerald, Thomas Cooper Library, University of South Carolina).

# TENDER IS THE NIGHT
*by* F. SCOTT FITZGERALD

This is Mr. Fitzgerald's first novel since the publication of "The Great Gatsby." That fine novel was unanimously acclaimed, and, long after its publication, Rebecca West said: "It has not been superceded in the common mind by better books, simply by more books." In "The Autobiography of Alice V. Toklas," Gertrude Stein said it "really created for the public the new generation" and that Fitzgerald would be real when many of his well-known contemporaries were forgotten. T. S. Eliot called it "the first step forward in the American novel since Henry James."

Now, in "Tender Is the Night," Mr. Fitzgerald takes another step forward, resumes his place among the leading American novelists of today, and supersedes "The Great Gatsby" with a book that is a complete departure from what has been the current fashion in novels.

The leading characters are Richard Diver, a young American psychiatrist, his rich and beautiful wife, Nicole, and Rosemary Hoyt, a young motion-picture star. It is all glitter and glamour, and nothing is more beautiful and satisfying than the opulent household of the Divers. But the reader soon senses that lurking behind the superficial beauty are horror and brutality. In the succeeding chapters the author savagely reveals the pseudo-sophistication and barbarism that underlie the smooth beautiful surface of the life of rich Americans and "intellectuals" abroad.

Basically, the story belongs to Dick Diver, whose career was thwarted and his genius numbed through his marriage to Nicole, child of a raw and rich Middle-Western family. The cause and development of this marriage lie at the bottom of the plot, and "Tender Is the Night" is one of the few novels which is completely based upon abnormal psychology and reveals the strangeness of psychoses and their treatment.

The plot is closely knit, the characters superbly portrayed and developed, the drama indescribably tense and fraught with emotion, the writing the best that has yet come from Fitzgerald's pen.

CHARLES SCRIBNER'S SONS, NEW YORK

---

F. SCOTT FITZGERALD

TENDER IS THE NIGHT

TENDER IS THE NIGHT

F. SCOTT FITZGERALD

SCRIBNERS

---

$2.50

Tender Is the Night
A Romance by
F. SCOTT FITZGERALD

To the generation that was young when "This Side of Paradise" came out, the name Fitzgerald is still perhaps associated with adolescence, and with the Jazz Age to which he gave the name in his "Tales of the Jazz Age." The author was twenty-two when he wrote "This Side of Paradise." He had attained to full maturity when he wrote "The Great Gatsby." The estimates of his present position and promise are suggested by these more recent opinions:

**T. S. Eliot:** "I have been waiting impatiently for another book by Mr. Scott Fitzgerald; with more eagerness and curiosity than I should feel towards the work of any of his contemporaries, except that of Mr. Ernest Hemingway."

**H. L. Mencken:** "His whole attitude has changed from that of a brilliant improvisateur to that of a painstaking and conscientious artist."

**Paul Rosenfeld:** "Not a contemporary American serves as thoroughly in every fiber the tempo of privileged post-adolescent America."

All who truly care about the future of American letters have awaited Mr. Fitzgerald's new novel with great expectations. Here these expectations are fulfilled.

A description of "Tender Is the Night" appears on the back of this jacket.

Dust jacket for Fitzgerald's 1934 fourth novel (Matthew J. and Arlyn Bruccoli Collection of F. Scott Fitzgerald, Thomas Cooper Library, University of South Carolina)

The dust jacket for Wolfe's 1929 first novel printed an excerpt from the author's "Note for the Publisher's Reader" in place of the publisher's usual flap copy (Rare Books and Special Collections, Thomas Cooper Library, University of South Carolina).

the
story of a
NOVEL
by
THOMAS WOLFE

author of "Of Time and the River"

•

How does a great novel come into being? What is its genesis? How does it develop? What are the sensations of a literary artist as characters take form beneath his pen? These and similar questions often come to the mind of every reader of fiction — and they have never been answered with such frankness, honesty, and conviction as in this brief "credo" of an outstanding American novelist. Here is the soul of an artist laid bare, with all his hopes, fears, doubts, and aspirations. But it is not only about Mr. Wolfe's own books — it is about all writing and all American writing especially, a book that every one directly interested in the art of fiction must read, and that every one of the many thousands who enjoyed Mr. Wolfe's novels will find permeated by the same "insatiable and enormous eagerness in life and living" that placed the stamp of genius on his novels.

The subject matter of this book created a literary sensation when it appeared in The Saturday Review of Literature. It inspired an editorial on Mr. Wolfe and his writing in The New York Times, John Chamberlain devoted his column to it, and it attracted favorable comment from critics all over the country.

The Story Of A Novel
Thomas Wolfe

the story of a NOVEL ═ Wolfe ═ Scribners

"In these days when some of our best writers are tired or short of breath it is thrilling to contemplate and to read the teeming novels of Thomas Wolfe."
BURTON RASCOE in The New York Herald Tribune

OF TIME AND THE RIVER

"He gives you an experience you can't just file away under Miscellaneous.... For decades we have not had eloquence like his in American writing.... At his best he is incomparable.... Of Time and the River is a wonderful, flashing, gleaming riot of characters, caricatures, metaphors, apostrophes, declamations, tropes, dreams."
CLIFTON FADIMAN in The New Yorker

LOOK HOMEWARD, ANGEL

"As interesting and powerful a book as has ever been made out of the circumstances of provincial American life. It is at once enormously sensuous, full of the joy and gusto of life, and shrinkingly sensitive, torn with revulsion and disgust."
MARGARET WALLACE in The New York Times

by Thomas Wolfe
Published by CHARLES SCRIBNER'S SONS

From Death
to Morning

Fourteen Stories by
THOMAS WOLFE

•

"These stories are Mr. Wolfe's peculiar property; they belong to him with the certainty of style and introspection — no other can match them: and they show the most striking literary personality of our day."
PETER MONRO JACK in The New York Times

"What stories they are! ... They are cumulative evidence of his right to be classed as one of the great American novelists, if not the greatest."
Philadelphia Ledger

"Reading the work of this genius is like listening to Wagner or watching the aurora borealis. It is an experience beside which the mill run of most fiction seems trivial and insignificant."
The Chicago Tribune

Dust jacket for Wolfe's 1936 account of writing Of Time and the River, which resulted in the charge that he could not write without Perkins's assistance (North Carolina Collection, Wilson Library, University of North Carolina at Chapel Hill)

Dust jacket for Wolfe's 1935 second novel, his best-selling book (North Carolina Collection, Wilson Library, University of North Carolina at Chapel Hill)

Wolfe with the manuscripts and typescripts for *Of Time and the River* in 1934 (North Carolina Collection, Wilson Library, University of North Carolina at Chapel Hill)

▲▼▲

*To: Wolfe*
*From: Perkins*                          *TLS, 1 p. Harvard*

Sept. 27, 1930

Dear Tom:

For Heaven's sake send us some word. I got your cable which said you were writing,– and said you were working. But no letter has come, and I am as worried again as I was before. I wish you would come back here now and live in the country. I could show you some fine country that would suit you. Please do write me the moment you get this. Send some word if only a postcard.

Ever yours,
Maxwell Perkins

▲▼▲

*To: Perkins*
*From: Wolfe*                           *ALS, 34 pp.[1] Princeton*

London, Tues Dec 9
1930

Dear Mr. Perkins:

. . . . .

. . . . .

. . . . . I want you to know this: I believe I have acted decently and honestly to everyone—certainly I have tried to—if you hear scurrilous and slanderous stories about me, about any action of mine, about anything to do with me spread by any of the ten million envenomed and reptilian Madame B—ds[2] who walk the streets of this earth full of hate, malice, and poison, put them down as lies: I have been in a hell of a jam this last year or so, and during the last six or eight months I have sweated out blood and agony—but I have behaved all right: I have done what I thought I had to do, and what people asked me to do, I have never betrayed or deserted anyone—in the end, if anyone gets betrayed or deserted it will be me. I have done the best I could, I have done some things badly, but please understand that I have behaved all right: if anyone thinks I have not let him come forward and say so to my face—otherwise let them hold their tongues in fairness, and someday they will know I have been square. You know me much better now than any of these people, you know what a nest of lies and venom New York is, for God's sake make any judgment or opinion on me for yourself, and out of our own relation——you are my friend, and one of the two or three people that I would not let any one in the world say a word against, so until I get back at least don't listen to opinions and judgments from

<u>people who</u> don't know a God damned thing about me, whether Scott Fitzgerald, Madame B, or anyone else.[3]— Please dont be alarmed at all this, or think I've gone suddenly mad—there's so much I want to say to you and so little I can say in a letter that part of it comes in convulsions and bursts—I seem to have to spend a maddening amount of time talking about dentists, and making foolish answers—I should like to tell you about the book, but I'll have to write another letter But here is the title, at any rate, and it seems to me to be a good and beautiful title and to say what I want it to say—if anything about it puzzles you I'll try to interpret all of it for you next time. Here it is:

The October Fair

or

Time and the River: <u>a Vision:</u>

Italics { The Son, The Lover, and The Wanderer;
The Child, The Mistress, and The Woman;
The Sea, The City, and The Earth.

"one generation passeth away,
and another generation cometh;
but the earth abideth for ever"

for title

page

Part One

ANTAEUS

"Who knoweth the spirit of man that goeth upward, and the spirit of the beast that goeth downward to the earth?"[4]—(small italics for title page of <u>Antaeus</u>)

(If this <u>argument</u> seems bad or inadvisable we wont use it. It gives a kind of key)

Argument: of the Libyan giant, the brother of Polyphemus, the one eyed, and the son of Gaea and Poseidon, whom he hath never seen, and through his father, the grandson of Cronos and Rhea, whom he remembereth. He contendeth with all who seek to pass him by, he searcheth alway for his father, he crieth out: "Art thou my father? Is it thou?" And he wrestleth with that man, and he riseth from each fall with strength redoubled, for his strength cometh up out of the earth, which is his mother. Then cometh against him Heracles, who contendeth with him, who discovereth the secret of his strength, who lifteth him from the earth whence his might ariseth, and subdueth him. But from afar now, in his agony, he heareth the sound of his fathers foot: he will be saved for his father cometh!

Now, don't get alarmed at all this and think I'm writing a Greek Myth. All of this is never mentioned once the Story gets under way, but it is a magnificent fable, and I have soaked myself in it over a year now: it says what I want to say, and it gives the most magnificent plot and unity to my book. The only other way in which the Antaeus legend is mentioned directly is in the titles to the various parts which are, tentatively, at present— ① Antaeus, ② Heracles, (or Faust or Helen, ③ Poseidon

To give you the key to all these symbols and people—Antaeus of course, is a real person, that he is in me but he is <u>not</u> me as the fellow in the first book was supposed to be—he is to me what Hamlet or Faust may have been to their authors—Thank God, I have begun to create in the way I want to—it is more completely <u>autobiographic</u> than anything I have ever thought of, much <u>more</u> than the first one—but it is also completely <u>fictitious</u>—nobody can identify me with Antaeus—whose real name is David Hawke, but who is called Monkey Hawke—except to say. "He has put himself into this character." It is a magnificent story, it makes use of all the things I have seen and known about, and it is like a fable—The other symbols are:

Heracles, who is the City: Poseidon, who is the Sea, eternal wandering, eternal change, eternal movement—but who is also a real person (<u>never</u> called Poseidon) of course, the father of Monkey Hawke, whom he has never seen, and whom, I have decided he shall never see, but who is near him at the end of the book, and who saves him (the idea that hangs over the book from first to last is that every man is searching for his father)—It is immensely long, I am bringing the Antaeus (which has two parts back home with me) and parts of the second —the City scenes are already written. The woman in various forms, at different times, is Gaea, Helen, or Demeter—but these things are never told you, and the story itself is direct and simple, given shape by this legend, and by the idea I told you—but it is also tremendously varied—it gives the histories of my people and it reconstructs old time—the idea of time—the lost and forgotten moments of peoples lives, the strange brown light of old time (i.e—America, say, in 1893— photographs of people coming across Brooklyn Bridge, the ships of the Hamburg American packet co, baseball players with moustaches, men coming home to lunch at noon in small towns, red barns, old circus posters) and many other phases of time is over all the book. I'd like to tell you of a chapter I'm now writing in the Second part of <u>Antaeus</u>—the chapter is called Cronos and Rhea (or perhaps simply <u>Time and the River</u>—that means <u>Memory and Change</u>)—my conviction is that a native has the whole consciousness of his people and nation in him—that he knows everything about it—every sight sound and memory of the people—don't get worried: I think this is going to be all right—you see, I <u>know</u> now past any denial, that <u>that</u> is what being an American or being anything means: it is not a government, or the Revolutionary War, or the Monroe doctrine—it is the ten million seconds and moments of your life—the shapes you see, the sounds you hear, the food you eat, the colour and texture of the earth you live in—I tell you <u>this</u> is what it is, and this is what homesickness is, and by God I'm the world's champion authority on the subject at present. <u>Cronos and Rhea</u> occurs on board an Atlantic liner—all the Americans returning home—and the whole intolerable memory of exile and nostalgia comes with it: it begins like a chant—first the smashing enormous music of the American names—first the names of the state—California, Texas, Oregon, Nebraska, Idaho, and the Two Dakotas—then the names of the Indian tribes—the Pawnees, the Cherokees, the Seminoles, the Penobscots, the Tuscaroras, etc—then the names of railways—the Pennsylvania, the Baltimore and Ohio, the Great Northwestern, the Rock Island, the Santa Fe, etc—then the names of the railway millionaires—the Vanderbilts, the Astors, the Harrimans; then the names of the great hoboes—Oakland Red, Fargo Pete, Dixie Joe, Iron Mike, Nigger Dick, the Jersey Dutchman etc—(the names of some of the great wanderers i.e)—then the great names of the rivers (the rivers and the sea standing for movement and wandering against the fixity of the earth)—the Monongahela, the Rappahannock, the Colorado, the Tennessee, the Rio Grande, the Missouri—when I get to the Mississippi I start the first of the stories of wandering and return—the woman floating down the river with her husband in flood time tells it, it is good—the whole thing is this pattern of meaning and narration—don't get alarmed, I think it's all right and fits in perfectly, I have plenty of straight story anyway I have told you too much and too little—I have had to scrawl this down and haven't time to explain dozens of things—but please dont be worried —its not anarchy, its a perfectly unified but enormous plan. I want to write again and tell you some more, especially about the last scene in Poseidon—it is the only fabulous scene in the book, he never sees his father but he hears the sound of his foot the thunder of horses on a beach (Poseidon and his horses) the moon drives out of clouds, he sees a print of a foot that can belong only to his father since it is like his own, the sea surges across the beach and erases the print, he cries out <u>Father</u> and from the sea far out, and faint upon the wind, a great voice answers "My Son!" That is briefly the end as I see it—but cant tell you anything about it now—the rest of the story is natural and wrought out of human experience—Polyphemus, by the way, the one eyed brother of Antaeus, represents the principle of sterility that hates life—i.e. waste landerism, futility-ism, one-eyedism (also a character in the book).

I don't know whether you can make anything out of this or not—I have worked all night it is 10:30 oclock as I finish this on the morning of Tues Dec 9, there is a fog outside that you can cut, you can't see across the street, I am dog tired—I want to come home when I know I have this thing by the well known balls—write me if you think its a good idea, but say nothing to anyone.

. . . . .

. . . . .

As Ever Faithfully,

Tom Wolfe

The Guaranty Trust Co

50 Pall Mall

London

<u>Address again</u>

Fred W. Wolfe

48 Spruce St

Asheville

N.C.

Don't tell anyone about this letter—If I've talked foolishness I'd rather keep it between us—at ten in the morning after being up all night you're not sane.

## Notes

1. 935 words have been omitted from this letter.

2. Madeleine Boyd had placed *Look Homeward, Angel* with Scribners; after Wolfe discharged her over mishandling of his royalties, she incurred his permanent enmity by claiming continuing commissions on this novel.

3. In his notebooks for 1930–31, Wolfe recorded his interpretation of Perkins's motivation for arranging a meeting between Wolfe and Fitzgerald:

> I will tell you a little story:
> There was once a young man who came to have a feeling of great trust and devotion for an older man. He thought that this older man had created liberty and hope for him. He thought that this older man was brave and loyal. Then he found that this older man had sent him to a drunken and malicious fellow, who tried to injure and hurt his work in every way possible. He found moreover that this older man had sent him to this drunk in order to get the drunk's "opinion" of him. That is the real end of the story (*Notebooks,* p. 511).

4. Ecclesiastes 3:21.

▲▼▲

*To: Perkins*

*From: Wolfe*                                           *ALS, 47 pp. Princeton*

London, Jan 19

1931

Dear Mr Perkins: You ask me to write to you and then I inundate you with long letters. But I have tried not to be too difficult or too much trouble: if you are willing to take the trouble with me now you may help me do something that will keep me forever.

I want you to help me do a very few simple physical things: I want to come back to my country in another month or so without anyone but yourself knowing about it; I want to find a quiet place to live in, and to live and work there in almost complete isolation for <u>at least</u> three months; during that time I should like to see and talk to you whenever you have time for it, and if there are a few simple kind and perfectly un-literary people that I could meet, I should like to meet them. Do you think it would be possible to do these things? It is of vital importance to me now that this should be so—I ask you humbly and earnestly to help me if you can. The isolation and privacy should certainly not be hard to get: I have achieved them almost perfectly here in England—some people say you cannot in America, as long as there is some little rag and bone of reputation + scandal that the curs can gnaw at—but I say that you can, and I'm going to have them. The reason I want to see one or two people is because I like people and need them, and this solitude has begun to prey upon me, I talk to myself, and when I sleep my mind continues to function with a kind of horrible comatose intelligence. I hear strange sounds and noises from my youth, and from America. I hear the million strange and secret sounds of Time.

Once you told me of a member of your family who had been "sort of wild" but who had now come through, chiefly, I believe because of your mother's intelligence and subtlety in dealing with him. Forgive me for mentioning this, but I mention it now because you told me you had never tried to find too definitely or exactly what he had done, because that kind of knowledge about a person embarassed you. But I think you do find out about a person more indirectly —sometimes I have talked to you about things I knew about by using a hypothetical way of speech.

—i.e. "If a certain person did so and so and if a person did so-and-so—what—" etc. But I suppose you know the two very ancient jokes about the young fellow who was suffering from one of the <u>physical</u> diseases of love, and who went to see his physician about it:

"I have a friend"—he began "All right, son." the doctor said, "take your friend out of your pants and we'll look at him" —or that other one who craftily asked his doctor "if it was possible for a man to get a venereal disease in a W. C."—"Yes, but that's a hell of a place to take a woman."[1]

You cant lie to your doctor, and you ought not to beat about the bush with your physician, and at the present moment, I am asking you to try to be my physician—I am not asking you to cure me of my sickness, because you can't do that, I must do it myself, but I am very earnestly asking you to help me to do certain things that will make my cure easier and less painful, at the present time, I am convalescent, but, as you know, in convalescence, you have occasional periods of relapse when everything sinks—vitality, hope, strength—and it is then that the patient must fight like hell. Well, I am a good boy and I have

fought like hell. I am not using simply an extended metaphor about this convalescence business, I'm speaking literally—just as the diseases of the spirit are
much more terrible than the diseases of the flesh, so their cure is more painful
and difficult. I have just passed through a two day period of relapse, which has
been attended by fever and fits of vomiting (physical facts, this time). This
relapse was caused by the visit of one of those bubonic rats of the spirit who live
by the destruction of others and who exist in such great numbers in New York.

So, here, bluntly and directly, is the cause of my present trouble, which I
think you may help me with: When I was twenty-four years old I met a woman
who was almost forty and I fell in love with her. I can not tell you here the long
and complicated story of my relations with this woman—they extended over a
period of five years, they began with me lightly and exultantly—at first I was a
young fellow who had got an elegant and fashionable woman for a mistress, and
I was pleased about it; then, without knowing how, when, or why, I was desperately in love with the woman, then the thought of her began to posess and
dominate every moment of my life, I wanted to own, posess, and devour her; I
became insanely jealous; I began to get horribly sick inside: and then all physical love, desire, passion ended completely—but I still loved the woman, I could
not endure her loving anyone else or having physical relations with anyone else,
and my madness and jealousy ate at me like a poison, like all horrible sterility
and barrenness. Twice I got away from New York and came abroad in an effort
to end it, and when I came back I would resume my life with the woman again.
I can  not say much about her here—and I am saying not one word of criticism
of her, the woman always swore she loved me and no one else, she always
insisted on her fidelity, and certainly she must have felt some strong passion,
because for years she would come every day, and stay with me, cook for me, and
do many lovely and beautiful things.

The anatomy of jealousy is the most complicated and tortuous anatomy on
earth: to find its causes, to explore its sources is more difficult and mysterious
than it was for the ancients to probe the sources of the Nile: people usually
attribute to it one cause, but comes from a terrible and bewildering complication of causes; there is usually in it the feeling of inferiority, induced by some
terrible shame, distrust, and humiliation of the past; there is in it also the horrible doubt that arises in the conflict of fact and ideal belief—it is true, for
example, that not war, Darwin, or science has destroyed the ancient conception
of God, so much as has the life of the modern city: the inhuman scenery, the
stony architecture, and the vast hordes of swarming maggots—crawling, paw-
ing, cursing, cheating, pushing, betraying, dying or living, swearing or pleading!
—the spectacle of the subway rush hour, for example, is sufficient to destroy all
ideas of man's personal destiny, his personal conversations with God, his personal importance and salvation. So it is with the other Ideal Beliefs—the beliefs

in Courage, Honor, Faithfulness, and Love—in that great stain of crawling filth
which is the city's life—that stain which is so horrible and yet has so much
beauty in it—we see the infinite repetitions of lust, cruelty, and sterility, of
hatred, defeat, and darkness, of gouging and killing!— We see, moreover, the
horrible chemistry of flesh, of millions of pounds and tons of flesh; we see flesh
soothed, or irritated, or maddened, or appeased in a million different patterns
daily, and our belief fails: how can one memory live here where a million memories pass before us in a second? How can one face be cherished and remembered out of the million faces? How can one grief, one joy, endure among ten
million griefs and joys? How, finally, can love endure here?—where treason can
be consummated in 30 seconds? How can faith live, where a million faiths have
died? If we surrender to this despair we are lost—the end of it all is futility and
death — at its cheapest, gin-party Van Vechtenism[2] or Madeleine Boydism,
which is not sinister as it wants to be, only cheap—as if the Saturday Evening
Post had suddenly turned nasty; at its worst it probably results in the death of
such a man as your friend, Mr. Brooks.[3] But here is the situation: I came away
finally, over eight months ago. I did not want to come, but I yielded to what
her friends wanted for her, and what it seemed to me would be best: I wrote her
from the boat, but since then I have not written her. The woman wrote and
cabled me often during the first four months, and then, quite properly, stopped.
I cannot tell you what distress and torment these letters + cables caused me—I
would get letters signed in her blood, and cables which said she was going to
die. Finally, about 3 mos. ago I got a cable which said:

"No word from you. Life impossible. Desperate. Cannot go on living like
this. Are you willing to accept the consequences?" For a few days, I thought I
would go mad. But I did not write or cable. Each day I would go for mail in
the most horrible state of nerves, wondering if I should see some cable which
carried the dreadful news. I longed for <u>no</u> news and I hoped for <u>some</u> news—
but nothing came, and that was almost worse than ever. I imagined that she had
died or killed herself, and that her embittered and griefstricken friends and family were saying nothing to me. I began to read the American papers for news. I
would buy the filthy rag they print in Paris—the Herald—and be afraid each
day that it would contain news of her death by leaping from a window, I began
to read the horrible mortuary columns of The New York Times, looking first in
that dense double column of names for one that began with <u>B</u>.

But then, in the theatrical columns of that same paper, at just about the date
when I feared this tragic act had happened, I read an account of a great success
she had scored in the theatre,[4] I met a man who asked me if I knew her, and
said he had seen her, looking very radiant and happy at a "party" in New York
several weeks before, other people wrote me telling me how well happy and pros-
perous she was looking, in Paris people would seek out café tables next to me

and the women, whom I did not know, would begin discussing the lady and me, hinting new interests for her very loudly so that I would not lose the benefit, and finally about a month ago (the middle of December) her cables began again: there had been two months silence, during which she had scored a great success—perhaps that had worn off again: anyway she had decided to begin dying again and I had done it. She said she was "desperate, hold out your hand to me in my hour of need. Impossible to face new year, I stood by you in bad years why have you deserted me? I love you and am faithful unto death, pain I bear too great to endure"—etc, etc. There were 8 or 10 of these messages: I felt the most enormous relief to know she was still alive + kicking, I cabled back, I asked her if it was fair to cable such messages when I was alone in a foreign land trying to write, I told her not to speak of hard years, that mine was harder than this, that I had no money, that her dentists + my family were getting it, and that if I didn't get peace and quiet to work now I was done for. She cabled that her family had "lost everything"—it pleases her to feel poor now, but while my family is living in actual want, hers is living in an expensive hotel apartment, they have two cars and a magnificent house in the country, and her sister is abroad now stopping at the Ritz in London. If this is poverty, then God knows what you would call what millions of people in America are enduring this winter. Her sister came to see me here in London, her sister hates me, but was unable to keep away out of bitter curiosity to see how I felt and how I was standing up under this hammering. Her sister made several shifty and hinting remarks about her, in order to draw me out, and of course I talked with complete frankness and honesty: I was too agitated and too horribly nervous to attempt concealment— I told this woman that it could not possibly be news to her that I had been in love with her sister and that she had been my mistress, I told her this could not possibly have gone on for years, with the woman coming to my place day after day without the family knowing it—at this she began to hedge and evade, saying she had suspected things, but that they knew nothing—in spite of the fact that a cable from the woman a few days before had said they knew all about it. Her sister at first, before these avowals of mine, had said she had been worried and upset and they knew something was wrong: now she said she had never been happier or calmer or more joyful and successful than this Fall: I then asked if her sister was a woman whose word could be believed—she said "yes"—and I demanded why, then, I should be driven mad by these cables threatening death, misery, and destruction. To this she made no reply but presently she said I must not take these things "too seriously"—that her sister was an "emotional woman" and might "think she meant these things" for five minutes or so, but that they were really not important. If this is true, I think it is one of the vilest and basest things I have ever heard, and to believe that a person that I have loved so dearly, and who has professed her love, faithfulness and faith for me so often, could deliberately and trivially do this ruinous and damnable thing to a young man without influence or money who is leading a desperately lonely life abroad, trying to get on with his work—this may strike her friends as an amusing thing, but I hope to God it seems to you to be a vile, cruel, and cowardly act. You may wonder why I come to you with this: my answer is that if I cannot come to you with it, there is no one in the world I can come to. I can not tell you what horrible pain and suffering this thing has caused me: I would wake up in the morning with a feeling of nausea in my guts, and my horror and fear would grow all day long until I went to the bank for mail—later, I would sometimes have to vomit from physical sickness. When her sister left the other night I vomited for two hours, I have lost two days on account of it, but tonight I am getting to my work again. But I am all right in spite of this weakness; during the past 3 mos (a little more) that I have been in this place I have written over 100000 words on my book—I have made myself work some time in the most ghastly state— but I have worked—and it has taken guts. I am a brave man, and I like myself: I am a good fellow, and I shall always like myself for what I did here, and I hope you like me, too, for I honor and respect you, and I believe you can help me to save myself. Also, I tell you this: I want to save not only myself, but by doing so, to save something else that is part of me, and without which no one can be saved; I mean my utter and absolute belief in love and in human excellence. No matter what breach of faith, truth, or honesty this woman may be guilty of, I want to come out of this thing with a feeling of love and belief in her—I remember full well countless acts of beauty, loveliness, and tenderness in this woman, there is the most enormous beauty and loveliness in her yet, and if she has learned craft, cunning, and treachery from these rats of the spirit—that is a matter for grief and pity rather than hate. But in this, the most passionate and devastating event of my life, I shall not be devoured at the end by hatred and bitterness and finally by cynicism and indifference. That is what the rats of the soul would like to see, it fits into all the trashiness of Sinister Van Vechtenism, etc—the young fellow who comes to New York, falls in love with a worldly and experienced woman, is made a fool of, and then either destroys himself or becomes one of the rats' club, eagerly awaiting the delightful entry of another visitor into the Spider's Parlor. But this is not going to happen to me— I think, during the early years of this affair, her friends were quite amused at the spectacle of a kid of 24 going around like a madman, eaten up with love and desperation, getting drunk and violent over a woman of 40. But I broke the rules of the game by doing a piece of work that had some little success; at this, their amusement turned to venom, they said I was making the woman unhappy, how badly I treated her, etc—and now, it seems, they are willing to do any dirty trick to destroy my work for the future—if my next book is no good, I assure you they will be immensely pleased; they will then say it is because I left her, etc.

Don't put this down simply to the suspicion and distrust of which I am accused. I admit that I am suspicious and distrustful but, in view of what I have seen during the past five or six years,—I think it is a God damned sane and solid principle to live by. I dont think I have ever mistrusted a man or woman who deserved to be trusted, and if I have lived almost entirely alone, these past eight or ten months it is because it was the only way I knew of meeting this thing. A man who has been sick and is convalescent must "lay low"—he can't play on football teams. In this solitude at present is my power and my way of healing myself—they hate me for it, they can not get at me: her sister venomously re-marked that it was "unnatural" to stay away from people like this, but I think staying away from people who make you vomit, and who hate life and love sterility is very natural: certainly if staying away from Paris Americans, and New York parties is unnatural I shall remain so now to the end of my days. But it is not a fair fight. These people talk of fairness, but they are rich, cunning, and powerful—they are a hundred against one, and I have no money nor influence. I have given this woman six of the best years of my life—madness, passion, good, bad—she had it all. Now, it is a rotten thing to try to ruin me when I must go on and use the little success I have gained. I have been fair—the one boastful thing I ever heard this woman say was that "she always got what she wanted in the end"—her sister repeated it the other day: I think it is a bad thing for any-one to say, it indicates something not to be trusted in people—if, by gentleness, sweetness, tears—by any means—she consciously "gets her way," it is bad and miserable in the end. You can "get your way" with people, but you can not "get your way" with life—she must grow old and die. Also, she has failed this time with me! I shall feel much more dreadful pain over this thing, but I am through. If I go back to her now, I am done for—it means real death—but I shall never go back, and I think she knows it. There are two courses left: one is a deep and abiding love and friendship, and the kind of relation I would like with her—I think this is possible and I am going to try to achieve it. The other to which her friends may counsel her is poison—the desire to "get back," to "show me," to see that rotten and malicious stories reach my ears, to launch out on new loves, to wound me through base trickery, and to [bring] the thing before me all they can. Also, to write lying letters and cables. If this is done, it will be a filthy thing, but I will not be made filthy by it; I am alone now, if I am brave and decent and have faith, and work, all will be well. I must not die. But I need help—such help as a man may hope to receive from a friend,—I turn to you for it now. You know how warmly and gratefully I feel toward Scribner's, but you are the only person there I can turn to. Mr Darrow is a good fellow but he calls me "Tom" when he gets an order for the book, and nods curtly when there are none. Dashiell does not know me and has no belief or faith in my work.

As for Jack, I have the warmest and deepest feeling for him: he is a kind + sensitive man, but he believes more in my defeat than in victory, he says he expects my next book to be good but I think he may rather expect a crash. I like Jack enormously, but I cannot take this to him I turn to you because I feel health and sanity and fortitude in you: try to help me to get away from this loneliness and to find a place in my own country where I can talk to a few people. Pain and sterility does not kill me, but it makes me vomit, and I cannot work while I am vomiting. If this is a frenzied appeal, understand that it is also a real and earnest one. I cannot tell you one tenth or one hundredth of this story, but, so help me God, I have told you the truth, I cannot begin to tell you the horrible pain and despair I have suffered over this.

The rats will say that "it serves him right" but, Mr. Perkins, I have never done anything to deserve this, I have never let anyone down, and at the end I have tried to do the best I could for this woman. I do not really mistrust people, in my heart I trust and believe in them, and I have trust and belief left in this woman even now, and I believe the beautiful part of her will win through in the end. Surely you cannot misunderstand what I have said in this letter; it is plain enough. I am in deep trouble, so deep that I may not get out of it, and I need a friend, I am not putting anything off on anyone, no one can say I have ever tried to get other people to live for me. Your last letter was only a note—well, write me another note: you need not discuss this letter, but if you understand my trouble, say simply that you do, and that you will try to help me.

I wish to God there were someone in the world who thought enough of me to go to see the woman, to ask her now to give me a decent chance for peace and hope in which to do my work. If she has an atom of the love and faith she protests, surely to God she does not want to ruin me now: I do not believe, if someone talked to her, that she would deny the things she has said to me, or have written these letters and cables—surely she is not so base as to lie about that.

Whatever else she has done or wants to do now I can not help, and I have given to this thing all the feeling I have in me—there's no more left. But at any rate, if she will not be my friend, and love me as a friend, she can at least give me a chance to do my work and get some joy and tranquility back into my heart again. I _must_ not be smashed this way at thirty—for God's sake, stand by me now, and I will be all right. The woman is surrounded by friends, wealth, success, luxury—she has a family—I can expect no help from these people: they will not only refuse to help, they will lie, cheat, and aid in anything that will cause me distress and failure. I swear to you that I have told the truth, and for God's sake do not think this is only a long speech: I am in terrible trouble, and I need a friend. This is the first appeal of this sort I have ever made. I do not know what to do, where to turn, but I want to live in my own country, and I want to forget this horrible business entirely. Someday, when we are both I hope, better and calmer, I trust I can see her again and be her friend.

You said that my letters sounded "unhappy." I hope this makes the reason plainer. Write me, please.

Tom Wolfe.

Mr Perkins, if I said anything here that I should not have said, be generous and lenient with me: I want to do what is decent and fair, and if I have spoken bitterly of this woman, please try to understand that she is a very wonderful woman, and I love her dearly, but she must get through this baseness of passion and the flesh which make people do terrible things. I know that there is in this world an excellence that will not compromise and some day I shall find it—when it says "love" it means it, when it says "forever" it does not mean four months—it will not talk of desperation and death unless it means those things, and the end of it will not be ruin and bitterness, but life and beauty.

Now, I shall get on with my work. But write me soon.

Would you like a foreigner's account of Merry England as it is today? They would have reached the second stage of degeneration, I know a dozen people in and out—and an interesting variety of lives it is:

① A Russian doctor, naturalized Englishman, an abortionist, who writes doctors stories. For 2 hrs in the afternoon the ladies come here in droves — what he has told me about it is highly interesting, as is the man.

② Mrs Lavis—my charwoman—she comes, cooks for me, looks after me, and loves me dearly for 14 shillings a week.[5] She is a good soul, and I know all about her sisters, cousins, aunts—the amazing story of her father—her own early life—and her whole philosophy, which is most curious and I think the same as that of the poor people all over England

③ A woman who is a spiritualist and spook writer in Chelsea—she is the daughter of the late Professor Darden?[6]—the gatherings at her house are very curious

④ A nurse in a "crazy house" at Basingstoke—her tales of the inmates and the conditions there.

⑤ A girl who is an alcoholic—merry Eng. Again

⑥ A publisher and his wife and a rich old American who lives with them.

⑦ The English wife of one of the great Russian Soviet Commissary's—this lady I understand has given me an undeserved notoriety[7]

⑧ The Hampstead Heath literary people and the present standard of sexual mawrals in merry England—which the boastful say is lower than at any time since the Restoration: in my opinion the Restoration was not in it.

⑨ Various Russian women, divorced ladies, cooks, bottlewashers, Piccadilly tarts, etc, etc.

No, I have not been entirely blind: the story of this little house in Ebury street and what comes in and out of it day by day might be interesting!

*Notes*

1. The jokes appear in *O Lost,* chapter 12, but were deleted from *Look Homeward, Angel.*
2. Van Vechten wrote novels about sophisticated New Yorkers; one of his best-known novels was *Parties* (1930).
3. Literary historian Van Wyck Brooks (1886–1963).
4. Bernstein designed the set for *Grand Hotel* (1931) by Vicki Baum.
5. She inspired the character Daisy Purvis in "'E, a Recollection," *New Yorker,* July 17, 1937.
6. Unidentified.
7. Ivy Litvinoff, with whom Wolfe had a brief affair. See *Notebooks,* p. 530.

▲ ▼ ▲

*To: Perkins*                         *February 24, 1931. London*
*From: Wolfe*                         *Wire. Princeton*

SAILING EUROPA THURSDAY NEED NO HELP NOW CAN HELP MYSELF MOST WORK SIX MONTHS ALONE BEST WISHES. TOM WOLFE.

▲ ▼ ▲

*To: Perkins*                         *1931. Brooklyn, New York*
*From: Wolfe*                         *ALS, 23 pp. Princeton*

Saturday—Aug 29

Dear Max: Thanks for your note which came this morning. I am glad you wrote me [    ] I have some definite idea of when you expect to see my book, and I can say some things about it that I wanted to say. You say you think I ought to make every conceivable effort to have the manuscript completely finished by the end of September. I know you are not joking and that you mean <u>this</u> September, and not September four, five, or fifteen years from now. Well, there is no remote or possible chance that I will have a completed Mss. of anything that resembles a book this September, and whether I have anything that I would be willing to show anyone next September, or any succeeding one for the next 150 years is at present a matter of the extremest and most painful doubt to me.[1]

I realize that it has been almost two years since my first book was published and that you might reasonably hope that I have something ready by this time. But I haven't. I believe that you are my true friend and, aside from any possible business interest, are disappointed because what hope you had in me has been weakened or dispelled. I want you to know that I feel the deepest regret on this account, but I assure you the most bitter disappointment is what I feel at present in myself. I don't want you to misunderstand me, or think that, aside from you and a few other people whose friendship has meant a great deal for me, I care one good God-damn of a drunken sailors curse whether I have "disappointed" the world of bilge-and-hog-wash-writers, Boyds,[2] Cohns,[3] or any of the other literary rubbish of sniffers, whiffers and puny, poisonous apes. If what I am about to lose because of my failure to produce was, as I once believed, something beautiful and valuable—I mean a feeling of deep and fine respect in life for the talent of someone who can create a worthy thing—then my regret at the loss of something so precious would be great. But do you really think that after what I have seen during the past 18 months I would cling very desperately to this 'stinking' remnant of a rotten bush, or any longer feel any sense of deference or responsibility to swine who make you sign books to their profit even while you break bread with them, who insolently command you to produce a book and "be sure you make it good or you are done for," who taunt and goad you by telling you to take care since "other writers" are getting "ahead of you", who try to degrade your life to a dirty, vulgar, grinning, servile, competitive little monkey's life—do you think I am losing anything so wonderful here that I can't bear the loss? You must know that I don't care a damn for all this now—I want you to know, Max, that the only thing I do care for now is whether I have lost the faith I once had in myself, whether I have lost the power I once felt in me, whether I have anything at all left—who once had no doubt that I had a treasury—that would justify me in going on. Do you think anything else matters to me? I have been a fool and a jack-ass—cheapened myself by making talks at their filthy clubs and giving interviews, but my follies of that sort were done long ago—for the rest I haven't tried to do anything but live quietly by myself without fancy mysterious airs, and there is as decent stuff within me as in anyone. I have kept my head above this river of filth, some of the dirty rotten lies they have told about me have come back to me, but I have yet to find the person who uttered them to my face. I want you to know that I consider that my hands are clean and that I owe no one anything—save for the debt of friendship for a few people. I did not write the blurbs, the pieces in the paper, the foolish statements, nor did I tell lies: no one can take anything from me now that I value, they can have their cheap nauseous seven-day notoriety back to give to other fools, but I am perfectly content to return to the obscurity in which I passed almost thirty years of my life without great difficulty. If anyone wants to know when I will have a new book out, I can answer without apology "when I have finished writing one and found some one who wants to publish it"—that is the only answer I owe to anyone (I don't mean you: you know the answer I have tried to make to you already)—and please, Max, if you can tactfully and gently, without wounding anyone, suggest to whoever is responsible for these newspaper squibs about my having written 500 000 words, and more all the time,—that he please for God's Sake cut it out, I will be grateful. I am sure it was intended to help, but it does no good, I assure you I am not at all afraid or depressed at the thought of total obscurity again,—

I welcome it, and I resent any effort to present me as a cheap and sensational person—in spite of my size, appetite, appearance, staying up all night, 500 000 words, etc—I am not a cheap and sensational person: if there is going to be publicity why can't it tell the truth—that I work hard and live decently and quietly, that no one in the world had a higher or more serious feeling about writing, that I made no boasts or promises, that I do not know whether I will ever do the writing I want to do, or not, or whether I will be able to go on at all, that I am in doubt and distress about it, but that I work, ask nothing from anyone, and hope, for my own sake, that I have some talent and power in me—I say, I am not afraid of publicity like this, because it would be truth, and it could not injure me save with fools.

I thank God I am in debt to no one: I have sent my family all I could, Mrs Boyd has had her full whack, the dentists are almost paid. Now, if they will all leave me alone, they can have the rest—if anything is left. I can't find out. I wish you'd find out for me and have Darrow send it to me. I've tried for a year to find out but I cant—I appreciate this paternal attitude, but it may be wasted on me, and I want to clear the board now. Above all, I don't want to owe you money. As thing stands, in my present frame of mind about my work, it is a blessing to me that I owe you no money and have no contract with you for a second book,—Max, won't you ask Darrow to send me whatever money is coming to me? As things stand now, it seems important to me that I should know where I stand financially and what I am going to have to do. I have earned my living teaching and in other ways before, and I believe I can earn my living again. As I told you the only thing that matters now would be to feel that the book has value and beauty for me, and that I have the power to do it—if I felt that I could do any work to support myself and feel good about it

Max, I have tried to tell you how I feel about all this, and now I want to sum it up this way:

Two years ago I was full of hope and confidence; I had compete within me the plans and ideas of at least a half dozen long books. Today I still have all this material, I have not the same hope and confidence; I have, on the contrary, a feeling of strong self-doubt and mistrust—which is not to say that I feel despair. I do not. Why this has happened I do not know—I think one reason is that I can not work in a glare, I was disturbed and lost self-confidence because of the notice I had, I think my success may have hurt me. Also, I had a personal trouble of which I told you something. I don't know whether this means I am unable to meet the troubles of life without caving in—this may be true, and in my doubt I think of some of the old books I read— "The Damnation of Someone or Another"[4]—"The Picture of Dorian Grey"[5]—in which spiritual decay, degeneration, and corruption destroys the person before he knows it—but I think that is literary night marishness—maybe these things happen, but I don't think they happened to me—I think I have kept my innocence, and that my feeling about living and working is better than it ever was. And I don't think I am unable to cope with the trial of life, but I think I may meet it clumsily and slowly, inexpertly, sweat blood and lose time. What I want to tell you is that I am in a state of <u>doubt</u> about all this.

Finally, the best life I can now dream of for myself, the highest hope I have is this: that I believe in my work and know it is good and that somehow, in my own way, secretly and obscurely, I have power in me to get the books inside me out of me. I dream of a quiet, modest life, but a life that is really high, secret, proud, and full of dignity for a writer in this country—I dream of a writer having work and power within him living this fine life untouched and uncoarsened by this filth and rabble of the gossip-booster sink—I dream of something permanent and fine, of the highest quality, and if the power is in me to produce, this is the life I want and shall have.

Thus, at great length, I have told you what is in my mind better than I could by talking to you, Max, do you understand that this letter is not bitter and truculent—save for these things and persons I despise. I want to tell you finally that I am not in <u>despair</u> over the book I have worked on—I am in <u>doubt</u> about it—and I am not sure about anything: I think I will finish it, I think it may be valuable and fine—or it may be worthless, I would like to tell you about it, and of some of the trouble I had with it—I can only suggest it: I felt if my life and strength kept up, if my vitality moved in every page, if I followed it through to the end it would be a wonderful book—but I doubted then that life was long enough, it seemed to me it would take ten books, that it would be the longest ever written, then, instead of paucity, I had abundance—such abundance that my hand was palsied, my brain weary, and in addition, as I go on, I want to write about everything and say all that can be said about each particular, the vast freightage of my years of hunger—my prodigies of reading, my infinite store of memories, my hundreds of books of notes return to devour me—sometimes I feel as if I shall compass and devour them, again, be devoured by them—I had an immense book and I wanted to say it all at once; it can't be done—now I am doing it part by part, and hope and believe the part I am doing will be a complete story, a unity, and part of the whole plan. This part itself has now become a big book: it is for the first time straight in my head to the smallest detail, and much of it is written—it is a part of my whole scheme of books as a smaller river flows into a big one.

As I understand it I am not bound now to Scribners or to any publisher by any sort of contract: none was ever offered me—neither have I taken money that is not my own. The only bond I am conscious of is one of friendship and loyalty to your house, and in this I have been faithful—it has been a real and serious thing with me.

I know that you want to see what I have done—to see if I had it in me to do more work after the first book, or whether everything burnt out in that one candle. Well, that is what I want to see, too, and my state of doubt and uneasiness is probably at least as great as your own. It seems to me that that is the best way to leave it now: the coast is clear between us, there are no debts or entanglements —if I ever write anything else that I think worth printing, or that your house might be interested in I will bring it to you, and you can read it, accept it or reject it with the same freedom as with the first book. I ask for no more from anyone. The life that I desire, and that I am going to try to win for myself, is going to exist in complete indifference and independence to such of the literary life as I have seen—I mean to all their threats either of glory or annihilation, to gin party criticism or newspaper blurbs and gossip, and to all their hysterical seven-day fames—If a man sets a high value on these things he richly deserves the payment he will get—as for me, I tell you honestly it is a piece of stinking fish to me—their rewards and punishments—I see what it did to writers in what they now call "the twenties"—how foolishly and trivially they worshipped this thing, and what nasty, ginny, drunken, jealous, fake-Bohemian little lives they had, and I see now how they have kicked those men out, after tainting and corrupting them and brought in another set which they call "the young writers"— among whom I have seen my own name mentioned. Well, I assure you I belong to neither group and I will not compete or produce in competition against any other person—No one will match me as you match a cock or a prizefighter, no one will goad me to show smartness or brilliance against another's—the only standard I will compete against now is in me: if I cant reach it, I'll quit.

It is words, words—I weary of the staleness of the words, the seas of print, the idiot repetition of trivial enthusiasms—I am weary of my own words but I have spoken the truth here; is it possible that we are all tainted with cheapness and staleness, is this the taint that keeps us sterile, cheap, and stale in this country—when I talk to you as here and say what I know is in my heart am I just another Brown[6]—a cheap stale fellow who pollutes everything he talks about —justice, [love], mercy—as he utters it. It isnt true—I am crammed to the lips with living, I am tired with what I've seen, I'm tired of their stale faces, the smell of concrete and [bent] steel, the thing that yellows, dries, or withers us—but did it mean nothing to you when I told you the beauty, exulting, joy, richness, and undying power that I had found in America—that I knew and believed to be the <u>real</u> truth, not the illusion?—the thing we had never found the pattern for, the style for, the true words to express—or was it only words to you; did you just think I was trying to be Whitman again. I know what I know, it crushes the lies and staleness like a rotten shell, but whether I can ever utter what I know, whether staleness + weariness has not done for me, I don't know—Christ, I am tired of everything but what I know to be the truth, and do not utter—I have it inside me, I even know the words for it but staleness and dullness have got into me,—I look at it with grey dullness and will not say it—it's not enough to see it: you've got to feel the thick snake-wriggle in each sentence—the heavy living tug of the fish at the line.

I'm out of the game—and it is a game, a racket: what I do now must be for myself,—I don't care who "gets ahead" of me—that game isn't worth a good god dam: I only care if I have disappointed you, but its very much my own funeral, too, I don't ask you to "give me a chance"—because I think you've given me one, but I don't want you to think this is a despairing letter, and that I've given up— I just say I don't know, I'm going to see: maybe it will come out right someday. By the way—I'm still working, I've been at it hard and will keep it up until I have to look for job: I may try to get work on Pacific coast. I'll come in to see you later, Max, please get Darrow to send me what money is coming to me.

When I was a kid we used to say of someone we thought the best and highest of—that he was "a high class gentleman." That's the way I feel about you. I don't think I am one—not the way you are—by birth, by gentleness, by natural and delicate kindness. But if I have understood some of the things you have said to me I believe you think the most living and beautiful thing on this earth is art, and that the finest and most valuable life is that of the artist. I think so, too; I don't know whether I have it in me to live that life, but if I have, then I think I would have something that would be worth your friendship. You know a good deal about me—the kind of people I came from (who seem to me, by the way, about as good as any people any where), and I think you know some of the things I have done, and that I was in love with a middle aged Jewish woman old enough to be my mother—I hope you understand I am ashamed of none of these things—my family, the Jewish woman, my life—but it would be a hard thing for me to face if I thought you were repelled by these things and did not know what I am like—I think my feeling about living and working and people is as good as you can find, and I want you to know how I feel: its so hard to know people and we think they feel inferior about things they really feel superior to, and the real thing that eats them we know nothing of.

I'm coming in to talk to you soon, but I can talk to you about some things better this way. Meanwhile, Max, good health and good luck and all my friendliest wishes.

Tom Wolfe

P.S.—I'm attaching a clipping a friend sent me from a Boston paper.[7] You see how quickly people can use an item like this injuriously—I think it has done harm, and I don't deserve it: Please get them to cut it out
and leave me alone—

*Notes*

1. This letter signals the beginning of Wolfe's suspicion that Perkins's responsibility to Scribners was in conflict with his loyalty to Wolfe, as indicated by Perkins's pressure for a second novel. In 1933 Wolfe delivered "The October Fair," which was partly used in *Of Time and the River* published in March 1935.

2. Probably Ernest Boyd.

3. Possibly Louis Henry Cohn, a New York rare-book dealer who wanted to publish a limited edition of Wolfe's work-in-progress under the House of Books imprint.

4. *The Damnation of Theron Ware* (1896) by Harold Frederic.

5. *The Picture of Dorian Gray* (1891) by Oscar Wilde.

6. Probably theatre critic and lecturer John Mason Brown.

7. Nowell quotes from this unlocated clipping: "Fiction is threatened with an epidemic of obesity. One of the latest symptoms in this country—the English situation is general and serious—is word from Thomas Wolfe who is working on a Maine coast island on a novel to be called *October Fair*. He confesses to a total of 500,000 words to date, and Charles Scribner's Sons are telegraphing their pleas for a process of selection, revision and condensation" (*Letters*, p. 310).

▲ ▼ ▲

To: *Perkins*                          ca. *January 15, 1932. Don Ce-Sar Hotel*
                                       *letterhead, St. Petersburg, Florida*
From: *Fitzgerald*                           *ALS, 2 pp. Princeton*

[*To right of letterhead*]    For three days only

Dear Max:

At last for the first time in two years + 1/2 I am going to spend five consecutive months on my novel. I am actually six thousand dollars ahead. Am replanning it to include what's good in what I have, adding 41,000 new words + publishing. Don't tell Ernest or anyone—let them think what they want—you're the only one whose ever consistently felt faith in me anyhow.

Your letters still sound sad. For God's sake take your vacation this winter. Nobody could quite ruin the house in your absense, or would dare to take any important steps. Give them a chance to see how much they depend on you + when you come back cut off an empty head or two. Thalberg[1] did that with Metro-Goldwyn-Mayer.

Which reminds me that I'm doing that "Hollywood Revisited" in the evenings + it will be along in, I think, six days—maybe ten.[2]

Have Nunnally Johnston's[3] humorous stories from the Post been collected? Every body reads them. Please at least look into this. Ask Meyers—he ought to search back at least a year which is as long as I've been meaning to write you about it.

Where in hell are my Scandanavian copies of <u>The Great Gatsby</u>?

You couldn't have sent me anything I enjoyed more than the Churchill book.[4]

Always Yours Devotedly
Scott Fitz

*Notes*

1. Movie producer Irving Thalberg; he became the model for Monroe Stahr, protagonist of Fitzgerald's unfinished Hollywood novel.

2. Not delivered to Perkins.

3. Nunnally Johnson, a prolific and highly successful screenwriter, published one collection of his *Saturday Evening Post* stories with Doubleday, Doran, in 1931.

4. Probably the one-volume abridgment of Winston Churchill's *The World Crisis,* published by Scribners in 1931.

▲▼▲

| | |
|---|---|
| *To: Perkins* | *March 16, 1932. Montgomery, Alabama* |
| *From: Fitzgerald* | *Wire. Princeton* |

PLEASE DO NOT JUDGE OR IF NOT ALREADY DONE EVEN CONSIDER ZELDAS BOOK UNTIL YOU GET REVISED VERSION LETTER FOLLOWS=[1]
SCOTT FITZGERALD.

*Note*

1. Zelda Fitzgerald sent her novel, *Save Me the Waltz,* to Perkins without showing it to Fitzgerald. When Fitzgerald read it he was angered by what he considered her appropriation of material that he planned to use in *Tender Is the Night.*

▲▼▲

| | |
|---|---|
| *To: Perkins* | *March 25, 1932. Montgomery, Alabama* |
| *From: Fitzgerald* | *Wire. Princeton* |

THINK NOVEL CAN SAFELY BE PLACED ON YOUR LIST FOR SPRING IT IS ONLY A QUESTION OF CERTAIN SMALL BUT NONE THE LESS NECESSARY REVISIONS MY DISCOURAGEMENT WAS CAUSED BY THE FACT THAT MYSELF AND DAUGHTER WERE SICK WHEN ZELDA SAW FIT TO SEND MANUSCRIPT TO YOU YOU CAN HELP ME BY RETURNING MANUSCRIPT TO HER UPON HER REQUEST GIVING SOME PRETEXT FOR NOT HAVING AS YET TIME READ IT AM NOW BETTER AND WILL WRITE LETTER TOMORROW IN MY OPINION IT IS A FINE NOVEL STOP WILL TAKE UP ARTICLE AS SOON AS I HAVE FINISHED CURRENT POST STORY WHICH WILL BE ON ARRIVAL BALTIMORE WEDNESDAY BEST REGARDS FAITHFULLY=
SCOTT FITZGERALD.

▲ ▼ ▲

*To: Perkins*                    *March 28, 1932. Montgomery, Alabama*
*From: Fitzgerald*                        *Wire. Princeton*

READ MANUSCRIPT BUT IF YOU HAVE ALREADY RETURNED IT
WIRE AND ILL SEND MY COPY STOP IF YOU LIKE IT AND WANT
TO USE IMMEDIATELY REMEMBER ALL MIDDLE SECTION MUST
BE RADICALLY REWRITTEN STOP TITLE AND NAME OF AMORY
BLAINE[1] CHANGED STOP ARRIVING BALTIMORE THURSDAY TO
CONFER WITH ZELDA WILL IMMEDIATELY DECIDE ON NEW
TITLE AND NAME CHANGES REVISING SHOULD TAKE FORT-
NIGHT=
    SCOTT FITZGERALD.

*Note*

1. Zelda Fitzgerald originally named her leading male character Amory Blaine, the
name of the protagonist of Fitzgerald's semi-autobiographical first novel, *This Side of
Paradise*.

▲ ▼ ▲

*To: Perkins*
*From: Hemingway*                *TLS with holograph additions and*
                                 *postscript, 5 pp.[1] Princeton*

                                 Key West, Fla.,
                                 April 4th, 1932

Dear Max,

. . . . .

    I have something over a hundred pictures necessary to make the book[2] com-
prehensive; having brought this number down from two hundred to, at present,
one hundred and twelve. What was it gave you the idea of suggesting sixteen
illustrations for the book after I spent all summer and my own money getting
the necessary illustrations and showed them to you in New York and we never
discussing on any terms except the use of a great amount of illustrations? I will
eliminate the colored frontispiece if you wish, in order to save expense, and have
no reproduction of painting in colour although I ordered and paid for the paintings on your authorization, but paid myself and would not suggest you pay
because I knew times were hard with you; but the book has to be properly illus-
trated. The reproductions in offset as you send them, printed flush with the page,
will do this splendidly if enough of them are used; but sixteen is a ridiculous
amount when I have written in the text that I have not described certain things

Willard Huntington Wright (S. S. Van Dine), Hemingway, Charles Scribner III, and Perkins at 597 Fifth Avenue (Princeton University Library)

in detail because photography has been brought to the point where it can represent some things better than a man can write of them, and when I spent the time that I spent ruining my eyes looking at negatives against an artificial light to get the pictures I needed after you had written and spoken about the scale you wanted to do the book on.

I spent a long time on that book, Max, over two years in the [actual] writing and rewriting and plenty of years in getting the material and to hell with getting it out now in a preoccupied with business worries manner and selling it down the river to the Book of the Month Club to get some one a sure seven thousand dollars to cover margins with. It may be that a hundred illustrations is a grotesque and impossible number, impossible to do in "these times," but Max, if you think about the trend in these times, other than their financial trend, you will know the value of pictures and that they will do more for the popularity of the book than any other thing. That is not what I want them for, but I know their value in that way. And I know the captions I can write.

If you read it over you will see that I wrote a pretty reasonable letter about the serialization. If you read it over five years from now you will see how much more reasonable it will seem. Since writing you about it I have not offered it anywhere nor done any negotiating for it. I turned down a thousand dollars to let Cosmopolitan read it with no option when I was in N.Y. plenty broke and I turned down seven thousand five hundred dollars when Lengel[3] was down here for them to publish some extracts from it. This quite possibly has no value but at least should show you I am serious.

Listen, you have troubles, and they are real troubles, and Scott has bad troubles, and I have had some troubles and if Mr. Thomas Wolfe lives long enough, great writer though he should be, he will have plenty of troubles too but I get my work done in spite of all troubles and when it is done to hell with it being bitched by somebody elses troubles. The first and final thing you have to do in this world is last in it and not be smashed by it and your work the same way.

Now, how much do the offset illustrations cost and what is the limit you can make and stillsell the book at 3.50 with a profit to yourself? I should not put it that way because that gives you an opportunity to say that sixteen is all you can make thank you very much and I can take it or leave it. As you did on the serialization. But Max it is getting a little too serious for that and if there has to be a compromise between sixteen and one hundred that compromise is not sixteen nor is it thirty two. If I have to borrow the money to pay for making the illustrations or take it out of my capital and spend it for that I will do so as I've already paid for getting them. But first would like to know at what price will you have to sell the book to make money for you with sixty offset illustrations? That is the irreducible minimum. It will be no fun for me to publish it with that but I do not care to publish it at all with less. Nor do I want to make it too expensive for people to buy. But what is the difference in sale between a book at 2.50–one at 3.50–one at 4.00 one at 5.00

. . . . .

. . . . .

Will do the proofs when I get them all since it is not just correcting mechanically but necessity to see it altogether in type so I can tell what I want to do with it. Do you know a Spanish proof reader competent to go over the spelling of the spanish words? This should be done. Setting them without italics is quite correct.

. . . . .

. . . . .

—Later—

I have been thinking over the book of the month business and this is how I stand—

If the book is offered to the book of the month through publishing necessity and against my natural wishes my advance is not to be deducted by Scribners from any payment made by Book of Month or other organization but is to remain as an advance against royalties on this book only to be deducted by Scribners from the money earned by the regular edition as sold by them. This to protect writer in times like these from publishers receiving seven thousands dollars from the book of month, recovering the 6500 advanced to the writer and then not being under the necessity to make as much of an effort to sell the book in times like these as the writer had to make to write it in the same times. The only reason for doing anything like this, as you say, is the depression. I do not mean it personally—only as a question of business policy in regard to Book of Month Club.

The second thing would be that if the book of the month club brought any pressure to bear for certain anglo saxon words or any portions of the text to be eliminated all these words, whenever eliminated, would be represented by blanks of the exact length of the word eliminated and all words or portions of the text eliminated would be restored in full in the regular trade edition to be published by the publishers and on which the advance of 6500 which I have received would apply.

Third thing would be that all review copies or presentation copies would be of the regular trade edition rather than the book of the month edition in case the book of the Month had eliminated any words from their text.[4]

How's that Max Or is it too business-like? You see I happen to believe in the book and it was you who said things were different in depressions and so on.

If the publishers need a sure 7,000 from that source all right—but I have to see that two things are not imperiled; the further sale, which helps you as much as it does me, and the integrity of the book which is the most important thing to me. If anyone so acts as to put themselves out as a book of the month they cannot insist in ramming the good word shit or the sound old word xxxx down the throats of a lot clubwomen but when a book is offered for sale no one has to buy it that does not want to—and I will not have any pressure brought to bear to make me emasculate a book to make anyone seven thousand dollars, myself or anyone else. Understand this is all business not personal. I'm only trying to be as frank as in talking so you will know how I stand and so we won't get in a jam and if I write too strongly or sound too snooty it is because I'm trying to make it frank and as honest and clear as possible. So don't let me insult you Max nor find any insults where none is intended but know I am fond of you and that we could not quarrel if we were together and if I'm rude I apologize sincerely.

If you want to publish two selections—the ones I outlined and Dashiell agreed to—in the magazine—Chapter Two—one was I believe—and the other the chapter on the bulls—saying they are from the book and giving them the place they should have in the magazine you can have them for nothing and use the money for illustrations for the book. Submitting proofs to me first of course. I won't sell them for less than they are worth but I will give them to you. That should show you whether I am friendly. But I am damned serious.

. . . . .
. . . . .

Yours always,
Ernest/

I know you didn't say you would do Book of Month or anything else against my wishes—but only asked how I felt and I have written so frankly so you would know how I feel about everything I mention.

### Notes

1. 398 words have been omitted from this letter.
2. *Death in the Afternoon.*
3. William Lengel, writer and literary agent, was an editor for *Cosmopolitan* in 1932.
4. *Death in the Afternoon* was not a Book-of-the-Month Club selection.

▲ ▼ ▲

To: Hemingway
From: Perkins                          CC, 3 pp.[1] Princeton

April 7, 1932

Dear Ernest:

I've just read your letter and I'm answering off hand to get things going and save time. You may get another giving specific figures before you answer. But answer these questions soon:

(1) Would it be possible with respect to placing the inserts to have them backed up, i.e. one picture on the back of another? This I think we could do even on the present basis and not increase the price. But the pictures I thought of as so close to the text that they ought to come close to particular passages.

(2) Would you rather revert to halftones in order to have a large number of pictures?

If we did, I should think we could have 32 inserts and if backed up 64 pictures, and perhaps not greatly increase the price.– But increase in the number of inserts does add greatly to costs, even in respect to binding.– Then too, each additional picture would add a page of text. We—and that means I—may have looked at the pictures too much by themselves,– as pictures rather than illustrations.– So we wanted to give each the best kind of reproduction possible for its own sake. But look at the Thomas book I sent you[2] (a good book, too) and see what you think of those pictures. That book we had to price at $5.00 even though he has a lower royalty than you, simply because a lower margin than that price yields was impossible.

In fact this question always ends with arithmetic, and the "hard times" makes that no different from what it always was. We don't try to increase the margin on account of that,– the tendency is the other way. The only influence of the bad times is on the retail price. We do want to keep the price at $3.50,– though we may have to give that up.[3] You know Steffens' book was a flat flop at its original price, but a great success when a Guild edition enabled Harcourt to bring it out anew and cheaper.[4]

Another point: we always want to bring books out the way you want them, partly because you want them that way, and partly because you do have a sure instinct in these things. But you seem to think that Scribners are looking out for themselves as opposed to you. That is not so. I am separating myself from them and am speaking with absolute honesty. They are not like that and never have been. That is known, and the Author's League rates them first in their treatment of authors' interests. They would not think of doing as you said about the advance. They never have done it, and never would. And the Magazine would never publish anything and not pay for it—but they can't pay higher prices now for things now than they could pay in good times. I know I've given you a wrong impression by glooming about the times to you. It was because of my own affairs. I always see things as too much one way or the other. I haven't had enough trouble, that's the trouble. But the slump only affects the question of retail price on the book and, on the Magazine, what we can't pay for we have to forget.

As for the Book Club, we don't like it any more than you do. And the limited likewise.– I wasn't urging a limited, but simply presenting an important possibility. At least that's what I should have been doing, and meant.

But write me quickly about the pictures and I'll write you more specifically before the week's over.

Yours,

. . . . .
. . . . .

*Notes*

1. 159 words have been omitted from this letter.
2. George Clifford Thomas Jr. and George C. Thomas III, *Game Fish of the Pacific* (Philadelphia: Lippincott, 1930).
3. *Death in the Afternoon* was published at $3.50.
4. *The Autobiography of Lincoln Steffens* was published in separate editions in 1931 by Harcourt, Brace, and by the Literary Guild.

▲▼▲

*To: Hemingway*
*From: Perkins*                                    *TS for wire. Princeton*

April 8, 1932

Mr. Ernest Hemingway
Key West, Florida
Shall publish book only as you want it though price must depend on method stop Wrote yesterday

Max

▲▼▲

*To: Perkins*         *April 15, 1932. Key West, Florida*
*From: Hemingway*     *Wire. Princeton*

AWFULLY HAPPY ABOUT PICTURES YOUR IDEA ABOUT PLACING THEM AT END SEEMS VERY INTELLIGENT AND EXCELLENT SOLUTION.[1]

*Note*

1. The eighty-one photographs were grouped in the book, which sold for $3.50.

▲ ▼ ▲

*To: Hemingway*
*From: Perkins*        *CC, 2 pp.[1] Princeton*

April 19, 1932

Dear Ernest:

I was mighty glad to get your telegram. Now send the pictures and captions whenever you can.– But we are all right for making up the dummy which is the only immediate problem, and you will soon have all of the proof. There is that matter about what they have come to call the four-letter words.– I won't argue with you about it because you know all of the arguments, except that you may not realize that spelling them out does technically make us guilty under the obscenity clause, and so it does give any legal authority that wants it, the right to act irrespective of anything but the more technical fact; and also that those words do prohibit completely all library sale but a very very small one. Dos Passos has gone beyond anyone else apparently, and I was told he had actually spelled out the words, but he has not in "1919" and I daresay that leaving two of the four letters blank was found by Harcourt to be enough to avoid the technical point of guilt.– though that certainly does make the law what Shakespeare said it was, a fool. But we knew that anyhow.

I read the story in the Cosmop, and I thought it was a very fine story.[2] Are they to have any more? I do not know why you should not publish those that you have written. I hope you will write others about Key West. I hope this means that you have got to the point where you can write about it.

What I meant about Scott is rather complicated and sometime I'll write you from home about it.– But Zelda has written a novel which was here in manuscript but later was withdrawn by Zelda to revise. It was very much autobiographical,– about herself, and biographical about Scott. In fact, she even named her hero Amory Blaine.– I did not say anything to Scott when it came, and felt very much perplexed what to do—it looked as if there were a great deal that was good in it, but it seemed rather as though it somewhat dated back to the days of "The Beautiful and Damned"—when I got a letter from Scott about it. Zelda had sent him a copy, and of course it would not do at all the way it was, with Amory Blaine the hero. It would have been mighty rough on Scott.– But this was written apparently very recently, and I think when Zelda was ill with her breakdown,– though that did not show in it in any obvious way, except that it was so much about Amory Blaine. This all must be a secret. I think the novel will be quite a good one when she finishes it. The thing is that she is evidently passionately fond of Alabama, and that gets into the early part of the book. I did not read any of it consecutively but the early part because of what Scott said in his letter. I think he must still be at the Rennert Hotel, Baltimore, Md. because mail I sent him to Montgomery has come back. Zelda wrote me a note about the manuscript which was of a sort which seemed to show that she was not very badly off this time, but Scott is greatly worried about her.[3]

. . . . .

Yours,

### Notes

1. 80 words have been omitted from this letter.
2. "After the Storm" appeared in the May 1932 issue of *Cosmopolitan*.
3. *Save Me the Waltz* was published by Scribners in October 1932 after Zelda Fitzgerald revised it. Sales were disappointing.

▲ ▼ ▲

To: Perkins                               *ca. April 30, 1932*
From: Fitzgerald                          *ALS, 3 pp. Princeton*

<u>Personal and Confidential</u> from F. Scott Fitzgerald
Hotel Rennert
Baltimore

Dear Max:

I was shocked to hear of your daughter's illness. If it is anything mental I can deeply sympathize for there is nothing so "terrifying + mysterious", as you say. I am somewhat of an amateur expert on the subject + if at any time things don't go well let us meet in New York and talk about it. I mean there were times in Zelda's illness where I needed a <u>layman</u>'s advice. If she is in good hands <u>do not make the criminal mistake of trying to hurry things</u>, for reasons of family affection or family pride.

---

Zelda's novel is now good, improved in every way. It is new. She has largely eliminated the speakeasy-nights-and-our-trip-to-Paris atmosphere. You'll like it. It should reach you in ten days. I am too close to it to judge it but it may be even better than I think. <u>But</u> I must urge you two things

(1.) If you like it please <u>don't</u> wire her congratulations, and please keep whatever praise you may see fit to give <u>on the staid side</u>—I mean, <u>as you naturally would</u>, rather than yield to a tendency one has with invalids to be extra nice to cheer them up. This seems a nuance but it is rather important at present to the doctors that Zelda does not feel that the acceptance (always granted you like it) means immediate fame and money. I'm afraid all our critical tendencies in the last decade got bullish; we discovered one Hemmingway to a dozen Callaghans and Caldwells (I think the latter is a wash-out) + probably created a lot of spoiled geniuses who might have been good workmen. Not that I regret it—if the last five years uncovered Ernest, Tom Wolfe + Faulkner it would have been worth while, but I'm not certain enough of Zelda's present stability of character to expose her to any superlatives. If she has a success coming she must associate it with work done in a workmanlike manner for its own sake, + part of it done fatigued and uninspired, and part of it done when even to remember the original inspiration and impetus is a psychological trick. She is not twenty-one and she is not strong, and she must not try to follow the pattern of my trail which is of course blazed distinctly on her mind.

(2.) Don't discuss contract with her until I have talked to you.

─────────────────

Ring's last story in the <u>Post</u> was pathetic, a shade of himself,[1] but I'm glad they ran it first and I hope it'll stir up his professional pride to repeat.

Beginning the article[2] for you on Monday. You can count on it for the end of next week.

Now <u>very important</u>.

(1.) I must have a royalty report for 1931 for my income tax—they insist.

(2.) I borrowed $600 in 1931. $500 of this was redeemed by my article. The other hundred should show in royalty report.

(3.) Since <u>Gatsby</u> was not placed with <u>Grosset</u> or <u>Burt</u> I'd like to have it in the <u>Modern Library</u>.[3] This is my own idea + have had no approach but imagine I can negotiate it. Once they are interested would of course turn negotiations over to you. But I feel, should you put obstacles in the way you would be doing me a great harm and injustice. <u>Gatsby</u> is constantly mentioned among memorable books but the man who asks for it in a store on the basis of such mention does not ask twice. Booksellers do not keep such an item in stock + there is a whole new generation who cannot obtain it. This has been on my mind for two years and I must insist that you you give me an answer that doesn't keep me awake nights wondering why it possibly benefited the Scribners to have me represented in such an impersonal short story collection as that of <u>The Modern Library</u> by a weak story,[4] + Ring ect by none at all. That "they would almost all have been Scribner authors" was a most curious perversion of what should have been a matter of pride into an attitude of dog-in-the manger.

Excuse that outburst, Max. Please write, answering all questions. Tell Louise I liked her story + hope she's better. Things go all right with me now. What news of Ernest? And his book?

Ever Your Friend<br>Scott

*Notes*

1. Either "Chicago's Beau Monde" (February 20, 1932) or "Alias James Clarkson" (April 16, 1932), both autobiographical articles.

2. Fitzgerald did not submit an article to *Scribner's Magazine* in the spring of 1932; his "Echoes of the Jazz Age" had been published by the magazine in November 1931.

3. *The Great Gatsby*, with an introduction by Fitzgerald, was republished by Modern Library in 1934.

4. "At Your Age."

▲▼▲

*To: Hemingway*
*From: Perkins*                    *CC, 3 pp.*[1] *Princeton*

July 22, 1932

Dear Ernest:

Everything seems now to be right with the book. And you will see when we send you the page proof, what we have done about the words, and it is not so bad. . . .

. . . Scott and I have got a grand tour of the Virginia battlefields planned, and although I do not see how I could take in more than two, it would be a great time if you were there. It all came from my going down to Baltimore and seeing Gettysburg, and really, Ernest, it was perfectly magnificent: you could understand every move in the whole battle if you had read about it. You could see the whole battlefield plain as day. There is a stone wall, as good as any in Connecticut, about two feet high, on Roundtop, built on the 3rd of July, by some Maine regiments. They knew all about stone walls.– It is as good as new today.

Scott and Zelda are living about forty minutes out from Baltimore in a house on a big place that is filled with wonderful old trees. I wanted to walk around and look at the trees, but Scott thought we ought to settle down to gin-rickeys.– But you could see the trees from the piazza where we sat, and a little pond there, too. It was really a fine sort of melancholy place. Zelda is not nearly as pretty, and is quite a little different, but I thought she was better, and that there was more reality in her talk, and that she seemed well. She was very nice. She has a whole lot of drawings and paintings that she gets out of her subconscious, and they are very expressive.– Whether they really are any good or not, I do not know, but they are not negative, anyhow. Scott did not look so well, but he was in fine spirits, and talked a lot. He told me that if I went to Key West he would certainly go next time.– You know he was in Florida, and he began inquiring about the fishing. It seems he caught an amberjack, I think, that weighed about forty pounds. He asked me how big the fish we caught were, and maybe I stretched it a little, but I could see it worried Scott. He said he had had an awful fight with this amberjack. It was mighty good to see him anyhow. I wish you would come and go to Antietam with us. It is beautiful country all around.– The depression seems simply silly when you motor all over that country and see the crops and all the rich foliage, and the orchards coming along, and even the villages looking all neat and fresh. It makes you feel as if it were all a lunacy, this depression.

. . . . .

. . . . .

There is one more thing, but I wouldn't worry about it. A man named Sidney Barth came in here with thirty-six manuscript pages of your letters to that Ernest Morehead.[2] I may have the name wrong, but to the same couple that those earlier letters were written to. He wants to sell these letters (written in 1925 and 1926) for $1800. I don't think you would want to spend that much, and the times are too bad to do it, and I wouldn't suppose he could sell them at that price at present. I ran over the letters in typewriting, and except that they are personal letters, I see nothing about them that ought to trouble you.– The only thing was some comments on McAlmon, but they were really all right. They were not hard on him. You did say in effect, that you did not think he was as good as Mark Twain, but that might almost be conceded! I thought they were mighty good letters. If there is anything you want me to do about it, let me know. I am sure there is nothing in them that need trouble you.[3]

Always yours,

*Notes*

1. 304 words have been omitted from this letter.
2. Perkins conflated the names Ernest Walsh and Ethel Moorhead, founders and editors of *This Quarter* in Paris. They published Hemingway, but the relationship turned sour. Hemingway attacked Walsh in *A Moveable Feast.*
3. This correspondence is at the University of Virginia Library.

▲ ▼ ▲

| | |
|---|---|
| *To: Perkins* | *1932. Cooke City, Montana* |
| *From: Hemingway* | *ALS, 2 pp.[1] Princeton* |

<u>July 27</u>

Dear Max—

. . . . .

Will you please erase the two cursings out of the compositors for still setting that Hemingway's Death[2] on those last galleys of the Dates of fights— I have the proof all packed and cant get to it— They are at the top of two of those last galleys— I wish to Christ you wouldnt have sent that slugged Hemingways Death again after all I'd written and wired— But want those erased as it does no good to slang the compositors— They arent responsible—

. . . . .

. . . . .
. . . . .
. . . . .
. . . . .

The letters you refer to are to Ernest Walsh and Ethel Morehead— The bastards I helped get out their magazine when he was supposed to be dying of TB. Did die finally and she sold his letters. Tell the man who wants to sell them that I said for him to stick them up his ass—

. . . . .

Poor old Scott— He should have swapped Zelda when she was at her craziest but still saleable back 5 or 6 years ago before she was diagnosed as nutty— He is the great tragedy of talent in our bloody generation—

. . . . .

So long Max— Good luck—
<u>Ernest</u>

### Notes

1. 179 words have been omitted from this letter.
2. The slug at the top of the galley proofs for *Death in the Afternoon* read "Hemingway's Death."

▲ ▼ ▲

*To: Perkins*
*From: Fitzgerald*                              *TLS, 1 p. Princeton*

"La Paix," Rodgers' Forge,
Towson, Maryland,
January 19, 1933.

Dear Max:

I was in New York for three days last week on a terrible bat. I was about to call you up when I completely collapsed and laid in bed for twenty-four hours groaning. Without a doubt the boy is getting too old for such tricks. Ernest told me he concealed from you the fact that I was in such rotten shape. I send you this, less to write you a <u>Rousseau's Confession</u> than to let you know why I came to town without calling you, thus violating a custom of many years standing.

Thanks for the books that you have had sent to me from time to time. They comprise most of the reading I do because like everybody else I gradually cut down on expenses. When you have a line on the sale of Zelda's book let us know.

Found New York in a high state of neurosis, as does everybody else, and met no one who didn't convey the fact to me: it possibly proves that the neurosis is in me. All goes serenely down here. Am going on the water-wagon from the first of February to the first of April but don't tell Ernest because he has long convinced himself that I am an incurable alcoholic, due to the fact that we almost always meet on parties. I am <u>his</u> alcoholic just like Ring is mine and do not want to disillusion him, tho even Post stories must be done in a state of sobriety. I thought he seemed in good shape, Bunny less so, rather gloomy. A decision to adopt Communism definitely, no matter how good for the soul, must of necessity be a saddening process for anyone who has ever tasted the intellectual pleasures of the world we live in.

For God's sake can't you lighten that pall of gloom which has settled over Scribner's?—Erskine Caldwell's imitations of Morley Callaghan's imitations of Ernest, and Stuart Chase's imitations of Earl Browder imitating Lenine.[1] Maybe Ring would lighten your volume with a monthly article. I see he has perked up a little in the New Yorker.[2]

All goes acceptably in Maryland, at least from the window of my study, with distant gun flashes on the horizon if you walk far out of the door.

Ever your old friend,<br>F. Scott Fitzgerald

### Note

1. Chase wrote books on government and economics. Browder was general secretary of the Communist Party U.S.A.
2. Lardner wrote a series of radio programs for the *New Yorker* beginning in June 1932.

▲ ▼ ▲

*To: Hemingway*
*From: Perkins*                                   *CC, 3 pp.*[1] *Princeton*

February 10, 1933

Dear Ernest:

. . . . .

. . . . .

. . . . .

Scott ended his last letter, of January 30th, with this sentence, "Will be getting in touch with you within the next few months on what I hope will be important business." I think that this means he thinks he will have his novel done. I wrote him that I had a hunch he would have published a novel within eighteen months, even allowing for serial. His letter sounded pretty good. But the best news I have is about Tom Wolfe. The day before you left I went to Baltimore. After you left Tom and me I said to him, "Why don't you come down to Baltimore and then we'll go to Washington too." He said he would, but I didn't expect him. But he did arrive there the next day and we had a good time out of it there and in Washington. On the way back he told me about a story he said he had written. He has a whole library of manuscripts, fragments of things. I said, "For Heaven's sake bring it in and let us publish it." Then there began all the regular series of procrastinations, but eventually he did turn up with about 60,000 words of his very best sort of thing, though far too much of the dithyrambic, too little of the dialogue and direct narrative.– But still the whole thing a unit. Some things had to go out of it obviously, too directly of the quality of autobiography, etc.; but even more obviously there were a lot of fragments I had already seen which fell right into it in place to complete the very motive of the manuscript. I called him up and said to him, "All you have to do now is to close your hand and you have your novel." We spent hours later talking about it, and of course Tom was all for breaking loose into all kinds of excursions away from the main thing, but I got him to promise that first he would put it together on the lines I suggested, with which he agreed.– If it needed enlargement thereafter (and it will need an awful lot of work in detail) he could do it, and see how it came. But he has promised first to deliver the manuscript. It does not seem possible now that he can avoid having a very fine book, in some ways better than "The Angel", much better structurally, for next fall.[2] I think it was a great piece of business having you and him meet. He did reproach him for some things, between ourselves. He said he thought it was pretty bad we had let him get within twenty dollars of starvation. I understood this, of course, from Tom perfectly well, but I did point out some of the other side of the matter;– but he said with a sly look he sometimes manages to take on, like the one his mother was described as having in the book,– he said, "Since we are talking business, how about the interest you earned on my $2,500 before it was spent?"

. . . . .
. . . . .

Ever yours,

*Notes*

1. 371 words have been omitted from this letter.
2. *Of Time and the River* was published in March 1935.

▲ ▼ ▲

*To: Perkins*               *Mid February 1933*
*From: Hemingway*         *ALS, 4 pp.*[1] *Princeton*

Box 406
Key West
<u>Monday</u>—          Florida

Dear Max:—

. . . . .
. . . . .

Glad about what you wrote of Tom Wolfe. He was awfully nice. He is like a great child and you must remember that. Genuises of that sort I guess are always children. Children, as you may have observed, Mr. Perkins, are a hell of a responsability. I liked him very, very much.

. . . . .

. . . . .

. . . . .

Will you tell me, please, ① about when to expect the royalty money on Death In Aft according to usual or present procedure.

② Whether I can draw on it before then.

③ What present sale is.

I distrust that present system but understand it.

Also are you or will you be prepared to advance me $6,000 on the book of stories—This is figured as 15% on 20,000 sale at $2.00. The 20,000 is the minimum sale I have to have Mr. Darrow carry in his mind. Also the minimum that will hold poor old Papa's affectionate loyalty. The advance mentioned is less than sale on day of publication of this last $3.50 masterpiece.

Would it be any more palatable to you to advance 3000 or 4000 and the balance at say $200 a month?

If I take an advance on the new book will not need the Death In Aft royalties until they are due. But anyhow let me know when they are due.

. . . . .

. . . . .

Because I tell you (personally) how broke I am dont think I am to be treated like all the poor little boys because my financial acumen (if necessary) is only equalled by my financial liberty of action (never necessary but present) and in reality I'm not asking any favor. You know that.

. . . . .

. . . . .

Am going well on a fine story. Have a fine plan for a novel. Will be working on the Gulf stream book from about 10th of April on— It may take 2 or 3 years more. Might get what I need this summer. Will see.[2]

Best to you always, Max

Ernest/

I dont know, frankly, whether Scott will ever come out of this thing or not. He seems so damned perverse. Does anyone think it is easy to get your work done properly? about wanting to fail—it's that damned, bloody romanticism. Why cant he grow up. That's a useless question. I wish to Christ I could see him sober. Tom Wolfe will be fine—always within the limits of his intelligence—He has a great talent and a very delicate fine spirit—You've got to be a big part of his intelligence so for Christ sake dont lose his confidence

*Notes*

1. 321 words have been omitted from this letter.
2. Hemingway did not write the Gulf Stream book.

▲ ▼ ▲

*To: Perkins*
*From: Wolfe*                                    *TS, 6 pp. Harvard*

*The following note apparently accompanied the work-in-progress that Wolfe submitted to Perkins in April 1933.*

NOTE

The concluding scenes of Anteus[1] which are to follow will require one or two weeks work to include them in the manuscript. This whole manuscript is a first draft. There are still many things to be woven into it as it is and is intended to be a web of a man's memory of the past, but I hope its final purpose and relation to the Proteus section which follows may be evident from this first copy.

The plan for these remaining scenes that end this book and that lead directly into the book which follows which is called <u>Proteus</u>: <u>The</u> <u>City</u>, the opening scenes of which I am including with this manuscript, are as follows:

1 — There is a scene in which the narrator describes the life and movement on the road by day and some of the people that his brother meets along the road, and the life that flows around them in the towns they go to. There is a scene that describes the return home into the hills again by night.

2 — There are the final scenes at home, the night before departure, a family party in a restaurant, the streets of the town by night and then a scene similar to the scene about October at the beginning of the book.

The purpose of all these concluding scenes whether in the panorama of furious movement and human unrest over the earth or in the streets of passing towns or in the scenes after the return home is to emphasize and complete the ideas already described in this book. These ideas are:

1 — the frenzied dissonance and the tortured unrest in the lives of people from which the strong figure of the father has been removed and who no longer have any great image to which they can unite their power and energy or any central and direct unity to gather and control them and who are being driven like leaves across the earth in a fury of wild unrest and longing without a door to enter or any goal or summit to attain.

2 — The impulse drives the narrator to flight from home and wandering. When having returned home again and found his father dead he finds that now he can inhabit this life which he has known only as a phantom or as someone walking in a dream who sees, feels and remembers and experiences all things with

a blazing vividness but who is unable to touch them, live in them or make them a part of him again.

The final scene begins at the moment of departure with the going of the train and concerns the journey of the train through the night and ends at morning as the train nears the city. This scene makes use of rhythms, memories and visions of time, the recurrent theme of wandering forever and the earth again, and the ideas concerning the eternity of the earth outside the train and the movement, unrest, and brevity of the lives of men who are being hurled across the earth in darkness which the movement of the train induces of which I already have the notes and to which I have already given the title — K-19.[2]

This scene and the end of this section ends at morning as the train begins to enter the tunnel to the city underneath the river, the first scene in Proteus: The City is about the river and the city and follows immediately upon this scene.

Finally, I want to give you the following information about the whole book. I have called this first section — Antaeus: Earth Again because Antaeus was a giant whose mother was the earth and who wrestled with Hercules. In my use of this fable I understand Hercules to be the million-visaged shape of time and memory, and it is with this figure that the narrator is contending in this whole section. According to the fable Hercules discovered when he threw Antaeus to the earth that his antagonist redoubled his strength each time he touched the earth and accordingly Hercules held him in his arms above the earth and conquered him that way. Accordingly, this part of my book is about a man who is conquered by the million shapes of time and memory which came to life around him with every step he takes and every breath he draws, the life which was once his own, but which now he can no longer make his own no more than if he were a ghost.

In the beginning of the book the feeling is expressed that when a man's father dies the man must then discover a new earth for himself and make a life for himself other than the life his father gave to him or die himself. Therefore, the final words of Antaeus spoken just as the train which is taking him to the city nears the tunnel are these: "Antaeus, Antaeus, there are new lands. Child, Child, go find the earth again." That new land, new life and new earth is the city, and <u>Proteus: The City</u> follows immediately after, and just as <u>Antaeus</u> is revisiting and going back into the life of time and memory and just as I want, much more than I have ever in this first draught, to loot my life clean, if possible of every memory which a buried life and the thousand faces of forgotten time could awaken and to weave it into <u>Antaeus</u> like a great densely woven web, so has <u>Proteus</u> a forward going movement into time and is filled with all the thousand protean shapes of life in the city going on around him. I am giving you here the first part of Proteus which concerns the first year of a young man's vision of the city. The remainder of Proteus which you have not seen is written either in whole or in part.

[*New page starts here; may not be continuation of the same memo.*]

The third³ part of the book I have called for the present <u>Faust and Helen</u>, and of that third part you have already seen most of the concluding section, which deals with springtime in the city. The first part of Faust and Helen is only partly written; it begins on a ship and introduces the figure of the woman.

The fourth and concluding part of the book which will be called either Oktoberfest or October Fair will occur entirely upon the continent of Europe. For this part I have made notes but have written almost nothing. Its purpose is to conclude the fury of movement, unrest and wandering that drives men across the earth and to show that whether any final peace or assuagement can be given to people who have ever felt the Faustian hunger to drink and eat the earth, they cannot find the peace and certitude they sought by wandering or beneath a foreign sky.

Finally the last book deals with the impulse in men's lives to return, to find a dwelling place at home and a door that they can enter and it includes the general movement of the book which is stated in the words "of wandering forever and the earth again."

Therefore, of these four books you have now seen in the first draft almost all of <u>Antaeus</u>, part of <u>Proteus</u> and the concluding part of <u>Faust and Helen</u>. The fourth part of October Fair, as I say, is still, save for notes, drafts and scenes, unwritten.

It is now my desire to call the whole book <u>Time And The River</u> instead of <u>October Fair</u> as I think that <u>Time And The River</u> better describes the intention of the whole book. By the time you have read this new manuscript and this note you should be able, with what you have seen of the whole, to judge if the project is feasible or just a mad delusion on my part.

I myself believe it is feasible and believe now that after all the despair and suffering of the last three years that I have not been chasing a phantom or deluding myself with the fragments of a disordered intelligence. I believe, on the contrary, that it is possible for me to complete this book and have a coherent legend of the savage hunger and unrest that drives men back and forth upon this earth and the great antagonist of fixity of everlasting change, of wandering and returning, that make war in our souls. If this is incoherent it does not seem so to me now; that the book if completed would be one of the longest books ever written I have no doubt, but that so far as I am concerned, is no valid objection to its being done and if it is worth being done it seems to me that it is the publisher and the world of practical mechanics and salesmanship that must somehow adapt itself and not the world of the creator.

You know that I am so desperately anxious to get this great weight off my soul, that I will yield to you on any point that can be yielded, and solicit and be grateful for any help of editing and cutting that you can give me, but what I want you to do now, and what is desperately important to me is that you be able to get from the manuscript which I have given you some coherent idea of what I intend, and just tell me with naked frankness if what I intend is worth intending and worth doing and whether I shall continue.

I ask you to bear in mind that I am in a desperate frenzy to get something finally accomplished. I have written in less than three months time over 300,000 words and this present manuscript which I am giving you now has been done in the last five weeks and has I believe something like 150,000 words in it. As a man works with this frenzied haste he cannot give the best and the utmost that is in him; he is tortured by the constant memory of all the things he can and should do to improve it and all the power and richness that long and painstaking effort will sometimes give to a piece of writing. But I earnestly hope that if I have lost some of this I have gained something by the very frenzy with which I have gone ahead and that whatever has been lost enough has been left to show that the thing <u>could</u> be done if it is worth doing at all.

Now finally it is up to you to tell me whether you understand what I am trying to do. Whether it is worth doing and if I shall go ahead and for God's Sake do it without delay and with merciful even if brutal honesty.

Finally look at this outline once again:

Book 1 -  Antaeus: Earth again (given to you here in rough draft with much left out that I want to put in, only the final three or four scenes lacking to make it a complete draft)

Book 2 -  Proteus: The City — given to you here in its first part and with most of the remainder written but still to be included in the manuscript.

Book 3 -  Faust and Helen — The final part of which you have read, of which you are printing two sections this spring in Scribner's Magazine;[4] the first part of which is mainly written either in full or in scenes and sections, still to be included.

Book 4 -  The October Fair — unwritten save for notes and rough drafts.

### Notes

1. Wolfe's novel that became *Of Time and the River.*

2. K-19 was the Pullman car on the New York–Asheville train. This section of the novel was broken up, but in 1932 Scribners expected to publish *K-19* as a separate novel. A facsimile of the publisher's dummy with the opening chapter has been published as *K-19: Salvaged Pieces,* edited by John L. Idol Jr. (Thomas Wolfe Society, 1983).

3. Typed as "first" but changed to "third" by an unidentified hand.

4. "Death, the Proud Brother," June 1933, and "No Door: A Story of Time and the Wanderer," July 1933.

▲▼▲

*To: Charles Scribner III*  *April 18, 1933*
*From: Perkins*  *CC, 4 pp. Princeton*

*From Perkins's four-page report to Scribner*

I do feel much encouraged about one thing though, although I can see unlimited work and struggle before it is fully accomplished;– that is Tom Wolfe's book. He brought me on Saturday something like 300,000 words of manuscript, considerable sections of which I had seen before. We already had here about 100, or 150,000 words. There is more to be done to fill in, but the book is really almost in existence now. There are many questions about it which will have to be argued out, and much revision and all that, just as was true of "The Angel".– But I really think that this book has half a dozen chapters in it that are beyond anything even in "The Angel"; and it may be a distinctly finer book than that. I had a sort of plan that after you come back, say in June or July, I might go off with Tom to the country and spend a couple of weeks, and get the book into shape.[1]

*Note*

1. Perkins did not go to the country with Wolfe.

▲ ▼ ▲

*To: Perkins*  *Havana, Cuba*
*From: Hemingway*  *Wire. Princeton*

1933 JUNE 11 PM 7 02

TITLE IS WINNER TAKE NOTHING STOP WITH THIS QUOTATION QUOTES UNLIKE ALL OTHER FORMS OF LUTTE OR COMBAT THE CONDITIONS ARE THAT THE WINNER SHALL TAKE NOTHING SEMICOLON NEITHER HIS EASE COMMA NOR HIS PLEASURE COMMA NOR ANY NOTIONS OF GLORY SEMICOLON NOR COMMA IF HE WIN FAR ENOUGH COMMA SHALL THERE BE ANY REWARD WITHIN HIMSELF CLOSE QUOTE[1] HOWS THAT TELL YOUR FRIEND EASTMAN WILL BREAK HIS JAW REGARDS=[2]
ERNEST

*Notes*

1. Hemingway wrote this passage in emulation of early English prose.
2. Hemingway was reacting to Eastman's review of *Death in the Afternoon*: "Bull in the Afternoon," *New Republic* (June 1933).

▲ ▼ ▲

*To: Perkins*          *1933. Hotel Ambos Mundos letterhead, Havana, Cuba*
*From: Hemingway*               *ALS, 4 pp.¹ Princeton*

June 13/

Dear Max

. . . . .

. . . . .

. . . . .

Eastman has given me a new slant on my so-called friends in N.Y. If he ever gets a solvent publisher to publish that libel between covers it will cost the publisher plenty of money and Eastman will go to jail. Moe Speiser² will see to that. I could use some of that dough.

If I ever see him anywhere or anytime, now or in the future, I will get my own redress myself.

I am tempted never to publish another damned thing. The swine arent worth writing for. I swear to Christ they're not. Every phase of the whole racket is so disgusting that it makes you feel like vomiting. Every word I wrote about the Spanish fighting bull was absolutely true and result of long and careful and exhaustive observation. Then they pay Eastman, who knows nothing about it, to say I write sentimental nonsense. He _really_ knows how bulls are. They are like this— (he explains) I am like this—etc. (he explains) I have seen 50 bulls do what that fool says—from his ignorance—no bull can do—Its Too disgusting to write about—

And it is a commonplace that I lack confidence that I am a man—What shit—And I'm supposed to go around with your good friends spreading that behind my back—And they imagine they will get away with it. Mr. Crichton³—Mr. Eastman etc. Why dont you give them space to write it in the magazine? Whenever and wherever I meet any one of them their mouths will make a funny noise when they ever try to say it again after I get through working over them. Mr. Crichton—the brave man who tells everybody things to their faces—We'll see—

They're a nice lot—The professional male beauties of other years—Max Eastman—a groper in sex (with the hands I mean) a traitor in politics and—hell I wont waste it on them.

It certainly is damned fine to have friends—They hear you are out of the country and they open up. Good. Bring on some more friends. I'll be a long way out of the country and they will all get very brave and say every thing they wish were true—Then I'll be back and we will see what will happen.

You see what they cant get over is 1 that I _am_ a man (2) that I can beat the shit out of any of them 3 that I can write. The last hurts them the worst. But they dont like any of it. But Papa will make them like it. Best to you—Ernest.

*Notes*

1. 200 words have been omitted from this letter.
2. Maurice Speiser was Hemingway's lawyer.
3. Kyle Crichton was a Scribners editor who also wrote leftist criticism as Robert Forsythe.

▲ ▼ ▲

*To: Perkins*
*From: Fitzgerald*                          *TLS, 4 pp. Princeton*

La Paix, Rodgers' Forge,
Towson, Maryland,
September 25, 1933.

Dear Max:

The novel[1] has gone ahead faster than I thought. There was a little set back when I went to the hospital for four days but since then things have gone ahead of my schedule, which you will remember, promised you the whole manuscript for reading November 1, with the first one-fourth ready to shoot into the magazine (in case you can use it) and the other three-fourths to undergo further revision. I now figure that this can be achieved by about the 25th of October. I will appear in person carrying the manuscript and wearing a spiked helmet.

There are several points and I wish you would answer them categorically.

1.   Did you mean that you could get the first fourth of the story into the copy of the magazine appearing late in December and therefore that the book could appear early in April?[2] I gathered that on the phone but want to be sure. I don't know what the ocean travel statistics promise for the spring but it seems to me that a May publication would be too late if there was a great exodus and I should miss being a proper gift book for it. The story, as you know, is laid entirely in Europe—I wish I could have gotten as far as China but Europe was the best I could do, Max (to get into Ernest's rhythm).

2.   I would not want a magazine proof of the first part, though of course I would expect your own proof readers to check up on blatant errors, but would want to talk over with you any small changes that would have to be made for magazines publication—in any case, to make them myself.

3.   Will publication with you absolutely preclude that the book will be chosen by the Literary Guild or the Book of the Month?[3] Whatever the answer the serial will serve the purpose of bringing my book to the memory and attention of my old public and of getting straight financially with you. On the other hand, it is to both our advantages to capitalize if possible such facts as that the editors of those book leagues might take a fancy to such a curious idea that the author, Fitzgerald, actually wrote a book after all these years (this is all said with the

reservation that the book is good.) Please answer this as it is of importance to me to know whether I must expect my big returns from serial and possibly theatrical and picture rights or whether I have as good a chance at a book sale, launched by one of those organizations, as any other best seller.

Ober is advancing me the money to go through with it (it will probably not need more than $2,000 though he has promised to go as far as $4,000) and in return I am giving him 10% of the serial rights. I plan to raise the money to repay him (if I have not already paid him by <u>Post</u> stories) by asking a further advance on the book royalties or on my next book which might be an omnibus collection of short stories or those two long serial stories about young people that I published some time ago in the <u>Post</u> as the Basil stories and the Josephine stories—this to be published in the fall.

You are the only person who knows how near the novel is to being finished, <u>please don't say a word to anyone</u>.

4. How will you give a month's advance notice of the story—slip a band on the jacket of the December issue? I want to talk to you about advertising when I see you in late October so please don't put even the publicity man at any work yet. As to the photographs I have a snap-shot negative of the three of us with a surf board, which enlarges to a nice 6 X 10 glossy suitable for rotogravures and also have a fine double profile of Zelda and me in regular cabinet photograph size and have just gotten figures from the photographer. He wants $18.00 for twelve, $24.00 for twenty-four and $35.00 for fifty and says he does not sell the plates, though I imagine he could be prevailed upon if we give him a "take it or leave it" offer. How many would you need? These two photographs are modern. I don't want any of the old ones sent out and I don't want any horrors to be dug up out of newspaper morgues.

Tell me how many you would need to cover all the press? Would it be cheaper if I sat when I came up there—the trouble is that in only one out of any three pictures is my pan of any interest.

5.   My plan, and I think it is very important, is to prevail upon the <u>Modern Library</u>, even with a subsidy, to bring out <u>Gatsby</u> a few weeks after the book publication of this novel. Please don't say that anybody would possibly have the psychology of saying to themselves "One of his is in the <u>Modern Library</u> therefore I will not buy another", or that the two books could be confused. The people who buy the <u>Modern Library</u> are not at all the people who buy the new books. <u>Gatsby</u>—in its present form, not actually available in sight to book buyers, will only get a scattering sale as a result of the success of this book. I feel that every time your business department has taken a short-sighted view of our community of interest in this matter, which is my reputation, there has been no profit on your part and something less than that on mine. As for example, a novel of Ernest's in the <u>Modern Library</u> and no novel of mine, a good short story

of Ernest's in their collection of the Great Modern Short Stories and a purely commercial story of mine. I want to do this almost as much as I want to publish this novel and will cooperate to the extent of sharing the cost.

There will be other points when I see you in October, but I will be greatly reassured to have some sort of idea about these points so that I can make my plans accordingly. I will let you know two or three days in advance when you may expect me.

One last point: Unlike Ernest I am perfectly agreeable to making any necessary cuts <u>for serial publication</u> but naturally insist that I shall do them myself.

You can imagine the pride with which I will enter your office a month from now. <u>Please do not have a band as I do not care for music.</u>

Ever yours,<br>
F. Scott Fitzgerald

### Notes

1. *Tender Is the Night.*
2. *Tender Is the Night* was serialized in four installments of *Scribner's Magazine,* January–April 1934. The book was published on April 12, 1934.
3. The novel was a Literary Guild alternate selection for June 1934.

▲ ▼ ▲

*To: Fitzgerald*
*From: Perkins*                               *CC, 4 pp. Princeton*

Oct. 6, 1933

Dear Scott:

I just read your piece on Ring.[1] Of course you could not do anything for Scribner's now. I thought it might have been only on one phase of him alone, but it says a great deal. I thought it was a very fine piece.

I am now writing to ask your advice.– I want to have us publish some sort of volume of Ring's material. The only possibilities I can think of are either a selection from his stories by somebody qualified to take out the best, and those most representative of his talent; or a selection from all of his writings, which would let in something from "You Know Me Al" and those little plays that you speak of, and some of the best of his lighter things. But whether we followed one of these plans, or the other, we would need an introduction, and I think only one that was written by someone really appreciative of him as a writer, and at the same time knew him well as a man, and was appreciative of him that way too, would do.– Grantland Rice would not do therefore, and the usual literary critic certainly would not.– So who would? Would you, do you think? And if so, would you be willing to undertake it?[2] It is true that you only knew Ring after what was the most typical part of his career was over,– when he was a sports writer, and a newspaperman, and all that. I suppose people like Grantland Rice might say, why didn't they ask someone who went through all those days with him? Anyhow, I wish you would either write me about this matter (it is a pure favor I am asking you) or else think it over until you appear here in the latter part of this month.– We could not publish a book until 1934. If we did it, I would want to get a really fine picture of Ring. I would almost rather have it after the Great Neck days because, although he did look terribly gaunt and ill, even before he went to the hospital, I do think that you could see better what a remarkable creature he was then.

John Bishop is back,– has a house in Connecticut.

Always yours,

### Notes

1. Lardner had died on September 25, 1933. Fitzgerald's tribute, "Ring," was published in the October 11, 1933, issue of the *New Republic.*

2. Scribners published *First and Last* in 1934, with an introduction by Gilbert Seldes.

▲ ▼ ▲

*To: Perkins*
*From: Fitzgerald*                    *Wire. Princeton*

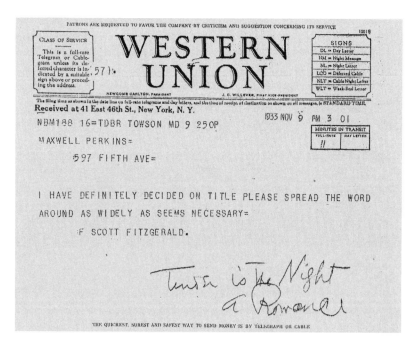

The title note is in Perkins's hand.

▲ ▼ ▲

*To: Perkins*
*From: Hemingway*                    *ALS, 6 pp.*[1] *Princeton*

November 17 1933
c/o Guaranty Trust Co. of N.Y.
4 Place de la Concorde
Paris
Cable address HEMINGWAY
GARRiTUS
PARIS

Dear Max:

· · · · ·

· · · · ·

· · · · ·

· · · · ·

· · · · ·

The bird,[2] when he labelled me as approaching middle-age was trying to get rid of me that way—Others having failed. So the advertizing department siezes on that to advertize the book by. If I write about ~~anybody~~—automatically they label that character as me—When I write about somebody that cant possibly be me—as in After The Storm, that unfortunate convert to Economics religion Mr. Chamberlain[3] says it is unusually imaginative or more imaginative than anything I've attempted. What shit.

When does Middle Age commience? That story—Wine of Wyoming is nothing but straight reporting of what heard and saw when was finishing A Farewell To Arms out in Sheridan and Big Horn— How old was I then? That was 1928 and I was just 30 years old while I was out there. Yet that bird says it is about middle aged people because <u>he himself</u> is middle-aged. I was 17 when first went to the war. (This for your own information) I write some stories absolutely as they happen ie Wine of Wyoming—The letter one, A Day's Wait The Mother of a Queen, Gambler, Nun, Radio, and another word for word as it happened, to Bra, After The Storm: |(Chamberlain found that more imaginative than the others)| others I invent completely Killers, Hills Like White Elephants, The Undefeated, Fifty Grand, Sea Change, A Simple Enquiry. <u>Nobody</u> can tell which ones I make up completely. The point is <u>I want</u> them all to sound as though they really happened. Then when I succeed those poor dumb pricks say they are all just skillful reporting.

I invented every word and every incident of A Farewell To Arms except possibly 3 or 4 incidents. All the best part is invented—95 per cent of The Sun Also was pure imagination. I took real people in that one and I controlled what they did—I made it all up—

A fool like Canby[4] thinks I'm a reporter. I'm a reporter <u>and an imaginative writer</u>. And I can still imagine plenty and there will be stories to write <u>As They Happened</u> as long as I live. Also I happen to be 35 years old and the last two stories I wrote in Havana were the best in the book—[5]. And this 15,000 word one[6] is better than either of them. Several miles better.— So if you let all the people who want me over with kid you into believing I'm through—or let the business office start to lay off me as a bad bet—You will be making a very considerable mistake because I havent started to write yet— (wont ever write you this again—)

I cant write better stories than some that I have written— What Mr. Fadiman[7] asks for—because you cant write any better stories than those—and nobody else can—But every once in a long while I can write one as good—And <u>all the time</u> I can write better stories than anybody else writing. But they want <u>better</u> ones and as good as <u>anyone ever</u> wrote.

God damn it. There cant be better ones. The one they pick out as "classic." Hills Like White Elephants not a damn critic thought <u>anything</u> of when it came out. I always knew how good it was but I'll be Goddamned if I like to have to say how good my stuff is in order to give the business office confidance enough to advertize it after they have read an unfavorable review and think I'm through

So I wont Ever again. Will do something else.

. . . . .
. . . . .
. . . . .
. . . . .
. . . . .
. . . . .

Yours always,

<u>Ernest</u>

### Notes

1. 564 words have been omitted from this letter.
2. Horace Gregory, "Ernest Hemingway Has Put on Maturity," *New York Herald Tribune Books,* October 29, 1933.
3. John Chamberlain, daily book reviewer for the *New York Times.*
4. Henry Seidel Canby, "Farewell to the Nineties," *Saturday Review of Literature* (October 28, 1933).
5. "A Way You'll Never Be" and "Fathers and Sons."
6. "One Trip Across" was published in *Cosmopolitan* (April 1934) before it was incorporated in *To Have and Have Not.*
7. Clifton Fadiman, "A Letter to Mr. Hemingway," *New Yorker* (October 18, 1933).

▲ ▼ ▲

*To: Perkins*
*From: Wolfe*                    *TLS, 2 pp. Princeton*

5 Montague Terrace, Brooklyn,
New York, December 15, 1933.

Dear Max:

I was pretty tired last night when I delivered that last batch of manuscript to you and could not say very much to you about it. There is not much to say except that today I feel conscious of a good many errors, both of omission and commission and wish I had had more time to arrange and sort out the material, but think it is just as well that I have given it to you even in its present shape.

I don't envy you the job before you. I know what a tough thing it is going to be to tackle, but I do think that even in the form in which the material has been given to you, you ought to be able to make some kind of estimate of its value or lack of value and tell me about it. If you do feel that on the whole I can now go ahead and complete it, I think I can go much faster than you realize. Moreover, when all the scenes have been completed and the narrative change to a third person point of view, I think there will be a much greater sense of unity than now seems possible in spite of the mutilated, hacked-up form in which you have the manuscript, and I do feel decidedly hopeful, and hope your verdict will be for me to go ahead and complete the first draft as soon as I can, and in spite of all the rhythms, chants—what you call my dithyrambs—which are all through the manuscript, I think you will find when I get through that there is plenty of narrative—or should I say when <u>you</u> get through— because I must shame-facedly confess that I need your help now more than I ever did.

You have often said that if I ever gave you something that you could get your hands on and weigh in its entirety from beginning to end, you could pitch in and help me to get out of the woods. Well, now here is your chance. I think a very desperate piece of work is ahead for both of us, but if you think it is worth doing and tell me to go ahead, I think there is literally nothing that I cannot accomplish. But you must be honest and straightforward in your criticism when you talk about it, even though what you say may be hard for me to accept after all this work, because that is the only fair way and the only good way in the end.

I want to get back to work on it as soon as I can and will probably go on anyway writing in the missing scenes and getting a complete manuscript as soon as I can. I wanted to write you this mainly to tell you that I am in a state of great trepidation and great hope also. Buried in that great pile of manuscript is some of the best writing I have ever done. Let's see to it that it does not go to waste.

Yours always, Tom Wolfe

Max, I think the total length of the manuscript I gave you is around 500,000 words.

▲ ▼ ▲

*To: Wolfe*                                      *Late 1933*
*From: Perkins*                                  *TS, 2 pp. Princeton*

*Undated memo to Wolfe, presumably from Perkins, for* Of Time and the River

### THINGS TO BE DONE IMMEDIATELY IN FIRST REVISION:

1–     Make rich man in opening scene older and more middle-aged
2–     Cut out references to previous book and to success
3–     Write out fully and with all the dialogue the jail and arrest scene
4–     Use material from Man on the Wheel[1] and Abraham Jones for first year in the city and University scenes
5–     Tell the story of love affair from beginning to end describing meeting with woman, etc.
6–     Intersperse jealousy and madness scenes with more scenes of dialogue with woman
7–     Use description of the trip home and the boom town scenes out of the Man on the Wheel.
      You can possibly use the trip home and boom town scene to follow on to the station scene. Play up desire to go home and feelings of homesickness and unrest and then develop idea that home town has become unfamiliar and strange to him and he sees he can no longer live there.
8–     Possibly ending for book with return to the city, the man in the window scene and the passages, "Some things will never change"
9–     In the Night Scene which precedes the station scene, write out fully with all dialogue the episodes of night including the death in the subway scene
10–    Cut out references to daughter
11–    Complete all scenes wherever possible with dialogue
12–    Fill in the memory of childhood scenes much more fully with additional stories and dialogue

*Note*

1. "The Man on the Wheel," part of the "Passengers" section of "K-19," was 90,000 words long in draft.

▲ ▼ ▲

To: *Hemingway*
From: *Perkins*                                    *CC, 3 pp.*[1] *Princeton*

January 12, 1933 [1934]

Dear Ernest:

The sale at the present moment amounts to thirteen thousand, six or seven hundred copies. We are now at that stage at which you came in last year,– many copies are on consignment of all the leading books, and we do not know what we may have sold out of the consignments. I hope we shall get to fifteen thousand by the time that is cleared up. It was not even a good depression year for publishers in general, but with the Longworth and Van Dine and Galsworthy and Sullivan[2] to help, we did a good deal better. We even sold about 3,000 of the first two volumes (which do not even touch the good part) of Churchill's Life of the Duke of Marlborough.–[3] But we gave a big advance on that book long ago, and I don't believe we shall ever get it back. We hope to carry on "Winner Take Nothing" through the winter and spring. The salesmen have just gone out and should get some good orders.

. . . . .

Have you heard what I was bound for some reason not to tell you, that Scott has finished his novel? A mighty fine one too. We are running it in Scribner's. I have had some hard but funny sessions with him in the last several months. The book is truly very fine as a whole. It has a very tight plot. Some people would pretend to misunderstand the adjective in view of the authorship, but not you,– though it does somewhat apply in the wrong sense. It is based upon a psychiatrical situation. The hero, one Dr. Diver, had prepared to be a psychiatrist;– and Scott could never have written it unless he had come into contact with sanitariums, psychiatrists, etc., etc., on account of Zelda's illness. It is the sort of story you can imagine Henry James writing, but of course it is written like Fitzgerald, and not James. If you were in a place where I could get it to you safely, I would send you the whole thing in proof. It really ought not to be serialized, but authors must eat, and magazines must live. I shall send you a set of complete proofs anyhow, when I have them, whether they get to you or not.

I went down to Baltimore and tried to read the manuscript here in an extremely unfinished and chaotic form, with Scott handing me Tom Collinses every few minutes, and taking out sections of the manuscript to read aloud to me. But we did get it finished. It was the serialization that made him do it. He had to do it once that was agreed upon.

Then Tom Wolfe's book.– I have got here about seven or eight hundred thousand words of it, and I am not going to let it get away from here. Tom is supposed to come here every afternoon at 4:30 and we work for two hours, and on Saturday afternoons, and the book will be published this summer. When it is, I am going to take a vacation.

. . . . .
. . . . .
. . . . .
. . . . .

Yours,

. . . . .

*Notes*

1. 220 words have been omitted from this letter.
2. Alice Roosevelt Longworth, *Crowded Hours*; S. S. Van Dine, *The Dragon Murder Case*; John Galsworthy, *One More River*; and Mark Sullivan, *Over Here: 1914–1918* (vol. 5 of *Our Times*).
3. *Marlborough: His Life and Times,* 4 vols. (Scribners, 1933–38).

▲ ▼ ▲

*To: Hemingway*
*From: Perkins*                              *CC, 4 pp.*[1] *Princeton*

Feb. 7, 1934

Dear Ernest:

As you know, Cosmop took your story, and I finally got them to give me a set of proof, and read it in excitement.[2] It is one of your big stories,– takes two or three days to shake it off. There are four stories in "Winner Take Nothing" that are anyhow as fine in their own ways, but this is one of those spectacular stories which everybody will feel to the full effect. I am mighty glad you wrote it, and I'll bet there will be a lot of talk about it.

. . . . .

I believe that Scott will be completely reinstated, if not more, by his "Tender Is the Night". He has improved it immensely by his revision—it was chaotic almost when I read it—and he has made it into a really most extraordinary piece of work.– And I believe when he gets through with revising the first quarter for the book, he will have a genuine masterpiece in its kind. He is in a much better psychological state of mind too, having done it,– I was down there about ten days ago. Domestically things are still bad with him, but about himself he feels like a new man, I could see. He has all kinds of plans now for writing,– wants to begin another novel immediately. I shall soon have the last of the book proof in type and will send you a set.– But you may not want to read it because the book itself will be better than this proof.

You know mighty well that I know you did right by us, as well as by Franklin.[3] He imposed rather hard terms—though not so bad really. But I was looking at the job as one of translation rather than of authorship, though his name was invaluable to it,– was in fact the biggest thing about it. But we never would have got the thing through at all if you had not been in it, I know that.

. . . . .

Always yours,

*Notes*

1. 142 words have been omitted from this letter.
2. "One Trip Across."
3. American bullfighter Sidney Franklin translated Spanish novelist Alejandro Pérez Lugín's novel *Currito de la Cruz* as *Shadows of the Sun* for Scribners (1934).

▲ ▼ ▲

❖❖❖❖❖❖❖❖❖❖❖❖❖❖❖❖❖❖❖❖❖❖❖❖❖❖

## SPRING PUBLICATIONS
### 1934

❖❖❖❖❖❖❖❖❖❖❖❖❖❖❖❖❖❖❖❖❖❖❖❖❖❖

**TENDER IS THE NIGHT**
by F. Scott Fitzgerald      *Publication Date, March.*   $2.50

**The Author:** *He is known to millions of readers as the most popular writer of short stories for "The Saturday Evening Post," and for his three famous novels: "This Side of Paradise," "The Beautiful and Damned," and "The Great Gatsby."*

**The Book:** One might be misled in the beginning of this book, just as was Rosemary Hoyt, the young movie star, by the glamorous beauty of the Riviera and the charm of the rich and leisured characters who first appear on the beach near Cannes. To Rosemary, Dick Diver's *ménage* and particularly himself, seemed all that the human heart could desire. So it all might seem to the reader, but there soon grows upon him amidst the revelry on the shore and then in Paris a sense that under the smooth and lovely surface there is lurking horror and brutality.

It is the story of Dr. Richard Diver, who had a great future before him and then was induced by the beauty and grace of Nicole, whom he met in a sanitarium at the beginning of the War, and by the pressure of her wealthy family, to marry her. He had had great plans for a career as a psychiatrist. By his marriage he was caught into the net of wealth, and the obligations, as they seemed, that go with it. He knew the dreadful secret behind Nicole's illness, but he did not realize all the implications of the position which he took.

This is the story of how he was captured in a silken coil and ultimately freed himself—but it is also a deeply ironic commentary upon the effects of wealth over all who possess it. It reveals increasingly as it advances the rottenness that underlies the most beautiful surface which is presented by the gay resorts of Europe and the people who frequent them.

**The Market:** *The market is obviously the entire reading public, but this book does have a special peculiar interest as being the first novel turning upon abnormal psychology caused by psychosis—the first full revelation of the nature and management of such a case.*

[ 3 ]

Catalogue entry for Fitzgerald's long-delayed fourth novel (Princeton University Library)

*To: Perkins*                                   *Key West, Florida*
*From: Hemingway*      *TLS with holograph inserts and postscript, 3 pp.¹ Princeton*

April 30, 1934

Dear Max:

. . . . .

I rushed a book last year because I had taken an advance. It was no fault of yours. I felt the obligation to get it out although my best judgement told me it needed another story of the kind I know it needed to have people think they were getting their moneys worth. It is not enough to just give them their two dollars worth, anybodys two dollars worth, if they will read them over. You have to give them just ten times more than anybody else ever gives them for the same amt. of money. And I had kidded myself that you didn't.

But I am a careerist, as you can read in the papers, and my idea of a career is never to write a phony line, never fake, never cheat, never be sucked in by the y.m.c.a. movements of the moment, and to give them as much literature in a book as any son of a bitch has ever gotten into the same number of words. But that isn't enough. If you want to make a living out of it you have to, in addition every so often, without faking, cheating or deviating from the above to give them something they understand and that has a story—not a plot—just a story that they can follow instead of simply feel, the way most of the stories are. The story is there but I dont tell it to them in so many words. I knew it then, too. But because I had taken the damned advance I thought what the hell —that's good enough for them and more—they won't know it is—but what the hell.

But I am a professional and professionals learn by their mistakes instead of justifying them. So that won't happen again.

. . . . .

Now about Scott's book. I finished it and it has all the brilliance and most of the defects he always has. In spite of marvellous places there is something wrong with it and, as a writer, this is what I believe is wrong. He starts with two people Gerald and Sara Murphy. He has the accent of their voices, their home, their looks marvellously. But he knows nothing about them. Sara Murphy is a lovely and a marvellously strong woman. Gerald is a man of great charm but very complicated emotionally and Scott depicts his charm very well at various times. He knows <u>nothing</u> about him emotionally.

But he takes these people who are formed by certain things, suffer from certain faults, which he knows nothing of because when he was with them he was busy making them into romantic figures instead of knowing what they were about (you do not learn about people by asking them questions), creating these romantic figures and then asking them concrete questions such as 'did you sleep with your wife before you married her?' in order to obtain "facts" to insert in the plasticine of his figures to try to make them seem true—it's awfully silly.

But anyway he takes a strong woman like Sara, a regular pioneer mother, and first arbitrarily makes her into a psychopathic case and then makes her into Zelda, then back into Sara, and finally into nothing. It's bloody hopeless.

Gerald is Gerald for a while, then made-up, the made-up part is good, then becomes Scott and has things happen to him that could never happen to Gerald. The beating up by the Carabiniere in Rome etc. So you are never convinced about him going to pieces.

He has taken a series of incidents, good incidents from his life and used them quite arbitrarily, made the story conform to the few wows he had saved up out of his life.

It isn't the way prose is written when the prose is any damned good—but then by Jesus he has so lousy much talent and he has suffered so without knowing why, has destroyed himself so and destroyed Zelda, though never as much as she has tried to destroy him, that out of this little children's, immature, misunderstood, whining for lost youth death-dance that they have been dragging into and out of insanity to the tune of, the guy all but makes a fine book, all but makes a splendid book.

But the hell of it is that you can't write Prose after you are thirty five unless you can think straight. And it is the flashes where he <u>does</u> think straight that carry this book in spite of all the worn christmas tree ornaments that are Scott's idea of literature.

The trouble is that he wouldn't learn his trade and he won't be honest. He is always the brilliant young gentleman writer, fallen gentleman writer, gent in the gutter, gent ruined, but never a man. If he is writing about a woman going crazy he has to take a woman who has gone crazy. He can't take one woman who would never go crazy and make her go. In life she wouldnt go crazy. Thats what makes it false. If he is writing about himself going to hell as a man and a writer he has to accept that and write about that. He can make it all up and imagine it all but he must imagine it truly. That is. If he wants it to be literature. You can make up every word, thought, and action. But you must make them up truly. Not fake them to suit your convenience or to fit some remembered actions. And you must know what things are about. He misunderstands everything. But he has this marvellous talent, this readability, and if he would write a good one now, making it all up, he could do it. But using actual stuff is the most difficult writing in the world to have good. Making it all up is the easiest and the best. But you have to know what things are about before you start and you have to have confidence. It is like navigating once you have dropped the shore out of sight astern. If you have confidence you are all right. But to have confidence you have to know your stuff.

. . . . .
. . . . .
. . . . .

Don't show any of this above to Scott or tell him I said anything I'll write him but have been too busy so far.

Best to you always,
Ernest

. . . . .
. . . . .

## Note

1. 512 words have been omitted from this letter.

▲▼▲

*To: Hemingway*
*From: Perkins*                        *CC, 3 pp.*[1] *Princeton*

May 3, 1934

Dear Ernest:

. . . . .

I was extremely interested in what you said about Scott and about the novel. I knew that a great deal of this was true, and yet a great deal of the good writing he has done has come from that very fact of a sort of adolescent romanticism. I saw Scott last week in Baltimore and things are very far from right with him, and it is all based on this confusion in himself. There are certain fundamental things about which he has the strangest, most unreal ideas. It has always been so of him. But about one of these delusions I think I made an impression. Here he is, only about thirty-five or six years old, with immense ability in writing, and in a state of hopelessness. But it is useless to try to talk directly to him about it.– The only way one could make an impression would be by some oblique method, and that takes a cleverer person than I am.

. . . . .

Yours,

. . . . .

## Note

1. 155 words have been omitted from this letter.

▲▼▲

*To: Hemingway*
*From: Fitzgerald*                    *TLS with holograph postscript, 1 p. Kennedy*

1307 Park Avenue,
Baltimore, Maryland,
May 10, 1934.

Dear Ernest:

Did you like the book? For God's sake drop me a line and tell me one way or another. You can't hurt my feelings. I just want to get a few intelligent slants at it to get some of the reviewers jargon out of my head.

Ever Your Friend
Scott

All I meant about the editing was that if I'd been in Max's place I'd have urged you to hold the book for more material.[1] It had neither the surprise of I.O.T (nessessessarily) nor its unity. And it did not have <u>as large a proportion</u> of 1st flight stories as M.W.W. I think in a "general presentation" way this could have been attoned for by sheer bulk. Take that opinion for what it's worth.

On the other hand: you can thank God you missed this publishing season!. I am 5th best seller in the country + havn't broken 12,000.

*Note*

1. Fitzgerald refers to Hemingway's story collection *Winner Take Nothing* (1933), which he compares to Hemingway's earlier collections *In Our Time* and *Men Without Women.*

▲▼▲

*To: Hemingway*
*From: Perkins*                         *CC, 3 pp.[1] Princeton*

May 23, 1934

Dear Ernest:

. . . . .
. . . . .
. . . . .

If ever I get down there to Key West I would like to talk about Scott's book. Anyhow it was a mighty notable book, and is quite furiously discussed. I know of course, that there is that conflict in Scott's character, and a kind of basic illusion which causes a defect in the book and did not cause one in "The Great Gatsby" which was completely fitted to the illusion and the conflict. The other difficulty came very largely from the fact that Scott was too, too long in getting the book written, and he could not bear to exclude all of the superfluous material which he had gathered up in those years. He did exclude a good deal that was in the first manuscript, but he could not—though he prides himself in his relentlessness in this regard—bring himself to exclude a good deal more that should have been left out.

. . . . .

Always yours,

*Note*

1. 168 words have been omitted from this letter.

▲ ▼ ▲

*To: Hemingway*
*From: Perkins*                                   *CC, 5 pp.*[1] *Princeton*

June 28, 1934

Dear Ernest:

. . . . .
. . . . .

I cannot come down now. I cannot leave as long as I can keep Tom going well, as he is doing now. We have over half the book finished,[2] except for a little touching up on another reading. We have got a good system now. We work every evening from 8:30 (or as near as Tom can come to it) until 10:30 or 11:00, and Tom does actual writing at times, and does it well,– where pieces have to be joined up. We are organizing the book.– That is the best part of the work we are doing. It will be pretty well integrated in the end, and vastly more effectively arranged. The fact is, Tom could do the work but his impulse is all away from the hard detailed revision. He is mighty ingenious at times, when it comes to the organization of material. The scheme is pretty clear in his own head, but he shrinks from the sacrifices which are really cruel often. A couple of nights ago I told Tom that a whole lot of fine stuff he had in simply ought to come out because it resulted in blurring a very important effect. Literally, we sat here for an hour thereafter without saying a word, while Tom glowered and pondered and figetted in his chair. Then he said, "Well, then will you take the responsibility?" And I said, "I have simply got to take the responsibility. And what's more," I said, "I will be blamed either way." But he did it, and in the end he knew he was right. We go over to "Chatham Walk" where you sit in the open, afterwards. Anyhow, we will have this book done by the end of July if we go on as we are going now.

. . . . .
. . . . .

Always yours,

*Notes*

1. 321 words have been omitted from this letter.
2. *Of Time and the River.*

▲ ▼ ▲

*To: Fitzgerald*
*From: Perkins*                                   *CC, 3 pp. Princeton*

Aug. 20, 1934

Dear Scott:

My personal idea of it would be that we should publish the book of stories as soon as we could, whenever it was.[1] I think it urgently important that you should bring out these stories close to "Tender Is the Night" for I think that the reviewers will be impressed by them, and that it will lead to a new discussion of "Tender Is the Night" and give a good many of them a chance to speak out more clearly than they did before. "Tender Is the Night" will have had time to sink in, and they will have had more conviction about it. Besides, the stories themselves show more sides of you than "Tender Is the Night".– They show that you understand more different sorts of people than are in that. I am very anxious to get them out for those reasons, especially.

You are in a position where you are compelled to think of immediate financial return beyond anything else. But if there is any conceivable way by which you could get these proofs read quickly and let us get the book out in October, it would in every other respect than that of immediate financial return be worth doing. You are smart about organizing your work, so you must have thought of everything. Is there any way that another person could work with you? The only question seems to be that of what you have used from the stories in "Tender Is the Night". I several times did notice things you had used. This ought to be avoided, of course, but I think it need not be avoided to the very uttermost. There is no reason a writer should not repeat a little in those respects. Hem has done it.[2] Anyhow, whatever would hasten the publication of this book would, I think, be worth doing if it could be done.

Always yours,

P.S. Just got your telegram about Pat O'Mara.[3] I know he has written well, and we shall look after his manuscripts well.

*Notes*

1. *Taps at Reveille,* Fitzgerald's fourth story collection, was published on March 20, 1935.
2. On August 24, 1934, Fitzgerald replied: "The fact that Ernest has let himself repeat here and there a phrase would be no possible justification for my doing the same.

Each of us has his virtues and one of mine happens to be a great sense of exactitude about my work. He might be able to afford a lapse in that line where I wouldn't be and after all I have got to be the final judge of what is appropriate in these cases. Max, to repeat for the third time, this is in no way a question of laziness. It is a question absolutely of self-preservation."

3. O'Mara was published by Vanguard Press, not by Scribners.

▲ ▼ ▲

*To: Hemingway*
*From: Perkins*                                    *CC, 3 pp.*[1] *Princeton*

Oct. 6, 1934

Dear Ernest:

That about the novel is wonderful news.[2] I won't worry about how it compares with other people's novels. I'd felt morally certain you were doing a novel, but not quite, because when you were here you spoke of having written a great deal on a narrative and of thinking you might reduce it to a story. Sidney Franklin did not know what you were writing, but he did tell me you had written a lot. You do a novel, and we shall strain every muscle for it. Things look better now too,– if only they don't break them down in some new way. But let me know soon if The First Fifty-Seven[3] could be published in the fall or the spring, or when. If the novel were imminent I would do the novel first.

. . . . .

. . . . .

That word in Tom's subtitle is Hunger,– "A Legend of Man's Hunger". I do think with Tom pretentiousness may be right. That is the idea anyhow,– at least in my accepting the subtitle. And it is a darn sight less pretentious than it was when Tom started. We have got over half the book now in type, and if we can only keep Tom from writing in a lot more, we shall soon have it all in type, and out in January. Of course twice as much ought to be done to it as he will let us. And then my conscience bothers me about it often. A man ought to understand his own book better than anyone else can. But I just have to follow my judgment regardless. Somebody has to do it. There is no question but it needs about fifty percent cutting, and Tom won't give it one-tenth of one percent.

Don't get into too much danger down there.

Always yours,

### Notes

1. 113 words have been omitted from this letter.
2. On October 3, 1934, Hemingway had written Perkins that he had "50,000 words on this long thing," a draft of *Green Hills of Africa*. Perkins assumed that Hemingway was writing a novel set in Africa.

3. Projected title for a collected edition of Hemingway's short stories.

▲ ▼ ▲

To: *Perkins*                          *1934*
From: *Hemingway*             *TLS, 2 pp.*[1] *Princeton*

Key West, Florida
November 16

Dear Max,

I finished the long bitch this morning, 492 mssspages, average, I suppose, something over a hundred and twenty words to the page. Feel pretty good about it. Will write you about it later. Too pooped to write about it now. Also about the first fifty-five or the first fifty-six, or whatever we call it. . . .

. . . . .
. . . . .
. . . . .

Glad you've got Tom Wolfe to the printers but I swear to God that last story in the magazine opened in the phoniest way and had the most Christ-awful grandiloquent title of anything I ever read.[2] You know why your geniuses stall so long and are afraid to publish may very well be because they have a big fear inside of them that it's phoney instead of being a World Masterpiece and are afraid somebody will find it out. It's better to write good ones one at a time and let the critics jump on what they don't like and have orgasms about what they do like and you know they're good yourself and write them and get them out and not give a good God-damn about what anybody says. But the only way you can do that is not to fake and most of the boys, if they don't fake, would be starved to death by Wednesday next. I suppose I'm getting to feel pretty good and may be a little snooty at having finished what started last April, so better sign off and not speak ill of my overassed and underbrained contemporaries, your World Geniuses. There's no feeling, Max, like knowing you can do the old stuff, even though it makes you fairly insufferable at the time to your publisher. On the other hand, I've never shot worse at birds in my life so I suppose what you make in Boston you lose in Chicago and after all I'm just a God-damned writer. . . .

Yours always
Ernest

### Notes

1. 610 words have been omitted from this letter.
2. "Dark in the Forest, Strange as Time," *Scribner's Magazine* (August 1934).

▲ ▼ ▲

*To: Wolfe*
*From: Perkins*                                    *ALS, 6 pp. Harvard*

Jany 21ˢᵗ, 1935

Dear Tom:– I'm committed to Key West now,[1] however impossible it seems, to go, + since, when I return, Of Time + the River will be a book, I'm taking this last moment to say what I've long been on the point of saying:–

Nothing could give me greater pleasure or greater pride as an editor than that the book of the writer whom I have most greatly admired should be dedicated to me if it were sincerely done. But you can not, + should not try to, change your conviction that I have deformed your book, or at least prevented it from coming to perfection. It is therefore impossible for you sincerely to dedicate it to me + it ought not to be done. I know we are truly friends + have gone through much in company + this matter, for my part, can have nothing to do with that, or ever shall. But this is another matter. I would have said this sooner but for some fear that you would misinterpret me. But the plain truth is that working on your writings, however it has turned out, for good or bad, has been the greatest pleasure, for all its pain, + the most interesting episode of my editorial life. The way in which we are presenting this book must prove our (+ my) belief in it. But what I have done has destroyed your belief in it + you must not act inconsistently with that fact. As for your preface[2] there is this obstacle to it at the start: a reader is meant to enter into a novel as if it were reality + so to feel it, + a preface tends to break down that illusion, + to make him look at it in a literary way. But perhaps that is in some degree a literary objection to a preface + when your's began so finely I thought you might be right to have it. But when I read more of it today it seemed to me you did the very things you meant to avoid doing in the novel: you made the book seem personal + autobiographical, + by showing resentment against those who objected to the apparent reality (as the preface implied) of the characters in the Angel you opened yourself to the same charge against this book + notified the whole public that it might rightly be brought.—And of the whole public not a handful can understand the artist's point of view or the <u>writer's</u> conscience. In these + other ways, I thought, you bared yourself to all the enemies you have + I told you so because I am your friend—

Max

P.S. I thought that woman looked dangerous![3]

<u>MP.</u>

### Notes

1. Perkins went to Key West to pick up the typescript for *Green Hills of Africa.*
2. Wolfe wished to add a preface that explained the novel's evolution and acknowledged Perkins's editorial role.
3. Possibly an intoxicated woman in a bar.

Perkins went to Key West in 1935 to discuss the publication of *Green Hills of Africa* with Hemingway (Princeton University Library).

▲ ▼ ▲

*To: Wolfe*                                    *1935. Perkins's personal letterhead*
*From: Perkins*                                          *ALS, 3 pp. Harvard*

Friday Feby 8<u>th</u>

Dear Tom:— I have seen the dedication in your book +, whatever the degree of justice in what it implies, I can think of nothing that could have made me more happy.[1] I won't go further into what I feel about it: I'm a Yankee + cannot speak what I feel most strongly, well. But I do wish to say that I think it a most generous + noble utterance. Certainly for one who could say that of me I ought to have done all that it says I did do.

I am glad the book is done because now it will be published.— But, although I had moments of despair + many hours of discouragement over it, I look back upon our struggles with regret that they are over. And, I swear, I believe that in truth the whole episode was a most happy one for me. I like to think we may go through another such war together.

Always Yours
Max

*Note*

1. One draft of TW's dedication read:

TO
MAXWELL EVARTS PERKINS

A great editor, and a brave and honest man, who stuck to the writer of this book through times of utter hopelessness and doubt and would not let him give in to his own despair, the dedication of a work to be known as *Of Time and the River* is offered with the hope that it may be in some part worthy of the devotion, skill, the loyal and unshaken friendship that was given to it, and without which it could never have been written, with the hope that all of it may be in some part worthy of the loyal faith, the skill, the patience and devotion, without which none of it could ever have been written, and which were given to it always by a great editor and a brave and honest man (*Notebooks*, p. 666).

▲ ▼ ▲

**To**

**MAXWELL EVARTS PERKINS**

A GREAT EDITOR AND A BRAVE AND HONEST MAN, WHO STUCK TO THE WRITER OF THIS BOOK THROUGH TIMES OF BITTER HOPELESSNESS AND DOUBT AND WOULD NOT LET HIM GIVE IN TO HIS OWN DESPAIR, A WORK TO BE KNOWN AS "OF TIME AND THE RIVER" IS DEDICATED WITH THE HOPE THAT ALL OF IT MAY BE IN SOME WAY WORTHY OF THE LOYAL DEVOTION AND THE PATIENT CARE WHICH A DAUNTLESS AND UNSHAKEN FRIEND HAS GIVEN TO EACH PART OF IT, AND WITHOUT WHICH NONE OF IT COULD HAVE BEEN WRITTEN

Dedication printed in *Of Time and the River,* reduced from Wolfe's original statement (Bruccoli Collection, Thomas Cooper Library, University of South Carolina)

*To: Perkins*  
*From: Hemingway*  

*Key West, Florida*  
*Wire. Princeton*  

FEB 18 1935

LETTER JUST RECEIVED SORRY UNABLE UNDERSTAND YOUR
ATTITUDE PRICE UNLESS YOU MEAN YOU WANT ME TO REFUSE
IT TO RELEASE YOU FROM PURCHASING¹ STOP WHAT DOES WE
DO NOT INTEND THERE SHALL BE ANY HARD FEELINGS ABOUT
PRICE MEAN STOP AND ON HOW SOUND AN ECONOMIC BASIS
DID I OFFER IT TO YOU STOP THE MAGAZINE HAS NEVER BEEN
ON A SOUND ECONOMIC BASIS AND NEITHER HAVE I BUT IVE
NEVER COST A PUBLISHER ANYWHERE ANY MONEY EITHER
EXCEPT LIVERIGHT BY LEAVING HIM STOP WHEN OFFERED YOU
FIFTY GRAND YOU WANTED TO CUT IT AS TOO LONG LATER
YOU GAVE FIVE THOUSAND DOLLARS FOR A LONG SHORT
STORY CONTEST STOP I TURNED DOWN THREE TIMES WHAT
YOU PAID ME TO PUBLISH FAREWELL IN THE MAGAZINE STOP
CAN YOU WONDER WHY DON'T UNDERSTAND THIS WHEN OUR
CLEAR AGREEMENTWAS YOU WERE TO WIRE ME AS SOON AS
YOU REACHED NEWYORK WHAT YOU COULD PAY

ERNEST

*Note*

1. Hemingway refers to the negotiations for serial publication of *Green Hills of Africa* in *Scribner's Magazine.*

▲▼▲

*To: Hemingway*  
*From: Perkins*  

*CC, 4 pp. Princeton*  

Feb. 19, 1935

Dear Ernest:

When there is a misunderstanding it never does any good to attempt explanations. It generally makes things worse. But the truth is my attitude has always been perfectly simple and there has never been in it any intention that it should be anything else. What I intended you to think was that we would make you the highest price we possibly could in view of the situation of the magazine, which I tried to explain, and that in order to do this, if the road was clear for the serial, we would have to spread it over as many numbers as we could without detriment to time of book publication, for the sake of spreading the payment. If I misled you, it was in not discussing the price more specifically when I was there at the time you mentioned five thousand. I had begun by saying between four and five thousand, and that was all that was said because I could not tell how many numbers we could run the serial in, and I thought it possible, though unwise, that we might be able to catch an earlier number to start with, and run it in eight, which would have made the five thousand easy. When I got back that was impossible. Anyway, it would have been too many numbers. Seven is a good many to stretch something over that ought, ideally, to be in one number. Surely I could never have given you the idea that we did not want the serial. I had never considered the possibility of serialization before you brought it up because I knew our price would seem low to you, and I simply regarded the thing as beyond our reach. In each of my letters I pretty clearly said that we would meet your price for we always have been completely for you since the first day we had anything here of yours,- unless you except the matter of "Fifty Grand" and the magazine of that day.

Dashiell was slower in reading the serial than I hoped he would be, but he was not unreasonably long as compared to any other magazine as I know, for I have dealings with them.– And the delay too, was inevitable on account of the situation he happened to be in. I daresay the editor of "Esquire"[1] runs a one man show where he can say Yes or No on an instant, without any regard to anyone else. But it cannot be that way in a house like this. The man who manages the magazine ought to have his say, and I do not believe that the Cosmop or anything but "Esquire" and perhaps not that, could have acted any more quickly. If you had suggested serialization to me before I came to Key West, I could have been prepared to deal with it entirely. As it was, all I could say was that I was positive of our wanting "The Green Hills" for a serial unless we were blocked by other things which was a slight danger, and if we could pay an adequate price.

We shall begin the serial in the May number which appears about April 20th. The last number, which will have the longest installment, as it should have (and I think installments break up very well) will appear October 20th, and we can publish it that moment, which is a good time.

### Note

1. Arnold Gingrich, editor of *Esquire,* had begun publishing Hemingway in autumn 1933.

▲ ▼ ▲

*To: Hemingway*
*From: Perkins*                          *CC, 2 pp.*[1] *Princeton*

Feb. 27, 1935

Dear Ernest:

. . . . .

. . . . .

The real reason I am writing is this: Scott has got back from four weeks in North Carolina and writes me "I have been on the absolute wagon for a month, not even beer or wine, and feel fine." He told Ober that he was never going to touch another drop. I thought maybe you could find some time and some reason to do something that would help him in the crisis he will have to meet after a bit. It would be a miracle if he could stop wholly and for good, but perhaps he will pull it off. I thought you might have some excuse to write him in a way that would do good. I suppose he is not telling people he has stopped, but I mean just something that would buck him up. His letter sounds fine and happy, but I know there will be a let down and a struggle.

Always yours,

*Note*

1. 114 words have been omitted from this letter.

▲▼▲

*To: Perkins*
*From: Fitzgerald*                         *TLS, 4 pp. Princeton*

1307 Park Avenue,
Baltimore, Maryland,
March 11, 1935.

Dear Max:

The second annoyance to you in two days—pretty soon I'm going to be your most popular author. (By the way we had sort of a Scribner congerie here last night. Jim Boyd and Elizabeth[1] came to supper and George Calverton[2] dropped in afterwards. Your name came up frequently and you would have probably wriggled more than at Wolfe's dedication. To prolong this parenthesis unduly I am sorry I mentioned Tom's book. I hope to God I won't be set up as the opposition for there are fine things in it, and I loved reading it, and I am delighted that it's a wow, and it may be a bridge for something finer. I simply feel a certain disappointment which I would, on no account, want Tom to know about, for, responding as he does to criticism, I know it would make us life long enemies and we might do untold needless damage to each other, so please be careful how you quote me. This is in view of Calverton's saying he heard from you that I didn't like it. It has become increasingly plain to me that the very excellent organization of a long book or the finest perceptions and judgment in time of revision do not go well with liquor. A short story can be written on a bottle, but for a novel you need the mental speed that enables you to keep the whole pattern in your head and ruthlessly sacrifice the sideshows as Ernest did in "A Farewell to Arms." If a mind is slowed up ever so little it lives in the individual part of a book rather than in a book as a whole; memory is dulled. I would give anything if I hadn't had to write Part III of "Tender is the Night" entirely on stimulant. If I had one more crack at it cold sober I believe it might have made a great difference. Even Ernest commented on sections that were needlessly included and as an artist he is as near as I know for a final reference. Of course, having struggled with Tom Wolfe as you did all this is old hat to you. I will conclude this enormous parenthesis with the news that Elizabeth has gone to Middleburg to help Mrs. White open up her newly acquired house.)

This letter is a case of the tail (the parenthesis) wagging the dog. Here is the dog. A man named John S. Martens writes me wanting to translate "Tender is the Night" or "This Side of Paradise" or "The Great Gatsby" into Norwegian. He has written Scribner's and met the same blank wall of silence that has greeted me about all publishing of my books in other countries. I am quite willing to handle continental rights directly but I cannot do it when I do not know even the name of the publisher of my books, having never had copies of them or any information on that subject. Isn't there somebody in your office who is especially delegated to seeing to such things? It is really important to me and if I should write a book that had an international appeal it would be of great advantage to have a foothold with translators and publishers in those countries. All I want from you is the status of "The Great Gatsby" in Scandinavia, Germany, etc. and a word as to whether I shall go ahead and make arrangements myself for the future in that regard.

I'd be glad to get a dozen or so copies of "Taps at Reveille" as soon as available.

Ever yours,<br>Scott

P.S. I haven't had a drink for almost six weeks and haven't had the faintest temptation as yet. Feel fine in spite of the fact that business affairs and Zelda's health have never been worse.

### Notes

1. Elizabeth Lemmon, Perkins's distant cousin, with whom he had a twenty-five-year platonic romance.

2. V. F. Calverton, born George Goetz, wrote and edited books on political and sociological subjects.

▲ ▼ ▲

*To: Perkins*
*From: Wolfe* *Wire. Princeton*

DEAR MAX TODAY IF I MISTAKE NOT IS WEDNESDAY MARCH THIRTEENTH I CAN REMEMBER ALMOST NOTHING OF LAST SIX DAYS YOU ARE THE BEST FRIEND I HAVE I CAN FACE BLUNT FACT BETTER THAN DAMNABLE INCERTITUDE GIVE ME THE STRAIGHT PLAIN TRUTH.[1]

    TOM.

### *Note*

    1. Wolfe was inquiring about the reviews for *Of Time and the River,* which had been published on March 8, 1935.

▲ ▼ ▲

*To: Wolfe* March 14, 1935
*From: Perkins* *Wire. Harvard*

GRAND EXCITED RECEPTION IN REVIEWS STOP TALKED OF EVERYWHERE AS TRULY GREAT BOOK STOP ALL COMPARISONS WITH GREATEST WRITERS STOP ENJOY YOURSELF WITH LIGHT HEART STOP WRITING

    MAX

▲ ▼ ▲

*To: Wolfe*
*From: Perkins* *CC, 3 pp. Princeton*

March 14, 1935

Dear Tom:

    Everybody outside of this house, outside the business, was amazed by the reception of "Of Time and the River". In the business it was expected, but even there, the excitement of the reviewers and their enthusiasm, was beyond the degree of expectation. You told me not to send you the reviews (I did send you a cable on the 8th which you must have got) but I am sending you herewith the first thing I can lay hands on that gives any kind of summary,– excerpts from some of the reviews. The reviews on the whole I think are much better than these excerpts could indicate. They all make parallels with the great writers, except in a few instances where no parallels are made. About the only one that mentions a contemporary is the one by Chamberlain[1] which mentions Lewis. Honestly, unless you expected no degree of adverse criticism at all, because of course there was that about too great length and the sort of things we all talked of, I cannot

imagine why you should have any restraint upon your happiness in this vacation. If any man could rest on laurels for a bit, the man is you. As for the sale,
we cannot tell yet how it will go on because a large number of copies—some
fifteen, seventeen thousand—were distributed to the stores, and it will take a little while for them to sell out. But we are getting some reorders now, and we have
printed five editions,– 30,000 copies. The Times, Tribune, and Saturday Review
gave you full front pages, and your picture was everywhere. People who went out
on Sunday afternoon to teas, etc., as Louise did, and Wheelock, where they were
not publishing people, but just regular people, the book was excitedly talked
about. We have a splendid window of which I have a copy to show you.[2] None
of the things you feared about the book were even hinted at, and your position
is enormously enhanced in every kind of way.– So for Heaven's sake, forget anxiety, which you haven't the slightest ground for but every ground for the greatest happiness and confidence, and enjoy yourself.

Always yours,

P.S. A lot of letters have accumulated for you, but I am holding them as you
directed. I am just writing this line the moment I got to the office and mailing
it immediately so as to get it to you as soon as can be done.

*Notes*

1. John Chamberlain previewed *Of Time and the River* in "Books of the Times,"
*New York Times,* March 8, 1935: "It is undoubtedly the richest American fiction since
'Arrowsmith' and 'An American Tragedy.'" Chamberlain formally reviewed the novel on
March 12: "As one makes the acquaintance of person after person, one feels like rising
to exclaim, 'Is there any living being whom Wolfe can't put before you in a novel?' Even
his Rotarian-minded business men have detail, and edge, a bite to their characterization
that might move Sinclair Lewis to homicidal envy."
2. Scribner's Bookstore window display.

▲ ▼ ▲

*To: Perkins*                    *St. George's Court letterhead, London*
*From: Wolfe*                         *ALS, 132 pp.[1] Princeton*

*This is Section one—<u>Am sending letter in sections</u><br>
Sunday March 31,<br>
1935

Dear Max: I know I should have written you before this, but until the last two
or three days I have written no one at all—— save for one or two, letters written on the ship—and of course have saved your letter to the last, because it was
probably the one which should have been written first.

—— Thursday——April 4th——I am picking this letter up again after
three or four days intermission—I seem to have a hell of a time getting on with

it, which is strange, as it is the one I most especially want to write— . . . . In Paris I couldn't sleep at all—I walked the streets from night to morning and was in the worst shape I have ever been in in my life—all the pent-up strain and tension of the last few months seemed to explode and I will confess to you that there were times there when I really was horribly afraid I was going mad—all the unity and control of personality seemed to have escaped from me—it was as if I were on the back of some immense rocketing engine which was running wild and over which I had no more control than a fly—I came home to my hotel one night—or rather at daybreak one morning—tried to get off to sleep— and had the horrible experience of seeming to disintegrate into at least six people —I was in bed and suddenly it seemed these other shapes of myself were moving out of me—all around me—one of them touched me by the arm—another was talking in my ear—others walking around the room—and suddenly I would come to with a terrific jerk and all of them would rush back into me again—I can swear to you I was not asleep—it was one of the strangest and most horrible experiences I've ever had—There were about three days of which I could give no clear accounting—and loss of memory of that sort is to me one of the worse things that can happen—That was the reason I sent you that frenzied telegram[2] —I had found your first cable when I got to Paris, but I wanted to know the worst—Your second cable cheered me up tremendously and at last when your letter with the excerpts from the reviews came I felt enormously relieved—I hope to God it all really is true as you said—that we have had a genuine and great success and then when I come back I will find my position enormously enhanced—If that is true I feel I can come back and accomplish almost anything—If that is true—if it is true that we have successfully surmounted the terrible, soul-shaking, heart-rending barrier of the accursed "second book"—I believe I can come back to work with the calm, the concentration, the collected force of my full power which I was unable to achieve in these frenzied, tormented, and soul-doubting last five years.—More than ever before, I have come to realize during this past month when I have had time to look back on that period and take stock of it—More than ever before, I have come to realize how much the making of a book, becomes an affair of honor to its maker. The honor of the artist—his whole life, all his character and personal integrity, all that he hopes and wants and dreams of, everything that gives his life any value to him— is at stake each time he produces any work—and that is really what the whole business of creation amounts to in the end—I hope to God that you and I have come through this ordeal honorably—I hope that we have won a true and worthy victory. You, I think, have done so in your great labors with me as an editor and a man—As for myself, the victory, if I have really won it, while a precious one, is not entire and whole as I would make it—If I have made my stamp come through, if through the ordeal and the agony of that book, the main outline of my full intention is revealed—that is a victory. But I can not ease my heart with the thought that I came through unshaken—I was badly shaken, time and again I was driven to the verge of utter self-doubt and despair by the sense of pressure all around me—the questions asked, the doubts expressed about my ability to write another book, the criticisms of my style, my adjectives, verbs, nouns, pronouns, etc, my length and fullness, my lack of Marxian politics and my failure to expound a set position in my writings—by all this, and countless other evidences of this pressure, I allowed myself so seriously to be disturbed and shaken that once or twice I [may] have been upon the very brink of total failure and submission. And now although, thanks to your great and patient efforts I may have won through to a victory—and pray to God this may be so!—that victory, as I say, is but a partial one, the full sum and import of my purpose has not been revealed.—I feel I have by no means begun to make a full and most effective use of my talent, and I hope this book will give me a position of some security, and freedom at last

This is Section <u>Two</u>

From the kind of perturbations that have tormented me these past five years, so that I may be able to achieve the concentration and totality I desire—

Sunday April 7—Well, here I go again—and I'm <u>bound</u> to finish this time—

. . .

  . . . . .

  . . . . .

  . . . . .

  . . . . .

This is Section <u>Three</u>

  . . . . .

—— Now, as to those excerpts from the reviews you sent me—They were splendid, wonderfully [    ], and I hope they were not too <u>hand-picked</u>—i.e. I hope that, as you said, they were taken more or less at random and if the reviews, on the whole were, as you say, better than these excerpts would indicate that would be wonderful—But even from these excerpts, good as they are, and from one or two indications in advance notices before I left New York I think I can spot the trend of some of the [    ] —Max, Max, perhaps you think I hate all forms of criticism, but the sad truth is, how much more critical am I, who am generally supposed to be utterly lacking in the critical faculty, than most of these critics are. God knows, I could profit by a wise and penetrating criticism as much as any man alive, but as I grow older I am beginning to see how rare— how much rarer even than Lear, Hamlet, the greatest productions of art—such criticism is—and how wrong-headed, false, and useless almost everything that passes as criticism is—I know for example that the great length of the book will be criticized—but the real, the tragic truth is that the book is not too long, but too short—I am not talking of page-length, word-length, or anything like that— as I told you many times, I did not care whether the final length of the book was 300, 500, or a 1000 pages so long as I had realized completely and finally my full intention—and that was not realized—I still sweat with anguish—with a sense of irremediable loss—at the thought of what another six months would have done to that book—how much more whole and perfect it would have been—Then there would have been no criticism of its episodic character—for, by God, in purpose and in spirit, that book was not episodic but a living whole and I could have made it so—the whole enwrought, inweaving sense of time and of man's past conjoined forever to each living [     ] moment of his life could have been made manifest—the thing that I <u>must</u> and <u>will</u> get into the whole thing somehow—Again, people will talk of the book having taken five years to write, but the real truth of the matter was that it was written practically in the whole in a year—it was written too fast, with frenzied maddened haste, under a terrible sense of pressure after I had written two other antecedent books and found I had not got back to a true beginning.—It is the work of frenzied, des- perate, volcanic haste after too much time had slipped away, and no one will know that—Even now, I not read the book, save for a page or two at a time— at every point the deficiency of my performance compared with the whole of my intent stares me in the face—the countless errors in wording and proof-reading —for which <u>I</u> alone am utterly to blame—but which in my frenzied state of mind I let pass by stab me to the heart—I was not ready to read proof, I was not through <u>writing</u>—the fault is my own. I fell down on that final job, the book was written and typed and rushed in to you in such frantic haste day after day that I did not even catch the errors in wording the typist made in an effort to decipher my handwriting—there are <u>thousands</u> of them—I don't know where to begin, but for God's sake, if it should be vouchsafed us that <u>more</u> editions will be printed, try to catch these:?[3]

. . . . .

Max, Max, I cannot go on, but I am sick at heart—we should have waited six months longer—the book, like Caesar, was from its mother's womb untimely ripped—like King Richard, brought into the world "scarce half made up"—[4]

Before I went away, you wrote me, in reference to the introduction I wanted to write, that you were trying to "save me from my enemies"—Max, my enemies are so much more numerous than you expect—they include, in addition to the Henry Harts,[5] Wassons,[6] and others of that sort, the Benets,[7] the I.M.P's,[8] the F.P.A's,[9] the Morleys,[10] the Nathans,[11] the Mark Van Dorens,[12] the Mike Golds,[13] and others of that sort—they include also the Lee Simonsons,[14] the Theatre Guilders,[15] the Neighborhood Playhousers,[16] the Hound and Horners, the Kir- stins,[17] Galantieres[18]—and all that crowd with all its power and wealth—and I fear we have played directly into their hands by our carelessness and by our frenzied haste—our failure to <u>complete</u> just when completion was in our grasp—I gravely fear that by the time this reaches you the reaction will have set in—the enemy will have gathered itself together and the attack begun—I can't go through five more years like this last five—my health is gone—my youth is gone—my energy is gone—my hair is going, I have grown fat and old—and for all my agony and anguish—the loss of my youth and health—what have I got?—I've got to have some security and repose—I've got to be allowed to finish what I've begun—I am no longer young enough, I have not energy or strength enough to go through it again—

——— For God's sake: try to kill false rumors

This is <u>Fourth</u> and
Last Section

When you hear them—before I left I saw that they were beginning to make another rubber stamp under the name of "criticism"—apparently they had discovered that I was six and a half feet tall, and very large—therefore it follows that all my characters are seven feet tall—bellow and roar when they talk—that I can create nothing but a race of gigantic monsters—Max, for Christ's sake, I beg and plead with you, don't let this horrible god-damned lie go unanswered— I have never created a monster in my life, none of my people are seven feet tall—the <u>fault</u> the <u>fault</u> always—as <u>you</u> should know—is not that we exceed the vital energy of life but that we fall short of it—and that a horrible misbegotten race of [    ] critics whose lies have grown underneath a barrel call out "monster" and "exaggeration" at you the moment you begin to approach the energy of life—You yourself told me you took one of your daughters through the Grand Central Station and showed her twenty people who might have stepped out of the pages of Dickens—and not a day of my life passes—a day spent in the <u>anguish of intense and constant speculation</u> and not at <u>literary cocktail parties</u> that I do not see a hundred—no, a thousand—who, if you put them in a book, would immediately bring down upon your head the sneers of the Patersons, the Benets, the Van Dorens, and all their ilk of "monsters," "seven feet tall," "untrue to life"—etc.

——— In Christ's name, Max, what is wrong with us in America? The whole world—not myself alone—wants to know. The English ask me, + the French ask me, everyone asks me, Why do we cry out that what we want is life, and then try to destroy and kill the best people that we have? Why do our best writers, poets, men of talent turn into drunkards, dipsomaniacs, charlatans, cocktail-cliquers, creators of Pop-eye horrors,[19] pederasts, macabre distortions etc—I tell you, it is not I alone who ask the question, but everyone here—all of Europe knows it. Why is it that we are burnt out to an empty shell by the time we are forty, that instead of growing in strength and power we are done for—empty burnt out wrecks at an age when men in other countries are just coming to their full maturity.—Is it because the seeds of destruction are <u>wholly</u> in ourselves— that there is something in the American air, the weather of the American life that burns the lives of men to rust as quickly as it rusts iron and steel—Or is it perhaps that there is in us a sterile, perverse, and accursed love and lust for death that wishes to destroy the very people that we set up—the people who have something to give that may be of value and honor to our life. Is it because we take a young man of talent—a young man proud of spirit, and athirst for glory, and full with the urge to create and make his life prevail—praise him up to the skies at first, and then press in upon him from all sides with cynics eyes and scornful [faces], asking him if he can <u>ever do it again</u> or is done for, finished, no good, through forever. Is it because we deal this [hand] of death to young proud people—telling them they are the lords of the earth one year, and the glory of their native's country—and the next year sneering, jeering, laughing, reviling, scorning and mocking them with the very tongues that sang their praises—just a year before. Is this the reason why we "fail." —the reason that our finest artists are destroyed?—Tell me, is this the reason—men in England also ask me; they all want to know—and then how easy for them all, when we <u>are</u> done for—when we have been driven mad, when we are drunkards, dipsomaniacs, perverts, charlatans, burnt out shell—how easy it is for the whole pack to pull the face of pious regret—to sigh mournfully—to say—"What a pity!—We had hoped once—He looked so promising at one time!—What a shame he had to go and waste it all!"—

I know your answer to these questions—that the strong man is as Gibraltar —that all these assaults will fall harmlessly against his iron front, the impregnable granite of his invincible soul—but, alas, no man is strong as that—it is a pleasant fable—his great strength is needed, to be concentrated on the work he does—and while his [     ] and every sinew of his life is is bent to the great labor of creation, what shall protect him from these coward-hordes who come to destroy his life from every side — Why should the artist—who is life's strongest man, earths greatest hero— have to endure this in America of all the countries of the earth—when his task alone is so cruel hard there—the need for a new language, the creation of a new form so stern and formidable—why should he have to do this great work and at the same time withstand the murderous attack of death-in-life when in every country in Europe the artist is honored, revered, and cherished as the proudest possession that a nation has?—

Take this for what it is worth—If you think it extravagant, then take it so, but see the core of truth in this as well—I have given my life to try to be an artist, an honor to my country, to create beauty, and to win fame and glory, and the honor of my people, for myself. What has it got me. At the age of 34 I am weary, tired, dispirited, and worn out. I was a decent looking boy six years ago—now I am a bald, gross, heavy, weary looking man.—I wanted fame—and I have had for the most part shame and agony—they continue to speak of me as a "writer of promise"—and if I only do 197 impossible things—which they doubt that I <u>can</u> do—something may come of my work in the end. The Paterson woman says my people are all seven feet tall and talk in bellowing voices— she says take away his adjectives, nouns, verbs, pronouns, words of violence, height, altitude, colour, size, immensity—and <u>where</u> would he be—the Mark Van Dorens say take away his own experience, the events of his own life, forbid him to write about what he has seen, known, felt, experienced—and where would he be? The Fadimans[20] say take away his apostrophes, declamations, lyrics, dreams, incantations—and where would he be?—The Rascoes[21] say he has no sense of humour—this to the man who created old Gant, wrote the lunch room scenes in the Angel, Bascom Hawke in the River, The Web of Earth, Oswald Ten Eyck, the countess, the Englishmen at the [     ] and all the others—the Communists say he is a romantic sentimentalist of the old worn-out romantic school with no Marxian code and the Saturday Reviewers a depicter of the sordid, grim, horribly unpleasant and [     ] school—and so it goes—in Christ's name what do these people want? Apparently, I would be a good writer if I would only correct 3,264 fundamental faults, which are absolutely, profoundly, and utterly incurable and uncorrectable—so what in Christ's name am I to do? —In God's name how am I to live?—What's before me?—I tell you, Max, I cannot put in another five years like the last—I must have some peace, security, and good hope—I must be left alone to do my work as I have planned and conceived it—or the game is up — I am tired and ill and desperate, I can't go on like this, forever—I got hurt somehow in Paris—how I dont know—during one of those three days I cant remember—I don't know whether I'm ruptured or not—I haven't the faintest idea, memory, or recollection of what happened—whether I got slugged in some joint or ran into something—but I woke up with a bruise above my groin. the size of a saucer, and ever since it felt as if something has been torn loose inside me—Forgive these wild and whirling words—you are the friend I honor and respect more than anyone else—I hope and pray to God you may have some use and credit from my life—in return for all you have done for it—just as I hope that I can make it prevail—as by God's will, I hope and trust I yet may do—

This is all for the present—if there is any great good news for God's sake send it to me—at any rate stay with me, be my friend, and all may yet be well,— Take this letter—or rather this Chronicle, this history, for what it is worth— weed the good from the bad—and consider what truth is in— I'm sending it to you in three or four installments because I cant get it in one letter— Goodbye, good luck and good health and love to all the family—Tom

Thomas Wolfe in 1935 (North Carolina Collection, University of North Carolina, Chapel Hill).

## Notes

1. 3,693 words have been omitted from this letter.

2. See March 13, 1935, cable.

3. Wolfe listed corrections required for twenty-nine pages. Scribner emended the text in the second, third, fifth, and sixth printings.

4. Perkins had put *Of Time and the River* into production before Wolfe was ready to relinquish it. See introduction.

5. Hart was an author and an editor at several New York publishing houses.

6. Ben Wasson was an author and literary agent.

7. William Rose Benét, editor of the *Saturday Review of Literature,* did not review any of Wolfe's novels.

8. Isabel M. Paterson (I.M.P.) was a literary columnist for the *New York Herald Tribune.* In her February 24, 1935, review of *Of Time and the River* Paterson wrote, "It might be an interesting experiment to take one of his chapters and eliminate all the superlatives, the adjectives, indicating altitude, volume, and violence. . . . Step it down again to life size, and see what would remain. . . . Let the characters say what they have to say, instead of roaring, whining, stuttering or gasping. . . . The remainder we feel sure, would still be interesting, but would it impress the genteel critics so much?" [the ellipses are in the original.]

9. Franklin Pierce Adams (F.P.A.) was writer of "The Conning Tower" column for the *New York Herald Tribune.*

10. Christopher Morley was a poet and novelist as well as an editor for the *Saturday Review of Literature* and a Book-of-the-Month Club judge.

11. Probably George Jean Nathan.

12. Mark Van Doren was a poet, critic, and editor for the *Nation.* In his essay "The Art of American Fiction" (*Nation,* April 25, 1934), Van Doren criticized *Look Homeward, Angel:* "Old Gant was the masterpiece of that work, and as such was testimony to Mr. Wolfe's undeniably huge talent in characterization. But Gant had a son, and the son so weakens the book with his self-pity that the public is justified in asking Mr. Wolfe whether he can keep himself out of the picture in books to come."

13. Michael Gold (Irving Granich) was a novelist (*Jews Without Money,* 1935) and editor of the *New Masses.*

14. Lee Simonson was scenic designer for the Theatre Guild, a theater company devoted in the 1920s and early 1930s to presenting artistic, noncommercial plays.

15. In 1923 the Guild had rejected Wolfe's play *Welcome to Our City.*

16. Neighborhood Playhouse was a New York theater company similar to the Theatre Guild. Aline Bernstein designed sets and costumes for many of their productions.

17. *Hound & Horn* was a literary magazine founded by Lincoln Kirstein, critic and ballet patron.

18. Lewis Galantière was a critic and translator.

19. Reference to William Faulkner's *Sanctuary* (1931).

20. Clifton Fadiman was book reviewer for the *New Yorker* and a Book-of-the-Month Club judge. In his March 9, 1935, review of *Time and the River* Fadiman criticized Wolfe's excessive language: "There are thousands of these prose Swinburne passages, all marvelous until you ask what they mean. Thus it is impossible to say any one thing of Mr. Wolfe's style. At its best it is wondrous, Elizabethan. At its worst it is hyper-thyroid and afflicted with elephantiasis. As Stevenson and Pater well knew, it is the blue pencil that creates the purple patch; but I suppose if Thomas Wolfe could use a blue pencil he would not be Thomas Wolfe. Still, he might be somebody even better."

21. Literary critic Burton Rascoe wrote at the end of an otherwise positive review of *Of Time and the River* that Wolfe "has no evident sense of humor; nor any true sense of comedy" (*New York Herald Tribune,* March 10, 1935).

▲▼▲

*To: Perkins*
*From: Fitzgerald*                    *TLS with holograph postscript, 4 pp. Princeton*

1307 Park Avenue,
Baltimore, Maryland,
April 17, 1935.

Dear Max:

Reading Tom Wolfe's story[1] in the current <u>Modern Monthly</u> makes me wish he was the sort of person you could talk to about his stuff. It has all his faults and virtues. It seems to me that with any sense of humor he could see the Dreiserian absurdities of how the circus people "ate the cod, bass, mackerel, halibut, clams and oysters of the New England coast, the terrapin of Maryland, the fat beeves, porks and cereals of the middle west" etc. etc. down to "the pink meated lobsters that grope their way along the sea-floors of America." And then (after one of his fine paragraphs which sounds a note to be expanded later) he remarks that they leave nothing behind except "the droppings of the camel and the elephant in Illinois." A few pages further on his redundance ruined some paragraphs (see the last complete paragraph on page 103) that might have been gorgeous. I sympathize with his use of repetition, of Joyce-like words, endless metaphor, but I wish he could have seen the disgust in Edmund Wilson's face when I once tried to interpolate part of a rhymed sonnet in the middle of a novel, disguised as prose. How he can put side by side such a mess as "With chitterling tricker fast-fluttering skirrs of sound the palmy honied birderies came" and such fine phrases as "tongue-trilling chirrs, plum-bellied smoothness, sweet lucidity" I don't know. He who has such infinite power of suggestion and delicacy has absolutely no right to glut people on whole meals of caviar. I hope to Christ he isn't taking all these emasculated paeans to his vitality very seriously. I'd hate to see such an exquisite talent turn into one of those muscle-bound and useless giants seen in a circus. Athletes have got to learn their games; they shouldn't just be content to tense their muscles, and if they do they suddenly find when called upon to bring off a necessary effect they are simply liable to hurl the shot into the crowd and not break any records at all. The metaphor is mixed but I think you will understand what I mean, and that he would too—save for his tendency to almost feminine horror if he thinks anyone is going to lay hands on his precious talent. I think his lack of humility is his most difficult characteristic, a lack oddly enough which I associate only with second or third rate writers. He was badly taught by bad teachers and now he hates learning.

There is another side of him that I find myself doubting, but this is something that no one could ever teach or tell him. His lack of feeling other people's passions, the lyrical value of Eugene Gant's love affair with the universe—is that going to last through a whole saga? God, I wish he could discipline himself and really plan a novel.

I wrote you the other day and the only other point of this letter is that I've now made a careful plan of the Mediaeval novel as a whole (tentatively called "Philippe, Count of Darkness" <u>confidential</u>) including the planning of the parts which I can sell and the parts which I can't.[2] I think you could publish it either late in the spring of '36 or early in the fall of the same year. This depends entirely on how the money question goes this year. It will run to about 90,000 words and will be a novel in every sense with the episodes unrecognizable as such. That is my only plan. I wish I had these great masses of manuscripts stored away like Wolfe and Hemingway but this goose is beginning to be pretty thoroughly plucked I am afraid.

A young man has dramatized "Tender is the Night' and I am hoping something may come of it.[3] I may be in New York for a day and a night within the next fortnight.

Ever yours,
Scott

Later—Went to N.Y. as you know, but one day only. Didn't think I would like Cape[4] that day. Sorry you + Nora Flynn[5] didn't meet. No news here—I think Beth[6] is leaving soon.

*Notes*

1. "Circus at Dawn."
2. Fitzgerald completed four installments of this work for *Red Book,* three of which were published during his lifetime.
3. Baltimore writer Robert Spofford seems not to have completed the dramatization.
4. Probably English publisher Jonathan Cape.
5. Nora Flynn, one of the celebrated Langhorne sisters, and her husband, former football star and actor Lefty Flynn, entertained Fitzgerald and his daughter, Scottie, in Tryon, North Carolina, during February of 1935.
6. Elizabeth Lemmon.

▲ ▼ ▲

*To: Perkins*                              *ca. February 15, 1936. Key West, Florida*
*From: Hemingway*              *TLS with holograph inserts, 1 p.[1] Princeton*

Dear Max;

. . . . .

. . . . .

. . . . .

Feel awfully about Scott. I tried to write him (wrote him several times) to cheer him up but he seems to almost take a pride in his shamelessness of defeat. The Esquire pieces seem to me to be so miserable. There is another one comeing too.[2] I always knew he couldn't think—he never could—but he had a marvelous talent and the thing is to use it—not whine in public. Good God people go through that emptiness many times in life and come out and do work. I always thought, from when I first met him, that if Scott had gone to that war that he always felt so bad about missing, he would have been shot for cowardice. But that has nothing to do with his writing, a writer can be a coward but at least he should be a writer. Hell I can't write about this and it is rotten to speak against Scott after all he had to go through. But I saw all the first part of it and it was so avoidable and self imposed and always from the one source—though the source spread into many channels and some of them you would never believe came from the same spring. Maybe the Church would help him. You can't tell.

Work would help him; noncommercial, honest work—aparagraph at a time. But he judged a paragraph by how much money it made him and ditched his juice into that channel because he got an instant satisfaction. While if you don't make so much and somebody said it was no good he would be afraid. It was a terrible thing for him to love youth so much that he jumped straight from youth to senility without going through manhood. The minute he felt youth going he was frightened again and thought there was nothing between youth and age. But it is so damned easy to criticize our friends and I shouldn't write this. I wish we could help him.

. . . .

Best to you always Max—Earnest/

*Notes*

1. 310 words have been omitted from this letter.
2. "The Crack-Up," *Esquire* (February 1936); "Pasting It Together," *Esquire* (March 1936); and "Handle With Care," *Esquire* (April 1936).

▲ ▼ ▲

*To: Hemingway*
*From: Perkins*                                          *CC, 4 pp.*[1] *Princeton*

Feb. 27, 1936

Dear Ernest:

I'll give you the hard and fast figure on the sale of "Green Hills" the moment we know it. As it is, on account of copies out on a returnable basis, we cannot yet know it exactly. The reason it is not on that last royalty statement is that it was not published until October 25th, and therefore no report is due on it until April 25th. But I do not think that it will be less than 10,000 copies.– Nor do I think that the reason it did not sell more was the reason you think.[2] It was mostly due to something that often happens in publishing: the public gets a superficial impression of what a book is, and the one they got of this book was that it was an account of a hunting expedition to Africa, covering a short space of time, and was therefore a distinctly minor piece of work. Anyone would have thought that who judged by the outside, superficially. That is what it would seem to be on its face. If all the reviews had emphatically argued otherwise, that impression would have been effaced, but the reviewers too are mostly superficial judges. The qualities of the book that made it fine were, as they should have been, not spectacular. Many of the reviewers took a superficial view, and all of the public except a few individuals of discrimination. I should have foreseen it. The public regards you as a novelist. "Death in the Afternoon" was so manifestly a work of years in accumulation and reflection that it stood by itself. But this the public took as an interlude.

. . . . .
. . . . .

I have just had an appeal for money from Scott, and I suppose I shall give it to him, but I wish I knew what could be done about him. The one thing that gives me some hope is that nobody would write those two articles in Esquire if they were really true. I doubt if a hopeless man will tell about it, or a man who thinks he is beaten for good. Those people I should think would not say anything at all, just as those who really intend suicide never tell anybody. So I thought that in some deep way, when he wrote those articles, Scott must have been thinking that things would be different with him. He may have lost that passion in writing which he once had, but he is such a wonderful craftsman that he could certainly make out well if he were able to control himself and be reconciled to life. He is only forty. It is absurd for him to give up.

Always yours,

*Notes*

1. 82 words have been omitted from this letter.
2. In a ca. December 20, 1925, letter to Perkins, Hemingway attributed the poor sales of *Green Hills of Africa* to his attack on critics in the book: "About the critics, offending same, I never thought about them at all. Only put down what I told the Austrian in response to questions and what I was thinking then. You remember Winner Take Nothing came out while we were away and I got the first reviews in Arusha and read them in the plane flying to Nairobi. That was how I happened to think about critics at all when I came back hunting after that time being ill in Nairobi. I didn't set out to offend them but to tell the truth and if the truth offended them tant pis. It is all to the good in a few years. But hard on you as publishers of present book."

▲ ▼ ▲

*To: Fitzgerald*
*From: Perkins*                    *CC, 2 pp. Princeton*

March 26, 1936

Dear Scott:

I remember your speaking to me about a collection of non-fiction. I did not think well of it as a collection. But do you remember at the time when you were struggling desperately with "Tender Is the Night" and it seemed as if you might not get through with it for long, that I suggested a reminiscent book? It might even have been before you published "Echoes of the Jazz Age" in 1931, which was a beautiful article. I have been reading that again lately, and have been hesitating on the question of asking you to do a reminiscent book,– not autobiographical, but reminiscent. Gertrude Stein's autobiography[1] is an apt one to mention in connection with the idea. I even talked to Gilbert Seldes about it, and he was favorable. I do not think the Esquire pieces ought to be published alone. But as for an autobiographical book which would comprehend what is in them, I would be very much for it. Couldn't you make a really well integrated book? You write non-fiction wonderfully well, your observations are brilliant and acute, and your presentations of real characters like Ring, most admirable. I always wanted you to do such a book as that. Whatever you decide, we want to do, but it would be so much better to make a book out of the materials than merely to take the articles and trim them, and join them up, etc.[2]

Always yours,

### Notes

1. *The Autobiography of Alice B. Toklas* (New York: Harcourt, Brace, 1933).
2. Fitzgerald did not undertake this project.

▲ ▼ ▲

To: Perkins                    *Wolfe's letterhead, 865 First Avenue, New York City*
From: Wolfe                    *TLS, 6 pp. Princeton*

April 21st, 1936

Dear Max:

I want to tell you that I am sorry I got angry last night and spoke as I did. The language that I used was unjustifiable and I want to tell you that I know it was, and ask you to forget it.

About the matter I was talking to you about however, I feel just as strongly today as I did last night. I don't want to re-hash the whole thing again. We have talked and argued about it too much already, but I do want to tell you honestly and sincerely that I am not arguing about the two or three hundred dollars which would be involved if I were given my old royalty of 15%, instead of the reduced one of 10%. I admit that there can be no doubt that I agreed to this reduction of my royalty before the publication of the book and at the time when estimates of cost of publication were being prepared, I told you that I hoped the book could be published at a very moderate price of 75¢ or a dollar. Not only because I thought it might be better for the success of the book itself, but also because I am not willing to make use of any past success I may have had, or take advantage of any present reputation I may have in the eyes of the public to publish so short and small a book at a high price. Now I don't want you to think that I am trying to dictate to my publishers the price for which I think my book ought to be printed. You told me an author had no right to dictate such prices and that in fact, the price the publisher put on his books was none of his business and although I think the subject is open to debate, I am on the whole, inclined to agree with you and was really not trying to dictate any prices, except what I told you when the publication of the book was discussed and I hoped personally, it would be brought out at a low price of 75¢ or a dollar.

You told me that it would be impossible to bring it out for as low a price as 75¢, but we all had hoped, I believe that it might be brought out for a dollar. Later, when estimates on the cost of publication came in, it was agreed that the price would have to be $1.25 and either then at that time, or previously I had agreed to a reduction of my customary royalty from 15% to 10% and I believe the 10% was to cover the first three thousand copies and that if the book sold more than that, I would get an increased royalty. The reason that I agreed to this reduction was because I knew the publisher was not likely to profit very much by the publication of so small a book and because I agreed with you the publication of the book was nevertheless, probably a good thing, and finally because you told me that even at the $1.25 price, the margin was very small and you thought I ought to accept the royalty of 10%, which I agreed to do.

Now the book has been published[1] and the other day when I got my own advance copy, I saw that the price had been still further raised from $1.25 to $1.50. This was the first knowledge that I had that the price had been raised. I agree with you that I probably have no right to argue with you about the price of a book or to have a say as to the price it ought to sell for. I also agree that if the book is successful and sells, I stand to profit in my share of the royalties at the increased price as well as does the publisher; but I don't think that either of these facts is the core of the matter, and they are certainly not what I am arguing about.

What I am arguing about is this,— that I agreed to accept a reduced royalty upon the basis of a dollar or dollar and a quarter book— and the reason that I agreed to accept the reduction was because it was presented to me that the cost of making the book was such that it would be difficult for the publisher to give a higher royalty and have him come out clear. Then after agreeing to this reduced royalty, upon my understanding that the book would be published at a dollar and a quarter, and having signed a contract accepting the reduced royalty, I find that the price of the book, without my knowledge, has been raised to $1.50, and is being published at that price. When I discussed that fact about a week ago, when I got my own advance copy, I told you that in view of the increase in price, I thought you ought to restore my former royalty of 15%. I still think that you ought to do so and have told you so repeatedly, and you feel you ought not to do so, and have refused to do so.

You have been my friend for seven years now and one of the best friends that I ever had, I don't think anyone in the world is more conscious than I am of what you have done for me, of how you stuck to me for years when I was trying to get another book completed and when so much time elapsed that people had begun to say I might never be able to write again. I think you stuck to me not only with material aid and support that Scribners gave me, during a large part of the time, when I had no funds of my own, but you stuck to me also with your own friendship and belief and spiritual support, and you not only gave me these price-less things, but you also gave me unstintedly, the benefits of your enormous skill and talent as an editor and a critic. I do not think a debt such as I owe you can ever sufficiently be repaid, but I have tried to do what I could through work, which I know you do value and through public acknowledgment which I know you do not want and on which you don't put the same value as you do upon the more important fact of work. So having said all this, and feeling this way toward you, and about what you and Scribners have done, I want to repeat again that I do not think it is right or proper for you to with hold from me my full and customary royalty of 15%, the circumstances being what they are.

I do not question your legal and contractual right to do this. I agreed to the reduction at the time and for the reason I have mentioned. I signed the contract and I am, of course compelled to abide by it. But I think it is up to you now in view of the facts I have mentioned, and since the reason of the reduction of the royalty— namely, the low price of the book is no longer true,— I think it is up to you and Scribners of your own accord to give me my 15%. It will not amount to much, even if you sell the entire three thousand copies, which the 10% roy-alty covers,— I don't think it will amount to more than two or three hundred dollars and I am not arguing with you about that. But just because you have been generous and devoted friends, and because my feeling toward you has been one of devotion and loyalty, I do not want to see you do this thing now which may be legally and technically all right, but is to my mind, a sharp business prac-tice. I know that you yourself, personally, do not stand to profit one penny whether I get 10% or 15%. I know that you yourself, probably did not suggest the reduction in royalty or fix the price of the book, but I also know the way I expect and want you to act now as my friend. It seems to me that it is impera-tive that you do this just exactly for the reason that I consider you all my friends and have always lived and felt and thought about you in that way and not as people with whom I had business dealings and who were going to use whatever business advantage they considered legitimate in their dealings with me.

You know very well that I am not a business man and have no capacity for business and that in matters of this sort, I am not able to cope with people who are skilled at it, but where it concerned you and Scribners, I have never thought for one moment, that I would have to cope with it. The thing I really feel and beleive is that at the bottom of your heart, you agree with me and my position in this matter and know that I am right as I know you agreed with me in the matter of almost $1.200, which I was charged for corrections in the proof of "Of time and the River." I'll admit that there too, I am legally responsible and signed the contract which had a clause in it stipulating the cost to the author if the changes and corrections in the proof exceed a certain amount. But the truth of the matter is as you know, and as you said at the time when the bill was first shown to me, that a great many of these corrections came as the result of the work we were both doing on the manuscript, and as a result of the editorial help and advice and the suggestions you made which were so generous and so invaluable. For this very reason perhaps, I ought not to harp upon the subject or complain about having to pay almost $1.200 for corrections that helped the book, but you said at the time the bill was shown to me that in view of the circumstances and the way the corrections were made and done, you didn't think I ought to have to pay as much money as that, and I understood you even to say that if I felt too strongly that I ought not to pay and that the bill was unfair, I would not have to pay it. Well, I don't feel that strongly about it, I think I made a lot of corrections on the proof on my own hook and I think that if these corrections were excessive, I ought to pay for them like anyone else. But I do feel that the bill of almost $1.200 is excessive and that I am being made to pay too much for corrections which I'll admit helped me and the book, but which were partly done with your collaboration.

I didn't mean to bring this into the letter at all. One of the main reasons for my whole feeling about this thing and about the reduced royalty is that, as you know, during the last year, I have been made the victim of almost every kind of unfair and dishonest procedure from people who have taken my money in the past, bringing suit against me, in an effort to get more money, to people walking off with my manuscript, making use of my name for public gatherings when I have not given my consent, appointing me judge to contests I know nothing about, selling my autograph and every other form of parasitism and skin game imaginable. The time has come when it has got to stop, I am not going to submit to it any longer if I can help it. And certainly I don't expect to see the people that I have considered the best friends I have, make use of any of the unfair advantages, however legal they may be, that some other people have made use of.

I want to ask you this; if your refusal in this matter is final and you insist on holding me to the terms of the contract I signed for The Story of a Novel, don't you think that I, or anyone else on earth for that matter, would be justified henceforth and hereafter, considering my relations with you and Scribners were primarily of a business and commercial nature, and if you make use of a business advantage in this way, don't you think I would be justified in making use of a business advantage too if one came my way? Or do you think it works only one way? I don't think it does and I don't think any other fairminded person in the world would think so either. As you know, I never gave a moment's serious consideration to any offers or persuasions that were made to me by other people and I think that you know very well that such offers were made. And that in one case at least, a very large sum of money was mentioned at a time when I, myself, had nothing. You not only knew of the occasion, but I telephoned you of it just as soon as the person telephoned and asked if he could talk to me. I informed you of the telephone call at once and told you I didn't know what it meant and you told me what it did mean, and furthermore told me I had a right to meet the man and listen to what he had to say and even consider what he had to offer.[2] Well, I suppose that's business practice and everyone agrees that it is fully justified and that a man has a right not only to listen, but to take the best and most profitable offer. That's business practice, maybe, but it has not been my practice. I did meet the man, I did listen to what he had to say and I paid no attention at all to his offer. What do you think about this any way? If people are going to get hard-boiled and business-like, should it all be on one side, or doesn't the other fellow have a right to get hard-boiled and business-like too?

I understand perfectly well that even publishers are not in business for their health, even though you have said that none of them make any great amount of money out of it. And I don't expect my relations with my publisher to be a perpetual love feast, into which the vile question of money never enters, but I do say, that you cannot command the loyalty and devotion of a man on the one hand and then take a business advantage on the other. I am sorry to have to say all this. I want to repeat how much I regret my language of last evening, but I also want to say that about this matter of the royalties, I feel as strongly and deeply now as I did then. I am writing this letter to you as a final appeal. You may think I am kicking up a hell of a row over nothing but I do think it is something, a great deal, not in a money way but in the matter of fair dealing, and I am writing to tell you so.

Sincerely,
Tom Wolfe

*Notes*

1. *The Story of a Novel* (Scribners, 1936), Wolfe's account of the writing and editing of *Of Time and the River*, had a first printing of 3,000 copies at $1.50. The 15 percent royalty on this printing amounted to $675. There was a small second Scribners printing in 1936.

2. After 1930 Wolfe was approached by several publishers, one of whom, he claimed, offered him a ten-thousand-dollar advance.

▲▼▲

*To: Wolfe*
*From: Perkins*                                    *TLS, 3 pp. Harvard*

April 22, 1936

Dear Tom:

I am giving directions to reckon your royalties on "The Story of a Novel" at 15% from the start. The difference in what you will receive if 3,000 copies are sold, between the ten and fifteen percent royalty, will be $225.00. We certainly do not think that we should withhold that sum of money if it is going to cause so much resentment, and so much loss of time and disquiet for all of us.

I would rather, simply agree to do this and say nothing further, but I should not have the right to do it without telling you that the terms as proposed on the $1.50 price are just, and that if the matter were to be looked upon merely as business, we should not be justified as business men in making this concession. You are under a misapprehension if you think that when we suggested a reduction of royalty—such as in similar cases have been freely made by writers of the highest rank, at least in sales—we were basing the suggestion on the question of price. I do remember that the price of $1.25 was mentioned as a desirable one, or a probable one, but the idea of the royalty was not dependent upon that. We could not at that time know what the price would have to be. We found that the price had to be higher because of the question of basic costs which come into every phase of the handling, advertising, promoting, and making of a book. Many of these basic costs do not vary at all because of the size of the book. We do not want to put our prices any higher than we are compelled to, and in fact more than most publishers, have tried to keep them low. We put them up only because we have to. The terms we proposed were therefore in my opinion just.

You return to the question of the excess corrections which were, I believe, $1100.00. If I gave you the impression that I thought this was unfair, it came from my dread of the resentment I knew you would feel to have them deducted from your royalties even though they have always been taken into account in every publisher's contract, and generally at only half the percentage that we allow for them. I once said to you in Charles Scribner's presence that you had a good technical argument for not paying these corrections because you did not make them, and therefore could say that they were not author's corrections, but publishers' corrections. This would be true, since you did not read your proof, but if you had done so, is there any doubt but what these corrections would have been much larger? They were almost wholly unavoidable corrections, like the change from the first to third person, and the changing of names. They were therefore rightly author's corrections and why should the author not pay for them? I think we began wrong by making no charge in the case of excess corrections on the "Angel," which amounted to seven hundred dollars, so that this charge came to you as a surprise.– And the truth is that many authors do resent being charged for such corrections because they cannot be got to consider them in advance. But if the author does not pay for this cost, after the publisher has paid the 20% allowance himself, the publisher will have to pay that too. Why should he have to do it?

As to the other matter you speak of, your freedom to do whatever you think is to your best interests in business, nobody could ever deny it, and I have often said that we did not. I certainly would not wish you to make what you thought was a sacrifice on my account, and I would know that whatever you did would be sincerely believed to be right by you,– as I know that you sincerely believe the contentions you make in this letter to me, to be right. I have never doubted your sincerity and never will. I wish you could have felt that way toward us.

Always yours,
Max

▲ ▼ ▲

To: Perkins     *Wolfe's letterhead, 865 First Avenue, New York City*
From: Wolfe       *TLS, 2 pp. Princeton*

April 23rd, 1936

Dear Max:

I got your letter this morning and I just want to write you back now to tell you that everything is settled so far as I am concerned, so let's forget about it.

Now that you have told me that you would restore my old royalty of 15%, I want to tell you that I don't want it and want to stick to the contract I signed. That goes for all my other obligations as well. I really made up my mind to this yesterday, and that was the reason I called you up last night and went around to see you.

I wanted to tell you and I am afraid I didn't succeed telling you very well that all the damn contracts in the world don't mean as much to me as your friendship means, and it suddenly occurred to me yesterday that life is too short to quarrel this way with a friend over something that matters so little. But I do want to tell you again just how genuinely and deeply sorry I am for boiling over the way I did the other night. We have had fireworks of this sort before and I am afraid it may occur again, but every time they do, I say something to a friend that is unjust and wrong and sweat blood about it later. So just help me along with this by forgetting all about it, and let's look forward to the future.

I suppose it is a good thing for me to have had this experience in the last year but there is something a little grotesque and tragic in the fact that the success I wanted and looked forward to having as a child, should have brought me so much trouble, worry, bewilderment and disillusion, but I am going to try to add the whole experience to the sum of things I have found out about all through my life and I hope that I will be able to make use of it, instead of letting it make use of me.

I see know what a terribly dangerous thing a little success may be because it seems to me the effort of an artist must always aim at even greater concentration and intensity and effort of the will where his work is concerned and anything that tends to take him away from that, to distract him, to weaken his effort is a bad thing.

I am now started on another book. I need your friendship, and support more than I ever did, so please forget the worst mistakes I have made in the past and let's see if I can't do somewhat better in the future.

                                        Sincerely,
                                        Tom

                              ▲ ▼ ▲

*To: Perkins*
*From: Hemingway*                    *TLS, 1 p.*[1] *Princeton*

                              July 23, 1936
                              Key West/

Dear Max:

        · · · · ·
        · · · · ·
        · · · · ·

I got a letter from Scott who was sore because I used his name in that Snows of Kilimanjaro[2] story. He has only been writing those awful things about himself since Feb. in Esquire but if I took issue with his analysis of his proclaimed break-up he gets sore. I told him that for five years I have not written a line about anybody I knew because I was so sorry for them all but that I felt time was getting short now and am going to cease being a gent and go back to being a novelist. Most of my friends were not of my own selection anyway. Can't wait to get out west and settled down to writing again. Have a big head of steam now.

        · · · · ·
        · · · · ·
        · · · · ·

                                        Yours always,
                                        Ernest/

                              *Notes*

    1. 325 words have been omitted from this letter.
    2. The *Esquire* text of "The Snows of Kilimanjaro" states that "poor Scott Fitzgerald" was "wrecked" by his "romantic awe" of the rich. "Snows" also quotes Fitzgerald's observation in "The Rich Boy" that the very rich "are different from you and me," followed by the rejoinder, presumably by Hemingway, that "they have more money." In reality, Hemingway was the recipient of the squelch delivered by Mary Colum and witnessed by Perkins. See Bruccoli, *Fitzgerald and Hemingway: A Dangerous Friendship,* pp. 190–94.

                              ▲ ▼ ▲

*To: Perkins*
*From: Fitzgerald*              *TLS with holograph revisions, 2 pp. Princeton*

Asheville, N.C.,
Sept. 19th, 1936

Dear Max:

This is my second day of having a minute to catch up with correspondence. Probably Harold Ober has kept you in general touch with what has happened to me but I will summarize:

I broke the clavicle of my shoulder, diving—nothing heroic, but a little too high for the muscles to tie up the efforts of a simple swan dive—At first the Doctors thought that I must have tuberculosis of the bone, but x-ray showed nothing of the sort, so (like occasional pitchers who throw their arms out of joint with some unprepared for effort) it was left to dangle for twenty-four hours with a bad diagnosis by a young Intern; then an x-ray and found broken and set in an elaborate plaster cast.

I had almost adapted myself to the thing when I fell in the bath-room reaching for the light, and lay on the floor until I caught a mild form of arthritis called "Miotosis," which popped me in the bed for five weeks more. During this time there were domestic crises: Mother sickened and then died and I tried my best to be there but couldn't. I have been within a mile and a half of my wife all summer and have seen her about half dozen times. Total accomplished for one summer has been one story—not very good, two <u>Esquire</u> articles, neither of them very good.

You have probably seen Harold Ober and he may have told you that Scottie got a remission of tuition at a very expensive school where I wanted her to go (Miss Edith Walker's School[1] in Connecticut). Outside of that I have no good news, except that I came into some money from my Mother, not as much as I had hoped, but at least $20,000. in cash and bonds at the materialization in six months—for some reason, I do not know the why or wherefore of it, it requires this time. I am going to use some of it, with the products of the last story and the one in process of completion, to pay off my bills and to take two or three months rest in a big way. I have to admit to myself that I haven't the vitality that I had five years ago.

I feel that I must tell you something which at first seemed better to leave alone: I wrote Ernest about that story of his, asking him in the most measured terms not to use my name in future pieces of fiction. He wrote me back a crazy letter, telling me about what a great Writer he was and how much he loved his children, but yielding the point—"If I should out live him—" which he doubted. To have answered it would have been like fooling with a lit firecracker.[2]

Somehow I love that man, no matter what he says or does, but just one more crack and I think I would have to throw my weight with the gang and lay him. No one could ever hurt him in his first books but he has completely lost his head and the duller he gets about it, the more he is like a punch-drunk pug fighting himself in the movies.

No particular news except the dreary routine of illness. Scotty excited about the wedding.[3]

As ever yours,
Scott Fitz

*Notes*

1. Ethel Walker School, Simsbury, Connecticut.
2. Hemingway's unlocated letter was described by Arnold Gingrich as "brutal."
3. Of Elisabeth ("Zippy"), Perkins's second daughter.

▲ ▼ ▲

*To: Fitzgerald*
*From: Perkins*                    *CC, 2 pp. Princeton*

Sept. 23, 1936

Dear Scott:

If you are sure to get $20,000 in six months, doesn't this offer you your big chance? You have never, since the very beginning, had a time free from the necessity of earning money.– You have never been free from financial anxiety. Can't you now work out a plan to get at least eighteen months, or perhaps two years, free from worry by living very economically, and work as you always wanted to, on a major book? Certainly it seems to me that here is your opportunity. I am glad Scotty is doing so well. I know the school in Simsbury, once thought of sending our girls out there. It is very good.

As for what Ernest did, I resented it, and when it comes to book publication, I shall have it out with him.[1] It is odd about it too because I was present when that reference was made to the rich, and the retort given, and you were many miles away.

Always yours,

*Note*

1. When the story was collected in *The Fifth Column and the First Forty-nine Stories* (Scribners, 1938), the name was changed to "Julian" at Perkins's insistence.

▲ ▼ ▲

To: Hemingway
From: Perkins                                    *CC, 4 pp.*[1] *Princeton*

Oct. 1, 1936

Dear Ernest:

You must have failed to get one letter I wrote you, because I told you in it that I thought "The Snows of Kilimanjaro" was a most extraordinary story. What's more, it showed a new vein in your talent, or at any rate showed it somewhat more clearly, though I can remember other stories that had it clearly. The last part of the story created a most curious and magical feeling which nobody will ever forget who has read it. I thought what a magnificent tale could be written of the defense of the Alcazar.[2] If you had been there, and got out of it safely, what a story! But I wish you would not go to Spain.[3] Those Alcazar boys made me pretty nearly decide to vote for the Rebels though I think they will bring no good to Spain if they win.– And if you aim to go there among the bullets, I shall hope that they hurry up and take Madrid and perhaps stop the fighting for a time. Anyhow, I hope you will let nothing prevent the publication of a novel in the Spring. And it should be early too.[4] I am awfully glad you wrote me about it. I had wondered how it was going. Let that big grizzly alone until you are finished.

. . . . .

I opened a telegram addressed to you to see whether it was important enough to forward, and it was from Scott. I don't know exactly what you could do for him, but the interview he gave the Post was frightful.[5] It gave me a chill to read it. It seemed as if Scott were bent upon destroying himself. He was trusting the reporter, and so was his nurse—when a man gets himself a trained nurse, it's time to despair of him—and both of them said things which the reporter must have known were not meant to go into print,– the nurse said them when Scott was out of the room. It gave you the impression of a completely licked and very drunk person, bereft of hope, acquiescing in his ruin. Scott had just written me that his mother had died, and that he was to come into twenty thousand dollars. I had known that this was a probability, and I had thought that there was his chance. So I wrote him that he must take that opportunity to work two years on ten thousand a year, without anxiety or the necessity of potboiling. I told him this was the only way to answer what this reporter had done. I hope Scott will turn up here tomorrow. It may be that having hit bottom, and having the shock of this story, he might rebound with the help of the money. Fortunately, hardly anybody reads the New York Post.

. . . . .

Always yours,

## Notes

1. 50 words have been omitted from this letter.

2. The Loyalist siege of Alcázar fortress in Toledo during the early months of the Spanish Civil War (July–September 1936). The Alcázar was held by the Franco forces referred to by Perkins as "the Rebels."

3. Hemingway first went to Spain to cover the Spanish Civil War for the North American Newspaper Alliance (NANA) in March 1937.

4. Hemingway was working on *To Have and Have Not,* which was published by Scribners in October 1937.

5. Michel Mok, "The Other Side of Paradise, Scott Fitzgerald, 40, Engulfed in Despair," *New York Post* (September 25, 1936).

▲ ▼ ▲

*To: Perkins*
*From: Fitzgerald*                                    *Wire. Princeton*

ASHEVILLE NCAR          1936 OCT 6          AM 2 23
EVEN THOUGH ADMINISTRATOR HAS BEEN APPOINTED BALTI-
MORE BANK WILL NOT ADVANCE MONEY ON MY SECURITIES
OF TWENTY THOUSAND. MARKET VALUE AT THEIR ESTIMATE
UNTIL SIX WEEKS BY WHICH TIME I WILL BE IN JAIL STOP WHAT
DO YOU DO WHEN YOU CANT PAY TYPIST OR BUY MEDICINES
OR CIGARETTS STOP ANY LOANS FROM SCRIBNERS CAN BE
SECURED BY LIEN PAYABLE ON LIQUIDATION CANT SOME-
THING BE DONE I AM UP AND PRETTY STRONG BUT THESE ARE
IMPOSSIBLE WRITING CONDITIONS I NEED THREE HUNDRED
DOLLARS WIRED TO FIRST NATIONAL BALTIMORE AND TWO
THOUSAND MORE THIS WEEK WIRE ANSWER=
      F SCOTT FITZGERALD.

▲ ▼ ▲

*To: Fitzgerald*
*From: Perkins*                              *CC, 3 pp. Princeton*

Oct 6, 1936

Dear Scott:

   We have been talking here for a long time as a result of getting your telegram. We have to have some business justification for the money we put out. With both Charlie and me there is a strong personal element in the matter, but there is none, or hardly any, with others who do not know you and who cannot understand why your account should look as it does. How are we to explain it to them? We greatly want to help you and always have, but you do not half help us to do it. In this case, if we send you the two thousand, we should have some degree of justification if you could give us a guarantee from the administrator that this, and the earlier loan of two thousand for which we hold your note, would be paid on liquidation of the Estate. But we should feel much better about the whole thing, and about you yourself, if you could now, with the respite which this inheritance will give you, work out some plan by which you would be producing something upon which we might hope to realize,– and you would too. One successful book would clear the whole slate for you all round. Couldn't you now make a regular scheme by which you would produce a book? I am not at all sure but what that biographical book I urged upon you would not be the most likely one to do what is needed. But you will now have this interval of a year, and you ought to make the fullest use of the opportunity. –If you only could tell us what you are planning, we should feel very much better about the whole matter,– and more on your account than on our own too.

Always yours,

▲ ▼ ▲

*To: Perkins*
*From: Fitzgerald*                    *TLS with holograph revisions, 3 pp. Princeton*

Grove Park Inn<br>Asheville, N.C.<br>October 16, 1936

Dear Max:

As I wired you, an advance on my Mother's estate from a friend makes it unnecessary to impose on you further.

I do not like the idea of the biographical book. I have a novel planned,[1] or rather I should say conceived, which fits much better into the circumstances, but neither by this inheritance nor in view of the general financial situation do I see clear to undertake it. It is a novel certainly as long as Tender Is The Night, and knowing my habit of endless corrections and revisions, you will understand that I figure it at two years. Except for a lucky break you see how difficult it would be for me to master the leisure of the two years to finish it. For a whole year I have been counting on such a break in the shape of either Hollywood buying Tender or else of Grisman getting Kirkland or someone else to do an efficient dramatization.[2] (I know I would not like the job and I know that Davis[3] who had every reason to undertake it after the success of Gatsby simply turned thumbs down from his dramatist's instinct that the story was not constructed as dramatically as Gatsby and did not readily lend itself to dramatization.) So let us say that all accidental, good breaks can not be considered. I can not think up any practical way of undertaking this work. If you have any suggestions they will be welcomed, but there is no likelihood that my expenses will be reduced below $18,000 a year in the next two years, with Zelda's hospital bills, insurance payments to keep, etc. And there is no likelihood that after the comparative financial failure of Tender Is The Night that I should be advanced such a sum as $36,000. The present plan, as near as I have formulated it, seems to be to go on with this endless Post writing or else go to Hollywood again. Each time I have gone to Hollywood, in spite of the enormous salary, has really set me back financially and artistically. My feelings against the autobiographical book are:

First: that certain people have thought that those Esquire articles did me definite damage and certainly they would have to form part of the fabric of a book so projected. My feeling last winter that I could put together the articles I had written vanished in the light of your disapproval, and certainly when so many books have been made up out of miscellaneous material and exploited material, as it would be in my case, there is no considerable sale to be expected. If I were Negly Farson[4] and had been through the revolutions and panics of the last fifteen years it would be another story, or if I were prepared at this moment to "tell all" it would have a chance at success, but now it would seem to be a measure adopted in extremis, a sort of period to my whole career.

In relation to all this, I enjoyed reading General Grant's Last Stand,[5] and was conscious of your particular reasons for sending it to me. It is needless to compare the difference in force of character between myself and General Grant, the number of words that he could write in a year, and the absolutely virgin field which he exploited with the experiences of four-year life under the most dramatic of circumstances. What attitude on life I have been able to put into my books is dependent upon entirely different field of reference with the predominant themes based on problems of personal psychology. While you may sit down and write 3,000 words one day, it inevitably means that you write 500 words the next. [Now, the suggestion that you have made me, Max, but that I have not gone over in my mind before, because while there are moments of pain and disappointment, I have not wanted to die enough to do anything about it (I came as close to it as ever in my life after that awful New York Evening Post article.)][6]

I certainly have this one novel, but it may have to remain among the unwritten books of this world. Such stray ideas as sending my daughter to a public school, putting my wife in a public insane asylum, have been proposed to me by intimate friends, but it would break something in me that would shatter the very delicate pencil end of a point of view. I have got myself completely on the spot and what the next step is I don't know.

I am going to New York around Thanksgiving for a day or so and we might discuss ways and means. This general eclipse of ambition and determination and fortitude, all of the very qualities on which I have prided myself, is ridiculous, and, I must admit, somewhat obscene.

Anyhow, that you for you willingness to help me. Thank Charlie for me and tell him that the assignments he mentioned have only been waiting on a general straightening up of my affairs. My God, debt is an awful thing!

Yours,

F. Scott Fitzgerald

Heard from Mrs Rawlins[7] + will see her.

*Notes*

1. Unidentified.
2. Theater producer Sam Grisman and playwright Jack Kirkland.
3. Owen Davis.
4. American journalist known for his autobiographical adventure books.
5. (Scribners, 1936) by Horace Green.
6. The bracketed sentences are crossed out but clearly readable.
7. Scribners author Marjorie Kinnan Rawlings visited Fitzgerald in Asheville in late fall 1936.

▲ ▼ ▲

*To: Perkins*           *Wolfe's letterhead, 865 First Avenue, New York City*
*From: Wolfe*                        *TLS, 2 pp. Princeton*

November 12, 1936

Dear Max:

I think you should now write me a letter in which you explicitly state the nature of my relations with Chas Scribners' Sons. I think you ought to say that I have <u>faith</u>fully and honorably discharged all obligations to Chas Scribners' Sons, whether financial, personal or contractual, and that no further agreement or obligation of any sort exists between us.

I must tell you plainly now what you must know already, that, in view of all that has happened in the last year and a half, the differences of opinion and belief, the fundamental disagreements that we have discussed so openly, so frankly, and so passionately, a thousand times, and which have brought about this unmistakable and grievous severance, I think you should have written this letter that I am asking you to write long before this. I am compelled by your failure to do so to ask you, in simple justice, to write it now.

I think it is unfair to put a man in a position where he is forced to deny an obligation that does not exist, to refuse an agreement that was never offered and never made. I think it is also unfair to try to exert, at no expense to oneself, such control of a man's future and his future work as will bring one profit if that man succeeds, and that absolves one from any commitments of any kind, should he fail. I also think it is unfair that a man without income, with little money, and with no economic security against the future, who has time and again, in the past, refused offers and proposals that would have brought him comfort and security, should now, at a time when his reputation has been obscured, and when there are no offers and little market for his work, be compelled to this last and sorrowful exercise of his fruitless devotion. And finally, I do not think that life is a game of chess, and if it were, I could not be a player.

I have nothing more to say here except to tell you that I am your friend and that my feeling toward you is unchanged.

Sincerely yours,<br>
Tom Wolfe

▲ ▼ ▲

*To: Wolfe*
*From: Perkins*                                     *ALS, 1 p. Harvard*

Perkins's initial response to Wolfe's November 12, 1936, announcement that he intended to leave Scribners (Harvard University Library)

▲ ▼ ▲

*To: Wolfe* *Perkins's personal Scribners letterhead*
*From: Perkins* *ALS, 2 pp. Harvard*

Nov 18ᵗʰ 1936

Dear Tom:—With this is a more formal letter which I hope is what you want. This is to say that on my part there has been no "severance." I can't express certain kinds of feelings very comfortably, but you must realize what my feelings are toward you. Ever since Look Homeward Angel your work has been the foremost interest in my life, + I have never doubted for your future on any grounds except, at times, on those of your being able to control the vast mass of material you have accumulated + have to form into books. You seem to think I have tried to control you. I only did that when you asked my help + then I did the best I could do. It all seems very confusing to me but, whatever the result I hope you don't mean it to keep us from seeing each other, or that you won't come to our house.

<u>Max</u>

▲ ▼ ▲

*To: Wolfe*
*From: Perkins* *TL, 2 pp. Harvard*

Nov. 18, 1936

Dear Tom:

You ask me to explicitly state the nature of your relations with Charles Scribner's Sons. To begin with, you have faithfully and honorably discharged all obligations to us, and no further agreement of any sort exists between us with respect to the future. Our relations are simply those of a publisher who profoundly admires the work of an author and takes great pride in publishing whatever he may of that author's writings. They are not such as to give us any sort of rights, or anything approaching that, over that author's future work. Contrary to custom, we have not even an option which would give us the privilege of seeing first any new manuscript.

We do not wholly understand parts of your letter, where you speak of us as putting you in a position of denying an obligation that does not exist, for we do not know how we have done that; or where you refer to 'exerting control of a man's future' which we have no intention of doing at all, and would not have the power or right to do. There are other phrases in that part of your letter that I do not understand, one of which is that which refers to us as being absolved from any commitments of any kind "should the author fail". If this and these other phrases signify that you think you should have a contract from us if our relations are to continue, you can certainly have one. We should be delighted to have one. You must surely know the faith this house has in you. There are, of course, limits in terms to which nobody can go in a contract, but we should expect to make one that would suit you if you told us what was required.

Ever sincerely yours,

▲ ▼ ▲

To: Wolfe
From: Perkins                    *TLS with holograph postscript, 1 p. Harvard*

Nov. 20, 1936

Dear Tom:

I thought I might as well send you the enclosed check since it has been drawn, together with a statement. About five hundred dollars more will be due in February, together with whatever else has accumulated in sales since the first of last August,– which may be a considerable sum.

Always yours,
Max

I wish I could see you but I don't want to force myself on you.
MP.

▲ ▼ ▲

To: Perkins
From: Fitzgerald                    *Wire. Princeton*

ASHEVILLE NCAR 3        1936 DEC 3        PM 7 44
CANT EVEN GET OUT OF HERE UNLESS YOU DEPOSIT THE REMAINING THOUSAND STOP IT IS ONLY FOR A COUPLE OF MONTHS STOP I HAVE COUNTED ON IT SO THAT I HAVE CHECKS OUT AGAINST IT ALREADY STOP PLEASE WIRE ME IF YOU HAVE WIRED IT TO THE BALTIMORE BANK STOP THE DOC-TORS THINK THAT THIS SESSION OF COMPARATIVE PROSTRA-TION IS ABOUT OVER=
SCOTT FITZGERALD.

▲ ▼ ▲

To: Perkins                    *Wolfe's letterhead, 865 First Avenue, New York City*
From: Wolfe                    *TLS with holograph postscript, 27 pp.[1] Princeton*

December 15, 1936

Dear Max:

I am sorry for the delay in answering your three letters of November 17th and 18th. As you know, I have been hard at work here day after day and, in addition, have recently been beset by some more of the legal difficulties, threats and worries which have hounded my life for the last year and a half. And finally, I wanted to have time to think over your letters carefully and to meditate my own reply before I answered you.

First of all, let me tell you that for what you say in your own two personal letters of November 17th and November 18th I shall be forever proud and grateful. I shall remember it with the greatest happiness as long as I live. I must tell you again, no matter what embarrassment it may cause you, what I have already publicly acknowledged and what I believe is now somewhat understood and known about in the world, namely, that your faith in me, your friendship for me, during the years of doubt, confusion and distress, was and will always be one of the great things in my life.

When I did give utterance to this fact in print — when I tried to make some slight acknowledgment of a debt of friendship and of loyalty, which no mere acknowledgment could ever repay — some of my enemies, as you know, tried to seize upon the simple words I had written in an effort to twist and pervert them to their own uses, to indicate that my acknowledgment was for a technical and professional service, which it was not, to assert that I was myself incapable of projecting and accomplishing my own purpose without your own editorial help, which is untrue.[2] But although such statements as these were made to injure me, and perhaps have done me an injury, I believe that injury to be at best only a temporary one. As for the rest, what I had really said, what I had really written about my debt to you, is plain and unmistakable, clearly and definitely understood by people of good will, who have a mind to understand. I would not retract a word of it, except to wish the words were written better, I would not withdraw a line of it, except to hope that I might write another line that would more adequately express the whole meaning and implication of what I feel and want to say.

As to those statements which were made, it seems to me malevolently, for what purpose I do not know, by people I have never met — that I had to have your technical and critical assistance "to help me write my books", etc, — they are so contemptible, so manifestly false, I have no fear whatever of their ultimate exposure. If refutation were needed, if the artist had time enough or felt it necessary to make an answer to all the curs that snap at him, it would not take me long, I think, to brand these falsehoods for the lies they are. I would only have to point out, I think, that so far from needing any outside aid "to help me write my books", the very book which my detractors now eagerly seize on as my best one, the gauge by which the others must be mentioned, and itself the proof and demonstration of my subsequent decline, had been utterly finished and completed, to the final period, in utter isolation, without a word of criticism or advice from any one, before any publisher ever saw it; and that whatever changes were finally made were almost entirely changes in the form of omission and of cuts in view of bringing the book down to a more publishable and condensed form. That book, of course, was "Look Homeward, Angel", and I believe that with everything else I ever wrote, the process was much the same, although the finality of completion was not so marked, because in later books I was working in a more experimental, individual fashion and dealing with the problem of how to shape and bring into articulate form a giant mass of raw material, whose proportions almost defeated me.

The very truth of the matter is that, so far from ever having been unsure of purpose and direction, in the last five years at any rate I have been almost too sure. My sense of purpose and direction is definite and overwhelming. I think, I feel and know what I want to do; the direction in which, if I live and if I am allowed to go on working and fulfill myself, I want to go, is with me more clear and certain than with any one that I have ever known. My difficulty has never been one of purpose or direction. Nothing is more certain than this fact, that I know what I want to do and where I want to go. Nothing is more certain than the fact that I shall finish any book I set out to write if life and health hold out. My difficulty from the outset, as you know, has never been one of direction, it has only been one of means. As I have already said and written, in language that seems to be so clear and unmistakable that no one could misunderstand it, I have been faced with the problem of discovering for myself my own language, my own pattern, my own structure, my own design, my own universe and creation. That, as I have said before, is a problem that is, I think, by no means unique, by no means special to myself. I believe it may have been the problem of every artist that ever lived. In my own case, however, I believe the difficulties of the problem may have been increased and complicated by the denseness of the fabric, the dimensions of the structure, the variety of the plan. For that reason I have, as you know, at times found myself almost hopelessly enmeshed in my own web.

In one sense, my whole effort for years might be described as an effort to fathom my own design, to explore my own channels, to discover my own ways. In these respects, in an effort to help me to discover, to better use, these means I was striving to apprehend and make my own, you gave me the most generous, the most painstaking, the most valuable help. But that kind of help might have been given to me by many other skilful people — and of course there are other skilful people in the world who could give such help, — although none that I know of who could give it so skillfully as you.

But what you gave me, what in my acknowledgment I tried to give expression to, was so much more than this technical assistance — an aid of spiritual sustenance, of personal faith, of high purpose, of profound and sensitive understanding, of utter loyalty and staunch support, at a time when many people had no belief at all in me, or when what little belief they had was colored by serious doubt that I would ever be able to continue or achieve my purpose, fulfill my "promise" — all of this was a help of such priceless and incalculable value, of such spiritual magnitude, that it made any other kind of help seem paltry by comparison. And for that reason mainly I have resented the contemptible insinuations of my enemies that I have to have you "to help me write my books". As you know, I don't have to have you or any other man alive to help me with my books. I do not even have to have technical help or advice, although I need it badly, and have been so immensely grateful for it. But if the worst came to the worst - and of course the worst does and will come to the worst - all this I could and will and do learn for myself, as all hard things are learned, with blood-sweat, anguish and despair.

As for another kind of help - a help that would attempt to shape my purpose or define for me my own direction,—I not only do not need that sort of help but if I found that it had in any way invaded the unity of my purpose, or was trying in any fundamental way to modify or alter the direction of my creative life — the way in which it seems to me it ought and has to go—I should repulse it as an enemy, I should fight it and oppose it with every energy of my life, because I feel so strongly that it is the final and unpardonable intrusion upon the one thing in an artist's life that must be held and kept inviolable.

All this I know you understand and will agree to. As to the final kind of help, the help of friendship, the help of faith, the help and belief and understanding of a fellow creature whom you know and reverence, not only as a person of individual genius but as a spirit of incorruptible integrity — that kind of help I do need, that kind of help I think I have been given, that kind of help I shall evermore hope to deserve and pray that I shall have. But if that too should fail — if that too should be taken from me, as so many rare and priceless things are taken from us in this life — that kind of dark and tragic fortitude that grows on us in life as we get older, and which tells us that in the end we can and must endure all things, might make it possible for me to bear even that final and irreparable loss, to agree with Samuel Johnson when he said: "The shepherd in Vergil grew at last acquainted with Love, and found him a native of the rocks".[3]

You say in one of your letters that you never knew a soul with whom you felt that you were in such fundamentally complete agreement as with me. May I tell you that I shall remember these words with proud happiness and with loyal gratefulness as long as I live. For I too on my own part feel that way about you. I know that somehow, in some hard, deep, vexed and troubling way in which all the truth of life is hidden and which, at the cost of so much living, so much perplexity and anguish of the spirit, we have got to try to find and fathom, what you say is true: I believe we are somehow, in this strange, hard way, in this complete and fundamental agreement with each other.

And yet, were there ever two men since time began who were as completely different as you and I? Have you ever known two other people who were, in almost every respect of temperament, thinking, feeling and acting, as far apart? It seems to me that each of us might almost represent, typify, be the personal embodiment of, two opposite poles of life. How to put it I do not know exactly, but I might say, I think, that you in your essential self are the Conservative and I, in my essential self, am the Revolutionary.

I use these words, I hope, in what may have been their original and natural meanings. I am not using them with reference to any of the political, social, economic or religious connotations that are now so often tied up with them. When I say that you are a Conservative, I am not thinking of you as some one who voted for Governor Landon,[4] for I can see how an action of that sort and your own considered reasons for doing it might easily have revolutionary consequences. When I say that I am a Revolutionary I know that you will never for a moment think of me as some one who is usually referred to in America as a "radical". You know that my whole feeling toward life could not be indicated or included under such a category. I am not a party man, I am not a propaganda man, I am not a Union Square or Greenwich Village communist. I not only do not believe in these people; I do not even believe they believe in themselves. I mistrust their sincerity, I mistrust their motives, I do not believe they have any essential capacity for devotion or for belief in the very principles of Revolution, of government, of economics and of life, which they all profess.

More than that, I believe that these people themselves are parasitic excrescences of the very society which they profess to abhor, whose destruction they prophesy and whose overthrow they urge. I believe that these people would be unable to live without the society which they profess to abhor, and I know that I could live if I had to, not only under this society but under any other one, and that in the end I might probably approve no other one more than I do this.

I believe further that these very people who talk of the workers with such reverence, and who assert that they are workers and are for the worker's cause, do not reverence the workers, are not themselves workers and in the end are traitors to the worker's cause. I believe that I myself not only know the workers and am a friend of the worker's cause but that I am myself a brother to the workers, because I am myself, as every artist is, a worker, and I am myself moreover the son of a working man. I know furthermore that at the bottom there is no difference between the artist and the worker. They both come from the same family, they recognize and understand each other instantly. They speak the same language. They have always stood together. And I know that our enemies, the people who betray us, are these apes and monkeys of the arts, who believe in everything and who believe in nothing and who hate the artist and who hate the living man no matter what lip service they may pay to us. These people are the enemies to life, the enemies to revolution. Nothing is more certain than that they will betray us in the end.

I have said these things simply to indicate to you a difference of which I know you must be already well aware. The difference between the revolutionary and the "radical," the difference between the artist and the ape of art, the difference between the worker and those who say they are the worker's friend. The same thing could be said, it seems to me, on your own side, about the true conservative and the person who only votes conservative and owns property and has money in the bank.

Just as in some hard, strange way there is between us probably this fundamentally complete agreement which you speak of, so too, in other hard, strange ways there is this complete and polar difference. It must be so with the South pole and the North pole. I believe that in the end they too must be in fundamentally complete agreement — but the whole earth lies between them. I don't know exactly how to define conservatism or the essential conservative spirit of which I speak here, but I think I might say it is a kind of fatalism of the spirit. Its fundaments, it seems to me, are based upon a kind of unhoping hope, an imperturbable acceptation, a determined resignation, which believes that fundamentally life will never change, but that on this account we must all of us do the best we can.

The result of all this, it seems to me, is that these differences between us have multiplied in complexity and difficulty. The plain truth of the matter now is that I hardly know where to turn. The whole natural impulse of creation — and with me, creation is a natural impulse, it has got to flow, it has got to realize itself through the process of torrential production — is checked and hampered at every place. In spite of this, I have finally and at last, during these past two months, broken through into the greatest imaginative conquest of my life — the only complete and whole one I have ever had. And now I dare not broach it to you, I dare not bring it to you, I dare not show it to you, for fear that this thing which I cannot trifle with, that may come to a man but once in his whole life, may be killed at its inception by cold caution, by indifference, by the growing apprehensiveness and dogmatism of your own conservatism. You say that you are not aware that there is any severance between us. Will you please tell me what there is in the life around us on which we both agree? We don't agree in politics, we don't agree on economics, we are in entire disagreement on the present system of life around us, the way people live, the changes that should be made.[5]

Your own idea, evidently, is that life itself is unchangeable, that the abuses I protest against, the greed, the waste, the poverty, the filth, the suffering, are inherent in humanity, and that any other system than the one we have would be just as bad as this one.[6] In this, I find myself in profound and passionate conflict. I hold no brief, as you know, for the present communist system as it is practiced in Russia today, but it seems to me to be the most absurd and hollow casuistry to argue seriously that because a good Russian worker is given a thicker slice of beef than a bad one, or because a highly trained mechanic enjoys a slightly better standard of living and is given more privileges and comforts than an inferior mechanic, the class system has been reestablished in Russia and is <u>identical</u>[7] with the one existing in this country, whereby a young girl who inherits the fortune of a five-and-ten-cent store king is allowed to live a life of useless, vicious idleness and to enjoy an income of five million dollars annually while other young girls work in the very stores that produce her fortune for ten dollars a week.[8]

It is all very well to say that the artist should not concern himself with these things but with "life." What are these things if they are not life — one of the cruelest and most intolerable aspects of it, it is true, but as much a part of the whole human spectacle as a woman producing a child. You, better than any one, have had the chance to observe during the past year how this consciousness of society, of the social elements, that govern life today, have sunk into my spirit, how my convictions about all these things have grown deeper, wider, more intense at every point. On your own part, it seems to me, there has been a corresponding stiffening, an increasing conservatism that is now, I fear, reached the point of dogged and unyielding inflexibility and obstinate resolve to try to maintain the status quo at any cost.[9]

Since that is your condition, your considered judgment, I will not try to change it, or to persuade you in any way, because I know your reasons for so thinking and so feeling are honest ones. But neither must you now try to change me, or to persuade me to alter or deny convictions which are the result of no superficial or temporary influence, no Union Square-Greenwich Village cult, but the result of my own deep living, my own deep feeling, my own deep labor and my own deep thought.

Had I given full expression to these convictions in "Of Time and the River" I believe it would have been a better book.[10] You do not think so. But I will say that these feelings, these convictions, are becoming deeper and intenser all the time, and so far from feeling that the world cannot be changed, that it cannot be made better, that the evils of life are unremediable, that all the faults and vices at which we protest will always exist, I find myself more passionately convinced than ever of the necessity of change, more passionately confirmed than ever in the faith and the belief that the life and the condition of the whole human race can be immeasurably improved. And this is something that grows stronger with me all the time. It has been my lot to start life with an obedient faith, with a conservative tradition, only to have that faith grow weaker and fade out as I grew older. I cannot tell you all the ways in which this came about, but I think I can indicate to you one of the principal ones.

I was a child of faith. I grew up in the most conservative section of America, and as a child I put an almost unquestioning belief and confidence in the things that were told me, the precepts that were taught me. As I grew older I began to see the terrible and shocking differences between appearance and reality all around me. I was told, for example, in church, of a Sunday morning, that people should love one another as their brothers, that they should not bear false witness against their fellow-man, that they should not covet their neighbor's wife, that they should not commit adultery, that they should not cheat, trick, betray and rob their fellows. And as I grew older and my knowledge of life and of the whole community increased, until there was hardly a family in town whose whole history I did not know, I began to see what a shameful travesty of goodness these lives were. I began to see that the very people who said on Sunday that one should not bear false witness against his neighbors bore false witness all the time, until the very air was poisonous with their slanders, with their hatreds, their vicious slanderings of life and of their neighbors. I began to see how the people who talked about not coveting their neighbors' wives did covet their neighbors' wives and committed adultery with them. I saw how the minister who got up and denounced a proposal to introduce a little innocent amusement in the Sunday life of the people — a baseball game or a moving picture show,—upon the grounds that it not only violated the law of God but was an imposition on our fellow-man, that we had no right to ask our fellows to do work on Sunday, had, at that very moment, two sweating negro girls in the kitchen of his own home, employed at meagre wages to cook his Sunday dinner for him. I saw how the wife of the town's richest man would go in for what was called social work and lecture the poor little shop-girls of the Y.W.C.A., telling them that no decent girl would take a drink, would stay out after nine o'clock at night, would tolerate the company of a young man without a chaperone — while her own daughter, unreproved, unchecked and licensed, was the heroine of five hundred fornications, was even at that moment lying in a state of drunken stupor in the embraces of another young town parasite.

Well, it is an old, old story, but to me it was a new one. Like every other boy of sense, intelligence and imagination, whoever first discovered these things for himself, I thought I was the first one in the world to see these things. I thought that I had come upon a horrible catastrophe, a whole universe of volcanic infamy over which the good people of the earth were treading blissfully and innocently with trusting smiles. I thought I had to tell this thing to some one. I thought I had to warn the world, to tell all my friends and teachers that all the goodness and integrity and purity of their lives was menaced by this snake of unsuspected evil.

I don't need to tell you what happened. I was received either with smiles of amused and pitying tolerance or with curt reprimands, admonitions to shut up, not to talk about my betters, not to say a word against people who had won a name and who were the high and mighty ones in town. Then slowly, like some one living in a nightmare only to wake up and find out that the nightmare is really true, I began to find out that they <u>didn't</u> mean it, they didn't mean what they said. I began to discover that all these fine words, these splendid precepts, these noble teachings had no meaning at all, because the very people who professed them had no belief in them. I began to discover that it didn't matter at all whether you bore false witness against your neighbor, if you only said that one should not bear false witness against his neighbor. I began to see that it didn't matter at all whether you took your neighbor's ox or his ass or his wife, if only you had the cunning and the power to take them. I began to see that it did not matter at all whether you committed adultery or not, so long as it did not come out in the papers. Every one in town might know you had committed it, and with whom, and on what occasions, the whole history might be a matter for sly jesting, furtive snickerings, the lewd and common property of the whole community, and you could still be deacon of the church provided you were not sued for alienation of affection. I began to see that you could talk of chastity, of purity, of standards of morality and high conduct, of loving your neighbor as yourself, and still derive your filthy income from a horde of rotting tenements down in niggertown that were so vile and filthy they were not fit to be the habitation of pigs. You could talk to a crowd of miserable, over-worked and under-paid shop-girls about their moral life and the necessity of chastity even though your own daughter was the most promiscuous, drunken little whore in town. And it didn't matter, it didn't matter — if you had the dough. That was all that mattered.

I discovered very early that people who had the money could do pretty damn near anything they wanted to. Whoredom, drunkenness, debauchery of every sort was the privilege of the rich, the crime of the poor. And as I grew older, as my experience of life widened and increased, as I first came to know, to explore, to investigate life in this overwhelming city, with all the passion, the hope, the faith, the fervor and the poetic imagination of youth, I found that here too it was just the same. Here too, if anything, it was more overwhelming because it was so condensed, so multiplied. Here too, if anything, it was even more terrible because the privileged city classes no longer pretended to cloak themselves in the spurious affirmations of religion. The result has been, as I have grown older, as I have seen life in manifold phases all over the earth, that I have become more passionately convinced than ever before that this system that we have is evil, that it brings misery and injustice not only to the lives of the poor but to the wretched and sterile lives of the privileged classes who are supported by it, that this system of living must be changed, that men must have a new faith, a new heroism, a new belief, if life is to be made better. And that life can be made better, that life will be made better is the heart and core of my own faith and my own conviction, the end toward which I believe I must henceforth direct every energy of my life and talent.

All this, I know, you consider elementary, and I agree with you. It is. These evidences of corruption in the life around me which I have mentioned to you, you consider almost childishly naive. Perhaps they are. But if they are, the anterior fundamental sources of corruption which have produced them are certainly neither childish nor naive. You have told me that you consider the life of a Smith Reynolds,[11] the vicious life of a young girl who, without ever having done a stroke of work herself, is privileged to enjoy an income of two million, or five million, or ten million a year, only a trifling and superficial manifestation and of no importance. With this, of course, I am in utter opposition. If these people, as you say, are only flies upon the tender of a locomotive, they are locomotive flies, and the locomotive that produced them should be scrapped.

I have gone into all this, not because these bases of contention are even fundamental to you and me, but because they are indicative of all the various widening channels of difference that have come up between us in recent years. Just as my own feeling for the necessity for change, for essential revolution in this way of life, has become steadily deeper and more confirmed, so too have you, hardened by the challenge of the depression, deeply alarmed by the menace of the times to the fortune of which you are the custodian[12] — not for yourself, I know, for you yourself I truly believe are not a man who needs material things, but alarmed by the menace of these times to the security and future of five young and tender creatures who, protected as they have been, and unprepared as they are to meet the peril of these coming times, are themselves, it seems to me, the unfortunate victims of this very system you must now try to help maintain — you have accordingly become more set and more confirmed in your own convictions.[13] With these personal affairs, these intimate details of your fine family, I have no intention to intrude save where it seems to me to have resulted in a bias that challenges the essence of my own purpose and direction.

What I really want to say to you most earnestly now is this: there has never been a time when I've been so determined to write as I please, to say what I intend to say, to publish the books I want to publish, as I am now. I know that you have asserted time and again that you were in entire sympathy with this feeling, that, more than this, you were willing to be the eager promoter and supporter of this intention, that you were willing to publish whatever I wanted you to publish, that you were only waiting for me to give it to you. In this I think you have deceived yourself. I think you are mistaken when you say that all you have waited for was the word from me, that you would publish anything I wanted you to publish. There are many things that I have wanted you to publish which have not been published.[14] Some of them have not been published because they were too long for magazine space, or too short for book space, or too different in their design and quality to fit under the heading of a short story, or too incomplete to be called a novel. All this is true. All this I grant. And yet, admitting all these things, without a word of criticism of you or of the technical and publishing requirements of the present time that make their publication impracticable, I will still say that I think some of them should have been published. I still think that much of the best writing that a man may do is writing that does not follow under the convenient but extremely limited forms of modern publication. It is not your fault. It is not Scribner's fault. It is just the way things are. But as I have been telling you, the way things are is not always the way, it seems to me that things should be; and one fact that has become plain to me in recent years and is now imbedded in my conviction, is that in spite of the rivers of print that inundate this broad land, the thousands of newspapers, the hundreds of magazines, the thousands of books that get printed every year, and the scores of publishers who assure you that they are sitting on the edges of their chairs and eagerly waiting, praying, that some one will come in with a piece of writing of originality and power, that all they are waiting for, all they ask for, is just for the opportunity of discovering it and printing it, the means of publication are still most limited for a life of the complexity, the variety, the richness, the fascination, the terror, the poetry, the beauty and the whole unuttered magnificence of this tremendous life around us, the means of publication are really pitifully meager, ungenerous, meanly, sterilely constricted.

Which brings me now to an essential point, a point that bears practically and dangerously on every thing that I have heretofore said to you.

About fifteen years ago, as you know, an extraordinary book was produced which startled the whole critical and publishing world. This book was the Ulysses of James Joyce. I know that you are well aware of the history of that book, but for the sake of the argument I am presently to make, let me review it again for you. Ulysses was published, if I mistake not, in 1921.[15] I have been informed dozens of times in the last few years by reputable and well-known publishers, including yourself, that they are eagerly waiting a chance to produce a work of originality and power, that they would produce it without question, without modification, if it were given to them. What are the facts concerning Ulysses? Was it published by Chas Scribner's Sons?[16] No, it was not. Was it published by Harper's, by Macmillan's, by Houghton-Mifflin, by one of the great English houses? It was not. Who published it then? It was published privately, obscurely, by a woman who ran a book shop in Paris.[17] And at first, as you know, it was treated by most critics as kind of literary curiosity — either as a work of deliberate pornography or as a work of wilfully complicated obscurity, of no genuine value or importance, save to a little group of clique adepts. And as you know, the book was taken up by clique adepts everywhere and used, or rather misused, in their customary way, as a badge of their snobbish superiority. But in addition to both these groups there was also a third group, I think, a very small group composed of those people scattered throughout the world who are able to read and feel and understand and form their own judgment without prejudice of the merits of a powerful and original work. It seems to me that almost the best, the most fortunate thing in life — in a writer's life at least — is that these people do exist. A great book is not lost. It does not get done to death by fools and snobs. It may be misunderstood for years. Its writer may be ridiculed or reviled or betrayed by false idolatry, but the book does not get lost. There are always a few people who will save it. The book will make its way. That is what happened to Ulysses. As time went on, the circle widened. Its public increased. As people overcame their own inertia, mastered the difficulty which every new and original work creates, became familiar with its whole design, they began to understand that the book was neither an obscene book nor an obscure book, certainly it was not a work of wilful dilettante caprice. It was, on the contrary, an orderly, densely constructed creation, whose greatest fault, it seems to me, so far from being a fault of caprice, was rather the fault of an almost Jesuitical logic which is essentially too dry and lifeless in its mechanics for a work of the imagination. At any rate, now, after fifteen years, Ulysses is no longer thought of as a book meant solely for a little group of literary adepts. The adepts of this day, in fact, speak somewhat patronizingly of the work as marking "the end of an epoch," as being "the final development of an out worn naturalism," etc., etc. But the book itself had now won an unquestioned and established place in literature. Its whole method, its style, its characters, its story and design has become so familiar to many of us that we no longer think of it as difficult or obscure. It seems no more difficult that Tristram Shandy. For my part, I do not find Ulysses as difficult as Tristram. Certainly it is no where near as difficult as The Ring and the Book.[18] Moreover, Ulysses can now be published openly in this country, sold over the counter as any other book is sold, without fear of arrest or action by the law. And at the present time, as you know, it is being sold that way, in what is known as "large quantities," by one of your fellow publishers. This man told me a year and a half ago that the sale up to that time, I believe, was something like 30,000 copies.[19] Ulysses, therefore, has made its way not only critically but commercially as well. These are the facts. I do not recall them in order to accuse you with them. I know you did not have the opportunity of publishing Ulysses. Perhaps no other well-known publisher, either in England or America, had that opportunity. I suppose furthermore that at that time it would have been impossible for any reputable publisher to have published that book openly. But the fact remains it did get published, didn't it — not by Scribner's, not by Houghton, not by any known publisher in England, but privately, by a little obscure bookseller in Paris.

And the reason your associates, the Modern Library, Inc., can now publish this book; in large quantities, openly, and derive a profit from it now, is because some private, obscure person took the chance fifteen years ago — took the chance, I fear, without the profits.

What, then? You say you are waiting eagerly to discover a manuscript of originality and power. You say that you are waiting eagerly to publish a manuscript of mine, that you will publish anything I want you to publish. I know you believe what you say, but I also think you deceive yourself. I am not going to write a Ulysses book. Like many another young man who came under the influence of that remarkable work, I wrote my Ulysses book and got it published too. That book, as you know, was Look Homeward, Angel. And now, I am finished with Ulysses and with Mr. Joyce, save that I am not an ingrate and will always, I hope, be able to remember a work that stirred me, that opened new vistas into writing, and to pay the tribute to a man of genius that is due him.

However, I am now going to write my own Ulysses. The first volume is now under way. The first volume will be called The Hound of Darkness, and the whole work, when completed, will be called The Vision of Spangler's Paul.[20] Like Mr. Joyce, I am going to write as I please, and this time, no one is going to cut me unless I want them to.[21] Like Mr. Joyce, and like most artists, I believe, I am by nature a Puritan. At any rate, a growing devotion to work, to purpose, to fulfillment, a growing intensity of will, tends to distill one's life into a purer liquor. I shall never hereafter — I hope that I have never heretofore — but I shall never hereafter write a word for the purpose of arousing sensational surprise, of shocking the prudish, of flaunting the outraged respectabilities of the middle-class mind. But I shall use as precisely, as truthfully, as tellingly as I can, every word I have to use, every word, if need be, in my vocabulary, every word, if need be, in the vocabulary of the foulest-mouthed taxi driver, the most prurient-tongued prostitute that ever screamed an obscene epithet. Like Mr. Joyce, I have at last discovered my own America, I believe I have found my language, I think I know my way. And I shall wreak out my vision of this life, this way, this world and this America, to the top of my bent, to the height of my ability, but with an unswerving devotion, integrity and purity of purpose that shall not be menaced, altered or weakened by any one. I will go to jail because of this book if I have to.[22] I will lose my friends because of it, if I will have to. I will be libeled, slandered, blackmailed, threatened, menaced, sneered at, derided and assailed by every parasite, every ape, every blackmailer, every scandalmonger, every little Saturday-Reviewer of the venomous and corrupt respectabilities. I will be exiled from my country because of it, if I have to. I can endure exile. I have endured it before, as you well know, on account of a book which you yourself published, although few — among them, some of the very ones who betrayed me then either by silence or evasion now try to smile feebly when I speak of exile, but it was the truth and may be true again. But no matter what happens I am going to write this book.

You have heard me talk to you before. You have not always been disposed to take seriously what I say to you. I pray most earnestly that you will take this seriously. For seven years now, during this long and for me wonderful association with you, I have been increasingly aware of a certain direction which our lives were taking. Looking back, I can see now that although Look Homeward, Angel gave you pleasure and satisfaction, you were extremely alarmed even then about its publication, and entertained the hope — the sincere and honest hope directed, I know, to what you considered my own best interests — that the years would temper me to a greater conservatism, a milder intensity, a more decorous moderation. And I think where I have been most wrong, most unsure in these past seven years, has been where I have yielded to this benevolent pressure. Because I think that it is just there that I have allowed myself to falter in my purpose, to be diverted from the direction toward which the whole impulsion of my life and talent is now driving me, to have failed there insofar as I have yielded to the modifications of this restraint. Restraint, discipline — yes, they were needed desperately, they are needed badly still. But let us not get the issues confused, let us not again get into the old confusion between substance and technique, purpose and manner, direction and means, the spirit and the letter. Restrain my adjectives, by all means, discipline my adverbs, moderate the technical extravagances of my incondite exuberance, but don't derail the train, don't take the Pacific Limited and switch it down the siding towards Hogwart Junction. It can't be done. I'm not going to let it happen. If you expected me to grow conservative simply because I got bald and fat and for the first time in life had a few dollars in the bank, you are going to be grievously mistaken. Besides, what is there longer for me to fear? I have been through it all now, I have seen how women can betray you, how friends can sell you out for a few filthy dollars, how the whole set-up of society and of justice in its present form permits the thief, the parasite, the scavenger, the scandal-monger to rob, cheat, outrage and defame you, how even those people who swear they are your sincerest and most enduring friends, who say they value your talent and your work, can sink to the final dishonor of silence and of caution when you are attacked, will not even lift their voices in a word of protest or of indignation when they hear you lied about by scoundrels or maligned by rascals. So what am I now to lose? Even the little money that I had, the greater part of it, has now been taken from me by these thieves and parasites of life. Well, they can take it, they can have it, they have got it. They can take everything I have, but no one henceforth shall take from me my work.

I am afraid of nothing now. I have nothing more to lose except my life and health. And those I pray and hope to God will stay with me till my work is done. That, it seems to me, is the only tragedy that can now stay with me.

The other day you were present when we were having an interview with a distinguished member of the legal profession.[23] I wonder what was going on in your mind when you saw that man and when you looked at me. When you saw that man, secure in wealth, in smugness, in respectability, even though all these authorities had come to him from his accursed profession, from shuffling papers, peering around for legal crevices, seeking not for truth or justice but for technical advantages. When you heard this man ask me if I had lived in certain neighborhoods, in certain kinds of habitation, if I ever drank, etc., and when you heard him cough pompously behind his hand and say that although he of course had never led "that sort of life" he was — ahem, ahem — not narrow-minded and understood that there were those that did. Understand? Why, what could he understand of "my kind of life"? He could no more understand it than a dog could understand the books in his master's library. And I have been forced to wonder of late, after some of the sad events of this last year, how much of it you understood. What I am trying to tell you, what I am forced to say, because it is the truth, is that I am a righteous man, and few people know it because there are few righteous people in the world.

But from my boyhood, from my early youth, I have lived a life of solitude, of industry, consecration. I have cost few people anything in this world, except perhaps the pains of birth. I have given people everything I had. I think that I have taken from no one more than I have given them. Certainly, I suppose that not even my bitterest enemies have ever accused me of living or working of thinking about money. During the time that you yourself have known me you have had ample demonstration of that fact. I known you have not forgotten them, and I hope that if anything should happen to me, if I should die, as indeed I have no wish to do, there would be some one left who had known me who would say some of these things I know to be true.

Please understand, that I neither intend nor imply any criticism of you, or of your friendship when I say these things. I know you are my friend. I value your friendship more than anything else in the world, the belief that you, above all people, respected my work and found happiness in being able to help me with it has been the greatest spiritual support and comfort I've ever known. I think further that if I ever heard you slandered or defamed or lied about I would assault the person who defamed you. But I know that that is not your way.[24] You believe that silence is the best answer, and perhaps you are right. At any rate, I want you to know that as long as I know you are my friend to the very hilt, to the very last, if need be, and I hope it never need be, to your own peril and security, that is all that matters. And that is the way I feel about you.

I do not know if you have always been aware of how I felt about these things, of what a naked, fiercely lacerated thing my spirit was, how I have writhed beneath the lies and injuries and at times, almost maddened to insanity at the treachery, the injustice and the hatred I have had to experience and endure, at what a frightful cost I have attained even the little fortitude I have attained. At times, particularly during the last year or two, the spectacle of the victim squirming beneath the lash has seemed to amuse you.[25] I know there is no cruelty in your nature. I do suggest to you, however, that where one is secure in life, when one is vested with authority, established in position, surrounded by a little world of his own making, of his own love, he may sometimes be a little unmindful of the lives of people less fortunate than himself. There is an unhappy tendency in all of us to endure with fortitude the anguish of another man. There is also a tendency among people of active and imaginative minds and temperaments who live themselves conventional and conservative lives to indulge vicariously their interest in the adventures and experiences of other people whose lives are not so sheltered as their own. And these people, I think, often derive what seems to be a kind of quiet, philosophic amusement at the spectacle of what is so falsely known as the "human comedy." But I might suggest to such people that what affords them quiet entertainment is being paid for by another man with blood and agony, and that while we smile at the difficulties and troubles in which an impulsive and generous person gets involved, a man of genius or of talent may be done to death.

I suppose it is very true to say that "every one has these troubles." I do think, however, that a man in my own position, of my own temperament, whose personality seems to penetrate his work in a peculiarly intimate way, so that he then becomes the target for intrigues and scandals of all sorts — such a man, I say, may have them to an exaggerated degree and through no essential fault of his own. Certainly, I do not think he could expect to be protected wholly from them. Certainly no one has the right to expect that his own life will be wholly free from the griefs and troubles that other people have. But I think a man who has not injured other people, who has not interfered with other people's lives or solicited their intrusion, has a right to expect a reasonable and decent amount of privacy — the reasonable and decent amount of privacy that a carpenter, a truck driver or a railroad engineer might have.

At any rate, in spite of all these things, I shall push forward somehow to the completion of my work. I feel that any more confusion or uncertainty might be ruinous to my purpose. There has been too much indecision already. We postponed the completion and publication of the October Fair, with some intention, I suppose, of showing the critics and the public I could create in a different vein, in a more objective manner than I had yet done. We also deferred completion and publication of The Hills Beyond Pentland. I know you said you were willing to go ahead and publish these books. You have always assured me on that point. But I did feel that your counsel and your caution were against their publication now.[26] I believe you may have allowed your apprehensions concerning who and what I might now write about at the period I had now reached in my writing to influence your judgments. I don't like to go into all this again.

The thing that happened last summer, your reaction to the manuscript Miss Nowell brought to you while I was in Europe, and your own comment as expressed to her in a note which she sent to me and which said, after she had cut all the parts you objected to in the manuscript out of it, that 'the only person it can now possibly hurt is Thomas Wolfe," was to me a shocking revelation.[27] I am not of the opinion now that the manuscript in question was one of any great merit. I know that I've done much better work. But the point, as I told you after my return from Europe, the point that we discussed so frankly and so openly, was that your action, if carried to its logical conclusions and applied to everything I write from now on, struck a deadly blow at the very vitals of my whole creative life.[28] The only possible inference that could be drawn from this matter was that from now on, if I wished to continue writing books which Charles Scribner's Sons were going to publish, I must now submit myself to the most rigid censorship, a censorship which would delete from all my writings any episode, any scene, any character, any reference that might seem to have any connection, however remote, with the house of Charles Scribner's Sons and its sisters and its cousins and its aunts. Such a conclusion, if I agreed to it, would result in the total enervation and castration of my work — a work which, as I have told you in this letter, I am now resolved must be more strong and forthright in its fidelity to purpose than ever. Again, in this whole situation there is a display, an almost unbelievable vanity and arrogance. It was first of all the vanity and arrogance that would lead certain people to suppose that I was going to "write about them," and then the vanity and arrogance of people who said that, although it was perfectly all right for me to write about other people "in humble walks of life," it was an unpardonable affront to all these important high-toned personages to be "written about" freely and frankly by a low scribbling fellow,[29] who is good enough no doubt to supply a publisher of manuscript, to give employment to his business, to add prestige to the reputation of his firm, but who must be put in his place when he overstepped the bounds of human sanctity.

Now, in the first place, as I told you before, whoever got the idea that I was going to write about him or her or them anyway? And in the second place, whoever got the idea that I was not going ahead and write as I damned please, about anything I wished to write about, with the complete freedom to which every artist is entitled, and that no one in the world is going to stand in the way of my doing this? I am certain at the present time not interested in writing about Chas Scribner's Sons or any one connected with Chas Scribner's Sons. It has at the present time no part of my creative plan or of my writing effort. And as you know very well, I don't "write about" people. I create living characters of my own — a whole universe of my own creation.[30] And any character that I create is so unmistakably my own that anyone familiar with my work would know instantly it was my own, even if it had no title and no name.

But, to go back to this simple, fundamental, inescapable necessity of all art, which I have patiently, laboriously, coherently explained a thousand times, in such language that no one misunderstand it, to all the people in this country, to all the people who, for some strange and extraordinary reason, in America and nowhere else that I have ever been on earth, keep harping forever, with a kind of idiot pertinacity, upon the word "autobiography" — you can't make something out of nothing. You can either say that there is no such thing as autobiographical writing or you can say that all writing is autobiographical, a statement with which I should be inclined to agree.[31] But you cannot say, you must not say that one man is an autobiographical writer and another man is not an autobiographical writer. You cannot and must not say that one novel is an autobiographical novel and another novel is not an autobiographical novel. Because if you say these things, you are uttering falsehood and palpable nonsense. It has no meaning.

My books are neither more nor less autobiographical than War and Peace. If anything, I should say that they are less, because a great writer like Tolstoi, who achieves his purpose, achieves it because he has made a perfect utilization of all the means, the materials at his disposal. This Tolstoi did in War and Peace. I have never yet succeeded in doing it completely and perfectly. Accordingly, Tolstoi is a more autobiographical writer than I am, because he has succeeded better in using what he had. But make no mistake about it, both of us, and every other man who ever wrote a book, are autobiographical. You are therefore not to touch my life in this way. When you or any man tries to exert this kind of control, to modify or shape my material in an improper way because of some paltry personal, social apprehension, you do the unpardonable thing. You try to take from the artist his personal property, to steal his substance, to defraud him of his treasure — the only treasure he has, the only property and wealth which is truly, inexorably, his own.

You can take it from him, but by so doing you commit a crime. You have stolen what does not belong to you. You have not only taken what belongs to another man, but you have taken what belongs to him in such a way that no one else can possibly claim ownership. No one owns what he has as does the artist. When you try to steal it from him he only laughs at you, because you could take it to the ends of the earth and bury it in a mountain and it would still shine straight through the mountain side like radium. You couldn't hide it. Any one on earth could find it and would know at once who the proper owner was.

That is what this final argument is about. I'm not going to be interfered with on this score. I get my material, I acquire my wealth as every artist does, from his own living, from his own experience, from his own observation. And when any outer agency tries to interpose itself between me and any portion of my own property, however small, and says to me "hands off," "you can't have that particular piece there," some one is going to get hurt.

You told me when I discussed these things with you in October, after my return from Europe, that you agreed with me, that in the last analysis you were always with the man of talent, and that if the worst comes to the worst you could resign your executive and editorial functions. Well, don't worry, you'll never have to. In the first place, your executive and editorial functions are so special and valuable that they can not be substituted by any other person on earth. They could not be done without by the business that employs them. It would be like having a house with the lights turned out. Furthermore, no one is going to resign on my account. There are still enough people in the world who value what I do, I believe, to support me freely, heartily and cheerfully, with no sense that they are enduring martyrdom on my account. So if there is ever any situation that might indicate any future necessity for any one to resign anything on my account, that situation will never arise, simply because I won't be there to be resigned about.[32]

This business about the artist hurting people is for the most part nonsense. The artist is not here in life to hurt it but to illuminate it. He is not here to teach men hatred but to show them beauty. No one in the end ever got hurt by a great book, or if he did the hurt was paltry and temporary in comparison to the immense good that was conferred.

Now, at a time when I am more firmly resolved than ever before to exert my full amount, to use my full stroke, to shine my purest and intensest ray, it is distressing to see the very people who published my first efforts with complete equanimity, and with no qualms whatever about the possibility of anybody getting "hurt," begin to squirm around uncomfortably and call for calf-rope and whine that their own toes are being stepped upon, even when nothing has been said, nothing written.[33] They have no knowledge or declaration of my own intention except that I intend in my own way to finish my own book. What are you going to do about it? You say you are not aware that there have been any difficulties or any severance. If these things I have been talking about are not difficulties, if this is not a threatened severance of the gravest nature, I should like to know what you consider difficult and what severance is? We can not continue in this irresolute, temporizing "Well now, you go ahead for the present — we'll wait and see how it all turns out —" manner. My life has been ravaged, my energy exhausted, my work confused and aborted long enough by this kind of miserable, time serving procrastination. I'm not going to endure it any longer. I'm not going to pour my sweat and blood and energy and life and talent into another book now, only to be told two or three years from now that it would be inadvisable to publish it without certain formidable deletions, or that perhaps we'd better wait a few years longer and see "how everything turns out".

We stalled around this way with October Fair, until all the intensity and passion I had put into the book was lost, until I had gone stale on it, until I was no longer interested in it — and to what purpose? Why, because you allowed your fond weakness for the female sex to get the better of your principle, because you were afraid some foolish female, who was inwardly praying for nothing better than to be a leading character in a book of mine, and who was bitterly disappointed when she was not, might get her feelings hurt — or that the pocketbook of the firm might get touched by suits for libel. Well, there would have been no suits for libel. I never libelled anybody in my life. Certainly, there was no remote danger of libel in The October Fair, but because of our weakness and irresolution the news got around that we were afraid of publication for this reason. The lying rumor was spread around in the column of a filthy gossip-writer, and the result now is that we have a libel suit on our hands from a person who was never libelled, who doesn't have a leg to stand on, but who is willing to take the chance and make the effort to get something because we were not firm and resolute in the beginning.[34]

Let's make an end of all this devil's business. Let's stand to our guns like men. Let's go ahead and try to do our work without qualification, without fear, without apology. What are you willing to do? My own position is now clear. I have nothing to be afraid of. And my greatest duty, my deepest obligation now is to the completion of my own work. If that can not be done any longer upon the terms that I have stated here, then I must either stand alone or turn to other quarters for support, if I can find it. You yourself must now say plainly what the decision is to be, because the decision now rests with you. You can no longer have any doubt as to how I feel about these matters. I don't see how you can any longer have any doubt that difficulties of a grave and desperate nature do exist.

I can only repeat here what I have told you before, that the possibility of an irrevocable and permanent severance has caused me the greatest distress and anguish of the mind for months, that if it occurs it will seem to me like death, but that whatever happens, what I have said and written about the way I feel towards you will remain.

I'm going South in a few days for the first time in seven years. It is a tremendous experience for me. Those seven years to me have been a lifetime. So much has been crowded into them — exile and vituperation from my own country, modest success and recognition, then partial oblivion, years of struggling and despairing, to conquer a new medium, to fashion a new world, partial success again, added recognition, partial oblivion again. It seems to move in cycles. Now I'm up against the same grim struggle, the same necessity for new discovery, new beginning, new achievement, as before. It will be strange to be back home again. I had but recently met you when I was there last. I was unknown then, but within a few weeks after my visit home a storm of calumny and abuse broke out that made me long for my former oblivion. Now that storm apparently has died down. They are willing to have me come back. So much has happened in those seven years. I've seen so many people that I know go down to ruin, others have died, others have grown up, some have lost everything, some have recovered something. People I knew well I no longer see. People who swore eternal love are now irrevocably separated. Nothing has turned out as we thought it would turn out. Nothing is the way we thought it was going to be. But Life, I now begin to see, moves in a great wheel, the wheel swings and things and people that we knew are lost, but some day they come back again. So it is a strange and wonderful event for me to be going back home. I knew so little of the world and people then, although I thought I knew so much of them. Now I really think I know a little more about the world and people than I knew then, and I think all of us understand a little more about one another.

I'm sorry this letter has had to be so long. It seemed to me there had to be some sort of final statement. I hope, now the statement has been made, the problem is more clear. I send all of you now all my best wishes for Christmas and for a New Year which I hope will bring to all of us an accomplishment and fulfillment of some of those things we most desire.

Meanwhile, with all friendship, all good wishes,

Sincerely yours,

Tom Wolfe

—Max, this is not a well-written letter, but it is a genuine and honest one. If you still have any interest in me, please attend to what I say here carefully!

P.S. New Orleans, Jan 10, 1937: I have with held this letter as long as possible. I had hoped against hope not to have to send it. But now, after the shocking events of the past two weeks since I left NY—Mitchell's letter conveying the blackmail threats of Dooher[35]—the growing peril of my situation in a mesh of scoundrelism—and your own telegram[36]—the increasing ambiguity and caution of your own statements—I have read the letter through again and decided that it must be sent. In spite of its great length there is much more to say—but let this stand now for a record![37]

## Notes

1. This letter has marginal comments, lines, and underlines presumably made by Perkins; they have been noted.

2. In "Genius Is Not Enough" (*Saturday Review of Literature*, April 25, 1936), a review of *The Story of a Novel*, Bernard De Voto wrote: "The most flagrant evidence of his incompleteness is the fact that, so far, one indispensable part of the artist has existed not in Mr. Wolfe but in Maxwell Perkins. Such organizing faculty and such critical intelligence as have been applied to the book have come not from inside the artist, not from the artist's feeling for form and esthetic integrity, but from the office of Charles Scribner's Sons."

In a November 13, 1935, letter to Wolfe's putative biographer John Terry, Perkins wrote: "The article or review by De Voto was the most important in its effect upon Tom's relation with me. It was that that set him to believe he must prove that I was not necessary to him. And I think that that was at the very root of our trouble" (University of North Carolina). See *Always Yours, Max: Maxwell Perkins Responds to Questions about Thomas Wolfe,* ed. Alice R. Cotton (Thomas Wolfe Society, 1997).

3. From Samuel Johnson's February 1755 letter to Lord Chesterfield quoted in James Boswell's *The Life of Samuel Johnson* (1791).

4. Alf Landon, governor of Kansas and the 1936 Republican presidential candidate. Although a Democrat, Perkins voted for Landon.

5. There are two vertical lines in the left margin at the end of this paragraph.

6. Vertical lines in left margin along the first three lines of this paragraph.

7. There is a mark in the left margin.

8. Reference to Barbara Hutton, heiress to the Woolworth fortune.

9. There is a vertical line in the left margin along the last three lines and "S Q."

10. Vertical line and "T R" in left margin.

11. This sentence is confusing because Wolfe omitted *and* after "Reynolds." Zachary Smith Reynolds, the heir to the R. J. Reynolds tobacco fortune, was the victim of an unsolved murder in 1932. The heiress Wolfe denounced was almost certainly Barbara Hutton, who inherited fifty million dollars in 1933.

12. Perkins's wife had a wealthy father.

13. Question mark in the left margin opposite reference to Perkins's five daughters.

14. Question mark in the left margin opposite this sentence.

15. *Ulysses* was published in 1922 by Shakespeare & Co. of Paris.

16. "Not offered" written in left margin.

17. Sylvia Beach, proprietor of Shakespeare & Co.

18. *Tristram* (1927), a long poem by Edwin Arlington Robinson, and *The Ring and the Book* (1868–69), a long poem by Robert Browning.

19. In 1933 Bennett Cerf and Donald S. Klopfer, partners in Random House, had successfully contested the American ban on *Ulysses.*

20. Wolfe's projected book about a writer's relations with his publishing house. Portions of the story are in *The Web and the Rock* and *You Can't Go Home Again.*

21. Vertical line and arrow in left margin opposite this sentence.

22. "Publisher" written in left margin.

23. Cornelius Mitchell.

24. Arrow and "NO" written in the left margin.

25. Question mark in the left margin.

26. Vertical line in the left margin opposite preceding three sentences.

27. "No More Rivers," a short story based on Scribners editor Wallace Meyer. Perkins was concerned about Wolfe's announced intention to use Scribner material that had come from Perkins in conversation. The cut version of "No More Rivers" was published posthumously in *Beyond Love and Loyalty* (Chapel Hill: University of North Carolina Press, 1983). The full version has never been published.

28. Vertical line and "No" in the left margin opposite beginning of this sentence.

29. Vertical line and question mark in left margin opposite this and preceding sentence.

30. "Yes but" in left margin.

31. Vertical line in left margin opposite first fourteen lines of this paragraph.

32. Vertical line and question mark in the left margin opposite last four lines of this paragraph.

33. In margin "Meyer Bridges Chapin," names of Scribner employees Wallace Meyer, Robert Bridges, and Joseph Hawley Chapin.

34. Vertical line in left margin opposite entire paragraph and "I did not tell." Wolfe refers to Walter Winchell in the *New York Daily Mirror* (September 21, 1936). The libel case was brought by Wolfe's former landlady, Marjorie Dorman, over "No Door" (*Scribner's Magazine,* July 1933).

35. Wolfe had allowed Muredach Dooher to act as his agent in selling the typescript of *Of Time and the River* to rare-book dealers. Wolfe mistakenly consigned Dooher unpublished manuscripts. After canceling his agreement with Dooher, Wolfe sued Dooher for return of the material; Dooher countersued, demanding an agent's fee for the unsold material.

36. Unlocated.

37. Wolfe sent a carbon copy of this letter to his trusted friend novelist Hamilton Basso with a handwritten postscript: "I've gone upon the record here—this is not perhaps the whole story—but in a general way it says some things I feel had to be said. I am leaving this copy of the letter in your care and, if anything should happen to me, I leave it to your discretion what should [be done] with this letter" (Hamilton Basso Papers, Yale University).

▲ ▼ ▲

| | |
|---|---|
| *To: Perkins* | *Wolfe's letterhead, 865 First Avenue, New York City* |
| *From: Wolfe* | *TLS with holograph postscript, 9 pp.*[1] *Princeton* |

December 23, 1936

Dear Max:

<u>I have already written you a long answer to your two personal letters of November 17th and November 18th which you should have received by the time you receive this</u>. Now, before I go away, I want to write an answer to your formal business letter of November 18th, in which you state the relations that now exist between myself and Charles Scribner's Sons.

First of all, let me thank you for acknowledging that I have faithfully and honorably discharged all obligations to you and that no further agreement of any sort exists between us with respect to the future. Then I want to tell you that I am sorry you found parts of my letter obscure and did not wholly understand them. I am sorry, because it seemed to me that the letter was clear. But if there has been any misunderstanding to what I meant, I shall try to clarify it now.

You say you do not wholly understand the part where "you speak of us as putting you in a position of denying an obligation that does not exist, for we do not know that we have done that." Well, what I said in my letter was "I think it is unfair to put a man in a position where he is forced to deny an obligation that does not exist, to refuse an agreement that was never offered and never made." That is a little different from the way you put it, but I thought it was clear, but if further explanation be needed, I can tell you that what I meant to say, by "I think it is unfair to put a man in a position where he is forced to deny an obligation that does not exist" is simply that no one has a right in my opinion to mix calculation and friendliness, business caution with personal friendship, financial astuteness with personal affection. The artist can not do that. Where his friendship, affection and devotion are involved, he cannot say "I think the world of all of you but of course business is business and I shall make such publishing arrangements as shall be most profitable to me." That is what I meant by "I think it is unfair to put a man in a position where he is forced to deny an obligation that does not exist." For, although you have acknowledged that no obligation does exist, after two years of delay since the publication of "Of Time and the River,"" no concrete proposal has ever been made to me concerning any novel or novels which were to follow it. I have waited in vain, with growing anxiety and bewilderment for such proposal to be made until the matter has now reached a point of critical acuteness which compelled me to write you as I have written you and say "I think it is unfair to put a man in a position where he is forced to deny an obligation that does not exist."

As to the next phrase, "to refuse an agreement that was never offered and never made," I think the meaning of that phrase is now sufficiently clarified by what has been already said.

To proceed: You say you also do not wholly understand the part of my letter where I refer to "'exerting control of a man's future' which we have no intention of doing at all, and would not have the power or right to do." What I said was "I think it is also unfair to try to exert, at no expense to oneself, such control of a man's future and his future work as will bring one profit if that man succeeds, and that absolves one from any commitments of any kind, should he fail." I thought that sentence was clear too. But if you require additional explanation I can only say that what I meant was that I did not think it fair again to play business against friendship, to accept the loyalty and devotion of an author to the firm that has published him without saying precisely upon what terms and upon what conditions you are willing to publish him in the future. In other words, if I must be still more explicit, I am now in the undeniable position of being compelled to tell people who ask me who my publisher is, of saying that my publisher is Charles Scribner's Sons, while Charles Scribner's Sons on their part, without risk, without involving criticism of any sort, are undeniably in the position where they are able to tell any one that they are my publishers, provided they want to be, but are not my publishers if they do not want to be.

You continue in your letter by saying "there are other phrases in that part of your letter that I do not understand, one of which is that which refers to us as being absolved from any commitments of any kind 'should the author fail.'" I do not see why you should have found this statement obscure or puzzling, but if you did I think that what I have already said in this letter precisely and exactly defines my meaning.

You continue by saying "if this and these other phrases signify that you think you should have a contract from us if our relations are to continue, you can certainly have one. We should be delighted to have one. You must surely know the faith this house has in you. There are, of course, limits in terms to which nobody can go in a contract, but we should expect to make one that would suit you if you told us what was required."

I think it is now my turn to be puzzled. I do not wholly understand what you mean when you say "we should expect to make one"—(a contract)—"that would suit you if you told us what was required." This really seems almost too good to be true. I have never heard of an author before being able and privileged to tell a publisher "what was required" in the terms of a contract. I cannot believe that is a practice of the publishing business. Authors do not dictate terms of a publisher's contracts. The publisher states the terms himself, and the author accepts them. For my part, so far as my relations with Scribner's are concerned, I have always accepted what was offered to me instantly and without question. It seems now a delightfully unexpected, overwhelming privilege to be suddenly told that it is now up to me to state "what is required" in the way of a contract.

Well, then, if I am to be allowed this privilege, may I ask for information on these specific points? When you say in your letter that "our relations are simply those of a publisher who profoundly admires the work of an author and takes great pride in publishing whatever he may of that author's writings"—in what sense and meaning am I going to understand the word "may"? I hate to quibble about words, but since you have yourself found it difficult and hard to understand phrases and sentences in my own letter which seem absolutely clear to me, it seems to me that the interpretation of even a little word like "may"—may be important. Neither of us surely is so ingenuous as to believe that this statement means that Scribner's is eagerly waiting my gracious permission to publish any and all manuscript that I may choose to give to them. We both know that such an interpretation as this would be ridiculous. We both know that in the past six or seven years I have written several million words of which Scribner's has published approximately seven or eight hundred thousand. We both know that you have seen and read millions of words of my manuscript which have never been published, which you rejected for publication flatly, or whose publication you advised against. We both know that I not only accepted your advice gratefully but that I also accepted your decision without question, even though it sometimes caused me grievous disappointment when I found that something I had thought good and worthy of publication was not thought good or worthy of publication by the person in whose judgment and critical authority I had and still have unqualified belief. We both know that there was never a time, there has never been a moment since I first walked into your office eight years ago when I have been in a position to hand you a piece of manuscript and arbitrarily demand that you publish it. The right of selection has always been yours. The right of rejection has always been yours. The right to say what you would or would not publish has always, and to my mind, properly, been finally and absolutely your own privilege. It seems manifest therefore that what you mean by the word "may" as used in your sentence must be interpreted as what you "may see fit" to publish. To this interpretation I have certainly never objected, but now that this misunderstanding and the danger of possible misinterpretation has arisen, I must ask you, secondly, if you won't try to specify, insofar as you are able, what it is you may see fit to publish of mine. I understand, of course, that there are obvious limits to what a publisher may be expected to publish—limits imposed by law and custom. But within those limits, how far are you willing to go?

You say in one of your personal letters that you "have never doubted for my future on any grounds except, at times, on those of being unable to control the vast mass of material I have accumulated and have to form into books." Alas, it has now become evident that this is not the only difficulty. It is not even any longer a fundamental one. As I have explained in my long letter to you, no matter how great a man's material may be, it has its limits. He can come to the end of it. No man can exceed his own material—it is his constant effort to surpass it, it is true—but he cannot spend money when he has not got it, he can not fish coin from the empty air, he cannot plank it down across the counter when his pockets are empty. No man has more than his one life, and no man's material is greater than his one life can absorb and hold. No man, therefore, not even the artist, can become the utter spendthrift with what he has. It is spitting straight in the face of fortune, and in the end he will get paid back for his folly. You say you have been worried about my being able to control my vast masses of material. May I tell you that in the past year one of my own chief and constantly growing worries has been whether I shall have any material left that I could use if you continue to advise against my present use of it, or if these growing anxieties and perturbations in the year past as to what I should use, as to what I should write about, continued to develop to the utter enervation and castration of my work. Therefore, having as you do some approximate knowledge, a far better one than any one else, at any rate, of the material at my command, can't you try, in view of all these doubts and misunderstandings, to specify what you think you may be able to publish and how much of it.

Third, at about what time would you now desire and expect to publish it, if I fulfilled my work in time? I know that I have been grievously at fault in meeting publication dates heretofore, but you know too it has not been through lack of effort or of application but rather through the difficulties imposed by my own nature and my imperfect understanding of the writer's art and the command of the tools of my profession. Nevertheless, and in spite of all these imperfections on my part, I should like to get some fairly definite notion of when it is you next expect to publish me, if ever. The reason that I am so earnestly and seriously concerned with this is that in former years, before the publication of "Of

Time and the River," you did show the greatest anxiety on this score. You were constant in your efforts to spur me on, to get me to complete and finish something for publication. Now, although almost two years have gone by since the publication of my last long book, you no longer show any anxiety whatever and, so far as I can judge, no immediate interest.

Finally, if you do want to publish another book of mine, if you can try to tell me what it is you think you want to publish, what you will be able to publish, and when you would like to publish it, what, finally and specifically, are these terms of which you speak?

You say "there are, of course, limits in terms to which nobody can go under contract, but we should expect to make one that would suit you if you told us what was required." I suppose, of course, that when you say that there are "limits in terms to which nobody can go in a contract" you mean that there are limits in terms beyond which no one can go. I understand this perfectly. But what, specifically, are these limits? What, specifically, are these terms?

Now I'm awfully sorry, Max, to have to try your patience with another long letter, and I am sorry if I seem to quibble over words and phrases, but I really do not think I quibble, since all these matters are of such vital and immediate concern to me and since we both have seemed to have trouble understanding sentences and phrases in each other's letters. I have gone to extreme lengths in this one to make everything I say as clear as possible. I shall be on my way South when you get this letter. I intend to be in New Orleans New Year's day, but since I am still uncertain whether I shall stay with friends or in a hotel, I suggest that you write me, if you have time and feel like writing, in care of General Delivery.

Meanwhile, until I hear from you, or until I see you again, with all my best and friendliest greetings to everyone at Scribners,

Sincerely yours,

Tom Wolfe

P.S. I am writing you this from Richmond. Frankly, I think we are at the end. I am sending this to you now—I should have sent it to you long ago, in view of the agony, the despair, the utter desolation this thing has cost me—but I must send it to you now. As to the other letter—the enormously long letter I wrote in answer to your two (over) personal ones I—I shall hold on to it a day longer—re-read it—perhaps make little revisions here and there—anything! anything!—to try to temper the sorrow and the grief of this final decision into which I—God knows—have been compelled without even the power of saying whether I wanted it or not. You must answer this straight![2]

Additional P.S.—As to your statement that anyone would want me—that, as you must now know, is not true. I am almost penniless, this suit for libel has appeared with almost sinister immediacy in the last month or two—I have turned down fortunes—$10,000 is a fortune to me, and you knew of that one at once.—the one that was made over two years ago when I was really penniless, and when you asked me to tell you what the offer was. I am broke—I have lost everything—I do not think we can go on— Who, then, are these <u>eager</u> publishers?—Answer at once please! Tom

*[Marginal notes from first page]*
1 I have deferred sending this, and accordingly am sending it from Richmond, Va. (But I deferred that too!)
2 P.S. Max: You'd better send the answer air mail to New Orleans—I am afraid you did not take this thing seriously but as I told you, it is like death to me— You'd better answer by wire—Tom—Atlanta, December 29, 1936.
You'd better say precisely what you can offer. Atlanta, December 29, 1936.
Max: This letter is imperative. I must have an <u>answer</u>—a definite one—at once!.

*Notes*

1. The first page of this letter has a holograph note by Wolfe around the margins: "I am keeping this letter to re-read and revise it; therefore you <u>will</u> <u>not</u> receive it at the same time as you get this letter."
2. "straight" is underlined four times.

▲▼▲

*To: Perkins*
*From: Hemingway*                           *Wire. Princeton*

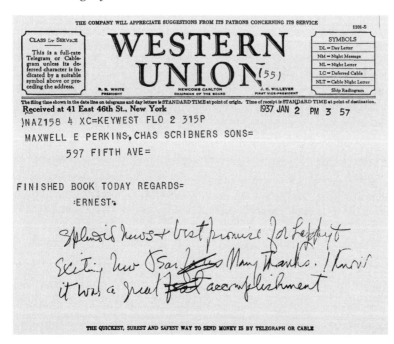

Hemingway's wire announcing completion of *To Have and Have Not,* with Perkins's draft reply (Princeton University Library)

▲ ▼ ▲

*To: Wolfe*                    *Perkins's personal Scribners letterhead*
*From: Perkins*                    *ALS, 4 pp. Harvard*

Jan 13th '37

Dear Tom:— I just got your long letter + have only glanced through it, so that I can't yet properly answer it.—The other came yesterday. I am dashing this off now to make clear two things.

My belief is that the one important, supreme object is to advance your work. Anything in furtherance of that is good + anything that impedes it is bad. What impedes it especially is not the great difficulty + pain of doing it,—for you are the reverse of lazy. You work furiously—but the harassment, the torment of outside worries. When you spoke to me about the settlement, it was, + had been before, very plain that this suit was such a worry, that it was impeding you in your work. It was only because of that that I gave the advice I did. I thought, then get rid of it, forget it, + clear the way more for what is really important supremely.—Now this blackmail talk puts a new face on that matter altogether.

As to my own self: I stand ready to help if I can whenever you want. You asked my help on Time + the River. I was glad + proud to give it. No understanding person could believe that it affected the book in any serious or important way,—that it was much more than mechanical help.—It did seem that the book was too enormous to get between covers. That was the first problem. There might be a problem in a book such as prohibited the publication of Joyce for years in this country. If you wished it we would publish any book by you as written except for such problems as those which prohibit,—some can't be avoided but I don't foresee them. Length could be dealt with by publishing in sections. Anyhow, apart from physical or legal limitations not within the possibility of change by us we will publish anything as you write it.

I simply want to quickly to put these points before you. You are not a private character though. No one whose work has been published, + has roused the interest + admiration of thousands of people can be that in the sense that a carpenter or truck driver are. To lose that kind of privacy is a consequence of important writing. In this case the writing is so important that it has to be done,— +, I know, at great cost to you

Yours,

Max

▲ ▼ ▲

To: Wolfe     *January 14, 1937. Perkins's personal Scribners letterhead*
From: Perkins      *ALS, 1 p. Harvard*

Dear Tom:– I've read your letter carefully. I think it's a wonderful letter. I have no quarrel with any of it,—except that you have greatly misunderstood some things I must explain.—But what a task you've put me to to search myself—in whom I'm not so very much interested any more—+ give you an adequate answer. Your position is right. I understand it + agree with it.

Always yours,
<u>Max</u>

▲ ▼ ▲

To: Wolfe
From: Perkins        *CCS, 6 pp. Princeton*

Saturday, January 16, 1937

Dear Tom:

In the first place I completely subscribe to what you say a writer should do, and always have believed it. If it were not true that you, for instance, should write as you see, feel, and think, then a writer would be of no importance, and books merely things for amusement. And since I have always thought that there could be nothing so important as a book can be, and some are, I could not help but think as you do. But there are limitations of time, of space, and of human laws which cannot be treated as if they did not exist. I think that a writer should, of course, be the one to make his book what he wants it to be, and that if because of the laws of space it must be cut, he should be the one to cut it:– and especially with you, I think the labour and discipline that would come from doing that without help or interference would further the pretty terrible task of mastering the material. But my impression was that you asked my help, that you wanted it.– And it is my impression too, that changes were not forced on you (You're not very forceable, Tom, nor I very forceful) but were argued over, often for hours. But I agree with you about this too, fully, and unless you want help it will certainly not be thrust upon you. It would be better if you could fight it out alone—better for your work, in the end, certainly;– and what's more, I believe you are now in a position to publish with less regard to any conventions of bookmaking, say a certain number of pages almost, whether or not it had what in a novel is regarded as an ending, or anything else that is commonly expected in a novel. I believe the writer, anyway, should always be the final judge, and I meant you to be so. I have always held to that position and have sometimes seen books hurt thereby, but at least as often helped. "The book belongs to the author."

I certainly do not care nor does this house—how revolutionary your books are. I did try to keep you from injecting radical, or Marxian beliefs into "Time and the River" because they were your beliefs in 1934 and 35, and not those of Eugene in the time of the book.– So it did not seem that they could rightly belong in the book. If they could have, then the times could not be rightly pictured, I thought. It must be so– Still, you were then and always conscious of social wrong and that is plainly in the book as you then saw it. There was the Astor story.[1] What was told was not heard by Eugene. It was second-hand, and second-hand material—something told, not heard and seen—is inferior to first-hand. If cutting had to be done, ought that not to be cut? I know your memory is a miracle, but it seems as if you must have forgotten how we worked and argued. You were never overruled. Do you think you are clay to be moulded! I never saw anyone less malleable.– And as for publishing what you like, or being prevented from it, apart from the limitations of space, you have not been, intentionally. Are you thinking of K 19? We would have published it if you had said to do it. At the time I said to Jack: "Maybe it's the way Tom is. Maybe we should just publish him as he comes and in the end it will all be right." But if we had, and the results had been bad at the moment, would you not have blamed me? Certainly I should have bitterly blamed myself. I do not want the passage of time to make you cautious or conservative, but I do want it to give you a full control—as it has done in the case of great writers in the past—over your great talent.– And if you can stand the struggle it will. But you must struggle too, and perhaps even more than in the writing, in the shaping and revising.– That might be the hardest thing of all to your nature. You have so much in you that the need with you is to get it uttered. Then to go back and polish and perfect seems petty, and goes against your nature, I guess.

Tom, you ought not to say some of the things you do,– that I find your sufferings amusing and don't take them seriously. I know something of them. I do try to turn your mind from them and to arouse your humor, because to spend dreadful hours brooding over them and in denunciation and abuse on account of them, seems to be only to aggravate them. It does no good. You have to suffer to write as you do, and the slings and arrows that strike you from outside madden you the more because you instinctively know that all that matters is your work and so why can't you be left to do it. I understand that. Have you seen me amused by other people's sufferings? You know that was unjust.

Then comes the question of your writing about the people here. I don't want to discuss it, because I agree that you have the same right to make use of them as of anyone else in the same way, and if there is an argument on it the whole thing may be bedevilled as was "October Fair" after Mrs. Bernstein protested.– (And by the way, wasn't it up to me to tell you of her visits? She went out saying I was her enemy. I conceded nothing to her.). But when I spoke of resigning after we published– and the moment I inadvertently said it I told Miss Nowell she must not repeat it, and she said she would not– I did not mean I would be asked or wanted to resign. That would never happen on any such ground. But it isn't the way you think, and it's up to you to write as you think you should.–

Your plan as outlined seems to me a splendid one too. I hope you will get on with it now.

There remains the question of whether we are in fundamental agreement. But it is no question if you feel it is not so. I have always instinctively felt that it was so, and no one I ever knew has said more of the things that I believed than you. It was so from the moment that I began to read your first book. Nothing else, I would say, could have kept such different people together through such trials. But I believe in democracy and not in dictators; and in government by principles and not by men; and in less government if possible rather than more; and that power always means injustice and so should be as little concentrated as is compatible with the good of the majority; and that violence breeds more evils than it kills; and that it's better to sizzle in the fryingpan until you're sure your jump won't take you into the fire; and that Erasmus who begged his friend Luther not to destroy the <u>good</u> in the Church because of the bad in it, which he thought could be forced out with the spread of education, was right, though not heroic, and the heroic Luther wrong.– and that Europe is the worse for his impetuosity today. I don't believe that things can't improve. I believe that the only thing that can prevent improvement is the ruin of violence, or of reckless finance which will end in violence.– That is why Roosevelt needs an opposition and it is the only serious defect in him. I believe that change really comes from great deep causes too complex for contemporary men, or any others perhaps, fully to understand, and that when even great men like Lenin try to make over a whole society suddenly the end is almost sure to be bad, and that the right end, the natural one, will come from the efforts of innumerable people trying to do right, and to understand it, because they are a part of the natural forces that are set at work by changed conditions.– It is the effort of man to adjust himself to change and it has to be led,– but the misfortune of man is that strong will almost always beats down intelligence, and the passionate, the reasonable. I believe that such as you can help on change, but that it ought to be by your writings, not by violent acts. I believe that wealth is bad but that it should not be confiscated, but reduced by law, and in accordance with a principle, not arbitrarily and in passion;– and if it is done in passion and violence the result will be a new privileged class made up of delegates of the man or the oligarchy that has seized the power. But it may be that the great underlying changes will dictate Communism as the best society for most people.– Then we ought to have it; but if we can evolve into it gradually how much better (though I know many on both sides say that is impossible) than if we go in by revolution and civil war. At least let us try the way of evolution first.– It seems to me that our Civil War and many of the great convulsions were caused by extremists on both sides, by those too hot-headed to wait for natural forces to disclose their direction, when the inevitable outcome could no longer be resisted. I do not believe the world can ever be perfect, of

course,– though it might in a sense approximate a political and economic perfection if conditions ceased from changing so that a long enough time was given
to deal with known and permanent factors.– But this is getting to be too much
of a philosophy of history or something, and I don't think it has anything to
do with fundamental agreement. I had always felt it existed– and I don't feel,
because you differ with me, however violently, on such things as I've said above,
that it does not, necessarily. It is more that I like and admire the same things and
despise many of the same things, and the same people too, and think the same
things important and unimportant,– at least this is the way it has seemed to me.

Anyhow, I don't see why you should have hesitated to write me as you did,
or rather to send the letter. There was mighty little of it that I did not wholly
accept and what I did not, I perfectly well understood. There were places in it
that made me angry, but it was a fine letter, a fine writer's statement of his beliefs,
as fine as any I ever saw, and though I have vanities enough, as many as most,
it gave me great pleasure too—that which comes from hearing brave and sincere beliefs uttered with sincerity and nobility.

Always yours,<br>MEP

*Note*

1. Unidentified.

▲▼▲

*To: Perkins*                          *ca. March 19, 1937. Tryon, North Carolina*
*From: Fitzgerald*                          *ALS, 1 p. Princeton*

Dear Max:

Thanks for the book[1]—I don't think it was very good but then I didn't go for
Sheean[2] or Negley Farson either. Ernest ought to write a swell book now about
Spain—real Richard Harding Davis reporting or better. (I mean not the sad
jocosity of P.O.M.[3] passages or the mere callender of slaughter.). And speaking
of Ernest, did I tell you that when I wrote asking him to cut me out of his story
he answered, with ill grace, that he would—in fact he answered with such un-
pleasantness that it is hard to think he has any friendly feeling to me any more.
Anyhow please remember that he agreed to do this if the story should come in
with me still in it.

At the moment it appears that I may go to Hollywood for awhile, and I hope
it works out. I was glad to get news of Tom Wolfe though I don't understand
about his landlady. What?

Ever Yours<br>Scott

Write me again—I hear no news. On the wagon since January + in good shape physically.

*Notes*

1. Unidentified.
2. Foreign correspondent Vincent Sheean.
3. In *Green Hills of Africa,* Hemingway referred to his wife Pauline as "Poor Old Mama" or "P.O.M."

▲ ▼ ▲

*To: Fitzgerald*
*From: Perkins*                    *CC, 2 pp. Princeton*

March 19, 1937

Dear Scott:

As for Ernest, I know he will cut that piece out of his story. He spoke to me a while ago about it, and his feelings toward you are far different from what you seem to suspect. I think he had some queer notion that he would give you a "jolt" and that it might be good for you, or something like that. Anyhow, he means to take it out.

Ober told me about the Hollywood possibility,[1] and I hope it goes through;– and as he told you, I took the liberty of sending three hundred to the Baltimore bank myself, in view of the situation.

I hope the Hollywood thing goes, but even if it does not, don't get discouraged now because your letters are beginning to look and sound the way they used to.

Always yours,

*Note*

1. In July 1937 Fitzgerald accepted a contract as a screenwriter with Metro-Goldwyn-Mayer; his beginning salary was $1,000 a week for six months.

▲ ▼ ▲

*To: Wolfe*            *[Mid July]. Hollywood*
*From: Fitzgerald*       *ALS, 1 p. Harvard*

Pure Impulse
U.S.A.
1937

Dear Tom: I think I could make out a good case for your nessessity to cultivate an alter ego, a more conscious artist in you. Hasn't it occurred to you that such qualities as pleasantness or grief, exuberance or cyniscism can become a plague in others? That often people who live at a high pitch often don't get their way emotionally at the important moment because it doesn't stand out in relief?

Now the more that the stronger man's inner tendencies are defined, the more he can be sure they will show, the more nessessity to rarify them, to use them sparingly. The novel of selected incidents has this to be said that the great writer like Flaubert has consciously left out the stuff that Bill or Joe, (in his case Zola) will come along and say presently. He will say only the things that he alone see. So Mme Bovary becomes eternal while Zola already rocks with age. Repression itself has a value, as with a poet who struggles for a nessessary ryme achieves accidently a new word association that would not have come by any mental or even flow-of-consciousness process. The Nightengale[1] is full of that.

To a talent like mine of narrow scope there is not that problem. I must put everything in to have enough + even then I often havn't got enough.

That in brief is my case against you, if it can be called that when I admire you so much and think your talent is unmatchable in this or any other country

Ever your Friend

Scott Fitzg

### Note

1. John Keats, "Ode to a Nightingale," from which Fitzgerald took the title *Tender Is the Night*. In August 1940 he wrote a letter to his daughter about this poem, "which I can never read through without tears in my eyes."

▲ ▼ ▲

*To: Fitzgerald*              *Oteen, N.C.*
*From: Wolfe*                 *TLS, 4 pp. Princeton*

July 26, 1937

Dear Scott:

I don't know where you are living and I'll be damned if I'll believe anyone lives in a place called "The Garden of Allah" which was what the address on your envelope said. I am sending this on to the old address we both know so well.[1]

The unexpected loquaciousness of your letter struck me all of a heap. I was surprised to hear from you but I don't know that I can truthfully say I was delighted. Your bouquet arrived smelling sweetly of roses but cunningly concealing several large-sized brick-bats. Not that I resented them. My resenter got pretty tough years ago; like everybody else I have at times been accused of "resenting criticism" and although I have never been one of those boys who break out in a hearty and delighted laugh when someone tells them everything they write is lousy and agree enthusiastically, I think I have taken as many plain and fancy varieties as any American citizen of my age now living. I have not always smiled and murmured pleasantly "How true," but I have listened to it all, tried to profit from it where and when I could and perhaps been helped by it a little. Certainly I don't think I have been pig-headed about it. I have not been arrogantly contemptuous of it either, because one of my besetting sins, whether you know it or not, is a lack of confidence in what I do.

So I'm not sore at you or sore about anything you said in your letter. And if there is any truth in what you say—any truth for me—you can depend upon it I shall probably get it out. It just seems to me that there is not much in what you say. You speak of your "case" against me, and frankly I don't believe you have much case. You say you write these things because you admire me so much and because you think my talent is unmatchable in this or any other country and because you are ever my friend. Well Scott I should not only be proud and happy to think that all these things are true but my own respect and admiration for your own talent and intelligence are such that I should try earnestly to live up to them and to deserve them and to pay the most serious and respectful attention to anything you say about my work.

I have tried to do so. I have read your letter several times and I've got to admit it doesn't seem to mean much. I don't know what you are driving at or understand what you are driving at or understand what you hope or expect me to do about it. Now this may be pig-headed but it isn't sore. I may be wrong but all I can get out of it is that you think I'd be a good writer if I were an altogether different writer from the writer that I am.

This may be true but I don't see what I'm going to do about it. And I don't think you can show me and I don't see what Flaubert and Zola have to do with it, or what I have to do with them. I wonder if you really think they have anything to do with it, or if this is just something you heard in college or read in a book somewhere. This either-or kind of criticism seems to me to be so meaningless. It looks so knowing and imposing but there is nothing in it. Why does it follow that if a man writes a book that is not like Madame Bovary it is inevitably like Zola. I may be dumb but I can't see this. You say that Madame Bovary becomes eternal while Zola already rocks with age. Well this may be true—but if it is true isn't it true because Madame Bovary may be a great book and those that Zola wrote may not be great ones? Wouldn't it also be true to say that Don Quixote, or Pickwick or Tristram Shandy "becomes eternal" while already Mr. Galsworthy "rocks with age." I think it is true to say this and it doesn't leave much of your argument, does it? For your argument is based simply upon one <u>way</u>, upon one <u>method</u> instead of another. And have you ever noticed how often it turns out that what a man is really doing is simply rationalizing his own way of doing something, the way he has to do it, the way given him by his talent and his nature into the only inevitable and right way of doing everything—a sort of classic and eternal art form handed down by Apollo from Olympus without which and beyond which there is nothing. Now you have your way of doing something and I have mine, there are a lot of ways, but you are honestly mistaken in thinking that there is a "way." I suppose I would agree with you in what you say about "the novel of selected incident" so far as it means anything. I say so far as it means anything because every novel, of course, is a novel of selected incident. There are no novels of unselected incident. You couldn't write about the inside of a telephone booth without selecting. You could fill a novel of a thousand pages with a description of a single room and yet your incidents would be selected. And I have mentioned Don Quixote and Pickwick and The Brothers Karamozov and Tristram Shandy to you in contrast to The Silver Spoon or The White Monkey[2] as examples of books that have become "immortal" and that boil and pour. Just remember that although Madame Bovary in your opinion may be a great book, Tristram Shandy is indubitably a great book, and that it is great for quite different reasons. It is great because it boils and pours—for the unselected quality of its selection. You say that the great writer like Flaubert has consciously left out the stuff that Bill or Joe will come along presently and put in. Well, don't forget, Scott, that a great writer is not only a leaver-outer but also a putter-inner, and that Shakespeare and Cervantes and Dostoievsky were great putter-inners—greater putter-inners, in fact, than taker-outers—and will be remembered for what they put in—remembered, I venture to say, as long as Monsieur Flaubert will be remembered for what he left out.

As to the rest of it in your letter about cultivating an alter ego, becoming a more conscious artist, by pleasantness or grief, exuberance or cynicism, and how nothing stands out in relief because everything is keyed at the same emotional pitch—this stuff is worthy of the great minds that review books nowadays—the Fadimans and De Votos—but not of you. For you are an artist and the artist has the only true critical intelligence. You have had to work and sweat blood yourself and you know what it is like to try to write a living word or create a living thing. So don't talk this foolish stuff to me about exuberance or being a conscious artist or not bringing things into emotional relief, or any of the rest of it. Let the Fadimans and De Votos do that kind of talking but not Scott Fitzgerald. You've got too much sense and you know too much. The little fellows who don't know may picture a man as a great "exuberant" six-foot-six clod-hopper straight out of nature who bites off half a plug of apple tobacco, tilts the corn liquor jug and lets half of it gurgle down his throat, wipes off his mouth with the back of one hairy paw, jumps three feet in the air and clacks his heels together four times before he hits the floor again and yells out "Whoopee, boys I'm a rootin, tootin, shootin son of a gun from Buncombe County—out of my way now, here I come!"—and then wads up three-hundred thousand words or so, hurls it at a blank page, puts covers on it and says "Here's my book!" Now Scott, the boys who write book-reviews in New York may think it's done that way; but the man who wrote Tender Is the Night knows better. You know you never did it that way, you know I never did, you know no one else who ever wrote a line worth reading ever did. So don't give me any of your guff, young fellow. And don't think I'm sore. But I get tired of guff—I'll take it from a fool or from a book reviewer but I won't take it from a friend who knows a lot better. I want to be a better artist. I want to be a more selective artist. I want to be a more restrained artist. I want to use such talent as I have, control such forces as I may own, direct such energy as I may use more cleanly, more surely and to a better purpose. But Flaubert me no Flauberts, Bovary me no Bovarys. Zola me no Zolas. And exuberance me no exuberances. Leave this stuff for those who huckster in it and give me, I pray you, the benefits of your fine intelligence and your high creative faculties, all of which I so genuinely and profoundly admire. I am going into the woods for another two or three years. I am going to try to do the best, the most important piece of work I have ever done. I am going to have to do it alone. I am going to lose what little bit of reputation I may have gained, to have to hear and know and endure in silence again all of the doubt, the disparagement, the ridicule, the post-mortems that they are so eager to read over you even before you are dead. I know what it means and so do you. We have both been through it before. We know it is the plain damn simple truth. Well, I've been through it once and I believe I can get through it again. I think I know a little more now than I did before, I certainly know what to expect and I'm going to try not to let it get me down. That is the reason why this time I shall look for intelligent understanding among some of my friends. I'm not ashamed to say that I shall need it. You say in your letter that you are ever my friend. I assure you that it is very good to hear this. Go for me with the gloves off if you think I need it. But don't De Voto me. If you do I'll call your bluff.

I'm down here for the summer living in a cabin in the country and I am enjoying it. Also I'm working. I don't know how long you are going to be in Hollywood or whether you have a job out there but I hope I shall see you before long and that all is going well with you. I still think as I always thought that Tender Is the Night had in it the best work you have ever done. And I believe you will surpass it in the future. Anyway, I send you my best wishes as always for health and work and success. Let me hear from you sometime. The address is Oteen, North Carolina, just a few miles from Asheville. Ham Basso, as you know, is not far away at Pisgah Forest and he is coming over to see me soon and perhaps we shall make a trip together to see Sherwood Anderson. And now this is all for the present—unselective, you see, as usual. Good bye, Scott, and good luck,

Ever yours,
Tom Wolfe.

*Notes*

1. Charles Scribner's Sons, 597 Fifth Avenue, New York, New York.
2. *The Silver Spoon* and *The White Monkey* are novels by John Galsworthy.

▲ ▼ ▲

*To: Fitzgerald*
*From: Perkins*                    *TLS, 4 pp. Princeton*

Aug. 24, 1937

Dear Scott:

Since the battle occurred in my office between two men whom I have long known, and for both of whom I was at the time acting as editor, I have tried to maintain a position of strict neutrality.– And I have said to every newspaperman, and to everyone that I did not know very well, that the "altercation" was a matter entirely between them, and that I had nothing to say about it. But here, for your own self alone, is what happened:

Max Eastman was sitting beside me and looking in my direction, with his back more or less toward the door, talking about a new edition of his "Enjoyment of Poetry". Suddenly in tramped Ernest and stopped just inside the door, realizing I guess, who was with me. Anyhow, since Ernest had often told me what he would do to Eastman on account of that piece Eastman wrote, I felt some apprehension.– But that was a long time ago, and everyone was now in a better state of mind. But in the hope of making things go well I said to Eastman, "Here's a friend of yours, Max." And everything did go well at first. Ernest shook hands with Eastman and each asked the other about different things. Then, with a broad smile, Ernest ripped open his shirt and exposed a chest which was certainly hairy enough for anybody. Max laughed, and then Ernest, quite good-naturedly, reached over and opened Max's shirt, revealing a chest which was bare as a bald man's head, and we all had to laugh at the contrast.– And I got all ready for a similar exposure, thinking at least that I could come in second. But then suddenly Ernest became truculent and said, "What do you mean by accusing me of impotence?" Eastman denied that he had, and there was some talk to and fro, and then, most unfortunately, Eastman said, "Ernest you don't know what you are talking about. Here, read what I said," and he picked up a book on my desk which I had there for something else in it and didn't even know contained the "Bull in the Afternoon" article. But there it was, and instead of reading what Eastman pointed out, a whole passage, Ernest began reading a part of one paragraph, and he began muttering and swearing. Eastman said, "read all of it, Ernest. You don't understand it,– Here, let Max read it." And he handed it to me. I saw things were getting serious and started to read it, thinking I could say something about it, but instantly Ernest snatched it from me and said, "No, I am going to do the reading," and as he read it again, he flushed up and got his head down, and turned, and smack,– he hit Eastman with the open book. Instantly, of course, Eastman rushed at him. I thought Ernest would begin fighting and would kill him, and ran around my desk to try to catch him from behind, with never any fear for anything that might happen to Ernest. At the same time, as they grappled, all the books and everything went off my desk to the floor, and by the time I got around, both men were on the ground. I was shouting at Ernest and grabbed the man on top, thinking it was he, when I looked down and there was Ernest on his back, with a broad smile on his face.– Apparently he regained his temper instantly after striking Eastman, and offered no resistance whatever.– Not that he needed to, because it had merely become a grapple, and of course two big men grappling do necessarily fall, and it is only chance as to which one falls on top.– But it is true that Eastman was on top and that Ernest's shoulders were touching the ground,– if that is of any importance at all. Ernest evidently thinks it is, and so I am saying nothing about it.

When both Ernest and Eastman had gone, I spoke to the several people who had seen or heard, and all agreed that nothing would be said.

It seems that Max Eastman for some reason wrote out an account of the thing and that the next night at dinner, where there were a number of newspaper people and various others of that kind, read it aloud. Apparently he was urged to do it by his wife, and it was supposed that it would go no further. But of course it did go further, and reporters came to Eastman for it and he gave them his own story. His story appeared in the evening papers on Friday, and reporters were calling me up all day, and when, late in the afternoon, Ernest came in I told him this. The reporters represented the story as saying, as indeed it did imply, the Eastman had thrown him over my desk and bounced him on his head, etc. And Ernest talked to one of these reporters and then agreed to be interviewed by him, and then a number of others turned up. I was talking to different people outside all the time and did not know what Ernest said until I read it in the papers. He talked too much, and unwisely. It would have been better to have said nothing, but at the time it seemed as though Eastman's story should not appear without proper qualification. Ernest really behaved admirably the moment after he had struck the blow with the book. He then talked more the next day at the dock before he sailed. That is the whole story. I think Eastman does think that he beat Ernest at least in a wrestling match, but in reality Ernest could have killed him, and probably would have if he had not regained his temper. I thought he was going to.

I am glad everything is going well with you. In rather troubled times I often think of that with great pleasure,– and with admiration.

All this I am telling you about the fight is in strict confidence.

Always yours,
Max

To: Perkins                          *MGM letterhead. Culver City, California*
From: Fitzgerald                  *TLS with holograph postscript, 1 p. Princeton*

Sept. 3, 1937.

Dear Max:

Thanks for your long, full letter. I will guard the secrets as my life.

I was thoroughly amused by your descriptions, but what transpires is that Ernest did exactly the asinine thing that I knew he had it in him to do when he was out here.[1] The fact that he lost his temper only for a minute does not minimize the fact that he picked the exact wrong minute to do it. His discretion must have been at low ebb or he would not have again trusted the reporters at the boat.

He is living at the present in a world so entirely his own that it is impossible to help him, even if I felt close to him at the moment, which I don't. I like him so much, though, that I wince when anything happens to him, and I feel rather personally ashamed that it has been possible for imbeciles to dig at him and hurt him. After all, you would think that a man who has arrived at the position of being practically his country's most imminent writer, could be spared that yelping.

All goes well—no writing at all except on pictures.

Ever your friend,
Scott

The Schulberg book[2] is in all the windows here.

### Notes

1. In July 1937 Hemingway had been in Hollywood raising funds to purchase ambulances for the Spanish loyalists.

2. *They Cried a Little* (Scribners, 1937), by Sonya Schulberg.

▲ ▼ ▲

To: Perkins                                    *New York City*
From: Wolfe          *RTLS with holograph postscript, 10 pp.[1] Princeton*

November 19, 1937

Dear Max:

My brother Fred has just written me, enclosing two letters that you wrote to him and to my mother, and a copy of a letter he wrote to you.

I want to go upon the record right now about several things. You told Fred that I had turned my back on you and Scribners. You told Miss Nowell that I had been going around town talking about you. And you told Basso that you were afraid now I was going to "write about" you and Scribners, and that if I did this you would resign and move to the country. I think that if you have said or felt these things you have been unjust and misleading. But what is a whole lot more important to me, I think they may have had an effect upon our friendship, which is the thing that matters to me most, and which I am willing to do anything I can to preserve.

Now, I am going to answer these specific things at once. In the first place, I did not "turn my back" on you and Scribners, and I think it is misleading and disingenuous for anyone to say this was the case. The facts of the matter are that the misunderstanding and disagreement between us had grown in complexity and difficulty for the past two years, and perhaps longer, and you and everybody else there at Scribners have known the situation as well as I. Furthermore, you have known for at least a year, and I think longer, that the possibility of this severance in our relations was a very real imminent one and we have talked about the situation many times. More than this, Charlie Scribner wrote me a letter last spring, at the time of the libel suit, and told me that although he would be sorry to lose me he would not try to hold me, if I wanted to go, and that I was free to go. Further, you told me once last winter to go, if I wanted to, but not to talk about it any more. Later you came to see me in my apartment on First Avenue and told me to go if I wanted to, but that the important thing was that you and I be friends. That is exactly my own position now. Finally, you have known for at least three months, since August, that my going was no longer a possibility, but an actual fact. You told Miss Nowell that I had communicated with various publishers and you asked her if it was true that I had signed up with Little, Brown & Company. It was not true.

Now that's the record. It is absurd for any one now to pretend that he is surprised, and that it has all come suddenly and is news to him.

You said in your letter to Fred that you could never understand about all this trouble, and that is the way I feel, too. But I do know that we both understood very definitely, and over a long period of time, that there was trouble, and I think it would be misleading and untruthful for either of us to say that he had absolutely no conception what it was all about. We did have a conception, and a very clear conception, too. There are so many things about it that are still puzzling and confusing to me, although I've spent a good part of the last year, and the better part of the last four months trying to think it out. But there are certain things that you knew and that I knew very clearly, and without going into the whole painful and agonizing business all over again, which we threshed out so many hundred times, beginning with Of Time and The River and continuing on with The October Fair and what I was going to do with it, and on to the book of stories and the Story of a Novel, and the lawsuits and the lawyers culminating in our final disagreement about the libel suit, the proper course to be taken, and the possible implications of the whole thing concerning my whole future life and work and the use of my material—there has been one thing after another, which we talked about and argued about a thousand times, so how can either of us truthfully say now that he has absolutely no idea what the misunderstanding is about.

You know that as a man and as a writer, I had finally reached a state of such baffled perplexity that I no longer knew what to do, what to try to accomplish and finish next, or whether, if I did finish and accomplish something I could ever have any hope under existing circumstances, of getting it published. You know and I know that beginning with Look Homeward, Angel, and mounting steadily there has been a constantly increasing objection and opposition to what I wanted to do, which phrased itself in various forms, but which had the total effect of dampening my hope, cooling my enthusiasm, and almost nullifying my creative capacity, to the work that I had projected, to the use I should make of my material, and even in some cases going so far as to oppose my possible use of material on personal rather than on artistic grounds. I am not trying to put all the blame for this on someone else, either. I know that I have often been unfair and unjust, and difficult to handle, but I do think that all this difficulty came out of these troubles I have mentioned. I felt baffled and exasperated because it really seemed to me I had a great creative energy which was being bottled up, not used, and not given an outlet. And if energy of this kind is not used, if it keeps boiling over and is given no way of getting out, then it will eventually destroy and smother the person who has it.

So that is why I think you are wrong when you tell my brother Fred and other people that I have turned my back on you and Scribners, and you don't know why. I am not going to do anything to carry on the debate of who left who—or whose back was turned, but I do know that there was no agreement of any sort between us concerning future work, no contract, and no assurance except perhaps that if I did something that satisfied you and that avoided the things you were afraid of, you would publish me. But, at the very least, under those same conditions any other publisher in the land would publish me, and I can't see that a connection is much of a connection when all the risk and obligation is on one side and there is none whatever on the other. This condition has persisted and developed for at least two years and I have said nothing to anyone about it outside of Scribners until very recently. If you are going to tell people that I turned my back on you and walked out on you, why don't you also tell them that three years ago when I didn't have a penny and was working on Of Time and The River I was approached by another publisher and offered what seemed to me a fortune. You know that I not only called you up and informed you of the matter instantly just as soon as it happened, but even asked you if I should even meet and talk to the people and that with great fairness you told me that it was certainly my right to meet and talk with them and listen to what they had to offer and then submit the offer to you and Scribners and give you a chance to meet it or to say you couldn't. You know when I did meet and talk with these people and heard their offer and rejected it on my own accord,[2] and told you all about it, I never once asked you or Scribners to meet the offer, although most writers apparently, and even publishers, would have considered that entirely fair and business like. So if you are going to say now that I walked out on you, why not tell some of the rest of the story too, and admit that I not only never tried to hold you up about anything, but never made approaches to anybody else, and rejected all that were made to me, even when I didn't have a cent. That is just the simple truth and I think in justice to me you ought to say so. But there is no use trying to go through all of this again, we have talked about it so many times, and both of us may be partly right and partly wrong, but how can either of us deny now that a situation has existed for months which had got into such a hopeless complex snarl, that at the end there was absolutely no way out of the mesh except by cutting it. That is the truth, and you know that is the truth. You have understood for a long time that it is the truth and that it existed, and I think you are now unjust to me if you pretend to anyone that you did not know it was the truth.

About your statement to Miss Nowell that I was going around "talking about you" in an injurious sense, I want to assure you that there is not an atom of truth in it. In the first place, I do not "go around"; I am not a gossip monger; I have no stories about any one to trade around. I am afraid that most of the gossip has come from the other side of the fence. You know better than I do that the profession in which you are employed and the circles in which you have to move are productive of rumor and much false report. I would injure myself before I injured you, but grim justice here compels me to remind you that those who live by the sword shall perish by the sword, and those who contemplate too often the play of the serpents fangs and find the spectacle amusing must run the risk some day of having those swift fangs buried in their own flesh.

I want to tell you now, if there were any further need of my going on the record, that if I have ever spoken about you to any man or woman, no one could have possibly construed my speech and meaning in any other way except in such a way as did you honor. And that was not only true when you were my publisher, but it is even more true now when you are my publisher no longer.

Fred told you in his letter that he had never heard me speak of you in any way except in such a way as to plainly indicate the affection and respect I felt for you. And I can assure you that has been true not only with Fred, but with everybody else; and not only in Asheville this summer but in New York since I returned to it in September, and if anyone has really given you any different idea, he has either deliberately lied or wickedly, wilfully and maliciously twisted or perverted something I said out of its context and its plain meaning for some bad purpose of his own. You owe me nothing, and I consider that I owe you a great deal. I don't want any acknowledgment for seeing and understanding that you were a great editor even when I first met you; but I did see and understand it, and later I acknowledged it in words which have been printed by your own house, and of which now there is a public record. The world would have found out any way that you were a great editor, but now, when people solemnly remind me that you are with an air of patiently enlightening me on a matter about which I have hitherto been unaware, I find it ironically amusing to reflect that I myself was the first one publicly to point out the fact in such a way that it could not be forgotten, that I, as much as any man alive, was responsible for pulling the light out from underneath the bushel basket, and that it is now a part of my privilege to hear myself quoted on every hand, as who should say to me: "Have you read Wolfe?"

About the rest of it, I came up here in September and for two full months I saw no one and communicated with no one except Miss Nowell. During all this time, I stayed alone and tried to think this whole thing out. And I want to tell you that one reason I now resent these trivialities and this gossip is that this may be a matter which is only important enough to some people to be productive of false and empty rumor or nonsensical statement, but to me it has been a matter of life and death. I can only tell you straight from the heart that I have not had anything affect me as deeply as this in ten years and I have not been so bereaved and grief stricken by anything since my brother's death. To hear, therefore, that at a time when I have eaten my heart out thinking of the full and tragic consequences of this severance with people with whom I have been associated for eight years, who printed my first work, and for whom I felt such personal devotion—the thing that chiefly was worrying you was the tremendous question of whether I am going to "write about you" and whether you could endure such a calamity is enough to make me groan with anguish.

I cannot believe you were very serious about this when there were so many more important and serious things to think about. But, if it will relieve your mind at all, I can tell you "writing about you" is certainly no part of my present intention. But what if it was, or ever should be?

What possible concern either as friend or editor, ought you to have, except to hope that if I ever "wrote about" you, I would write about you as an artist should, add something to my own accomplishment, and to the amount of truth, reality, and beauty that exists. This I thought was your only concern when you considered Look Homeward, Angel, and not whether it was about possible persons living in a specific little town. This I thought was also, with one or two reservations, your chief concern with Of Time and The River. This, I think, has been less and less your concern ever since—with the October Fair, with perturbations about other work that I have projected since, and finally with the crowning nothingness of this. I don't know how or why this thing has come about—or what has happened to you—but I know my grief and bewilderment have grown for two years and are immense.[3]

Like you, I am puzzled and bewildered about what has happened, but in conclusion can offer this:– that maybe for me the editor and the friend got too close together and perhaps I got the two relations mixed. I don't know how it was with you, but maybe something like this happened to you too, I don't know. If this is true, it is a fault in both of us, but it is a fault that I would consider more on the side of the angels, than the devil's side.

I think, however, that what is even more likely to be a fault in modern life is when the elements of friendship and of business get confused, and when there is likely to be a misapprehension on the part of one or both of the parties as to which is which. I won't pretend to be naive about business or to tell you that the artist is a child where business matters are concerned. The artist is not a child where business is concerned, but he may seem to be so to business men, because he is playing the game with only one set of chips, and the other people are sometimes playing the game with two sets of chips. I don't want you to understand by this that I think playing the game with two sets of chips is always wrong and wicked and playing the game with one set of chips is always right. I do not think so. But I do think that when the players sit down to play, each of them ought to know what kind of game is being played—with one set of chips or two. I think this is important, because I think most of the misunderstanding comes from this. To give you a simple hypothetical example, which, let us say, I invented for purposes of illustration, and which I assure you certainly does not dig into the past or concern my relations with my former publishers: a publisher,[4] let us say, hear's an author is without a publisher and writes him. It is a very nice and charming letter, and says that the publisher has heard that the writer no longer has a publisher and tells him, if that is the case, he would like to see him and to talk to him. He goes on further to say that everybody in his office feels as he does personally about the work that he has done and about the work that he is going to do, and that it would be a privilege and an honor to publish him.

Do I suppose that this letter is hokum and that it is only a part of a publisher's formula when approaching any author. By no means. I think the publisher is sincere and honest and means what he says.

But to proceed with this hypothetical case: The author replies to the publisher that it is true he is without a publisher, but that he is in a great state of perplexity and puzzlement about his work, about a great amount of manuscript involving the material of several books and the labor of several years, and about what he is going to do next. He tells the publisher that what he needs most of all first is someone of editorial experience and judgment he can talk to. He tells him further that he is not at all sure that the work he has in mind would be the kind of work the publisher of this house would care to publish. But he asks the man if he wants to talk it over and find out what the situation is.

The upshot of it is the publisher telephones and comes to see him right away. They go out to dinner together, they have a good meal and some good drinks, and they talk the situation over. The publisher tells the author again how he and his house feel about the author's work and repeats and emphasizes his warm interest. The author then lays the matter before the publisher, tells him so far as he can, the problems and the perplexities that have been bothering him about his work and his manuscript. The publisher then asks which part of this manuscript the author thinks is nearest to completion. The author tells him and the publisher says where is the manuscript. The author tells him that the manuscript is packed up and in storage, and the publisher asks the author to get it out and show it to him. The author replies that he would like to, but that he is living in a small rented room and that the bulk and magnitude of the manuscript is such that it would be impossible to get it out and work on it in his own place. The publisher replies that in the offices of his company there is loads of space, and that he would be delighted if the author would make use of it. He can move his manuscript here and be free to work without disturbing anyone.

The author agrees to this proposal, and before they part the publisher addresses the author by his first name.

Now, so far so good: This hypothetical story must have a very familiar sound to you and you must agree as I do that so far everything is fine. Both parties are not only sincere and mean everything they say, but both sides are also playing with one set of chips.

Now to proceed: in a day or two, the publisher calls up again and tells the author that a young man in his publishing house is free and would be very glad to help the author move the manuscript that very afternoon. The author agrees to this, meets the young man and together they go to the storage warehouse, get the manuscript and bring it back to the publisher's office, where it is left. The next day, the author goes to the publisher's office, the crates and boxes of manuscript have been opened up, everything is ready, and the author sets to work. The publisher comes in, jokes about the size and bulk of the manuscript, repeats again his eagerness to see it and his desire to get at it as quickly as possible, and asks the author if he may call him by his first name, Jim. The author replies that this is his name and that he would be delighted if the publisher called him Jim. The publisher is catching a train in a few minutes, the two men shake hands very warmly, just before he leaves the publisher says: "Oh, by the way," and hands the author an envelope. When the author asks him what the envelope is, the publisher says it is nothing, just an acknowledgment that he has received the manuscript and to put it away among his papers. The author sticks the envelope into his pocket without looking at it. That night, however, in his room he sees the envelope upon his table and opens it: It reads as follows, "Dear Jones—this is to acknowledge that we have received one large packing case of manuscript, nine pasteboard cartons, and two valises, which are now stored in our offices. In view of the possible value of this material, we wish to inform you that this house can assume no responsibility for it, and that you leave it here entirely at your own risk."

Now, what is the truth about this situation? Is the publisher wrong? By no means. Apparently, he is justified in writing such a letter by all the standards of good business practice, and it would be hard to find a business person who would say that he was anything except exactly right. Furthermore, the publisher may have acted as he did out of a scrupulous observance of what seemed to him the rules of business fairness and honesty. Nevertheless, the author cannot help remembering that the publisher asked if he could call him Jim when they were having drinks together over the dinner table, but calls him Jones when he writes a business letter. The author also cannot help remembering when the publisher talked to him over the dinner table, he told him it was not the money he hoped to make out of the author's books or the sales he hoped the books would have that concerned him principally, but rather the pride he would have in publishing the author's works, the privilege and the honor it would be to publish them, regardless of any commercial advantages that might accrue. He has told the author also that he can rest assured that if he comes to his house, he need not worry about the economic future, that no matter whether his next book sold or not, the house was a house which would stand by its authors through disappointments and vicissitudes and was willing to back its faith with its support. Furthermore, I believe that the publisher was sincere and meant what he said.

But the author is puzzled, and I think he has a right to be puzzled. Any business man would tell you the publisher was right not only about what he said over the dinner table, but right also when he wrote the letter about who should assume the risk and responsibility for the manuscript. The author can understand both conversations, but what he cannot understand is both conversations together. What he objects to is "Jim" over the dinner table, and in editorial relations, but "Jones" where business is concerned. From my own point of view, the author is right. The publisher did not tell him that it was going to be Jim in friendship and in editing, but Jones in business. He led the author to believe, with his talk of faith and belief and support and the privilege and the honor of publishing the author, that it was going to be Jim all the time.

Now, from my own point of view, Max, I think the publisher was wrong. I know that many people will not agree with me and will say that the publisher was right, that it was business, and that he was justified in everything that he did. I do not think so, and I think that much of the misunderstanding between publishers and authors comes from just this fact. I think the trouble comes when one side is playing with one set of chips, and the other side with two. Please understand that I am not accusing the side that plays the two of dishonesty or of unscrupulous practices. But I do think they are wrong in not making it clear at the beginning, the kind of game they are playing. And I have used deliberately a trifling and relatively unimportant example to illustrate my meaning. When you multiply this example by scores of much more important and vital examples, and when Jim finds that it is always Jones when a question of business advantage, of profit or loss, is concerned, when Jim finds that friendship and business are not equal and balance each other, but that business always gets the upper hand when a question of advantage is concerned, then there is likely to be trouble.

I want to say also that I think Jim was wrong in the very beginning when he allowed his personal feelings to get so involved that he lost his perspective. I think Jim was wrong in that he based his publishing relationship too much on friendship, on feelings of personal loyalty and devotion, no matter at what cost to himself. I think in doing this Jim was unfair to himself and unfair to his publishers. I think that perhaps the best publishing relation would be one in which Jim felt friendship and respect and belief for his publishers, and they for him, but in which neither side got too personally involved. In the end, it is likely to involve too great a cost of disillusionment and grief and disappointment for someone, perhaps upon both sides. Please believe that I have offered this not by way of criticism of anyone, but just as possibly throwing some light upon a confused and troubled problem.

Now I am faced with one of the greatest decisions of my life and I am about to take a momentous and decisive step. You are no longer my publisher, but with a full consciousness of the peril of my position, and the responsibility of the obligation I am now about to assume, I want to feel that you are still my friend, and I do feel that in spite of all that has happened. I feel that you want me to go on and grow in merit and accomplishment, and do my work; and I believe that you would sincerely wish for my success and high achievement, and be sorry for my failure, no matter who became my publisher. I believe other people there at Scribners feel the same way. You said a year ago that the important thing, regardless of who published me is that we remain friends. That expresses my own feeling now, and I am writing to tell you so and to tell you that I hope it is the same with you. This letter is a sad farewell, but I hope also it is for both of us a new beginning, a renewal and a growth of all the good that has been.

You told Fred that I had not been to see you but that you would like to see me. I want to see you, but I do not think that now is the right time. I think you ought to see by now that I am not "sore" at anybody, but I am sore inside, and I want to wait until things heal. And my whole desire now is to preserve and save, without reservation, without any rankling doubt or bitterness, the friendship that we had, and that I hope we shall forever have. This is about all that I can say. I have felt pretty bad, and for a time my eyes went back on me but I am wearing glasses when I work now, and am now back at work again. If I can keep on working, without interruptions and the costly experiences of the last two years, I think everything may yet turn out all right.

You don't need to answer this letter. I wrote it to you just to go upon the record, to tell you how things really were, and let you know what was in my mind and heart. I hope that I have done so.

With all good wishes to you, to Louise, and the children, and to Scribners,

Sincerely yours,

Tom Wolfe

I am your friend, Max, and that is why I wrote this letter—to tell you so. If I wrote so much else here that the main thing was obscured—the only damn one that matters—that I am your friend and want you to be mine—please take this last line as being what I wanted to say the whole way through—Tom

[*Wolfe's holograph copy of his postscript written on his CC of the letter*]:
Max, I am your friend, and I have written this letter to tell you that I am—This is the only damn thing that matters—to let you know that I am your friend, and I hope that you are mine—and if I have written so much else that this is obscured—that I am your friend—then please take this last line as being what I was trying to say through the whole letter—Tom

### Notes

1. This letter also survives in a five-page single-spaced typed draft dated November 18, 1937 (Harvard).

2. Charles A. Pearce, an editor at Harcourt, Brace, may have approached Wolfe but was not authorized to do so.

3. Wolfe's portrayal of Perkins as Foxhall Edwards was posthumously published in *The Web and the Rock* (New York: Harper, 1939) and *You Can't Go Home Again* (New York: Harper, 1940). See appendix 1.

4. Not a "hypothetical example." The editor was Robert N. Linscott of Houghton Mifflin. Wolfe had deposited his manuscripts with the publishing house in October 1937, in anticipation of a contract.

▲ ▼ ▲

*To: Wolfe*                                       *Perkins's personal Scribners letterhead*
*From: Perkins*                                              *ALS, 3 pp. Harvard*

Nov. 20ᵗʰ '37

Dear Tom:—I am your friend + always will be, I think, + it grieved me deeply that you should even have transacted the little business that needed to be done through an intermediary instead of face to face.—But it made no difference otherwise + I hope we may soon meet as friends. Of course I had to tell Fred + others, when they asked me about you what the situation was. It was humiliating + had to be faced. I could not properly, even by silence, let it be assumed that things were as they had been. I told Fred truly too when I said I did not understand about it. I don't,—but that need make no difference between us, + I wont let it on my side. Miss Nowell should never have told you of my concern as to your writing about <u>us</u>—it was not <u>me</u>—though I think her motive was a kind one. I know the difficulty of your problem + I never meant this point to come up to confuse you. But don't you see that serious injury to this house + to my long time association here, for which I was responsible, would make me wish to be elsewhere? I hate to speak about this, but I can't have you misunderstand it.

I've missed you, + felt badly about it. I want to hear you tell of all you saw in the South sometime. I'm sorry about your eyes. Anyone who reads + writes so much must wear glasses though. —The worst thing about them is that they are always getting lost, but in the end one masters even that.

Anyhow I'm glad to have seen your hand writing again

Always yours

Max

▲ ▼ ▲

To: Hemingway
From: Perkins                                          CC, 4 pp.[1] Princeton

Feb. 3, 1938

Dear Ernest:

I am glad you wrote. I had been expecting you would turn up almost any day because I thought you would have to come about the play.[2]– By the way: I don't know how matters stand in that regard, but if for any reason it would help for us to publish the play before it was produced, which has sometimes been done, we could do it, of course. But the general scheme is to publish immediately on production because the production is generally what makes the play sell, and it sells most while the run is going on. We sold about 10,000 of "Idiot's Delight" by Robert Sherwood that way,– even though he did not give us the copy until the play had run for quite a while.– But this play of yours would sell without a production, and it is possible that its publication might have some value in connection with arranging for production. I am only saying this because I know almost nothing except the little that Speiser told me, and it was that that made me think you would have to come up to New York right off.

I am getting up the figures you want, and I shall send them all tomorrow. I shall send a statement of everything.– There is that loan of a thousand dollars which can go on as a loan if you want, or be put as an advance against a new book. And there is some income tax point about which I have to get clear and explain. I shall also send you a list of the advertising we did on "To Have".– We spent $9,500 in newspaper and magazine advertising, and we sent out hundreds of thousands of lists and circulars and Bookbuyers.[3] We sent out through our own store, and other stores, imprinted 87,000 postcards announcing the book to individuals, to arrive on the day of publication. We kept the book at the top of every ad. through the season. Of course it would have sold more if it had not been for what they politely call the "recession". We cannot publish it in any big way, but we shall carry it along in all our regular advertising through the Spring. I know plenty people who call this your best book, and I am sure that whether it was that or not—and comparisons always seem pointless to me, each book being something by itself alone—it did represent a breaking through into new territory, and an enlargement of technique. It showed a lot of things.

The Tom business is very curious and confused. The libel suit that Tom thinks we got him into was one feature. But another one came certainly from the fact that he had now got to a book in which he wanted to write about us.– When I saw him the other night, he said that he was writing a book that Scribners would be proud of!! I didn't say anything, but felt apprehensive. Another thing was that Tom may perhaps go through cycles like in manic-depressive, and for a long time he seemed almost insane,– like believing that we fomented a libel suit. In those stages he gets terribly desperate, and completely doubts his abilities. I had reassured him for so many years that it was no longer effective. I really think that when he put himself up to be bid for, he did it partly to restore his confidence,– and I think it has restored it. Another element was one that might be in an obscure way greatly in his favor: he had become dependent upon us to a degree that was never dreamed of with any other author that I ever heard of, so that we looked after all sorts of things for him, and he could not make a decision without referring it here – I think that although he brought this about, he came to resent it, without perhaps being completely conscious of his resentment, and he determined to break himself loose and be his own man, and do his own work.– And if he only can do his own work, all of it, it will be his salvation, and it will be the only thing that could make him really top-notch. I believe that this had a lot to do with the whole thing.– I know he resented that silly dedication. Anyhow, I have to go over and testify for him in a lawsuit next week, and what's more, I think I put his lawyers in possession of material that will insure him of winning it. I ought to have been a lawyer,– maybe.

Scott was here twice last week, but I never saw him alone. He is sticking to his job well and has paid off a great deal of his debt, and has a better contract for another year which should clear him up.–[4] And then if only we have another boom, he might get going. He has not been drinking at all, and he looked well. He hoped you were in town. He said you were the most dynamic personality at present,– in the world, I think it was, or anyhow in this country.

We did give a big tea, and invited all the authors, and almost all of them came. It was for Molly Colum. Thirteen years after beginning her book she finished and published it.[5] (I am sending you a copy). One time a couple of years ago, Nancy Hale, whose book of stories we were publishing,[6] was making what seemed to be unreasonable requirements about advertising and exploitation, and so I said sarcastically, "And wouldn't you like us to give you a tea?" and she took me right up, and I did it.– And Molly Colum came to it, and said, "Why don't you give me a tea, Maxwell?" And I said, "Well, we will when the book is out." Then I forgot about it until Molly didn't let me.– But we really have had good times at both those teas, except that there was such a mob of people.– And now, having given two of the women authors teas, I have got to keep it up with all of them, I suppose, and plan one for Marjorie Rawlings in late March or April. You will get an invitation, and I suppose Eastman will too, since he is on the list.– So what? I hope, nothing.

. . . . .

If we published a book of stories this Fall—that is, the omnibus book[7]—we could do it quite early, even in August, and in that connection we could always carry it along as of equal importance with "To Have and Have Not". If we publish the play in the Fall too, I think it would do no harm either to the stories or to the play. A play is looked upon as a different thing altogether, generally speaking.

It must be mighty hard to settle down to a quiet and writing life after all that.

Always yours,

### Notes

1. 120 words have been omitted from this letter.

2. *The Fifth Column and the First Forty-nine Stories* was published by Scribners in October 1938. Benjamin Glazer's adaptation of the play opened on Broadway to disappointing reviews on March 7, 1940. It closed on May 18, 1940, after eight-seven performances.

3. *The Bookbuyer* was a Scribners promotional publication.

4. Fitzgerald's MGM contract had been renewed for one year at $1,250 per week.

5. *From These Roots: The Ideas That Have Made Modern Literature* (Scribners, 1937).

6. *The Earliest Dreams* (Scribners, 1936).

7. Hemingway was considering a volume that would collect his short stories and other writings.

▲ ▼ ▲

*To: Fitzgerald*
*From: Perkins*                    *TLS, 4 pp. Princeton*

March 9, 1938

Dear Scott:

I was mighty glad to get your letter. I'll bet you find the work out there very interesting. Don't get so you find it too interesting and stay in it. I don't believe anyone could do it better, and I should think doing "Infidelity"[1] would be really worthwhile.

You know my position about Ernest's story "The Snows".– Don't be concerned about it. We do aim to publish a book of his stories in the Fall and that would be in it. His play will presumably be put on in the Fall but I cannot find out definitely whether it has yet been arranged for. I think Ernest is having a bad time, by the way, in getting re-acclimated to domestic life, and I only hope he can succeed.[2]

I am sending back the letter about Gatsby.– You might want to have it for some reason. What a pleasure it was to publish that!. It was as perfect a thing as I ever had any share in publishing.– One does not seem to get such satisfactions as that any more. Tom was a kind of great adventure, but all the dreadful imperfections about him took much of the satisfaction out of it. I think that at bottom Tom has an idea now that he will go it alone, doing his own work, and if he could manage that, it would be the one and only way in which he could really achieve what he should.

Scott, I ought not to even breathe it to you because it will probably never turn out, but I have a secret hope that we could some day—after a big success with a new novel—make an omnibus book of "This Side of Paradise," "The Great Gatsby," and "Tender Is the Night" with an introduction of considerable length by the author. Those three books, besides having the intrinsic qualities of permanence, represent three distinct periods.– And nobody has written about any of those periods as well. But we must forget that plan for the present.[3]

I understand about your brief holiday, and thought it was justified, and greatly enjoyed seeing you the little I did. I wish you were to be here on April first when we are giving a party for Marjorie Rawlings, whose "South Moon" you liked.– She has written one called "The Yearling" which the Book of the Month Club has taken for April.–[4] I planned the party before the Club did take it, though. They also took "South Moon" but that only sold about 10,000 copies even so, because it appeared on the day the bank holiday began.[5]

Yours,

Max

*Notes*

1. Fitzgerald worked on this unproduced screenplay for Joan Crawford.
2. Hemingway's marriage to Pauline was under pressure because of his relationship with Martha Gellhorn, who became his third wife.
3. This volume was not published.
4. *South Moon Under* was published by Scribners in 1933 and *The Yearling* in 1938.
5. In order to prevent further bank failures, President Franklin D. Roosevelt closed the banks for four days beginning March 5, 1933.

▲▼▲

*To: Fitzgerald*
*From: Perkins      TLS, 4 pp. Bruccoli Collection, University of South Carolina*

[*holograph note by Fitzgerald*] If you think you have the only troubles contemplate Ernest as revealed

April 8, 1938

Dear Scott:

You know Ernest went back to Spain, and I think he did it for good reasons. He couldn't reconcile himself to seeing it all go wrong over there,– all the people he knew in trouble—while he was sitting around in Key West. It was a cause he had fought for and believed in, and he couldn't run out on it. So he went back for a syndicate, and he wrote me on his arrival in France ten days ago. He wrote from the ship,[1] and in a quite different vein from what he ever did before, in apology for having been troublesome—which he hadn't been in any serious sense—and thanking me for "loyalty" and then sending messages to different people here, and also to you and John Bishop. In fact, his letter made me feel depressed all through the weekend because it sounded as if he felt as if he did not think he would ever get back from Spain.– But I haven't much faith in premonitions. Very few of mine ever developed. Hem seemed very well, and I thought he was in good spirits, but I guess he wasn't. I thought I would tell you that he especially mentioned you.

But the good news is that the play, which came right after the letter, is very fine indeed, and it shows he is going forward. At the end, after "Philip" has gone through all kinds of horrors and carried on an affair with a girl who is living in a Madrid hotel writing trivial articles, he says to his side-partner, "There's no sense babying me along. We're in for fifty years of undeclared wars, and I've signed up for the duration. I don't exactly remember when it was, but I signed up all right."

And then later the girl, who has disgusted him by turning up with a silver fox cape bought for innumerable smuggled pesetas, tries to persuade him to marry her, or anyhow to go off with her to all the beautiful places on the Riviera and

Paris and all that. And Philip says finally, "You can go. But I have been to all those places and I have left them all behind, and where I go now I go alone, or with others who go there for the same reason I go."

This isn't much to give you an idea from, but you have intuition, and you know Ernest. He has grown a lot in some way. I don't know where he is going either, but it is somewhere. But anyhow, I felt greatly moved by the play, but melancholy after his letter. One thing that worries him a lot is Evan Shipman who was in that foreign brigade, whatever they called it.[2] Anything may have happened to him, and Ernest felt responsible about his being there. I hope everything will turn out all right, but I thought you would like to hear. Anyhow, the play is really splendid. It should be produced in September.

Always yours,<br>
<u>Max</u>

[*holograph note by Fitzgerald*]    <u>Please</u> return This with your next letter![3]

*Notes*

1. This letter is unlocated.
2. The Abraham Lincoln Brigade.
3. Fitzgerald probably sent Perkins's letter to his daughter, Scottie.

▲ ▼ ▲

*To: Perkins*          *Garden of Allah letterhead, Hollywood, California*
*From: Fitzgerald*                    *TLS, 4 pp. Princeton*

April 23, 1938

<u>PERSONAL AND CONFIDENTIAL</u>
Dear Max:

I got both your letters and appreciate them and their fullness, as I feel very much the Californian at the moment and, consequently, out of touch with New York.

The Marjorie Rawlings' book[1] fascinated me. I thought it was even better than "South Moon Under" and I envy her the ease with which she does action scenes, such as the tremendously complicated hunt sequence, which I would have to stake off in advance and which would probably turn out to be a stilted business in the end. Hers just simply flows; the characters keep thinking, talking, feeling and don't stop, and you think and talk and feel with them.

As to Ernest, I was fascinated by what you told me about the play, touched that he remembered me in his premonitory last word, and fascinated, as always, by the man's Byronic intensity. The Los Angeles Times printed a couple of his articles, but none the last three days, and I keep hoping a stray Krupp shell hasn't knocked off our currently most valuable citizen.

In the mail yesterday came a letter from that exquisitely tactful co-worker of yours, Whitney Darrow, or Darrow Whitney, or whatever his name is. I've never had much love for the man since he insisted on selling "This Side of Paradise" for a dollar fifty,[2] and cost me around five thousand dollars; nor do I love him more when, as it happened the other day, I went into a house and saw someone reading the Modern Library's "Great Modern Short Stories" with a poor piece of mine called "Act Your Age"[3] side by side with Conrad's "Youth," Ernest's "The Killers" because Whitney Darrow was jealous of a copyright.

His letter informs me that "This Side of Paradise" is now out of print. I am not surprised after eighteen years (looking it over, I think it is now one of the funniest books since "Dorian Gray" in its utter spuriousness—and then, here and there, I find a page that is very real and living), but I know to the younger generation it is a pretty remote business, reading about the battles that engrossed us then and the things that were startling. To hold them I would have to put in a couple of abortions to give it color (and probably would if I was that age and writing it again). However, I'd like to know what "out of print" means. Does it mean that I can make my own arrangements about it? That is, if any publisher was interested in reprinting it, could I go ahead, or would it immediately become a valuable property to Whitney again?

I once had an idea of getting Bennett Cerf to publish it in the Modern Library, with a new preface. But also I note in your letter a suggestion of publishing an omnibus book with "Paradise," "Gatsby" and "Tender." How remote is that idea, and why must we forget it? If I am to be out here two years longer, as seems probable, it certainly isn't advisable to let my name sink so out of sight as it did between "Gatsby" and "Tender," especially as I now will not be writing even the Saturday Evening Post stories.

I have again gone back to the idea of expanding the stories about Phillippe, the Dark Ages knight, but when I will find time for that, I don't know, as this amazing business has a way of whizzing you along at a terrific speed and then letting you wait in a dispirited, half-cocked mood when you don't feel like undertaking anything else, while it makes up its mind. It is a strange conglomeration of a few excellent over-tired men making the pictures, and as dismal a crowd of fakes and hacks at the bottom as you can imagine. The consequence is that every other man is a charlatan, nobody trusts anybody else, and an infinite amount of time is wasted from lack of confidence.

Relations have always been so pleasant, not only with you but with Harold[4] and with Lorimer's Saturday Evening Post, that even working with the pleasantest people in the industry, Eddie Knopf and Hunt Stromberg,[5] I feel this lack of confidence.

Hard times weed out many of the incompetents, but they swarm back— Herman Mankiewicz,[6] a ruined man who hasn't written ten feet of continuity in two years, was finally dropped by Metro, but immediately picked up by Columbia! He is a nice fellow that everybody likes and has been brilliant, but he is being hired because everyone is sorry for his wife—which I think would make him rather an obstacle in the way of making good pictures. Utter toughness toward the helpless, combined with super-sentimentality—Jesus, what a combination!

I still feel in the dark about Tom Wolfe, rather frightened for him; I cannot quite see him going it alone, but neither can I see your sacrificing yourself in that constant struggle. What a time you've had with your sons, Max—Ernest gone to Spain, me gone to Hollywood, Tom Wolfe reverting to an artistic hill-billy.

Do let me know about "This Side of Paradise." Whitney Darrow's, or Darrow Whitney's letter was so subtly disagreeable that I felt he took rather personal pleasure in the book being out of print. It was all about buying up some second-hand copies. You might tell him to do so if he thinks best. I have a copy somewhere, but I would like a couple of extras.

Affectionately always,

Scott

*Notes*

1. *The Yearling.*
2. *This Side of Paradise* was priced at $1.75.
3. The story was titled "At Your Age." The word *Act* is a secretarial error.
4. Ober, with whom Fitzgerald broke in July 1939.
5. Edwin Knopf and Hunt Stromberg were MGM producers.
6. Mankiewicz, who had a long career as a screenwriter, wrote *Citizen Kane* (1941).

▲ ▼ ▲

*To: Fitzgerald*
*From: Perkins*                                    *CC, 2 pp. Princeton*

May 24, 1938

Dear Scott:

You know I wish you would get back to the Phillippe.– When you were working on that you were worn out, and I thought could not do it justice.– But if you could get at it now it would be different, and you could make a fine historical novel of that time, and the basic idea was excellent and would be appreciated and understood now better than when you were writing it.– But I must say I should think your present work would take all the time you have, pretty much. Does it ease off any in the summer?

You do the gentleman you particularly write about a wrong in regard to the short story.– That was not his fault, but that of A.H.S.[1] who was very much rooted in the past, as you know. He could not catch the new idea and felt as if the use of material we had published was always more or less of a robbery. In fact, W.D. wanted to do the book of stories we finally published in order rather to offset the decision in regard to the Modern Library.– But that too was based on a misunderstanding of the situation. For a short story in those days one could not do much of anything.

I am sure that to put the three books in one now would be hopeless. We are really in as deep a depression as we ever saw, and you know how bad that was. It means books sell about a third of what they otherwise would, and we are mighty lucky in having "The Yearling".– It goes to the very tip top by the way, next week. And we have a splendid new first novel for the Fall too.[2] But books in general do not get much of anywhere, and I would not want to waste the possibilities for this three-in-one volume in these adverse conditions. It would come to nothing and would merely spoil an opportunity for good.– What's more, I think it is a little too soon anyway. There comes a time, and it applies somewhat now to both "Paradise" and "Gatsby," when the past gets a kind of romantic glamour. We have not yet reached that with "Tender Is the Night" and not to such a degree as we shall later even with "Paradise" I think. But unless we think there never will be good times again—and barring a war there will be better times than ever, I believe—we ought to wait for them. We shall lose nothing by it except that when one has an idea it is hard to postpone the execution of it.

I just had a letter from Ernest and he is about to come back. It was a fine and characteristic letter, and he wants to get back and wri[te. He] has plenty that is grand, he says. He has been right in it apparently,– says that "Nobody's got any social standing now who has not swum the Ebro at least once." He may have sailed by this time, but he wrote from Marseilles and was about to fly back to Madrid. I have seen dispatches of his from there. He was just going to look things over and then start for the U.S.A.

I had a mighty nice lunch with John Bishop. He gets better as he ages—he does age though for his hair is pretty white. I think he is now going to write a novel.– Its scene is to be Paris at the time when you were all over there, the post-war period.– It isn't really about that, but rather human relations of certain individuals.[3] Bunny they say is very happy and I have always meant to get him and his wife[4] over to New Canaan, but the trouble is that I have to do all my work at home. No one could do it here.

Always yours,

*Notes*

1. Arthur Hawley Scribner, head of Scribners from 1930 to 1932.
2. Possibly Taylor Caldwell's *Dynasty of Death*.
3. Bishop did not write this novel.
4. Wilson married writer Mary McCarthy in 1938.

▲ ▼ ▲

To: *Perkins*          *Providence Hospital letterhead, Seattle, Washington*
From: *Wolfe*                    *ALS, 4 pp. Princeton*

Aug 12,
1938

Dear Max: I'm sneaking this against orders—but "I've got a hunch"—and I wanted to write these words to you.

—I've made a long voyage and been to a strange country, and I've seen the dark man very close; and I don't think I was too much afraid of him, but so much of mortality still clings to me—I wanted most desperately to live and still do, and I thought about you all a 1000 times, and wanted to see you all again, and there was the impossible anguish and regret of all the work I had not done, of all the work I had to do—and I know now I'm just a grain of dust, and I feel as if a great window has been opened on life I did not know about before—and if I come through this, I hope to God I am a better man, and in some strange way I can't explain I know I am a deeper and a wiser one—If I get on my feet and out of here, it will be months before I head back, but if I get on my feet, I'll come back.

—Whatever happens—I had this "hunch" and wanted to write you and tell you, no matter what happens or has happened, I shall always think of you and feel about you the way it was that 4th of July day 3 yrs. ago when you met me at the boat, and we went out on the cafe on the river and had a drink and later went on top of the tall building and all the strangeness and the glory and the power of life and of the city were below[1]—Yours Always

Tom

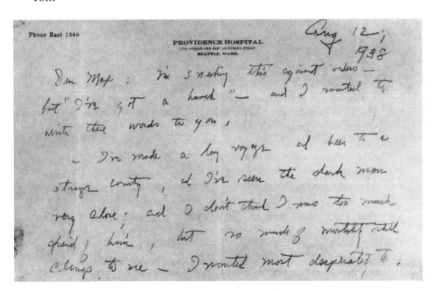

First page of Wolfe's last letter (Harvard)

*Note*

1. After Wolfe's death Perkins wrote about the Fourth of July episode Wolfe described; Perkins may have intended this material for his article "Thomas Wolfe" published in the *Harvard Library Bulletin* (Autumn 1947), but it was not included:

> Once, some three months after the triumphant publication of "Of Time and the River" Tom landed from a steamer on a blazing hot Fourth of July, and I met him. For all his good times abroad, his overwhelming reception in Germany, no child could have been more happy to be home, more eager to see all of New York at once. And that afternoon and night we did range from the floating restaurant on the East River at 55th Street, to the roof of the Prince George Hotel in Brooklyn where the whole shining city and the harbor were spread out. In the course of our wanderings we passed a doorway somewhere near Tenth Street close to Third Avenue. Tom caught me by the shoulder, swung me round and pointed to the top of a house. "There," he said, "is where a young man, six years ago began to write his first novel in an attic." And he added eagerly, "Let's go up and see it." But when we got to the top floor under its low ceiling and Tom knocked, and then rattled the door, no one was within. Meanwhile I was looking out a rear window, I saw that by going up one fire escape and down another, you could enter the so-called attic. I said, "Tom if we want to see the eyrie where the young eaglet mewed his mighty youth we can do it," and we did. Maybe it was burglary but the window was open and the statute of limitations must now obtain. There it was that he had begun to write "Look Homeward, Angel" and it was an attic but a comfortable one, and in the spacious dimensions of Thomas Wolfe himself.
>
> *The House of Scribner, 1905–1930*. Dictionary of Literary Biography Documentary Series, vol. 16, ed. John Delaney (Detroit: Bruccoli Clark Layman/ Gale Research, 1997), p. 330.

▲ ▼ ▲

| | |
|---|---|
| *To: Wolfe* | *Mid-August 1938. Perkins's personal Scribner's letterhead* |
| *From: Perkins* | *ALS, 1 p. University of North Carolina.* |

Dear old Tom:– I'm mighty sorry you've been ill + now you've won out so well for God's sake take care for a while + get really strong again.—If you do, this bad business may well turn out to have been a good one. You've needed rest ever since I've known you + your recuperation should give it to you, + you'll come to you work a refreshed + new man. I'm writing you a letter in type[1] because my hand is so illegible.—But I wanted to tell you how happy I was to know that you were getting well

Always yours,

Max

*Note*

1. Perkins refers to his August 19, 1938, letter.

▲▼▲

To: *Wolfe*
From: *Perkins*                    *TLS, 3 pp. Harvard*

Aug. 19, 1938

Dear Tom:

I was most happy to get your letter, but don't do it again. That is enough, and will always be valued. And I remember that night as a magical night, and the way the city looked. I always meant to go back there, but maybe it would be better not to, for things are never the same the second time. I tried to find you some good picture books, and found three good in their way. But maybe I shall find something better. I'll keep my eyes open for it.

Everyone hereabouts is greatly concerned over your illness, and that means many people who do not even know you too. Don't get impatient about loss of time. You don't really lose time, in the ordinary sense.– Even six months would not be important. Even if you were really relaxing, as they call it, all that time, you would be getting good from it, even as a writer.– I hope you will manage to do it too.

I am expecting to go up with Louise tomorrow to Windsor, for over Sunday, mostly to see my mother, and to see my uncle who has now passed ninety, and is in better shape than he was ten or twelve years ago. He was next to the oldest in that family of twelve, just barely too young for the Civil War to which his older brother ran away, from Yale, and joined the cavalry and got his health destroyed by it, but I think Uncle Ally would have come through that all right. I do not think though, that he is going to cheer me up about the state of the nation and the prospects for the human race. He foretold the downfall of 1929, but said that he did not expect anyone to listen to him. And they didn't.

I could send you some good books to read, but I don't think you will want to do any reading for yet awhile. What you ought to do is to realize that by really resting now, you are in fact actually gaining time, not losing it.

Always yours,
Max

▲▼▲

To: *Fitzgerald*
From: *Perkins*                    *CC, 3 pp. Princeton*

Sept. 1, 1938

Dear Scott:

I went over to see Harold Ober the other day and heard about you, what you are working on now, that you had a plan for a novel, that Scottie got safely into Vassar, etc. I hope something may bring you back this way again before long, but I suppose you will have to stay on that job for another year or eighteen months or so. I have a long letter from Elizabeth[1] today, to tell about how she bought that church house on the place and made it all over and is just about getting it finished.– She is living in it now. She seems very happy, but it seems all wrong that she should be living alone.

Hem went through here like a bullet day before yesterday, to sail for France. He is going to take at least another look at Spain, but his real purpose was to work. I wish I could talk to you about him: he asked me about a plan he has, and I advised him quite vigorously, and yet had some doubts of the wisdom of it afterward. But I think it is right enough. I only would like to talk to someone who really would understand the thing. We are publishing, after a great deal of argument and frequent changes of plan which were made to meet Hemingway's wishes mostly, a book which is to be called "The Fifth Column and the First Forty-Nine Stories". It is the play, "The Fifth Column", the four new stories, and then all the old ones, in an omnibus volume. The play appears simply as if it were a story, and it can be read that way mighty well.– If later it is produced, we shall publish separately the version used, for there will be a demand for it in that form.– But here it appears as if it were one of his stories, you might say. There is a good introduction. One of the new stories is "The Snows of Kilimanjaro" and you are not in it. By the way, the O'Brien collection containing that, had nothing whatever to do with us, and I did not even know that that story was in it until the book was out.[2] Hem was really in better shape and spirits than I have seen him in for years, and there were not so many people around,– all that rabble from Esquire has generally been hanging around recently, and I never really got a good chance to talk to him quietly. I did this time. I think his home problems are working out somehow or other, but having got into all this Spanish business, with all the partisanship there is around it, he could not work over here because so many people were bothering him to do things for this cause or that.– The communists seem to regard him as one of themselves now, and they keep pestering him for all kinds of reasons.

Couldn't you get time to write the old lone Wolfe? He went on an odyssey of the Northwest, not having seen it before, and after six or eight weeks of it, he found himself in Seattle, and mighty ill.– It turned out he had bronchial pneumonia and he is still far from well, and has a fever, though some seven weeks have passed. I think he came pretty close to death. He wrote me a very nice letter in answer to one I wrote him, and that apparently brought back his fever again. He needs support and encouragement now for I know he will begin to get into a panic about the time he is wasting. If this illness should result in his getting a really long rest, it would perhaps have been good fortune, and not bad,– for he has never rested a moment since I have known him hitherto. I think if he does what he should, he will go to California, and lay off for some months.– But I hope he won't go down your way, for then he would find too much that was exciting from Hollywood.

I am just sending you one book because it is so good. It is not in your line at all, and judged as a whole, it does not quite come off in a story sense. But really it is not a story. It is directly derived from experience, and it is excellent. It is a book you will remember pieces of for years.– But you do not have to read it if you haven't the time. It is called "The Captain's Chair".[3] It is too bad it had to be called that, and be presented as if it were a novel, but I could not contend against the English publishers, or do anything with the author when he was dealing with them first,– but I tried to get this man to write a book about this region twenty years ago, before he had ever done anything, and I still have in the safe the thirty pages that he did bring in as an example of what he could do.

I think I have Louise moved back to Connecticut for good.– She may insist upon an apartment or a suite in a hotel, or something, for a month or two, but the house is filled up with children and grandchildren so that we cannot get back there, thank Heaven. I am glad to be a commuter again.– It is the way I began, and I never lost the habit. Zippy has a magnificent boy with a Napoleonic head, and red hair. Peggy is delighted with her job in Bergdorf Goodman, but just the same I told her plainly that if she did not watch her step she would find herself engaged. He is a very nice and attractive boy, but he has no money. Now she is getting an apartment on 78th Street.

Always yours,

### Notes

1. Elizabeth Lemmon.
2. "The Snows of Kilimanjaro" was reprinted in Edward J. O'Brien's *The Best Short Stories 1937* (Boston and New York: Houghton Mifflin, 1937) with the reference to Fitzgerald retained.
3. By Robert J. Flaherty (Scribners, 1938).

▲▼▲

To: *Perkins*                          *September 11, 1938. Baltimore*
From: *Fred Wolfe*                      *Wire. Princeton*

PLAN OPERATING ON TOM TOMORROW MORNING FEEL YOUR PRESENCE WOULD HELP IF YOU CAME TONIGHT COME TO MARBURG BUILDING RECEPTION ROOM HOPKINS
   FRED W WOLFE.

▲▼▲

*To: Fred Wolfe*                                    *September 15, 1938*
*From: Perkins*                                    *File copy of wire. Princeton*

DEEPLY SORRY[1] MY FRIENDSHIP WITH TOM WAS ONE OF THE
GREATEST THINGS IN MY LIFE  GIVE MY LOVE TO MABEL[2] AND
YOUR MOTHER  I ADMIRED YOU ALL SO MUCH  ONE CAN SEE
HOW TOM CAME BY HIS GREAT QUALITIES
                    MAXWELL PERKINS

*Notes*

    1.  Thomas Wolfe died of tuberculosis of the brain on September 15, 1938, at Johns
Hopkins Hospital, Baltimore, Maryland.
    2.  Mabel Wolfe Wheaton, Wolfe's sister.

▲ ▼ ▲

*To: Perkins*                              *MGM letterhead, Culver City, California*
*From: Fitzgerald*                              *TLS, 1 p. Princeton*

Sept. 29th 1938

Dear Max:

    I feel like writing to you about Tom as to a relation of his, for I know how
deeply his death must have touched you, how you were so entwined with his
literary career and the affection you had for him. I know no details. Shortly after
I got your letter that he was in Seattle I read in the paper that he was starting
East sick. This worried me and it seemed a very forlorn and desolate and grievous experience yet something which his great vitality would somehow transcend
and dominate—and then the end at Baltimore and that great pulsing, vital frame
quiet at last. There is a great hush after him—perhaps even more than after the
death of Ring who had been moribund so long.

    I would like to know something about the situation. You, as his literary
executor, are I suppose oddly enough more in control of his literary destiny than
when he was alive. I don't suppose that his "million words" rounds out his great
plan but I am not so sure that that matters because the plan must have been a
mutating and progressive thing. The more valuable parts of Tom were the more
lyrical parts or rather those moments when his lyricism was best combined with
his powers of observation—those fine blends such as the trip up the Hudson in
"Of Time And The River". I am curious to know what his very last stuff was
like, whether he had lost his way or perhaps found it again.

    With deepest sympathy for you and also for his family. Do you think it would
do any good to write them a letter and to whom should I address it?

Ever, your friend—
Scott
F. Scott Fitzgerald

▲ ▼ ▲

*To: Hemingway*
*From: Perkins*                              *CC, 3 pp.*[1] *Princeton*

Oct. 14, 1938

Dear Ernest:

. . . . .

You must have had a dreadful time trying to work over there in the midst of the war crisis,– though perhaps you discovered sooner than the rest of us, that nobody really meant to have a war. Or did they? I can't understand it. But everything seems now to be worse than ever so far as human decency is concerned.

You will have read, of course, of Tom's death which was an awful business too. I never want to go through such a day as I did at Baltimore when he was operated on, [with that terrific, emotional family,- like a day out of "Look Homeward, Angel".][2] But I am enclosing a copy of Tom's last letter, which he wrote just before his illness took its fatal turn. It is a remarkable and beautiful letter, I think.

I hope you have been able to write, but I swear I do not see how you could have done much recently. Maybe you have, though. You wrote "The Fifth Column" in Madrid. You ought to be back here by Thanksgiving anyhow. . . .

Yours always,

*Notes*

1. 115 words have been omitted from this letter.
2. Bracketed material is crossed out in the carbon copy.

▲ ▼ ▲

*To: Perkins*                                   *1938.*
*From: Hemingway*              *TLS with holograph postscript, 3 pp.*[1] *Princeton*

c/o Guaranty Trust Co. of N.Y.
4 Place de la Concorde
Paris
Oct 28/

Dear Max;

I should have written you a long time ago how sorry I was about old Tom. But I knew you would know and it never does any good to discuss casualties. You must have had a hell of a time with it all. That was a good letter he wrote. Everybody writes you fond letters when they think they are going to die. You ought to get quite a collection. Hope I'll write you a lot of them in the next fifty years.

. . . . .

. . . . .

. . . . .
. . . . .
. . . . .
. . . . .
. . . . .

I worked like a bastard right up until that Wednesday. Thought maybe it would be last chance ever to write and wrote well. Did two long stories. One was just unfinished when the war was called off. Finished it afterwards. Since, in the mess everything's in, the sort of let down and carnival of treachery and rottenness that's going on, coupled with being upset about the damn book (not hearing anything and then everything I hear being bad) it's been hard to work. But I have two Chapters[2] done on the novel. Look like will be back pretty soon now. Ask Pauline to show you the copy of one of the stories I sent her—Night Before Battle. It is ten thousand some words long.[3]

Will work again on the novel today. Writing is a hard business Max but nothing makes you feel better.

. . . . .

I haven't written the Napoleonic story yet. But will.[4] Going to look in on Bercelona next week before comeing home. Max I am a little bit gloomy so I will terminate this.

Remember if anything ever happens to me I think just as much of you as Tom Wolfe even if I can't put it so well.

So long Max.
Ernest

. . . . .

*Notes*

1. 436 words have been omitted from this letter.
2. Hemingway did not continue work on this unidentified novel.
3. *Esquire* (February 1939).
4. This story was not written.

▲▼▲

To: Perkins                          MGM letterhead, Culver City, California
From: Fitzgerald                          TLS, 2 pp. Princeton

December 24, 1938.

Dear Max:

Since the going-out-of-print of "Paradise" and the success (or is it one?) of the "Fifth Column" I have come to feel somewhat neglected. Isn't my reputation being allowed to let slip away? I mean what's left of it. I am still a figure to many people and the number of times I still see my name in <u>Time</u> and the <u>New Yorker</u>

ect. make me wonder if it should be allowed to casually disappear—when there are memorial double deckers to such fellows as Farrel and Stienbeck.[1]

I think something ought to be published this Spring. You had a plan for the three novels and I have another plan, of which more hereafter, for another big book; the recession is over for awhile and I have the most natural ambition to see my stuff accessible to another generation. Bennet Cerf obviously isn't going to move about <u>Tender</u> and it seems to me things like that need a spark from a man's own publisher. It was not so long ago that "Tender" was among the dozen best of a bad season and had an offer from the Literary Guild—so I can't be such a long chance as say, Callaghan. Either of the two books I speak of might have an awfully good chance to pay their way. A whole generation now has never read "This Side of Paradise". (I've often thought that if Frank Bunn at Princeton had had a few dozen copies on his stands every September he could have sold them all by Christmas).

But I am especially concerned about <u>Tender</u>—that book is not dead. The <u>depth</u> of its appeal exists—I meet people constantly who have the same exclusive attachment to it as others had to <u>Gatsby</u> and <u>Paradise</u>, people who identified themselves with Dick Diver. It's great fault is that the <u>true</u> beginning—the young psychiatrist in Switzerland—is tucked away in the middle of the book. If pages 151–212 were taken from their present place and put at the start the improvement in appeal would be enormous. In fact the mistake was noted and suggested by a dozen reviewers. To shape up the ends of that change would, of course, require changes in half a dozen other pages.[2] And as you suggested, an omnibus book should also have a preface or prefaces—besides my proposed glossary of absurdities and inaccuracies in <u>This Side of Paradise</u>. This last should attract some amused attention.

The other idea is this:

A Big collection of stories leading off with <u>Phillipe</u>—entirely rewritten and pulled together into a 30,000 word novelette. The Collection could consist of:

1. Phillipe
2. Pre-war (Basil & Josephine)
3. May Day
4. The Jazz Age (the dozen or so best Jazz Stories).
5. About a dozen others including Babylon.

The reason for using <u>Phillipe</u> is this: He is to some extent completed in the 4th story (which you have never read) and in spite of some muddled writing, he is one of the best characters I've ever "drawn". He should be a long book—but whether or not my M.G.M. contract is renewed I'm going to free-lance out here another year to lay by some money, and then do my modern novel. So it would be literally <u>years</u> before I got to <u>Phillipe</u> again—if ever.

In my work here I can find time for such a rewrite of <u>Phillipe</u> as I contemplate—I could finish it by the first of February. The other stories would go in to the collection unchanged. Unlike Ernest I wouldn't want to put in <u>all</u> the stories from all four books but I'd like to add four or five never published before.

I am desperately keen on both these schemes—I think the novels should come first and, unless there are factors there you haven't told me about, I think it is a shame to put it off. It would not sell wildly at first but unless you make some gesture of confidence I see my reputation dieing on its feet from lack of nourishment. If you could see the cards for my books in the public libraries here in Los Angeles continually in demand even to this day, you would know I have never had wide distribution in some parts of the country. When <u>This Side of Paradise</u> stood first in the <u>Bookman's Monthly List</u> it didn't even appear in the score of the Western States.

You can imagine how distasteful it is to blow my own horn like this but it comes from a deep feeling that something could be done if it is done at once, about my literary standing—always admitting that I have any at all.

Ever your friend,

Scott

### Notes

1. James T. Farrell, author of the Studs Lonigan trilogy (1932–35). Fitzgerald had a low opinion of John Steinbeck's proletarian novels.

2. Malcolm Cowley's edition of "The Author's Final Version" of *Tender Is the Night* was published by Scribners in 1951; it was not well received and went out of print.

▲ ▼ ▲

To: Perkins                           *MGM letterhead, Culver City, California*
From: Fitzgerald                           *TLS, 2 pp. Princeton*

January 4, 1939.

Dear Max:

Your letter rather confused me. I had never clearly understood that it was the Modern Library who were considering doing my three books as a giant volume. I thought it was an enterprise of yours. If they show no special enthusiasm about bringing out "Tender" by itself, I don't see how they would be interested in doing a giant anyhow. You spoke of it last year as something only the recession kept you from doing.

What I don't like is the out-of-print element. In a second I'm going to discuss the <u>Philippe</u> business with you, but first let me say that I would rather have "This Side Of Paradise" in print if only in that cheap American Mercury book edition than not in print at all. I see they have just done Elliot Paul's "Indelible". How do you think they would feel about it? And what is your advice on the subject?

Maxwell Perkins at Charles Scribner's Sons. He customarily wore a hat in his office (Charles Scribner's Sons Archives, Princeton University).

Now about <u>Philippe</u>. When I wrote you I had envisaged another year of steady work here. At present, while it is possible that I may be on the Coast for another year, it is more likely that the work will be from picture to picture with the prospect of taking off three or four months in the year, perhaps even more, for literary work. <u>Philippe</u> interests me. I am afraid though it would have to be supported by something more substantial. I would have to write 10,000 or 15,000 more words on it to make it as big a book as "Gatsby" and I'm not at all sure that it would have a <u>great</u> unity. You will remember that the plan in the beginning was tremendously ambitious—there was to have been Philippe as a young man founding his fortunes—Philippe as a middle-aged man participating in the Captian founding of France as a nation—Philippe as an old man and the consolidation of the feudal system. It was to have covered a span of about sixty years from 880 A.D. to 950. The research required for the second two parts would be quite tremendous and the book would have been (or would be) a piece of great self-indulgence, though I admit self-indulgence often pays unexpected dividends.

Still, if periods of three or four months are going to be possible in the next year or so I would much rather do a modern novel. One of those novels that can only be written at the moment and when one is full of the idea—as "Tender" should have been written in its original conception, all laid on the Riviera. I think it would be a quicker job to write a novel like that between 50 and 60,000 words long than to do a thorough revision job with an addition of 15,000 words on "Phillipe". In any case I'm going to decide within the next month and let you know.

Thanks for your letter. I wish you'd send me a copy of the Tom Wolfe article because I never see anything out here. John wrote about me in the Virginia Quarterly, too.[1]

Ever your friend,

Scott

P.S. I hope Jane and Scottie see a lot of each other if Scottie stays in, but as I suspected, she has tendencies toward being a play-girl and has been put on probation. I hope she survives this February.[2]

*Notes*

1. John Peale Bishop, "The Sorrows of Thomas Wolfe," *Kenyon Review* (Winter 1939). Bishop had published a condescending article, "The Missing All," about Fitzgerald in the *Virginia Quarterly Review* (Winter 1937).
2. Both Scottie Fitzgerald and Jane Perkins, Maxwell Perkins's fourth daughter, were attending Vassar College.

▲ ▼ ▲

*To: Perkins*
*From: Fitzgerald*                              *TLS, 2 pp.*[1] *Princeton*

5521 Amestoy
Encino, California
February 25, 1939

Dear Max:

. . . . .

· · · · ·

· · · · ·

I have several plans, and within a day or so will be embarked on one of them. It is wonderful to be writing again instead of patching—do you know in that "Gone With the Wind" job I was absolutely forbidden to use any words except those of Margaret Mitchell, that is, when new phrases had to be invented one had to thumb through as if it were Scripture and check out phrases of her's which would cover the situation![2]

Best wishes always,

Scott

P. S. I am, of course, astonished that Tom Wolfe's book[3] did what you told me. I am sure that if he had lived and meant to make a portrait of you he would at least have given it a proper tone and not made you the villain. It is astonishing what people will do though. Earnest's sharp turn against me always seemed to have pointless childish quality—so much so that I really never felt any resentment about it. Your position in the Wolfe matter is certainly an exceedingly ironic one.

*Notes*

1. 184 words have been omitted from this letter.
2. In January 1939 Fitzgerald worked briefly on the screenplay for *Gone With the Wind*.
3. Wolfe's portrait of Perkins as Foxhall Edwards—"The Fox"—in the posthumously published *The Web and the Rock* (1939), edited by Edward Aswell for Harper.

▲ ▼ ▲

To: Perkins                                   *1939*
From: Hemingway          *TLS with holograph postscript, 2 pp.*[1] *Princeton*

Key West                          March 25

Dear Max;

· · · · ·

· · · · ·

I don't like to talk about this because it's bad luck but have been going awfully well writing. Got to Cuba intending to write these three stories. Instead wrote one about the war, Pauline thinks among best I've ever written, called Under The Ridge.[2] And then started on another I'd had no intention of writing for a long time and working steadily every day found I had fifteen thousand words done; that it was very exciting; and that it was a novel.[3] So I am going to write on on that until it is finished. I wish I could show it to you so far because I am very proud of it but that is bad luck too. So is talking about it. Anyway I have a wonderful place to work in Cuba with no telephone, nobody can possibly bother you, and I start work at 8.30 and work straight through until around two every day. I'm going to keep on doing that until this is finished. I turned down a lot of Hollywood money and other money and I may have to draw on you to keep going. If you want to see the collateral you can—but you don't need to so far. I promise you that. Have worked very slowly reading everyword over from the start every day. I hope it will be a good novel. Anyway it will be as good as I can write, being in good shape, putting all worries aside, and writeing as carefully and well as I can. It is 20 times better than that Night Before Battle which was flat where this is rounded and recalled where this is invented.

Am going to stay in one place now and work no matter what. After the way the French treated the Spanish Republic I feel no obligation to fight for the French and anyhow it is more important now for me to write and that is what am doing. To hell with comeing to N.Y. Have figured out that in any personal problems I am no good to anyone if I do not work. So am working where can work and not be interfered with. Bumby is here for his Easter vacation. Then I Am going back to Cuba. So it looks like we will have a book of stories and a novel. Have five new stories so far. The Denunciation. The Butterfly and The Tank. Night Before Battle. Nobody Ever Dies. Landscape With Figures. and this new one. Hell, that makes six.[4]

· · · · ·

· · · · ·

Ernest

I found Scotts Tender Is The Night in Cuba and read it over. It's amazing how excellent much of it is. If he had integrated it better it would have been a fine novel (as it is) Much of it is better than anything else he ever wrote. How I wish he would have kept on writing—Is it really all over or will he write again? If you write him give him my great affection (I always had a very stupid little boy feeling of superiority about Scott like a tough durable little boy sneering at a delicate but talented little boy) But) Reading that novel much of it was so good it was frightening——

*Notes*

1. 178 words have been omitted from this letter.
2. *Cosmopolitan* (October 1939).
3. *For Whom the Bell Tolls.*
4. "The Denunciation," *Esquire* (November 1938); "The Butterfly and the Tank," *Esquire* (December 1938); "Night Before Battle," *Esquire* (February 1939); "Nobody Ever Dies!" *Cosmopolitan* (March 1939); "Landscape with Figures," first published in *The Complete Short Stories of Ernest Hemingway: Finca Vigia Edition* (New York: Scribners, 1987).

▲ ▼ ▲

*To: Perkins*          *1939*
*From: Fitzgerald*         *Wire. Princeton*

ENCINO CALIF     JUL 3
MAXWELL PERKINS=
NEW CANAAN, CONN.
=HAVE BEEN WRITING IN BED WITH TUBERCULOSIS UNDER DOCTORS NURSES CARE SIS ARRIVING WEST. OBER HAS DECIDED NOT TO BACK ME[1] THOUGH I PAID BACK EVERY PENNY AND EIGHT THOUSAND COMMISSION. AM GOING TO WORK THURSDAY IN STUDIO AT FIFTEEN HUNDRED[2] CAN YOU LEND ME SIX HUNDRED FOR ONE WEEK BY WIRE TO BANK AMERICA CULVERCITY. SCOTTIE HOSPITAL WITH APPENDIX AND AM ABSOLUTELY WITHOUT FUNDS. PLEASE DO NOT ASK OBERS COOPERATION=
          SCOTT
         JUL 4 730A.

### Notes

1. Harold Ober, who had been Fitzgerald's literary agent since 1919, handled magazine sales and advanced him payments against unsold stories. In 1939 Ober declined to make further advances/loans, and Fitzgerald terminated their business relationship. Harold and Anne Ober continued to provide a home for Scottie Fitzgerald.

2. In December 1938 Fitzgerald's MGM contract was not renewed. Between March 1939 and October 1940, he took freelance screenwriting jobs with other studios.

▲▼▲

*To: Perkins*        *October 14, 1939. Encino, California*
*From: Fitzgerald*           *Wire. Princeton*

PLEASE DO GET IN TOUCH WITH LITTAUER[1] HAVE OUTLINED EVERY SCENE AND SITUATION AND I THINK I CAN WRITE THIS BOOK AS IF IT WAS A BIOGRAPHY BECAUSE I KNOW THE CHARACTER OF THIS MAN EVER YOURS =
SCOTT FITZGERALD.

### Note

1. Kenneth Littauer, editor at *Collier's,* had negotiated with Fitzgerald for serial rights to his Hollywood novel. The deal fell through because Littauer required a larger sample of the book than Fitzgerald could provide and because Fitzgerald expected a bigger upfront payment than *Collier's* was willing to offer.

The unfinished novel, edited by Edmund Wilson, was published by Scribners in 1941 under the title *The Last Tycoon,* which was provided by Wilson. The novel was reedited by Bruccoli and published under Fitzgerald's working title *The Love of the Last Tycoon: A Western* (New York & Cambridge: Cambridge University Press, 1993).

▲ ▼ ▲

*To: Perkins*
*From: Fitzgerald*                              *TLS, 1 p. Princeton*

October
20
1939

Dear Max:=

I have your telegram but meanwhile I found that Collier's proposition was less liberal than I had expected. They want to pay $15,000. for the serial. But (without taking such steps as reneging on my income tax, letting go my life insurance for its surrender value, taking Scottie from college and putting Zelda in a public asylum) I couldn't last four months on that. Certain debts have been run up so that the larger part of the $15,000. has been, so to speak, spent already. A contraction of my own living expenses to the barest minimum, that is to say a room in a boarding house, abandonment of all medical attention (I still see a doctor once a week) would still leave me at the end not merely penniless but even more in debt that I am now. Of course, I would have a property at the end, maybe. But I thought that I would have a property when I finished "Tender Is the Night"! On the other hand, if I, so to speak, go bankrupt, at least there will not be very much accumulating overhead.

However, if Collier's would pay more it would give the necessary margin of security and it would give me $2,000. in hand when I finish the novel in February. I feel quite sure that if I wasn't in such a tight spot Collier's would not figure that $20,000. was exorbitant for such a serial.

The further complication of money to get started with—to take me through the first ten thousand words, was something I hope you might be able to work out between you. Certainly there is no use approaching Harold with it in any way. I would have to pay the piper in the end by paying him a cut on a deal on which he has done nothing. He is a stupid hard-headed man and has a highly erroneous idea of how I live; moreover he has made it a noble duty to piously depress me at every possible opportunity. I don't want him to know <u>anything about the subject of the novel</u>.

Meanwhile I have sold in the last few months ten short stories to <u>Esquire</u>, at the munificent sum of $250. a piece. Only two of these were offered to another magazine because when you're poor you sell things for a quarter of their value to realize quickly—otherwise there wouldn't be any auctioneers.

Have you talked to Charlie Scribner or mulled over the question further? If you come to any decision which is possibly favorable, would you put it in the form of a night letter? I am enclosing a letter to Kenneth Littauer which will keep you up with the situation at present.

Ever yours,<br>Scott

5521 Amestoy Avenue
Encino, California

▲ ▼ ▲

*To: Fitzgerald*
*From: Perkins*                      *Typed draft for wire. Princeton*

Nov. 29, 1939

A beautiful start. Stirring and new. Can wire you two hundred fifty and a thousand by January.

Max.

▲ ▼ ▲

*To: Fitzgerald*
*From: Perkins*                          *CC, 3 pp. Princeton*

Nov. 30, 1939

Dear Scott:

I had meant to write you right after I wired you, but was too terribly rushed. I thought the book had the magic that you can put into things. The whole transcontinental business, which is so strong and new to people like me, and to most people, was marvelously suggested, and interest and curiosity about Stahr was aroused, and sympathy with the narratress. It was all admirable, or else I am no judge any more. I think Littaur had a preconception. He had not read "Tender Is the Night" and he was thinking that it was way back to Gatsby since you last wrote. Anyhow he is wrong,– though for all I know he may be right as to serialization.

I sent you $250 because Littaur told me—and I hope you won't mind this —that you had wanted it. And I thought you might need it badly. I spoke of a thousand more. Before the first of January I ought to receive a small bequest. I need most of it to pay off a debt that I got into by going on a man's note.– I didn't do it like a fool, but because he had to have the help at the time, and I realized he almost certainly would not ever be able to meet it himself. But anyhow, I shall be left with a thousand which is what they used to call "velvet" and you are welcome to it if it will help with this book. I can believe that you may really get at the heart of Hollywood, and of what there is wonderful in it as well as all the rest.

I got your telegrams and I called up Leland Hayward[1] so as to try to arrange to show him the outline.– But although it is a quarter of three, he has not yet come in. I shall follow instructions though, and I hope you will push on with courage, for you have a right to. I also sent the manuscript to Braun.[2] I'll give you any pertinent news as it comes along.

Shut your eyes and ears to the war if you can, and go ahead.

Always yours,

### Notes

1. Motion-picture and theatrical agent.
2. Joseph Bryan, an editor at the *Saturday Evening Post*, which declined *The Love of the Last Tycoon* because the material was too strong for that magazine.

▲ ▼ ▲

*To: Hemingway*
*From: Perkins*                              *CC, 2 pp.*[1] *Princeton*

Nov. 30, 1939

Dear Ernest:

Scott is in great despondency but he has a short book all planned, and partly done. I saw 6,000 words, and mighty good, new and stirring. It makes you aware of new transcontinental ways of life. This may not make sense, but the nature of the Gatsby like story is secret.

. . . . .
. . . . .

Always yours,

### Note

1. 95 words have been omitted from this letter.

▲ ▼ ▲

*To: Fitzgerald*
*From: Perkins*                              *CC, 1 p. Princeton*

Dec. 7, 1939

Dear Scott:

I don't want to keep bothering you but I do want you to know how deeply interested I am in this book. I think what you have done is most excellent, and if anyone thinks differently, he is wrong. I am not interested in it only for Scribners or even only for you, but because I want to see what you have in you justify itself.– So any time you have a chance to tell me how things go on, do it as briefly as you please.

Always yours,

▲ ▼ ▲

*To: Perkins*
*From: Fitzgerald*                    *TLS, 1 p. Princeton*

December
19
1939

Dear Max:

The opinion about the novel seems half good and half bad. In brief, about four or five people here like it immensely, Leland likes it and you like it. Collier's, however, seems indifferent to it though they like the outline. My plan is to just go ahead and dig it out. If I could interest any magazine, of course it would be a tremendous help but today a letter from the Post seems to indicate that it is not their sort of material. The plan has changed a bit since I first wrote the outline, but it is essentially as you know it.

Your offering to loan me another thousand dollars was the kindest thing I have ever heard of. It certainly comes at the most opportune time. The first thing is this month's and last month's rent and I am going to take the liberty of giving my landlady a draft on you for $205., for January 2nd. This with the $150. that you have already sent me is $335. For the other $645., will you let me know when it is available?

I am not terribly in debt as I was in 1935–7, but uncomfortably so. I think though my health is getting definitely better and if I can do some intermittent work in the studios between each chapter of the novel instead of this unprofitable hacking for Esquire, I shall be able to get somewhere by spring.

Max, you are so kind. When Harold withdrew from the questionable honor of being my banker I felt completely numb financially and I suddenly wondered what money was and where it came from. There had always seemed a little more somewhere and now there wasn't.

Anyhow, thank you.

Ever your friend,
Scott

5521 Amestoy Avenue
Encino, California

▲▼▲

*To: Fitzgerald*                    *TSL, 2 pp. Princeton*
*From: Perkins*

Dear Scott:

I hope you got safely through the so-called holidays. I feel pretty exhausted though I didn't do much but read manuscripts.—Only one party.

Now these drafts are raising Cain. I think we have at last got them straightened out, but they wouldn't take a Connecticut bank check, and I have had to

improbable.  It appears that the sum
was badly invested some twenty-five
years ago, and at least has seriously
diminished.  I just have to tell you
about it because of the way things are.

Always yours,

To Mr. F. Scott Fitzgerald

Perkins drew this self-portrait at the end of his January 2, 1940, letter to Fitzgerald
(Princeton University Library).

do a lot of shifting things around. But Scott, do remember that I have done all I can for the present. There was one draft more than I expected at that. I am still in debt in that matter I told you of, though not much; and the bequest I told you of begins to seem somewhat improbable. It appears that the sum was badly invested some twenty-five years ago, and at least has seriously diminished. I just have to tell you about it because of the way things are.

Always yours,

Max

▲ ▼ ▲

*To: Perkins*                                   *Havana, Cuba*
*From: Hemingway*                          *Wire. Princeton*

1940 APR 22 AM 8 17

PROVISIONAL TITLE IS QUOTES FOR WHOM THE BELL TOLLS UNQUOTE FROM PASSAGE JOHN DONNE OXFOR BOOK OF ENGLISH PROSE BOTTOM PAGE ONE SEVENTY ONE STARTING QUOTES NO MAN AS AN ISLAND ETC STOP PLEASE REGISTER TITLE=IMMEDIATELY STOP SENT BURTON[1] FOLLOWING WIRE WHAT PERKINS EYE HAVE TO KNOW TO DECIDE WHETHER SERIALIZATION MONTHLY MAGAZINE JUSTIFIES DELAYING PUBLICATION IS WHAT WILL YOU PAY HOW MANY INSTALLMENTS WHEN WOULD START AND WHEN FINISH STOP SCRIBNERS= MAKEING UP CATALOGUE MONDAY STOP BETWEEN FIFTEEN AND TWENTY THOUSAND MORE WORDS COMEING COMPLETING END MAY STOP BEST

ALWAYS ERNEST.

*Note*

1. Harry Burton, editor of *Cosmopolitan*. *For Whom the Bell Tolls* was not serialized.

▲ ▼ ▲

*To: Hemingway*
*From: Perkins*                            *Typed draft for wire, 2 pp. Princeton.*

April 22, 1940

Ernest Hemingway
Hotel Ambos Mundos
Havana, Cuba
All knocked out by first five hundred twelve pages. Think absolutely magnificent strange and new stop. Would never show to outsider. Title beautiful. Congratulations

Max

▲ ▼ ▲

*To: Hemingway*
*From: Perkins*                          *CC, 2 pp.*[1] *Princeton*

April 24, 1940

Dear Ernest:

I am just sending you a line to say that I have read all of the manuscript there is here, and am still in a kind of daze, half in that land, and half in this,– which has happened to me twice before in reading your manuscripts. I think this book has greater power, and larger dimensions, greater emotional force, than anything you have done, and I would not have supposed you could exceed what you had done before. It is a surprising book too. You know right off that you are in Spain, and the war, and then you expect something so different from what you get. You just naturally expect what you do conventionally get in a book that is in a war, what they call battle pieces, and all. Well, by God, that fight piece, where El Sordo dies, is a wonder. That surprises you, and you know for dead sure that that is the way it would be. The nearest thing I ever saw to that fight was perhaps one or two pieces in Tolstoi, one in a book that was called, I think, "The Thistle".[2] You might not have seen it. But the way you write about war— nobody will ever forget the apparition of the cavalryman, his horse stepping along in the snow, and not seeing Robert until too late—all seems strange. And then you realize that that is because it is so utterly real. If the function of a writer is to reveal reality, no one ever so completely performed it. It was wonderful, too, to give this war—though of course that is not the point of the book—in the way you did, with these partisans, all extraordinarily solid people. A reader feels that it gives you people of Spain, as the war was to them, in a more real way than if it had been about the actual enlisted men. There isn't a person in it that anyone would ever forget, including old Goltz, the General. As for the girl, she is lovely, and as if one had known her.

Anyhow, reading it is an experience, that's all. Even now it has got so these things go through my head as if I had seen them. It is truly amazing. Well, I'll read it in proof, and I know I'll find greater depths in it the second time. It has them. All the memories that go through Jordan's head, which nobody can equal you in giving anyhow, are beautiful. It is an astonishing achievement. You are always in suspense because of the frame of the story.

As to the title, I don't believe you could possibly improve it, and I almost hope you won't try to,– and especially when you read that passage. Now the book has the spirit of that passage in it. I never read that before. But nobody who ever did would ever forget that either.

. . . . .

Yours,

. . . . .

*Notes*

1. 167 words have been omitted from this letter.

2. Tolstoy's *Hadji Murad* (1912) opens with a long description of a thistle in a field; the novella, set in the early 1850s, is about the ongoing war between the Chechens and the Russians.

▲ ▼ ▲

*To: Perkins*
*From: Fitzgerald*                                     *TLS, 2 pp. Princeton*

> c/o Phil Berg Agency
> 9484 Wilshire Blvd.
> Beverly Hills, Calif.
> May 20, 1940

Dear Max:

I've owed you a decent letter for some months. First—the above is my best address though at the moment I'm hunting for a small apartment. I am in the last week of an eight week movie job for which I will receive $2300. I couldn't pay you anything from it, nor the government, but it was something, because it was my own picture Babylon Revisited[1] and may lead to a new line up here. I just couldn't make the grade as a hack—that, like everything else, requires a certain practised excellence—

The radio has just announced the fall of St. Quentin! My god! What was the use of my wiring you that Andre Chamson has a hit when the war has now passed into a new stage making his book a chestnut of a bygone quiet era.[2]

I wish I was in print.[3] It will be odd a year or so from now when Scottie assures her friends I was an author and finds that no book is procurable. It is certainly no fault of yours. You (and one other man, Gerald Murphy) have been a friend through every dark time in these five years. It's funny what a friend is— Ernest's crack in The Snows, poor John Bishop's article in the Virginia Quarterly (a nice return for ten years of trying to set him up in a literary way) and Harold's sudden desertion at the wrong time, have made them something less than friends. Once I believed in friendship, believed I could (if I didn't always) make people happy and it was more fun than anything. Now even that seems like a vaude-villian's cheap dream of heaven, a vast minstrel show in which one is the per-petual Bones.

Professionally, I know, the next move must come from me. Would the 25 cent press keep Gatsby in the public eye—or is the book unpopular. Has it had its chance? Would a popular reissue in that series with a preface not by me but by one of its admirers—I can maybe pick one—make it a favorite with class rooms, profs, lovers of English prose—anybody. But to die, so completely and unjustly after having given so much. Even now there is little published in American fiction that doesn't slightly bare my stamp—in a <u>small</u> way I was an original. I remember we had one of our few and trifling disagreements because I said that to anyone who loved "When Lilacs last—" Tom Wolfe couldn't be such a <u>great</u> original. Since then I have changed about him. I like "Only the Dead" and "Arthur, Garfield etc.",[4] right up with the tops. And where are Tom and I and the rest when psychological Robespierres parade through American letters elevating such melo as "Christ in Concrete"[5] to the top, and the boys read Steinbeck like they once read Mencken! I have not lost faith. People will <u>buy</u> my new book and I hope I shan't again make the many mistakes of <u>Tender</u>.

Tell me news if you have time. Where is Ernest and what doing? How about Elizabeth Lemmon, the lovely, & unembittered and sacrificed virgin, the victim of what I gradually and depressingly found was the vanity of her family. How I disliked them—the heavily moustached Mrs. Doctor, the panting Virginian hausfrau sister who fancied herself an aristocrat, the Baltimore bond-salesman who will inherit. And, in the midst, the driven snow of Elizabeth. It was too sad to bear.

Love to all of you, of all generations.<br>Scott

### Notes

1. Fitzgerald wrote this screenplay for producer Lester Cowan, who did not make a movie of it; the screenplay was later published (New York: Carroll & Graf, 1993).

2. The French town St. Quentin fell to German armor on May 18, 1940. Chamson published *La galère* in 1939 and *Quatre mois* in 1940; it is unclear to which book Fitzgerald is referring.

3. Fitzgerald's books were in print but not stocked in bookshops.

4. "Only the Dead Know Brooklyn" and "Four Lost Men."

5. A 1939 novel by Pietro Di Donato.

▲ ▼ ▲

*To: Hemingway*
*From: Perkins*                              *CC, 4 pp. Princeton*

August 14, 1940

( Hemingway wouldn't like this )[1]

Dear Ernest:

Here are the very few things I have to say,– though some of them, being little more than typographical may duplicate on marks you have on the reader's set of proof, or those I sent you read by Meyer.

On galley 2, a little below the middle you say, "The man who will go with you (that was Anselmo)". I think that that parenthesis is entirely unnecessary,– that the reader would know this meant Anselmo. Still it would do no harm in there excepting that the reader is listening to Goltz's talk. He is under the illusion of being present in the person of Robert. This parenthesis tends to break the illusion somewhat. Anyhow I don't think it is needed at all.

On galley 5, I have marked two instances where it seems to me the verb should be changed to conform to the pronoun. I must say I am shaky on this "thee" and "thou" matter and the verbs that go with them, and besides I have taken it that you are perhaps somewhat modifying usage, as they call it in colleges, to suggest the way of Spanish speech. But there is no harm in pointing out these two instances.

On galley 17 in the paragraph considerably below the half-way point, beginning "not in joke" you put in a parenthesis to translate "la gente". I think this is wholly superfluous,– that that is one word everybody, however unfamiliar with any foreign language, would know. I think everyone could be expected to realize it meant "the people" and if so it is superfluous, and it too is in a direct quotation where one is hearing the person speak and tends to injure the effect and illusion.

On galley 18 I questioned whether the last paragraph might not be omitted. It is hard to take it out because it is very good. The reason to do it, if it should be done, is that so far in the story everything has been told as seen, and heard, and all, by Robert. This is the first place where you take the reader from him into someone else, apart from what he realized about the other person. I know it is good. The only point is whether it does not break the reader out of the story by the change from one person to another.[2]

The next time that happens is where Pablo talks to the horses. There it becomes perfectly right, and thereafter as you get to doing it, and very smoothly and rightly, it is always all right. It is just in this one instance where the change comes suddenly. In this book one gets to know all about Pilar, and I don't know that this is needed here because she is completely revealed as you go on.

On galley 19, where the gypsy is singing, about one-third down the galley, they have failed to italicize the third line in the verse, "But still I am a man". Probably this is already marked on the reader's set, though I do not remember its being

On galley 29, about thirty lines down, you use the word "scretological".[3] It is all right, of course. The only point is that it comes as a surprise. Since you have been using the word "obscenity" it comes as a surprise and makes the reader think out of the book for a minute. It might be better to stick to the regular word.

On galley 42 it seems to me that the first two words of the second line might better be "them from" instead of "from them". This may have been queried on the reader's set.

On galley 50, the fourth paragraph from the bottom, about bigotry. It is certainly very shrewd psychology all the way through, but when I read this and came to that about being married, etc., I thought that Robert was married. But he was not. The reason one thinks this is that a young man, and not married, would not be likely to reflect upon that point of being married, etc., or so it seems to me. I think the reader when he reads that would get the impression that

Robert was married. But he wasn't, and it is better that he should not be thought so, even for the moment.[4]

Galley 54 has a few typographical suggestions on it, and so does galley 59.

Somewhere a little previous to galley 71 Robert is sitting in the cave and thinking and remembering. It is extraordinarily good. And then right after that comes that about the smell of death which finally leads Pilar into a long and exceedingly effective and alive talk. I am not sure whether, despite the fact that there is nothing in all this which is not interesting to read, and deeply so, you might not find some way of shortening the thinking and the talk about the smell of death, etc. The point is only that the two long passages, though in a way very different, are of a sort that delay the story possibly longer than is advantageous.– I mention this with great trepidation, and wouldn't dare to suggest any specific point of cutting. I am doubtful if it can be done, and certainly it should only be done purely for the sake of the whole book, and not at all for the sake of the episodes themselves.[5]

On galley 73, in remembering about Gaylords and Karkov, you come to "a certain American journalist" who turns out to be named Mitchell, and about whom Karkov implies embezzlement. I haven't an idea who this man is, but you must consider the libel question. You will know whether it is safe. If the man is one whom many would recognize, unless the implication against him could be proved, and with the burden on us to do it, I think this passage is certainly libelous. But maybe the man is not recognizable, or if he is and is a bad egg, there may be reasons why he could not sue. But if he is recognizable and could, you might do something which would make him unrecognizable,– it is a point to consider anyhow.[6]

Galley 75 has some typographical suggestions on it.

Galley 94 is about El Sordo's fight, and nobody will ever forget it who reads it. It is all about El Sordo and his companions and the Spaniards who are attacking them. Nothing is known about it to Robert or his band, except that the fight is going on, and how it is bound to end. You say in it, (second paragraph galley 94) that "he had killed the young officer . . . the same one who had ridden up the pass that lead to Pablo's camp". Doesn't this take you out of it a little? El Sordo didn't know about what had happened at Pablo's camp. If it added to the effect to know that this was the same officer, it would be different. I don't think it does. The point is that everything is told as it seemed to El Sordo, and this takes you away from how it seemed to him. I thought it a point worth considering whether that ought not to be omitted.[7]

There is nothing later than this. The last chapters I did read very fast for they were the ones I had read last, and I thought too that I would read them over again when the last 1500 words came. But all the last chapters are magnificent, and I don't think there would be anything to be said about them beyond those little typographical matters, etc., that would be marked on the galleys read by Meyer.

Always yours,

MEP

P.S. I am sending you this entire set of galleys, but those I have referred to I have clipped together and put on top of the others.[8]

### Notes

1. Written in holograph by Perkins.
2. The last paragraph of chapter 4; Hemingway did not revise this paragraph.
3. Perkins's secretary misheard the word "scatological" in dictation.
4. Hemingway cut the following passage from the galleys (chapter 13, p. 164): "But what was the other thing that made as much for bigotry as continence? Sure. Being married to an unattractive wife and being faithful to her. Being married to such a woman and working at it was twice as strong a force for bigotry as continence. Twice as strong. Sure. But look at that old one from home with a beautiful wife who seemed, when you talked to her, twice as bigoted and witch-hunting as he was. Sure, he told himself. You'll have quite a time writing a true book. You better confine yourself to what happens. Now, back to Maria."
5. Hemingway disregarded Perkins's advice.
6. Hemingway changed "American journalist who wrote for an American publication" to "British economist who had spent much time in Spain." He also deleted anecdotes about Mitchell's being a fund-raiser for the Communists and close to Roosevelt. The source for this character has not been definitely identified.
7. Hemingway deleted the line.
8. Perkins's marked galleys are unlocated.

▲▼▲

To: Perkins      *Hollywood, California*
From: Fitzgerald      *TLS, 1 p.*[1] *Princeton*

December
13
1940

Dear Max:

Thanks for your letter. The novel progresses—in fact progresses fast. I'm not going to stop now till I finish a first draft which will be some time after the 15th of January. However, let's pretend that it doesn't exist until it's closer to completion. We don't want it to become—"a legend before it is written" which is what I believe Wheelock said about "Tender Is the Night". Meanwhile will you send me back the chapters I sent you as they are all invalid now, must be completely rewritten etc. The essential idea is the same and it is still, as far as I can hope, a secret.

Bud Shulberg, a very nice, clever kid out here is publishing a Hollywood novel with Random House in January. It's not bad but it doesn't cut into my material at all.[2] I've read Ernest's novel[3] and most of Tom Wolfe's[4] and have been doing a lot of ruminating as to what this whole profession is about. Tom Wolfe's failure to really explain why you and he parted mars his book but there are great things in it. The portraits of the Jacks (who are they?)[5] Emily Vanderbilt are magnificent.

No one points out how Saroyan[6] has been influenced by Franz Kafka. Kafka was an extraordinary Czchoslovakian Jew who died in '36. He will never have a wide public but "The Trial" and "America" are two books that writers are never able to forget.

This is the first day off I have taken for many months and I just wanted to tell you the book is coming along and that comparatively speaking all is well.

Ever your friend,
Scott

P.S. How much will you sell the plates of "This Side of Paradise" for? I think it has a chance for a new life.

### Notes

1. F. Scott Fitzgerald died of a heart attack on December 21, 1940. This is his final letter to Perkins.

2. *What Makes Sammy Run?* (1941). Budd Schulberg and Fitzgerald briefly collaborated on a screenplay for *Winter Carnival*. They were fired by producer Walter Wanger for getting drunk during a trip to Dartmouth College. In 1950 Schulberg published a novel, *The Disenchanted,* whose protagonist was based on Fitzgerald.

3. *For Whom the Bell Tolls.*

4. *The Web and the Rock* (New York: Harper, 1939).

5. The Jacks were portraits of Aline Bernstein and her husband.

6. Short-story writer and playwright, William Saroyan.

▲ ▼ ▲

*To: Fitzgerald*
*From: Perkins*                    *CC, 2 pp.*[1] *Princeton*

Dec. 17, 1940

Dear Scott:

That is mighty good news your letter brings.– I am sending back what I had of the manuscript, and the outline. I don't think it makes much difference what is written about Hollywood. Your book is sure to be all by itself.

If you want to know why Tom and I parted, read the enclosed[2] which I wrote out for a man who had thought it was because he got ten thousand dollars from Harpers. I think this was certainly the real reason though I doubt if Tom ever acknowledged it to himself,- although he would have had a perfect right to in a sense.

I'll try to look up Kafka. I know nothing about him.

Ernest is still in town, but he is leaving Thursday with Martha who is heading soon for the Burma Road for Collier's, and Ernest has some plan himself to join her in the eastern part of the world a month later. Of course he has been having a fine time with the extraordinary sale of his book and all.

Well, I hope that "some time after January 15th" will come soon.

Always yours,

### Notes

1. Perkins's last letter to Fitzgerald.
2. Unlocated.

▲▼▲

*To: Zelda Fitzgerald*          *Perkins's personal Scribners letterhead*
*From: Perkins*                  *TLS, 2 pp. Princeton*

December 26, 1940

Dear Zelda:

It was most good of you to write me, and to telephone too. Only a few days before I heard the news, less than a week, I had a short but confident sounding letter from Scott. He had hoped to finish his novel in January. Well, when we see the manuscript we can see what may be done about it. The first chapter was beautiful, equal to anything Scott had ever written, I thought, when I saw it some months ago.

Gilbert Seldes just came in to talk to me, deeply moved; and I had a telegram from John Bishop which said that he wished he could come to Baltimore tomorrow,[1] but that he found that no means of getting there from the Cape were quick enough to make it possible.

I'll see Scottie tomorrow, and I want to tell her that she must go through at least this year at Vassar. Jane has told me about her often, and how deeply interested she has become in her studies. She is so young too, that I think she should go through the next year, and that means will be found to make it possible. It is too soon to tell exactly what the situation is financially, though I have been in touch with John Biggs. I shall be able to talk to him tomorrow too.[2]

Louise is going down with me. She was mighty fond of Scott, and of you too. At any rate, everything will be done that possibly can be done for Scott's sake and yours and Scottie's. I never had a better friend. He did many things for me, and he was always loyal. I shall always miss him.

Affectionately yours,

Max

### Notes

1. Fitzgerald's funeral was held in Bethesda, Maryland, on December 27, 1940; he was buried in Rockville, Maryland, the same day.
2. Biggs, Perkins, and Gerald Murphy loaned Scottie Fitzgerald money that allowed her to complete her studies at Vassar. She later repaid them.

▲ ▼ ▲

*To: Hemingway*
*From: Perkins*                                    *CC, 3 pp. Princeton*

Dec. 28, 1940

Dear Ernest:

I thought of telegraphing you about Scott but it didn't seem as if there were any use in it, and I shrank from doing it. Anyhow, he didn't suffer at all, that's one thing. It was a heart attack and his death was instantaneous,– though he had had some slight attack, as they realize now, a short time before. The Catholics would not allow a funeral from a Catholic church, or burial in a Catholic cemetery.– So I was glad Zelda did not come, for she has grown to be deeply religious, and would have been shocked by that.

One thing about it, Scott did leave something like forty thousand dollars, and there will be at least enough left I should suppose, to get Scottie through college and pay all his debts, and perhaps more than that. The will is very much confused and difficult. John Biggs and I are named as executors.–[1] I am afraid this ends my last chance of getting to Cuba for awhile, for it will take some weeks to clear up confusions in the Will. It may be necessary for me to go to California. It will be in the end if I am executor. The point is that Harold Ober was first named, and then Scott changed him to me, and whether he did it legally is somewhat doubtful. But even apart from that, things must be done for Scottie. She ought at least to finish this year, and I think since she is so young, she should finish the next one, and means will be found for that, whatever happens. There is no use talking about Scott now.

The Murphys were on the train to and from Baltimore. I had met Gerald before. I think you told me what a person Sarah was. Anyhow, she is. It made you feel good to talk to such a one.

Well, our sale to a couple of days ago comes to 189,000 copies. I am enclosing herewith five of the bulletins sent out by Paramount to theatre people, etc. We think that this big Life feature will be next week.[2]

Yours always,

*Notes*

1. To avoid conflict-of-interest problems, Perkins withdrew as executor but continued to help Biggs manage Fitzgerald's literary properties.
2. "The Hemingways in Sun Valley: The Novelist Takes a Wife" and "*Life* Documents His New Novel with War Shots," *Life,* 10 (January 6, 1941): 49–57.

▲ ▼ ▲

*To: Hemingway*
*From: Perkins*                    *CC, 2 pp.*[1] *Princeton*

Dec. 31, 1940

Dear Ernest:

   . . . . .

   . . . . .

I hope you didn't feel too badly about Scott. I am trying to think of some way that something could rightly be done to bring his writings forward.– But the novel appears to have been very far from finished. In a way that is the worst thing about it all because this book might have vindicated Scott completely. It was going good. Well, I'll tell you all about it when you come up.

Yours always,

*Note*

1. 66 words have been omitted from this letter.

▲▼▲

*To: Zelda Fitzgerald*            *Perkins's personal Scribners letterhead*
*From: Perkins*                 *TLS, 2 pp. Princeton*

Jan. 3, 1941

Dear Zelda:

I have been thinking a great deal about what can be published,– for something must be published that will show Scott's true significance. In a way he got caught in the public mind in the age that he gave a name to,– and there are many things that he wrote that should not belong to any particular time, but to all time. We'll find some way to do him justice in a book, but I must wait to see the manuscript of the book he was writing.– The first part of it that I did see, was as good as anything he ever did do. We must not move too fast. I am thinking a great deal of what Bunny Wilson might do, but possibly Hemingway might help as well.[1] Gilbert[2] came in to see me, most deeply moved about it all, as much as any of them. He was a true friend, and a great admirer,– and I don't know whether he didn't see more truly the meaning of what Scott did than any of them.

As for Scottie, though I haven't seen very much of her, I have kept track of her, and I believe she should have a good life.– And what's more, she is assured of the devotion and effort of myself and several others for your sake, and Scott's, and her own.

I always thought of Montgomery, Alabama, as a place of peace and loveliness,– although I think I may have got my impressions wholly from you, the only one from there I ever did know. Louise and I both will always try to see you whenever it can be possible. By the way, Scott and many other people always praised Sarah Murphy to me. I don't know why it is that when you hear a person greatly praised you almost always are disappointed in them.– But she seemed to be all that anybody ever said about her.

Always yours,<br>Max

Notes

1. Zelda Fitzgerald resisted the idea of inviting Hemingway's help: "May I suggest that rather than bringing into play another forceful talent of other inspiration it would be felicitous to enlist a pen such as that of Gilbert Seldes, whose poetry depends on concision of idea and aptitude of word rather than on the spiritual or emotional transport of the author" (*The Last of the Novelists,* p. 116).

2. Seldes.

▲ ▼ ▲

*To: John Biggs*                    *Perkins's personal Scribners letterhead*
*From: Perkins*                         *TLS, 2 pp.[1] Princeton*

March 4, 1941

Dear John:

. . . . .

Scottie came in here yesterday and I urged her to plan for her final year in college. She agreed that her father had wished her to complete the course. She is to send me letters from her father,– especially those about writers and writing.

You will have plenty of trouble, and for no compensation, I suppose, in managing this estate, and I don't like to add to it. But I would sometime like to consult you about what book should be published for Scott. The unfinished novel is most interesting. It is a tragedy it is unfinished. It was a clear step forward. I don't say that it was better in actual writing itself, or even that it would have been, than "The Great Gatsby". But it has the same old magic that Scott got into a sentence, or a paragraph, or a phrase. It has a kind of wisdom in it, and nobody ever penetrated beneath the surface of the movie world to any such degree. It was to have been a very remarkable book. There are 56,000 words. If they were published alone, it would only be read as a curiosity, and for its literary interest, because people won't read an unfinished book. But it ought somehow to be published for the sake of Scott's name. My idea was to publish "The Great Gatsby", five or six of the best stories, and then this unfinished book in one volume. But Bunny Wilson, whom Scott so deeply trusted, wants to make a sort of miscellaneous book with those terrible cracked plate pieces from "Esquire" (I am sure Scott would not want them in a book) and perhaps some things from the letters.[2] People won't buy a miscellaneous book like that anyhow, and apart even

FICTION · 7

•••••★★★★★★★★★★★★★★★★★★★★★★★★★★★★★★★★★★★★★★★★★★★★★★

# The Last Tycoon;

Together with "The Great Gatsby" and Selected Stories

## F. SCOTT FITZGERALD

*Edited with an Introduction by* EDMUND WILSON

*Publication date: October* $2.75

**THE AUTHOR AND THE BOOK:** The most tragic element in Scott Fitzgerald's death was that he was approaching the end of what might well have been his greatest novel.

*The Last Tycoon,* whose hero was a man of genius, a movie director, was written to the extent of some 50,000 words and with notes showing how it was to be carried on, and concluded. It was more after the pattern of *The Great Gatsby* than any other of the novels. The heroine, Celia, the daughter of a Hollywood producer, tells the story of the talented Stahr, a man of vision, and enormous executive capacity too. Celia marries him at the point at which the narrative stops after many scenes of extraordinary brilliance which reveal the inner nature of the movie world and the fascinating character of Stahr.

The stories selected are those which show how Fitzgerald transcended the material and the temper of the time to which he gave the name, the Jazz Age. He had been so amazingly successful in representations of that time that he had become identified with it. This collection with that masterpiece *The Great Gatsby* shows his true place in literature, his real greatness.

**THE MARKET:** Readers of the better grades of fiction.

Fall 1941 catalogue (Princeton University Library)

from the money question,– from the question of reputation,– we want whatever is published to be as widely read as we can make it be. I don't think Bunny takes a practical view of the matter. Then he is reluctant to write an introduction to the book—though he would write a fine one to the unfinished book as it appeared in a collection. He thinks Dos Passos ought to do it. I wish Bunny would do it because, as he said and would say, each book Scott wrote, including this last one, showed marked progress. Scott never thought so highly of "The Beautiful and Damned" but in revealing his command of structure and organization, at any rate, it was an advance over "This Side of Paradise".

I would be mighty interested to know what you thought of those cracked plate articles in "Esquire" if you read them.

Always yours,<br>Max

### Notes

1. 40 words have been omitted from this letter.

2. Wilson edited and provided an introduction for Fitzgerald's unfinished novel, which was published by Scribners as *The Last Tycoon* in 1941. Wilson later edited a collection of Fitzgerald's nonfiction, some of his notebook items and letters, and tributes to him by other writers, which was published as *The Crack-Up* by New Directions in 1945.

▲ ▼ ▲

To: *Hemingway*
From: *Perkins*                  *CC, 3 pp.*[1]

April 4, 1941

Dear Ernest:

. . . . .

Everything goes along all right. The sale, which has slowed up, of course, in the face of a lot of big books like Marquand and Glasgow,[2] has reached barely less than 491,000,[3] and the printings including one now under way, come to 565,000. . . .

We finally got a plan worked out about Scott's novel. It is the most tragic thing that it wasn't finished, for it broke into wholly new ground and showed Scott as advancing and broadening. But it is very much unfinished, both in that the last third of it anyhow was not written at all, and also internally. But it has to be published, and should be, and what we finally decided was that Bunny Wilson should edit it and comment on it, with an introduction, and with explanations at the end, and anything else that would help. Then we should publish it as "The Last Tycoon: An Unfinished Novel by Scott Fitzgerald" together with "The Great Gatsby" and selected stories. Wilson's introduction would also cover Scott's career as a writer and show his importance. It will be kind of an omnibus book of his best writings in fiction.– Bunny wanted to put in "Tender Is the Night". But even apart from the physical difficulty of such a large volume as that would make it, "Tender Is the Night" was too recently published. The Princeton Press too is planning to make up some kind of book of writings about Scott, and of some of his writings.[4] I hate to think of the crack-up pieces going into it.– For one thing Scott was dramatizing his situation there. This novel shows that except for the physical side of it, he didn't crack up. He was just getting into a good state of mind. You ought sometime to talk to that Sheilah Graham[5] about it. I think she was mighty good for him, and a mighty good girl herself. I don't know that you ever saw her. We'll fix it up for Scottie to go through college if we can make her do it. Scott wanted her to finish and she is only nineteen, with one more year to go.

. . . . .
. . . . .
. . . . .
. . . . .

Yours,

*Notes*

1. 747 words have been omitted from this letter.
2. John P. Marquand, *H. M. Pulham, Esquire* (Boston: Little, Brown, 1941) and Ellen Glasgow, *In This Our Life* (New York: Harcourt, Brace, 1941).
3. "Book of Mo 252,000 paid for; We 239,000" (Perkins's note).
4. The Princeton University Press volume was not published.
5. Graham, a Hollywood columnist, was Fitzgerald's companion for the last three and one-half years of his life.

▲ ▼ ▲

*To: Perkins*          *Havana, Cuba*
*From: Hemingway*      *Wire. Princeton*

1941 SEP 1 AM 7 41

AGREE RANDOM HOUSE RIDICULOUS QUOTES SIX BEST QUOTES EDITION IF FEE SPLIT FOUR HUNDRED ME AND ONE HUNDRED YOU[1] STOP ALSO DENY PERMISSION ANY REPRINTS OF ANY KIND EVER WITHOUT MY WRITTEN PERMISSION STOP SINCE SCRIB NERS STANDING ON CONTRACT AND DEDUCTING ALL THEIR LEGAL EXPENSES FROM MY ROYALTIES RATHER THAN GOING ON STRAIGHT ETHICAL BASIS AS FORMERLY AM PERFECTLY WILLING COMMIT HARIKARI RATHER THAN SUBMIT TO FUR-THER GYPPING STOP AS TO LEGAL PROCEDURE SPEISERS LET-TER TO ME CONDEMNS SCRIBNERS PROCEDURE IN CHARGING MY ROYALTIES WITHOUT DISCUSSION ON BOTH LEGAL AND ETHICAL GROUNDS BUT EVIDENTLY THOSE NO LONGER FIG-URE STOP IF IT IS COWARDICE ABOUT ASSUMING ANY CORE-SPONSIBILITY IN DEFENDING OUR JOINT PROPERTY AGAINST A SUIT BY A LUNATIC[2] AM GLAD TO HAVE THAT CLEAR NOW STOP PLEASE TELL CHARLIE THAT IT IS NOT GOOD POLICY TO CUT STEAKS OUT OF HIS RACE HORSES TO MAKE A DIME OR WHAT-EVER HORSE MEAT BRINGS A POUND STOP TELL CHARLIE IF HE NEEDS ANY MONEY WILL BE GLAD TO LOAN IT TO HIM RATHER

THAN HAVE HIM STEAL IT FROM ME AND IN THE END WE
WOULD BE BETTER FRIENDS AND HE WOULD HAVE MORE
MONEY BEST REGARDS=
       ERNEST

*Notes*

1. Apparently a response to proposed terms for including "The Snows of Kilimanjaro" in *Great Modern Short Stories* (New York: Modern Library, 1942).

2. John Igual de Montijo had filed an action alleging that Hemingway had based part
of *For Whom the Bell Tolls* on his movie script titled *Viva Madero*. The suit was thrown out
of court, but the $1,000 bill for legal fees was deducted from Hemingway's royalty account.

▲ ▼ ▲

| | |
|---|---|
| To: Perkins | *Havana, Cuba* |
| From: Hemingway | *Wire. Princeton* |

                     1941 SEP 1 AM 10 11

SORRY SENT LONG ANGRY NIGHT LETTER PLEASE DISREGARD
IT=

      ERNEST.

▲ ▼ ▲

| | |
|---|---|
| To: Perkins | *Sun Valley, Idaho* |
| From: Hemingway | *TLS with holograph inserts, 5 pp.*[1] *Princeton* |

                         November 15, 1941

Dear Max,

   . . . . .

I read all of Scott's book[2] and I don't know whether I ought to tell you what
I truly think. There are very fine parts in it, but most of it has a deadness that
is unbelievable from Scott. I think Bunnie Wilson did a very credible job in
explaining, sorting, padding and arranging. But you know Scott would never
have finished it with that gigantic, preposterous outline of how it was to be. I
thought the part about Stahr was all very good. You can recognize Irving Thalberg, his charm and skill, and grasp of business, and the sentence of death over
him. But the women were pretty preposterous. Scott had gotten so far away from
any knowledge of people that they are very strange. He still had the technique
and the romance of doing anything, but all the dust was off the butterfly's wing
for a long time even though the wing would still move up until the butterfly
was dead.[3] The best book he ever wrote, I think, is still "Tender Is The Night"
with all of its mix-up of who was Scott and Zelda and who was Sara and Gerald Murphy. I read it last year again and it has all the realization of tragedy that
Scott ever found. Wonderful atmosphere and magical descriptions and none of
the impossible dramatic tricks that he had outlined for the final book.

Scott died inside himself at around the age of thirty to thirty-five and his creative powers died somewhat later. This last book was written long after his creative power was dead, and he was just beginning to find out what things were about.

I read over the stories and I think Bunnie Wilson made a very poor selection. "The Rich Boy" if you read, it is really profoundly silly. "The Diamond As Big As The Ritz" is simply trash. When you read in "The Rich Boy" about his gradual decay and suddenly see that Scott has given twenty-eight as the age for this oldness setting in, it is hardly credible that he could write that way.

I am happy the book had such a fine review by J. Donald Adams in the Sunday Times with such a good picture of Scott.[4] I think that should please Scotty very much and be very good for her because she never really knew how good Scott was. But J. Donald Adams is not really a very intelligent man, and to someone who knew Scott truly well and is in the same trade, the book has that deadness, the one quality about which nothing can be done in writing, as though it were a slab of bacon on which mold had grown. You can scrape off the mold, but if it has gone deep into the meat, there is nothing that can keep it from tasting like moldy bacon.

When you wrote Martha,[5] you said that Hollywood had not hurt Scott. I guess perhaps it had not because he was long past being hurt before he went there. His heart died in him in France, and soon after he came back, and the rest of him just went on dying progressively after that. Reading the book was like seeing an old baseball pitcher with nothing left in his arm coming out and working with his intelligence for a few innings before he is knocked out of the box.

I know you're impressed by all the stuff about riding in aeroplanes on account of you not doing that and Scott had done it so recently that it impressed him too and he got something of the old magic into it. But in the things between men and women, the old magic was gone and Scott never really understood life well enough to write a novel that did not need the magic to make it come alive.

This sounds gloomy and critical, but I know you would want me to write what I really thought about it. You've had three guys. Scott, Tom Wolfe and me. Two of them are already dead, and no one can say what will happen to the third one. But I think it is best to criticize strongly so when you get the new ones that will come along afterwards, you can talk to them truly.

. . . . .

. . . . .

. . . . .

That's all I know about to write now. Please excuse the long letter, and if I sound deprecatory about Scott, remember I know how good he is and was only criticizing Wilson's selections and the posthumous work.

Best to you always,

Ernest/

## Notes

1. 463 words have been omitted from this letter.
2. *The Last Tycoon.*
3. Hemingway recycles this comment on Fitzgerald in *A Moveable Feast.*
4. "Scott Fitzgerald's Last Novel," *New York Times Book Review,* November 9, 1941,
p. 1.
5. Writer Martha Gellhorn, whom Hemingway married in November 1940.

▲ ▼ ▲

*To: Perkins*
*From: Hemingway*                     *ALS, 6 pp.*[1] *Princeton.*

June 10. 1943
At Sea

Dear Max:

. . . . .
. . . . .
. . . . .
. . . . .
. . . . .
. . . . .
. . . . .
. . . . .
. . . . .

Max please dont get sore at me. I need your sound advice, your judgement and your help—If Charley Scribner ever wants to pick a fight with me because I am insuffecently respectful or more bother than I am worth, or simply for any good reason at all that is okay—but dont <u>you</u> pick any fights because you are my most trusted friend as well as my God damned publisher and dont get yourself confused in your mind with too many institutions or I wont be able to speak ill of Harvard, Connecticut, the Confederate Army, Scribners, God or God knows what without being accused of imputive skunkhood and will only be able to curse women and still be your pal.[2]

Which I still hope I am—

　　　Ernest　　　Ernest Hemingway.

. . . . .

## Notes

1. 671 words have been omitted from this letter.
2. In a May 18, 1943, letter to Perkins, Hemingway accused Scribners of not promoting *The Fifth Column and the First Forty-nine Stories* because the house could earn more money by selling reprint rights for the collection and its individual stories. On

May 28, Perkins responded to this charge: "Ernest, there is one thing of which I only speak because we ought not by silence to seem to agree that we had followed a policy which really would make us out to be skunks as well as fools. Perhaps we are sometimes fools, but we are not skunks. We would be both if we took a book of yours, or of any other writer's, and said, 'We'll do nothing for this because we'll make plenty of money out of the permissions and reprints from it.'"

▲ ▼ ▲

*To: Hemingway*
*From: Perkins*                                  *CC, 4 pp.*[1] *Princeton*

June 21, 1943

Dear Ernest:

· · · · ·

I could not, and would not have any right to get sore at you. And you have a right any time to cuss at Harvard, or the Army of Northern Virginia, or me, to any extent you want.– It is only that I wanted to have the record right. I don't mind your cussing out Scribners either. I didn't mind it when you did it. I just wanted you to know. As for women, you can even cuss them out to me without making me mad. You wouldn't even have to <u>smile</u>, when you did it.

I keep hearing that the picture is very wonderful, not only good for a movie, but really good.[2] And I know that everything is set for the Grosset & Dunlap edition. The danger now is about paper, and that is getting serious.[3] But I understand that they are perfectly safe for an edition of 100,000 copies,– and of course by next year they get a new lease on their allowance.

I do so well remember that night on the fishing snack, and the way the lights and the shadows looked in that cabin.– And I remember when we got back and you hailed John, and we could tell by his voice that he had been hitting the bottle, and you asked him about it, and he said, "I used my own judgment." And we found that he had, too. Once you wrote me about that little boy, I suppose he is now in the Army or the Navy, or something. All that now seems long ago.

I am sending you a copy of a book that is fascinating to read,– "The Shock of Recognition" which Bunny Wilson edited.[4] He is the damnedest fellow. Once Scott told me he was a god-devoured man. But he talked to me not long ago as if he were a man-devouring god. He is getting the Jehovah complex. He always had it, but it is growing on him. But he truly is what we used to call "a man of letters".– And he says he made them make the book the way it is, physically I mean, and it is a beautiful little book.

· · · · ·

Always yours,
MAXWELL E. PERKINS

Late photograph of Perkins (Al Ravenna)

*Notes*

1. 130 words have been omitted from this letter.
2. *For Whom the Bell Tolls* (1943).
3. Paper supplies for publishers were rationed during World War II.
4. (Garden City, N.Y.: Doubleday, Doran, 1943); a collection of American writers' statements on other American writers.

▲▼▲

*To: Perkins*          *November 16, 1943. Finca Vigia letterhead, Havana, Cuba*
*From: Hemingway*                          *TL, 2 pp.¹ Princeton*

Dear Max:

　· · · · ·
　· · · · ·
　· · · · ·
　· · · · ·

. . . A woman ruined Scott. It wasn't just Scott ruining himself. But why couldn't he have told her to go to hell? Because she was sick. It's being sick that makes them act so bloody awful usually and it's because they're sick you can't treat them as you should. The first great gift for a man is to be healthy and the second, maybe greater, is to fall with healthy women. You can always trade one healthy woman in on another. But start with a sick woman and see where you get. Sick in the head or sick anywhere. But sick anhwere and in a little while they are sick in the head. If they locked up all the women who were crazy—but why speculate I've known god-damned good ones; but take as good a woman as Pauline—as hell of a wonderful woman—and once she turns mean. Although, of course, it is your own actions that turn her mean. Mine I mean. Not yours. Anyway let's leave the subject. If you leave a woman, though, you probably ought to shoot her. It would save enough trouble in the end even if they hanged you. But you can't do it on account of the children and so there isn't any solution actually to anything except to get so nobody can hurt you and by the time you get to that you've usually been dead for some time.

. . . . .

. . . . .

Best to you always,

*Note*

1. 655 words have been omitted from this letter.

▲ ▼ ▲

*To: Hemingway*
*From: Perkins*                                   *CC, 4 pp.*[1] *Princeton*

Feb. 17, 1944

Dear Ernest:

. . . . .

. . . . .

. . . . .

Ernest, I have wonderful letters from Scott. Many long ones, about his own work and about other writers. Brilliant letters. I had no idea of it. In retrospect it had seemed as if all our correspondence was about money, and almost all by cable. I remember most of the things that I read, but I would have thought that I had got them in conversation. The reason I got the letters out was that Bunny is still fussing with that miscellaneous book in which I think he had meant to include letters from you. I never liked the idea of that book. It had things in it that I know Scott would not like himself, and that I did not think were right, and then it was <u>so</u> miscellaneous. Made up of so many scraps.– Bunny knew I disapproved of it. We declined it in fact, and he was mad at me on that account.[2] But if it were to be done, I wanted it to be as good as it could be, and so had all Scott's correspondence got together, looked at it a little and saw its possibilities. Bunny wanted to take it away with him. I told him he could he could read it all here at any time during office hours. He said it was too noisy, and I said he could have a private room where it was completely silent.– But he thought I was most unreasonable,– though I don't see how anybody could think we could let a part of our records, the property of the House, be taken away from here. He wanted me to go through it, and I am trying to do it gradually, at odd moments. But a selection from it of four or five letters would be extremely difficult.

I don't think I told you that my other sister lost a boy in the war, shot down over Wake Island. I guess I showed more sense than anyone in the family after all, in choosing the sex of my children. It always seems as if the boy that was lost was the best one of the lot, too.

. . . . .

Always yours,
MAXWELL PERKINS

*Notes*

1. 284 words have been omitted from this letter.
2. *The Crack-Up* has never gone out of print.

▲ ▼ ▲

To: Perkins                          *Finca Vigia letterhead, Havana, Cuba*
From: Hemingway                      *TLS, 2 pp.*[1] *Princeton*

February 25 1944

Dear Max:

. . . . .

I wish you would keep all the Scott letters for a definitive book instead of letting Bunny Wilson pee them away in his usual malicious driblets. He never asked me for any letters from Scott and I have very many; unfortunately all packed in Key West but available anytime I have something to do besides this war. Have letters from Gatsby period all through the Paris time and all the rest. All of them about writing and showing Scotts great strength and most of his weaknesses. I should suggest you save all of your letters; don't give permission for any of them to be used; until we could get out a good book n Scott and his letters. I know him, through some periods, better than anyone and would be glad to write a long, true, just, detailed (all of those I mean in the measure that anyone can do any such thing) account of the years I knew him. It might be better to wait and write it for my own memoirs but my memoir expectancy has been so slight these last years that might be good to write a good piece about Scott before I get too punchy to remember.[2] Would suggest that John Peale Bishop who knew, loved, and understood Scott much better than Wilson ever did edit the letters. John is unfailably kind, impersonal and disinterested while Wilson is usually twisting the facts to cover some expressed error of critical judgement he has made in the past or some prejudice or lack of knowledge or scholarship. He is also extremely dishonest; both about money and about his friends and other writers. I know no one who works so hard at being honest and less true inner honesty within himself. His criticism is like reading second rate gospels written by some one who is out on parole. He reads most interestingly on all the things one does not know about. On the things one knows about truly he is stupid, inaccurate, uninformative and pretentious. But because he is so pretentious his inaccuracies are accepted by all those with less knowledge of what he is writing about than he has. He is the great false-honest, false-craftsman, falsegreatcritic of our exceedingly sorry times which, if every one was honest in himself and what he writes, have no need to be sorry in any way. You can trace the moral decay of his criticism on a parrallel line with the decline in DosPassos's writings through their increasing dishonesty about money and other things, mostly their being dominated by women. But let us not attack that theme with limited time available. Anyway above is my suggestion with regard to Scott's letters. When I am through with this war will have to get in training and shape again to write and would be glad to help on the Scott book to warm up and get going.

I miss writing very much Max. You see, unlike the people who belaboured it as a dog's life <u>ce metier de chien</u> Conrad and old Ford were always suffering about I loved to write very much and was never happier than doing it. Charlie's[3] ridiculing of my daily word count was because he did not understand me or writing especially well nor could know how happy one felt to have put down properly 422 words as you wanted them to be. And days of 1200 or 2700 were something that made you happier than you could believe. Since I found that 400 to 600 well done was a pace I could hold much better was always happy with that number. But if I only had 320 I felt good.

. . . . .
. . . . .
. . . . .
. . . . .

Best Always to Charlie and your local mob,
Ernest
E. Hemingway

*Notes*

1. 292 words have been omitted from this letter.
2. Hemingway's contemptuous recollections of Fitzgerald were posthumously published in *A Moveable Feast.*
3. Charles Scribner III.

▲ ▼ ▲

*To: Perkins*                                    *Havana, Cuba*
*From: Hemingway*                         *TLS, 2 pp.*[1] *Princeton*

July 23 1945

Dear Max:

. . . . .
. . . . .
. . . . .
. . . . .
. . . . .
. . . . .

Will you have them send me Bunny's book on Scott? I feel badly not to write anything about Scott when I knew him, possibly, the best of any of them. But you cannot write anything true as long as Zelda is alive anymore than I can write with my bitch of a mother still able to read. When I was liveing with Georgie Wertenbaker's P47 group there was a man named Jonah something or other (a preposterous name) maybe not even Jonah; who gave me all the Gen on Scott's last time.[2] He was with him when he died etc. Also at the terrible thing with Sheilah. He never would have finished the book of course. It was more an outline to draw advances on; a mock-up of a project than a book. That was why the wonderful grandiloquence of it so impresses those people who are not in the secret of how writers are. The Epic, as we know, is usually false. And he pitched that at an Epic note that would be impossible for anyone to sustain. In wasn't by accident that the Gettysburg address was so short. The laws of prose writing are as immutable as those of flight, of mathematics, of physics. Scott was almost completely uneducated. He knew none of the laws. He did everything wrong; and it came out right. But geometry, always catches up with you. I always feel that you and I can talk truly about Scott because we both loved him and admired him and understood him. Where other people were dazzled by him we saw the good, the weakness and the great flaw that was always there. The cowardice, the dream world that was not a late symptom as (reading the reviews Bunny seems to feel). He always had the dream of football greatness, war (which he knew <u>nothing</u> of) (The Sour Science) and when he couldn't walk across Fifth Avenue in traffic he thought 'with what I <u>know</u> now what a great broken field runner I would be.'

Next time I'll write what was good in him. But we take it for granted people should be good. And in a horse, a regiment, a good writer I look for what is wrong. Take it for granted they are good or would not be looking at them.

. . . . .
. . . . .
. . . . .

Ernest/

*Notes*

1. 856 words have been omitted from this letter.
2. Jonah Ruddy was the legman for Sheilah Graham's column. His memories of Fitzgerald were never published. Graham told Bruccoli that Ruddy appropriated Fitzgerald's manuscripts.

▲▼▲

*To: Hemingway*
*From: Perkins*                *CC, 1 p.[1] Princeton*

June 5, 1947

Dear Ernest:

This is just a line to tell you that after I telephoned you, though I could hardly hear, I gathered that things were going on well. I now have heard that although that seems to be true, you have had a very devil of a time.[2] I am mighty sorry about it. I know how horrifying such things are, but in my case they have been brief.– I could not have taken it for the length of time you have. But you are always good that way. There is no sense in my saying all this, but it is impossible not to say something. It has been mighty tough, and I do greatly hope the situation is now better.

Yours always,

*Notes*

1. This was Perkins's last letter to Hemingway.
2. Hemingway's son Patrick had been dangerously ill in Cuba.

▲▼▲

*To: Charles Scribner III*
*From: Hemingway*                                    *Wire. Princeton*

THE COMPANY WILL APPRECIATE SUGGESTIONS FROM ITS PATRONS CONCERNING ITS SERVICE          1280

| CLASS OF SERVICE | | SYMBOLS | |
|---|---|---|---|
| This is a full-rate Cablegram unless its deferred character is indicated by a suitable symbol preceding the address. | **WESTERN UNION** **CABLEGRAM** JOSEPH L. EGAN PRESIDENT | LC | Deferred Cablegram |
| | | NLT | Cable Night Letter |
| | | Ship | Radiogram |

Received at

)N274 INTL=N HAVANA VIA WUCABLES 22 17 704P

LC CHARLES SCRIBNER=

:SCRIBNERS 979 FIFTH AVE NYK=          1947 JUN 17 PM 8 25

:WHAT AWFUL LUCK DEEPEST SYMPATHY YOU AND ALL AT SCRIBNERS
HAVE CABLED LOUISE=

:ERNEST.

.597.

THE QUICKEST, SUREST AND SAFEST WAY TO SEND MONEY IS BY TELEGRAPH OR CABLE

Perkins died of pneumonia on June 17, 1947 (Princeton University Library).

▲▼▲

*To: Charles Scribner III*              *Finca Vigia letterhead, Havana, Cuba*
*From: Hemingway*              *TLS with holograph postscript, 2 pp.[1] Princeton*

June 28 1947

Dear Charlie:

Don't worry about me kid. . You have troubles enough without that. I didn't write you after I cabled because what the hell can you say. We don't need to talk wet about Max to each other. The bad was for him to die. I hadn't figured on him dying; I'd just thought he might get so completely damn deaf we'd lose him that way. Anyway for a long time I had been trying to be less of a nuisance to him and have all the fun with him possible. We had a hell of a good time this last time in New York and wasn't it lucky it was that way instead of a lot of problems and arguments. Anyway he doesn't have to worry about Tom Wolfe's chickenshit estate anymore, or handle Louise's business, nor keep those women writers from building nests in his hat. Max had a lot of fun, anyway I know we had a lot of fun together, but useing up all his resistance that way by not takeing some lay offs to build up is a good lesson to us and don't you get to overworking now, at least until young Charlie gets to know the business for quite a long time because I want to be able to see your alcohol ravaged face when I come in the office for at least the next twenty two years to help me feel someone in N.Y. has a worse hangover than I have.

Charlie don't worry about me at all. I never liked that son of a bitch Darrow but he's out. Wallace and I like and understand each other very well.[1] You and I get along damn well. A lot better than people know and you don't have to worry about writing me letters. I'd have to work and try to write well if I were in jail, or if I had 20 million dollars, or if I was broke and working at something else to keep going, or if I was going to die, or if I had word I was going to live forever. So don't worry about me. I'm not going to succomb to any temptations and I don't flatter easy any more. You've got enough dough to back me to extent that I have to ask for it while I write this book and I will borrow as little as I can and write as good as I can. Have been working out ways for my existant stories to be sold to pictures on a non-whoreing basis to keep me going while write, same as always, with no regard for whether it is to sell; but only on a basis of how well I can write it. At least have been working on that and if Speiser doesn't blow it up by over-extending his negociatory ability should be o.k. within this month. However things go I have dough now to last me until Sept. But if the deal with Hellinger[2] goes through I am set for all the time I will need on the book and some afterwards.

If it would do any good you might let it be known that while Max was my best and oldest friend at Scribners and a great, great editor he never cut a paragraph of my stuff nor asked me to change one. One of my best and most loyal friends and wisest counsellors in life as well as in writing is dead. But Charles Scribners Sons are my publishers and I intend to publish with them for the rest of my life.

Malcom Cowley can tell you what he and Max and I and later he and Max were lineing up of getting out a three vol. edition of Farewell To Arms, Sun Also Rises, and For Whom The Bell Tolls showing the relationship between the three with illustrations and an introduction by Cowley. That might come after the new edition of A Farewell To Arms you said you and Max were talking about. I think it is g od policy to keep these books going in our own editions and the three comeing out together with the Cowley tie-up of them would insure g od reviews. Might do better hitting with all three than throwing in piecemeal.[3]

If only the boys hadn't done away with Ben Siegal[4] we might have put him in charge of getting me the Nobel prize. He asked me one time, "Ernie why don't you ever get any of these prizes? I see other writers getting prizes what's the trouble Ernie? There's certainly someway that can be rigged."[5]

> TO CHARLIE SCRIBNER
> AND
> TO MAX PERKINS

Dedication in *The Old Man and the Sea,* 1952 (Bruccoli Collection, Thomas Cooper Library, University of South Carolina)

Won't bother you with any more of this with everything you have on your hands. If young Charlie is going good in the advertizing end why not leave him there for a while instead of yanking him?

. . . . .

. . . . .

. . . . .

We have real Gordon's gin at 50 bucks a case and real Noilly Prat and have found a way of makeing ice in the deep-freeze in tennis ball tubes that comes out 15 degrees below zero and with the glasses frozen too makes the coldest martini in theworld. Just enough vermouth to cover the bottom of the glass, ounce 3/4 of gin, and the spanish cocktail onions very crisp and also 15 degrees below zero when they go in the glass.

This has been rugged as I said but there are better ways of sweating it out than putting your head on the wailing wall.

Did Max get the invitation to the Bronze Star thing?[6] Gen.Lanham who I was with from Normandy on when he was commanding 22nd Inf.Regt. said I should have turned it down but I thought that would be rude and also imply I thought I should have something better which I thought sort of chickenshit. One time in the war got drunk at a dinner because was to get DSC but it got turned down at the top. So thought better take this before it got cancelled.

So long Charlie. Take care of yourself.

Best always

Ernest

Have you heard anything from Martha?[7] I havent heard from her since Christmas. Have a new house-maid named Martha and certainly is a pleasure to give her orders. Marty was a lovely girl though. I wish she hadnt been quite so ambitious and war crazy. Think it must be sort of lonesome for her without a war.

## Notes

1. Scribners editor Wallace Meyer.

2. Mark Hellinger, the movie producer who made *The Killers* (1946), agreed to pay Hemingway $50,000 a year for four years for rights to four unwritten short stories; but the deal fell through when Hellinger died.

3. This plan was never implemented.

4. Ben "Bugsy" Siegel, a Las Vegas racketeer, was murdered in 1947.

5. Hemingway was awarded the Nobel Prize for Literature in 1954.

6. In June 1947 Hemingway was awarded a Bronze Star for meritorious service as a war correspondent.

7. Hemingway and Gellhorn had been divorced in December 1945, and he married his fourth wife, Mary Welch, in March 1946. Ernest Hemingway committed suicide on July 2, 1961, in Ketchum, Idaho.

# Appendix I

## Thomas Wolfe's Portrait of Maxwell Perkins
### in *You Can't Go Home Again*

*Wolfe was the only one of the three sons who wrote a tribute to Maxwell Perkins. Hemingway did not write about him, except in letters. Publisher George Jaggers in Fitzgerald's "Financing Finnegan" (1938) is based on Perkins, but this story is mainly a private joke. It was inevitable that Wolfe would write about Perkins in recognizable detail. This portrait of George Webber's editor was posthumously published in* You Can't Go Home Again *(New York: Harper, 1940). As Wolfe's literary executor, Perkins was required to approve publication of this work assembled by another editor. Perkins didn't think that "The Fox" was an accurate portrait of him, but his family told him that Wolfe had got him right.*

### From Chapter 28, "The Fox"

During all these desperate years in Brooklyn, when George lived and worked alone, he had only one real friend, and this was his editor, Foxhall Edwards. They spent many hours together, wonderful hours of endless talk, so free and full that it combed the universe and bound the two of them together in bonds of closest friendship. It was a friendship founded on many common tastes and interests, on mutual liking and admiration of each for what the other was, and on an attitude of respect which allowed unhampered expression of opinion even on those rare subjects which aroused differences of views and of belief. It was, therefore, the kind of friendship that can exist only between two men. It had in it no element of that possessiveness which always threatens a woman's relations with a man, no element of that physical and emotional involvement which, while it serves nature's end of bringing a man and woman together, also tends to thwart their own dearest wish to remain so by throwing over their companionship a constricting cloak of duty and obligation, of right and vested interest.

The older man was not merely friend but father to the younger. Webber, the hot-blooded Southerner, with his large capacity for sentiment and affection, had lost his own father many years before and now had found a substitute in Edwards. And Edwards, the reserved New Englander, with his deep sense of family and inheritance, had always wanted a son but had had five daughters, and as time went on he made of George a kind of foster son. Thus each, without quite knowing that he did it, performed an act of spiritual adoption.

So it was to Foxhall Edwards that George now turned whenever his loneliness became unbearable. When his inner turmoil, confusion, and self-doubts overwhelmed him, as they often did, and his life went dead and stale and empty till it sometimes seemed that all the barren desolation of the Brooklyn streets had soaked into his very blood and marrow—then he would seek out Edwards. And he never went to him in vain. Edwards, busy though he always was, would drop whatever he was doing and would take George out to lunch or dinner, and in his quiet, casual, oblique, and understanding way would talk to him and draw him out until he found out what it was that troubled him. And always in the end, because of Edwards' faith in him, George would be healed and find himself miraculously restored to self-belief.

What manner of man was this great editor and father-confessor and true friend—he of the quiet, shy, sensitive, and courageous heart who often seemed to those who did not know him well an eccentric, cold, indifferent fellow—he who, grandly christened Foxhall, preferred to be the simple, unassuming Fox?

▲▼▲

The Fox asleep was a breathing portrait of guileless innocence. He slept on his right side, legs doubled up a little, hands folded together underneath the ear, his hat beside him on the pillow. Seen so, the sleeping figure of the Fox was touching—for all his five and forty years, it was so plainly boylike. By no long stretch of fancy the old hat beside him on the pillow might have been a childish toy brought to bed with him the night before—and this, in fact, it was!

It was as if, in sleep, no other part of Fox was left except the boy. Sleep seemed to have resumed into itself this kernel of his life, to have excluded all transitions, to have brought the man back to his acorn, keeping thus inviolate that which the man, indeed, had never lost, but which had passed through change and time and all the accretions of experience—and now had been restored, unwoven back into the single oneness of itself.

And yet it was a guileful Fox, withal. Oh, guileful Fox, how innocent in guilefulness and in innocence how full of guile! How straight in cunning, and how cunning-straight, in all directions how strange-devious, in all strange-deviousness how direct! Too straight for crookedness, and for envy too serene, too fair for blind intolerance, too just and seeing and too strong for hate, too honest for base dealing, too high for low suspiciousness, too innocent for all the scheming tricks of swarming villainy—yet never had been taken in a horse trade yet!

So, then, life's boy is he, life's trustful child; life's guileful-guileless Fox is he, but not life's angel, not life's fool. Will get at all things like a fox—not full-tilt at the fences, not head-on, but through coverts peering, running at fringes of the wood, or by the wall; will swing round on the pack and get behind the hounds, cross them up and be away and gone when they are looking for him where he's not—he will not mean to fox them, but he will.

Gets round the edges of all things the way a fox does. Never takes the main route or the worn handle. Sees the worn handle, what it is, says, "Oh," but knows it's not right handle though most used: gets right handle right away and uses it. No one knows how it is done, neither knows the Fox, but does it instantly. It seems so easy when Fox does it, easy as a shoe, because he has had it from his birth. It is a genius.

Our Fox is never hard or fancy, always plain. He makes all plays look easy, never brilliant; it seems that anyone can do it when Fox does it. He covers more ground than any other player in the game, yet does not seem to do so. His style is never mannered, seems no style at all; the thrilled populace never holds its breath in hard suspense when he takes aim, because no one ever saw the Fox take aim, and yet he never misses. Others spend their lives in learning to take aim: they wear just the proper uniform for taking aim, they advance in good order, they signal to the breathless world for silence—"We are taking aim!" they say, and then with faultless style and form, with flawless execution, they bring up their pieces, take aim—and *miss!* The great Fox never seems to take aim, and never misses. Why? He was just born that way—fortunate, a child of genius, innocent and simple—and a Fox!

"And ah!—a cunning Fox!" the Aimers and the Missers say. "A damned subtle, devilish, and most cunning Fox!" they cry, and grind their teeth. "Be not deceived by his appearance—'tis a cunning Fox! Put not your faith in Foxes, put not your faith in this one, he will look so shy, and seem so guileless and so bewildered—but he will never miss!"

"But how——" the Aimers and the Missers plead with one another in exasperation—"how does he do it? What has the fellow got? He's nothing much to look at—nothing much to talk to. He makes no appearance! He never goes out in the world—you never see him at receptions, parties, splendid entertainments—he makes no effort to meet people—no, or to talk to them! He hardly talks at all! . . . What has he got? Where does it come from? Is it chance or luck? There is some mystery——"

"Well, now," says one, "I'll tell you what my theory is——"

Their heads come close, they whisper craftily together until——

"No!" another cries. "It is not that. I tell you what he does, it's——"

And again they whisper close, argue and deny, get more confused than ever, and finally are reduced to furious impotence:

"Bah!" cries one. "How does the fellow do it, anyway? How does he get away with it? He seems to have no sense, no knowledge, no experience. He doesn't get around the way we do, lay snares and traps. He doesn't seem to know what's going on, or what the whole thing's all about—and yet——"

"He's just a *snob!*" another snarls. "When you try to be a good fellow, he high-hats you! You try to kid him, he just looks at you! He never offers to shake hands with you, he never slaps you on the back the way real fellows do! You go out of your way to be nice to him—to show him you're a real guy and that you think he is, too—and what does he do? He just looks at you with that funny little grin and turns away—and wears that damned hat in the office all day long—I think he *sleeps* with it! He never asks you to sit down—and gets up while you're talking to him—leaves you cold—begins to wander up and down outside, staring at everyone he sees—his own associates—as if he were some half-wit idiot boy—and wanders back into his office twenty minutes later—stares at you as if he never saw your face before—and jams that damned hat further down around his ears, and turns away—takes hold of his lapels—looks out the window with that crazy grin—then looks at you again, looks you up and down, stares at your face until you wonder if you've changed suddenly into a baboon—and turns back to the window without a word—then stares at you again—finally *pretends* to recognize you, and says: 'Oh, it's you!' . . . I tell you he's a *snob,* and that's his way of letting you know you don't *belong!* Oh, I know about him—I know what he is! He's an old New Englander—older than God, by God! Too good for anyone but God, by God!—and even God's a little doubtful! An aristocrat—a rich man's son—a Groton-Harvard boy—too fine for the likes of us, by God!—too good for the 'low bounders' who make up this profession! He thinks we're a bunch of business men and Babbitts—and that's the reason that he looks at us the way he does—that's the reason that he grins his grin, and turns away, and catches at his coat lapels, and doesn't answer when you speak to him——"

"Oh, no," another quickly interrupts. "You're wrong there! The reason that he grins that grin and turns away is that he's trying hard to hear—the reason that he doesn't answer when you speak to him is that he's deaf——"

"Ah, deaf!" says still another in derision. "Deaf, hell! Deaf as a Fox, *he* is! That deafness is a stall—a trick—a gag! He hears you when he wants to hear you! If it's anything he wants to hear, *he'll* hear you though you're forty yards away and talking in a whisper! He's a Fox. I tell you!"

"Yes, a Fox, a Fox!" they chorus in agreement. "That much is certain—the man's a Fox!"

So the Aimers and the Missers whisper, argue, and deduce. They lay siege to intimates and friends of Fox, ply them with flattery and strong drink, trying thus to pluck out the heart of Fox's mystery. They find out nothing, because there's nothing to find out, nothing anyone can tell them. They are reduced at length to exasperated bafflement and finish where they started. They advance to their positions, take aim—and miss!

And so, in all their ways, they lay cunning snares throughout the coverts of the city. They lay siege to life. They think out tactics, crafty stratagems. They devise deep plans to bag the game. They complete masterly flanking operations in the night-time (while the great Fox sleeps), get in behind the enemy when he isn't looking, are sure that victory is within their grasp, take aim magnificently—and fire—and shoot one another painfully in the seats of their expensive pants!

Meanwhile, the Fox is sleeping soundly through the night, as sweetly as a child.

Night passes, dawn comes, eight o'clock arrives. How to describe him now as he awakes?

A man of five and forty years, not really seeming younger, yet always seeming something of the boy. Rather, the boy is there within that frame of face, behind the eyes, within the tenement of flesh and bone—not imprisoned, just held there in a frame—a frame a little worn by the years, webbed with small wrinkles round the eyes—invincibly the same as it has always been. The hair, once fair and blond, no longer fair and blond now, feathered at the temples with a touch of grey, else-where darkened by time and weather to a kind of steel-grey—blondness really almost dark now, yet somehow, still suggesting fair and blond. The head well set and small, boy's head still, the hair sticking thick and close to it, growing to a V in the center of the forehead, then back straight and shapely, full of natural grace. Eyes pale blue, full of a strange misty light, a kind of far weather of the sea in them, eyes of a New England sailor long months outbound for China on a clip-per ship, with something drowned, sea-sunken in them.

The general frame and structure of the face is somewhat lean and long and narrow—face of the ancestors, a bred face, face of people who have looked the same for generations. A stern, lonely face, with the enduring fortitude of gran-ite, face of the New England seacoast, really his grandfather's face, New England statesman's face, whose bust sits there on the mantel, looking at the bed. Yet some-thing else has happened on Fox's face to transfigure it from the primeval naked-ness of granite: in its essential framework, granite still, but a kind of radiance and warmth of life has enriched and mellowed it. A light is burning in the Fox, shin-ing outward through the face, through every gesture, grace, and movement of the body, something swift, mercurial, mutable, and tender, something buried and withheld, but passionate—something out of his mother's face, perhaps, or out of his father's, or his father's mother's—something that subdues the granite with warmth—something from poetry, intuition, genius, imagination, living, inner radiance, and beauty. This face, then, with the shapely head, the pale, far-misted vision of the eyes, held in round bony cages like a bird's, the strong, straight nose, curved at the end, a little scornful and patrician, sensitive, sniff-ing, swift-nostriled as a hound's—the whole face with its passionate and proud serenity might almost be the face of a great poet, or the visage of some strange and mighty bird.

But now the sleeping figure stirs, opens its eyes and listens, rouses, starts up like a flash.

"What?" says Fox.

The Fox awake now.

· · · · · · · · · ·

*From Chapter 30, "The Anodyne"*

· · · · · · · · · ·

Wherever he was, Fox was one to get the little things—the little, most important things that tell you everything. He never picked a little thing because it was a little thing, to show he was a devilish cunning, subtle, rare, and most aesthetic fellow: he picked a little thing because it was the *right* thing—and he never missed.

Fox was a great fox, and a genius. He was no little Pixy of the Aesthetes. He did not write nine-page reviews on "How Chaplin Uses Hands in Latest Picture" —how it really was not slap-stick, but the tragedy of Lear in modern clothes; or on how Enters* enters; or on how Crane's[†] poetry can only be defined, reviewed, and generally exposited in terms of mathematical formulae—ahem! ahem, now! —as:

$$\frac{\sqrt{an + pxt}}{237} = \frac{n - F3(B^{18} + 11)}{2}$$

(Bring on the Revolution, Comrades; it is Time!)

Fox did not go around making discoveries nine years after Boob McNutt[‡] had made them. He didn't find out that Groucho was funny seven years too late, and then inform the public *why* he was. He did not write: "The opening *Volte* of the Ballet is the historic method amplified in history, the production of historic fullness without the literary cliché of the historic spate." He had no part in any of the fine horse-manure with which we have allowed ourselves to be bored, maddened, whiff-sniffed, hound-and-hornered, nationed, new-republicked, dialed, spectatored, mercuried, storied, anviled, new-massed, new-yorkered, vogued, vanity-faired, timed, broomed, transitioned,[§] and generally shat upon by the elegant, refined, and snobified Concentrated Blotters of the Arts. He had nothing to do with any of the doltish gibberings, obscene quackeries, phoney passions, and six-months-long religions of fools, joiners, and fashion-apes a trifle

*Theatrical performer Angna Enters (1907–1989).

[†] Hart Crane (1899–1932).

[‡] Comic-strip character who became a model of stupidity.

[§] In this catalogue of magazines Wolfe refers to *Hound and Horn, The Nation, The New Republic, Dial, The Spectator, The American Mercury, Story, The Anvil, The New Masses, The New Yorker, Vogue, Vanity Fair, Time, Broom,* and *transistion.*

brighter and quicker on the uptake than the fools, joiners, and fashion-apes they
prey upon. He was none of your little franky-panky, seldesey-weldesey, cowley-
wowley, tatesey-watesy, hicksy-picksy, wilsony-pilsony, jolasy-wolasy, steiny-weiny,
goldy-woldly, sneer-puss fellows. Neither, in more-conventional guise, was he
one of your groupy-croupy, cliquey-triquey, meachy-teachy, devoto-bloato* wire-
pullers and back-scratchers of the world.

*Wolfe's targets include writer Waldo Frank (1889–1967), critic Gilbert Seldes (1893–
1970), critic Malcolm Cowley (1898–1989), writer and poet Allen Tate (1899–1979),
critic Granville Hicks (1901–1982), critic Edmund Wilson (1895–1972), editor Eugene
Jolas (1894–1952), Gertrude Stein (1874–1946); editor and critic Michael Gold (1893–
1967), and critic Bernard De Voto (1897–1955).

# Appendix 2

## Thomas Wolfe
### A Writer for the People of His Time and Tomorrow
by Maxwell Perkins

*Wings* [The Literary Guild] (October 1939)

I knew Thomas Wolfe for some ten years about as intimately as one man can know another, and yet I understood him better after he died when I visited Asheville.*

It is ringed around by mountains of such height and mass and impregnability that one feels imprisoned within them, and the whole world is without. The train gets you there by long windings through cuts and passes and in the end by a series of spirals, or so it seems. The mountains are so great and silent that Asheville, a considerable and active city, is like a small town, and all the great world of the North and South and West, and of the past too, was beyond. When the train whistled often in the night and Tom listened as it swung around those many curves, it signified more to him than distance: it was winding its way out through the folds of the mountains into the unknown, not just into more of the same thing that was in and around Asheville.

By this imprisonment, one can think, Tom's imagination was intensified, and his desire for experience, by being pent up, was increased and sharpened. It was not this that made him what he was, of course, but the character of what he did and wrote was qualified by it. This gave his writings their particular intensity and violence, and later increased his sense, as with one released from a prison, that there was not enough time, and so made him wild to see, read, taste, feel and record everything.

And so it was this perhaps—and hearing the trains wind out around the labyrinthe mountain walls—that gave him his first great continental vision of America which was always his obsession. His imagination vaulted the mountains, and, fed by what he heard and read, and later saw, made him view the whole vast,

---

* *The Web and the Rock,* published by Harper in 1939, was offered for sale by The Literary Guild. Although Perkins was no longer editing and publishing Thomas Wolfe, he was executor of Wolfe's literary estate.

sprawling, lonely land at once. For Tom was a poet in the largest sense though he never knew it, never would believe it. He used often to say, "Any man would be a poet if he could." But he thought instinctively of a poet as one who wrote in rhyme and adhered to the strictest rules of metre.

When we were preparing his books for the press and came upon those passages, sometimes half narrative like "The Four Lost Men—Garfield, Arthur, Harrison, and Hays"—and sometimes wholly lyrical like "October Has Come Again," and others like "The Names of the Nation," the question was what to do with them. They did not belong in a novel in the conventional view. They were not in any sense narrative, they broke into the story. And yet they were too lovely or too magnificent to dispense with. We used to talk of setting them apart as interludes, in italics, but they were perhaps more of the essence of what Tom had to say than the narrative itself. They were the poet speaking and we rightly ended by letting them stand as they came. Even then I hoped for a time when they could be taken out and published together in a separate book like *The Face of a Nation.* *

Perhaps no one in our day has written finer narrative than Wolfe—take, for example, half a dozen episodes in the first part of *The Web and the Rock*— especially that of the killing of the heroic negro who ran amuck. But Tom's essential nature was that of a poet, even as the child who exulted in the colors and smells and tastes and sounds and feelings; and when I knew him as for the moment free from the torment of the struggle with his work, he always showed that nature.

What would he want to do, for instance, after a night of work when he was in New York, was to visit the markets way down off West Street in the early morning when the drays pulled by big horses, like percherons, were bringing in the produce, and the blue-green cabbages, the piled-up fruit, the purple eggplant, crowded the stalls under the glaring lights; and there was the clatter of hooves and the rattle of wheels, and the shouts of the boisterous drivers and grocers' boys. Tom loved to walk through all that and smell the vegetables, walking in his slow, swinging, countryman's stride, in the swaying raincoat he always wore, and the shabby black felt hat.

Or in the late afternoon, after he came round to get his mail, we would go to Beekman Towers and up to the roof to lean on the parapet at dusk and look far down toward the slender bridges, and the docks of Brooklyn, to see the white night boats come slowly through the haze up the East River headed for the Sound. From that tower you could see all Manhattan. Tom never saw it so but he compared it—as in his books—to a great ship, with its sharp prow pointed toward the sea.

* Subtitled *Poetical Passages From the Writings of Thomas Wolfe* (New York: Scribners, 1939).

On the way to some such place as that he would go roundabout to visit the Grand Central Station when it was thronged with people and all the movement of the place was strongest. I think there was nowhere in New York he loved so much. He never tired of it. He would linger and watch and listen, head and shoulders above the crowd. It was not only the hurry and the hum that held him—the sound of life and time—but the vision he had of the great continental locomotives of the New York Central and the New York, New Haven & Hartford, sliding out with their tons of lighted cars.

He frequented saloons, and drank there, and knew a hundred bartenders as friends; but it was not because of the drink. He listened. He loved the live, expressive talk of natural people at a bar when their tongues are loosened a little or much, and they speak in the language of life. But his own talk was the best talk. He would call up at some incredible hour to say he had not eaten all day and would we not go somewhere with him. He knew all the New York restaurants, German, French, Turkish, Chinese, and whenever we went he would often forget the troubles which beset him and tell of what had moved him most —the mists over the river Cam in Cambridge, for instance, or the flaming fields of tulips in Holland, or the sound of the bells of Oxford—and his face would light up and he would forget everything but the one thing, and tell of it so that you felt it all as it had seemed to him. Even one who knew his writings well would later remember what he heard in talk as vividly as what he had read, and not at first be able to recall whether Tom had told him of it or whether it was in his books.

And mostly Tom talked of America. No one so loved this nation, and yet no one denounced it more bitterly—its injustice and violence and waste and inequality. He seemed at times to hate it—but it was the hatred that comes from love. He knew Europe well from his wanderings, and though he said the French were "a race of cats" and "the teeth of the English are loose" he warmed to those lands and knew full well what they had that we have not. And he still thought always of America and knew that it was different from anywhere else. He knew the lights and colors were different here, and the character of the varied land and all the multiplicity of its peoples.

It was this that made him feel so desperately that the work of the artist in America—he might have said specifically the poet—was not yet even begun, and that the revelation of America to Americans was yet to be made; and it was in those poetical passages, his dithyrambs especially, that he showed his continental vision.

Once, some three months after the triumphant publication of *Of Time and the River*, Tom landed from a steamer on a blazing hot Fourth of July, and I met him. For all his good times abroad, his overwhelming reception in Germany, no child could have been more happy to be home, more eager to see all New York

again and at once. And that afternoon and night we did range from the floating restaurant on the East River at 55th Street, to the roof of the Saint George
Hotel in Brooklyn where the whole shining city and the harbor were spread out
below.*

Tom must have lived in eight or nine different parts of New York and
Brooklyn for a year or more. He knew in the end every aspect of the City—he
walked the streets endlessly—but he was not a city man. The city fascinated him
but he did not really belong in it and was never satisfied to live in it. He was
always thinking of America as a whole and planning trips to some part that he
had not yet seen, and in the end taking them. His various quarters in town
always looked as if he had just moved in, to camp for a while. This was partly
because he really had no interest in possessions of any kind, but it was also
because he was in his very nature a Far Wanderer, bent upon seeing all places,
and his rooms were just necessities into which he never settled. Even when he
was there his mind was not. He needed a continent to range over, actually and
in imagination. And his place was all America. It was with America he was most
deeply concerned and I believe he opened it up as no other writer ever did for
the people of his time and for the writers and artists and poets of tomorrow.
Surely he had a thing to tell us.

# Ernest Hemingway
## by Max Perkins

*Book-of-the-Month Club News* (October 1940)[†]

In spite of Ernest Hemingway's repugnance to publicity—his first and most
emphatic request to his publishers was that nothing about his personal life
should be given out—he is one of those about whom legends gather; and since
he is disinclined to talk about himself it is hard to disentangle truth from rumor.*

But one of the earliest stories significant of his character I do know to be
fact. When still a boy, but large for his age and strong, his father, yielding to his
urgency, gave him as a present the price of an advertised course in boxing. You
paid the ex-fighter in advance and he turned you over to a pug. In the first lesson Young Hemingway got rough treatment. His nose was broken. Few returned
for a second lesson, but Hemingway did, and he finished the course. It never
even occurred to him that this was a racket—that you weren't supposed to come
back ever.

---

* See Wolfe's last letter to Perkins, 12 August 1938.
† *For Whom the Bell Tolls* was a Book-of-the-Month Club selection.

That was in Chicago when he lived in Oak Park. Only a little later—he was certainly below sixteen—he left home, determined to take care of himself. In a surprisingly few years later he was taking care of a number of other people toward whom he thought he had loyalties. His first established job was that of reporter on the *Kansas City Star*—though if his size had not beguiled a city editor into overestimating his age by several years, he would never have got it. Before this he had shown some inclination to write, for pieces by him had appeared in his school paper, but in Kansas City he really began to learn.

Then came the World War. Even when it ended Hemingway would have been barely old enough to enlist, but he was bound to see it, and finally got into the Ambulance Service on the Italian front, later to command a section, and then to transfer to the Infantry with a lieutenant's commission. He was wounded, and in the end received as high a decoration as the Italian army gives. It is commonly thought that the war scenes in *A Farewell to Arms* came directly from that experience. They didn't. The most famous ones of all, those in the account of the Caporetto Retreat, were wholly his own creations. He wasn't there.

War is, we know, a revelation to one who can retain impressions. The Book of Common Prayer says: "In the midst of life we are in death," but one could also say of war that in the midst of death we are in life. Many writers, like Tolstoy, have largely learned of life from war—for then life is quickened and intensified, and the qualities of men come sharply out. Hemingway saw it again after Versailles when, as correspondent for an American syndicate, he covered the Graeco-Turkish War, and he said he learned far more of war from that, as an observer, than from the World War as a participant.

Then in Paris he turned wholly to writing, and lived for several years in poverty. This was in the post-war renaissance which so deeply affected American literature. When about 1927, he came to America, it was by way of Cuba, for economy's sake. Then he crossed to Key West, liked it, and stayed.

Hemingway became a great fisherman in those waters through which runs the deeply blue gulf stream: the fishing was needed as relief from the hardest work in the world, that in which everything is presented in final truth, where the essential quality of each thing told of is perceived and fixed. And that's why it was done—that and the need of such a man for action. Obviously his first interest was in writing, and not *his* writing only.

Once when he came to New York and Tom Wolfe was in an agony to master the material of *Of Time and the River* I asked Ernest to talk to him. No writers could have been so far apart in style and method, yet Ernest was fully appreciative of Tom and he understood his torment in his work. I remember, at that luncheon which so encouraged Tom, Ernest told him some helpful things—always, for instance, to break off work when you "are going good." Then you can rest easily and on the next day easily resume. For such as Tom, however

critical he might be of some qualities in his work, Hemingway had a deep
sympathy because of Wolfe's artistic honesty—but not for the literary writers.
When told of one who could not go on with his work until he found the right
place to work in, he said, "There's only one place for a man to work. In his
head."

Hemingway has too largely appeared as a man of force and action. He is that
too and when he thought the people who were Spain were fighting for what was
Spain, he gave all he could and was quite prepared to give his life. But his writings are surely enough to show what he is besides that, and what one soon learns
who sees him is that he is always at his work; always aware.*

---

*Perkins was not immune to the Hemingway mythologizing process. This article repeats
lies Hemingway told about himself: he did not run away from home; his father did not
pay for boxing lessons; he obtained his job at age eighteen on the *Kansas City Star* through
a family connection; he did not command troops in the Italian army; and he greatly
exaggerated his Paris poverty.

# APPENDIX 3

## Sources and Background Reading

Baker, Carlos. *Ernest Hemingway: A Life Story.* New York: Scribners, 1969.

———, ed. *Ernest Hemingway: Selected Letters, 1917–1961.* New York: Scribners, 1981.

Berg, A. Scott. *Max Perkins: Editor of Genius.* New York: E. P. Dutton/Thomas Congdon Books, 1978.

Bruccoli, Matthew J. *Fitzgerald and Hemingway: A Dangerous Friendship.* New York: Carroll & Graf, 1994.

———. *Some Sort of Epic Grandeur: The Life of F. Scott Fitzgerald,* Second Revised Edition. Columbia: University of South Carolina Press, 2002.

———, ed. *F. Scott Fitzgerald's The Great Gatsby: A Documentary Volume, Dictionary of Literary Biography Volume 219.* Detroit: Bruccoli Clark Layman/The Gale Group, 2000.

——— with Judith S. Baughman, eds. *F. Scott Fitzgerald: A Life in Letters.* New York: Scribners, 1994.

——— with the assistance of Robert W. Trogdon, eds. *The Only Thing That Counts: The Ernest Hemingway/Maxwell Perkins Correspondence, 1925–1947.* New York: Scribners, 1996.

——— and Park Bucker, eds. *To Loot My Life Clean: The Thomas Wolfe-Maxwell Perkins Correspondence.* Columbia: University of South Carolina Press, 2000.

——— and George Parker Anderson, eds. *F. Scott Fitzgerald's Tender Is the Night: A Documentary Volume,* Dictionary of Literary Biography, vol. 273. Detroit: Bruccoli Clark Layman/Thomson/Gale, 2003.

Burlingame, Roger. *Of Making Many Books: A Hundred Years of Reading, Writing and Publishing.* New York: Scribners, 1946.

Cowley, Malcolm. "Unshaken Friend," *The New Yorker,* 20 (1, 8 April 1944), 32–36, 39–42; 30–34, 36–43. Reprinted, Boulder, Colo.: Roberts Rinehart, 1972.

Delaney, John, ed. *The House of Scribner, 1905–1930: Dictionary of Literary Biography Documentary Series Volume 16.* Detroit: Bruccoli Clark Layman/Gale Research, 1997.

———, ed. *The House of Scribner, 1931–1984: Dictionary of Literary Biography Documentary Series Volume 17.* Detroit: Bruccoli Clark Layman/Gale Research, 1998.

Donald, David Herbert. *Look Homeward: A Life of Thomas Wolfe.* Boston: Little, Brown, 1987.

Frothingham, Bertha Perkins, Louise Perkins King, and Ruth King Porter, eds. *Father to Daughter: The Family Letters of Maxwell Perkins.* Port Townsend, Wash.: Empty Bowl, [1995].

Kuehl, John and Jackson R. Bryer, eds. *Dear Scott/Dear Max: The Fitzgerald-Perkins Correspondence.* New York: Scribners, 1971.

Mitchell, Ted, ed. *Thomas Wolfe: A Documentary Volume, Dictionary of Literary Biography 229.* Detroit: Bruccoli Clark Layman/The Gale Group, 2001.

Nowell, Elizabeth. *The Letters of Thomas Wolfe.* New York: Scribners, 1956.

———. *Thomas Wolfe: A Biography.* Garden City, N. Y.: Doubleday, 1960.

Perkins, Maxwell. "Scribner's and Thomas Wolfe." *Carolina Magazine,* 68 (October 1938), 15–17.

———. "Thomas Wolfe." *Scribner's Magazine,* 105 (May 1939), 5.

———. "Thomas Wolfe: A Writer for the People of His Time and Tomorrow." *WINGS* [The Literary Guild] (October 1939).

———. "Ernest Hemingway." *Book-of-the-Month Club News* (October 1940), 4.

———. "Thomas Wolfe." *Harvard Library Bulletin,* 1 (Autumn 1947), 269–277.

Reynolds, Michael. *Hemingway: The American Homecoming.* Oxford, UK and Cambridge, Mass.: Blackwell, 1992.

———. *Hemingway: The 1930s.* New York: Norton, 1997.

———. *Hemingway: The Final Years.* New York: Norton, 1999.

Tarr, Rodger L., ed. *Max + Marjorie: The Correspondence between Maxwell E. Perkins and Marjorie Kinnan Rawlings.* Gainesville: University Press of Florida, 1999.

———, ed. *As Ever Yours: The Letters of Max Perkins and Elizabeth Lemmon.* University Park: Pennsylvania State University Press, 2003.

Trogdon, Robert W., ed. *Ernest Hemingway: A Documentary Volume, Dictionary of Literary Biography 210.* Detroit: Bruccoli Clark Layman/The Gale Group, 1999.

Wheelock, John Hall, ed. *Editor to Author: The Letters of Maxwell E. Perkins.* New York: Scribners, 1950.

———. *The Last Romantic: A Poet Among Publishers,* ed. Matthew J. Bruccoli with Judith S. Baughman. Columbia: University of South Carolina Press, 2002.

Wolfe, Thomas. *The Story of a Novel.* New York and London: Scribners, 1936.

———. *O Lost: A Story of the Buried Life,* text established by Arlyn and Matthew J. Bruccoli. Columbia: University of South Carolina Press, 2000.

# INDEX

"Gambler, the Nun, and the Radio, The"
(EH), 169
*Game Fish of the Pacific* (Thomas &
Thomas), 148, 149n2
Garland, Hamlin, 51
Gauss, Christian, 53, 55n16
Gellhorn, Martha, xviiin, 276n2, 308, 317,
318n5, 329, 329n5
*General Grant's Last Stand* (Green), 218,
219n5
"Genius Is Not Enough" (De Voto),
242–43n2
*"Genius," The* (Dreiser), 111n2
*Germinal* (Zola), 51
"Ghost Story (As Sherwood Anderson
Would Write It If He Weren't Prevented),
A" (Benchley), 64, 64n2
Gingrich, Arnold, 188n, 214n2
Glasgow, Ellen, 314, 315n2
Glazer, Benjamin, 274n2
*Gods* (Desmond), 34n3
Godwin, Murray, 109
Gold, Michael (Irving Granich), 195,
200n13, 337n
Golding, Louis, 47
*Gone with the Wind* (Mitchell), 293, 293n2
Gordon, Caroline, xix
Graham, Sheilah, 314–15, 315n5, 325n2
*Grand Hotel* (Baum), 136n4
*Great Gatsby, The* (FSF), xxiiin, xxiv, xxix,
54, 62n2, 190, 280, 289, 297, 303, 312,
314, 322
    composition and revision, 16, 17n8, *17,*
    20–21, 23, 25n1, 30–31, 32–33,
    34n9, 35–36, 37, 37n, 40–41 (see
    also *Great Gatsby:* Perkins and)
    dramatization, 50, 55n5, 57, 217
    dust jacket, 22, 22n1, 27, 27n1, 27n2,
    41, 47
    later editions, 36n1, 107, 142, 152,
    153n3, 166
    Perkins and, xvii, 21–22, 27–29, *39,*
    39–40, 56, 179, 275
    reviews, 41, 42n5, *43,* 44, 45n, 46,
    47n1, 48, 48n2, 50, 55n2, 55n3, 79,
    80n3, 97, 99n4
    royalties, 29, 30n3, 31
    sales, 34, 40, *43,* 44, 45, 61
    Scribners catalogue entry, *37*
    serialization proposed, 36n2, 40n1
    sources, 33, 34n4, 34n6

stories related to, 46n, 53
title, 22, 23, 27, 30, 36, *39,* 45
*Great Modern Short Stories,* 278, 316n
*Green Hat, The* (Arlen), 47n2
*Green Hills of Africa* (EH), 184n1, *185,* 255
    composition, 182, 182n2, 183
    reviews and sales, 203, 204n2
    serialization, 187–88
Green, Horace, 219n5
*Green Pastures, The* (Connelly), 111, 111n2
Gregory, Horace, 169, 170n2
"Gretchen's Forty Winks" (FSF), 53
Grisman, Sam, 217, 218n2
Grosset & Dunlap (publisher), 152, 319
*Growth of the Soil, The* (Hamsun), 81
*Gullible's Travels* (Lardner), 46

*H. M. Pulham, Esquire* (Marquand), 314,
315n2
"Haircut" (Lardner), 40, 40n3, 41, 46, 50
Hale, Nancy, xix, 274
"Ham-American" (Lardner), 48n8
Hamsun, Knut, 51, 55n8, 81
"Handle with Care" (FSF), 203n2
Harcourt, Alfred, 56, 57n1, 60, 108
Harcourt, Brace (publisher), 57, 57n1, 59,
62, 64, 148, 149n4, 150, 271n2
Hardy, Thomas, 42n1, 51
Harper (publisher), xxvi, 293n3, 308, 339n
Hart, Henry, 195, 199n5
*Harvard Advocate,* xx
*Harvard Library Bulletin,* 282n1
Harvard University, xx, 318, 319
Hayward, Leland, 297, 298n1, 299
*Hearst's International,* 53, 55n15
Hellinger, Mark, 327, 329n2
Hemingway, Clarence, xvii, 343, 344n
Hemingway, Ernest, 50, 81, 109, 120, 152,
156, 308–9
    on critics, 164, 169–70, 183, 204n2
    death, xxviii, 329n7
    Eastman, Max, brawl with, 260–61
    finances, 145, 158, 343, 344n
        Scribners royalties and advances, xxvii,
        60, 63, *66,* 76–77, 89, 92, 93, 98,
        146–47, 158, 176, 203, 294,
        315n3, 315–16, 316n, 318–19n2
    Fitzgerald, Scott, and, vii, xiv, xxv–xxvi,
    34, 57, 59, 120, 142, 158, 262, 277,
    293, 294, 322–23, 324n2, 324–25
    EH on FSF's writing, xxv–xxvi, 50,